SURVEYING THE EXPANDING CO... W9-BSU-779
Europe during one of his famous fireside chats
in 1940, Presidents Franklin Roosevelt
ominously warned that "we know of other
methods, new methods of attack. The Trojan
horse. The fifth column that betrays a nation
unprepared for treachery. Spies, saboteurs,
and traitors are the actors in this new
strategy." Having identified a new type of
war—a shadow war—being perpetrated by
Hitler's Germany, FDR decided to fight fire
with fire, authorizing the formation of the
Office of Strategic Services (OSS) to organize
and oversee covert operations. Based on an
extensive analysis of OSS records, including
the vast trove of records released by the
CIA in the 1980s and '90s, as well as a new set
of interviews with OSS veterans conducted
by the author and a team of American
scholars from 1995 to 1997, *The Shadow War
Against Hitler* is the full story of America's far-
flung secret intelligence apparatus during
World War II.

In addition to its responsibilities generating,
processing, and interpreting intelligence
information, the OSS orchestrated all manner
of dark operations, including extending
feelers to anti-Hitler elements, infiltrating
spies and sabotage agents behind enemy lines,
and implementing propaganda programs.
Planned and directed from Washington, the
anti-Hitler campaign was largely conducted in
Europe, especially through the OSS's foreign
outposts in Bern and London. A fascinating
cast of characters made the OSS run: William
J. Donovan, one of the most decorated
individuals in the American military who

(continued on back flap)

THE SHADOW WAR AGAINST HITLER

THE SHADOW WAR
AGAINST HITLER

The Covert Operations of America's Wartime
Secret Intelligence Service

Christof Mauch

TRANSLATED FROM THE GERMAN BY
JEREMIAH M. RIEMER

COLUMBIA UNIVERSITY PRESS

NEW YORK

Columbia University Press
Publishers Since 1893
New York   Chichester, West Sussex

Copyright © 1999 Deutsche Verlags-Anstalt GmbH, Stuttgart
Translation Copyright © 2003 Jeremiah M. Riemer
All rights Reserved

Library of Congress Cataloging-in-Publication Data
Mauch, Christof.
[Schattenkrieg gegen Hitler. English]
The Shadow war against Hitler : the covert operations of America's
wartime secret intelligence service / Christof Mauch ; translated from
the German by Jeremiah M. Riemer.
p.   cm.
Includes bibliographical references and index.
ISBN 0–231–12044–3 (cloth : alk. paper)
1. United States.   2. World War, 1939–1945 — Secret service — Germany.
3. World War, 1939–1945 — Secret service — United States.   I. Title.

D810.S7 M34613 2003
940.54'8673 — dc21

2002041115

Columbia University Press books are printed on permanent and durable acid-free paper
Printed in the United States of America

c 10 9 8 7 6 5 4 3 2 1

For Ian Maxwell,
Alexander Morgan,
and Wendy

CONTENTS

ACKNOWLEDGMENTS

I discovered the the OSS while researching the German resistance to Hitler. To my surprise, Allen Dulles, the chief OSS agent in Bern, had been extremely well informed about the German resistance generally and the "Stauffenberg circle" in particular. If Dulles was so well-connected, I wondered what else I might find about Nazi Germany in U.S. intelligence records. I thus decided to make "The OSS and Germany" the subject of my *Habilitationschrift*. Like most *Habilitationschriften*, mine was heavier than a telephone book, and prospective publishers—and readers—would have been well advised against trying to read it cover to cover. I therefore prepared a "lighter" version, which was published in German under the title *Schattenkrieg gegen Hitler* in 1999.

To investigate the wartime activities of the OSS required several lengthy stays in the United States. In all, I spent a year and a half at the National Archives in Washington, D.C., and many months working in other archives and libraries in the U.S. and Europe. During this time, I examined close to two miles of records, much of which were not catalogued at the time. (Since the completion of this study, more than 5 million pages of World War II related records have been declassified through the Interagency Working Group, as required by the Nazi War Crimes Disclosure Act. These documents will certainly stimulate new research and writing in the field of World War II intelligence.)

I would never have been able to complete this study without the help of the following organizations and individuals. My greatest debt of gratitude is to the

Deutsche Forschungsgemeinschaft (DFG), to the American Council of Learned Societies (ACLS), to the Volkswagen Foundation, and to the Franklin D. Roosevelt Library for a Beeke-Levy Grant. I am also grateful for being able to draw upon a major oral history project—a series of interviews with 40 OSS veterans—supported by the Center for the Study of Intelligence and by Georgetown University. Many staff members at the archives I visited offered stimulating and useful advice. I owe particular thanks to Lawrence McDonald, Timothy Mulligan, and John E. Taylor of the National Archives, College Park, Maryland, as well as Robert Parks and Nancy Snedeker in Hyde Park for their help.

Colleagues and friends provided much encouragement over the years. Arnold H. Price, an historian and OSS veteran, took an interest in my work from the very outset. Special thanks go to my mentor Jürgen Heideking who passed away much too early, and to Jost Dülffer and Günter Kahle at the University of Cologne. I would also like to thank Gerhard L. Weinberg, who read the original German edition and provided me with valuable comments. Many other scholars shared their relevant research and insights, especially Siegfried Beer, Richard Breitman, Erica Brown, Betty Dessants, Donald Detwiler, Barry Katz, George Kent, Petra Marquardt-Bigman, Kenneth McDonald, Betty McIntosh, Armin Mruck, Timothy Naftali, Beate Ruhm von Oppen, Neal Petersen, Kevin Ruffner, Nicholas Sheetz, Bradley F. Smith, James Srodes, Thomas F. Troy, John Waller, Robert Wolfe, and Maochun Yu.

Without William J. Strachan, the President of Columbia University Press, this book would not exist. I am grateful that he suggested it for translation from German into English, and I am grateful to his staff, in particular to Leslie Bialler who edited the manuscript, and to Kim Callihan who prepared the index.

In particular, I must single out Jeremiah Riemer, who prepared this translation. He clarified many points that were ambiguous or confusing in the German text and thereby improved this study immensely. He has enlightened me on any number of issues, and for this I owe him my sincere gratitude. Jeremiah is a first-class translator.

In my *Habiliationschrift* and the German version of this book, I translated all quotations from documents in English into German. For this English edition, I needed to check the original wording of all those quotations. I cannot thank Christoph Bottin and Jennifer Rogers enough for their help in this tedious task.

Finally, my greatest debt of all is to my wife, Wendy Lower, for her patience and understanding, and to our children, who keep me from losing touch with life. To the three of them, this book is dedicated.

C.M.
Washington, D.C.
January 2003

THE SHADOW WAR AGAINST HITLER

Introduction

In an in-house radio play for the OSS, recorded in September 1945 in order to convey to future generations of secret agents what the political mission of the wartime secret intelligence service had been, the announcer explained (against the background strains of "America the Beautiful"): "We were blind in 1941 and that needn't have been. . . . Wake up, man. We've got to know what *they're* doing, as soon as they do—before they do! . . . The greatest nation in the world cannot rely upon physical strength alone. . . . We've got to beat them at *any* game they may plan."[1] This appeal to watchfulness and for better global information reflected the change of consciousness that had taken place during the Second World War, both in American government circles and the population at large. Unlike European governments, which were already outdoing each other in an arms race at the beginning of the century, before 1941 the United States had thought about foreign countries' political and military goals in only a limited way; even American interest in estimating national strengths or weaknesses was decidedly small. By 1945 the situation looked completely different. At a single stroke, and for all to see, the Americans had become the strongest nation in the world, and from now on they would be worrying about their global rank.

The years between 1941 and 1945—the period during which the American secret intelligence service, the Office of Strategic Services (OSS) and its predecessor, the Coordinator of Information (COI), were at work—were truly a turning point for political, institutional, social, and economic developments, a juncture without comparison before or since in American history. From an ideological perspective, the brilliant U. S. military victory, which achieved "the greatest gains with the smallest [indigenous] sacrifices,"[2] had brought about the defeat of National Socialism and, in its place, a confrontation with its wartime ally, the Soviet Union. The "Imperial Presidency" (as Arthur Schlesinger called it) and federal government acquired far-reaching influence on social developments, and the structural changes caused by the war established an economic recovery that would continue into the postwar period. Pearl Harbor and Hiroshima—symbolic dates for an era of catastrophes—characterized the trauma of a world war from whose shocks and wounds the world would take decades to recover. Pearl Harbor demonstrated to Americans that even they were not invulnerable to attack and that the era of isolation belonged (at last) to the past. Hiroshima and Nagasaki, by contrast, showed how the atom bomb now gave the U.S. military superiority. The weapon's brutality, however, seemed to prohibit its future use; there could be no harmless playing with nuclear fire. The dangerous new weapons, the unspeakable loss of life, and the horrors of the Second World War had presented the major powers with a dilemma: Their wish to defend political spheres of influence and economic interests demanded, in case of war, a toll so high that doubts arose everywhere about the reasonableness of that centuries-old principle (engraved into the French and Prussian canons) that war—"última razón de reyes" (Calderón)—was the last word of the rulers.[3]

Here the methods of a "shadow war"[4] seemed to offer an alternative, one that had been employed and tested during the Second World War by both Axis and Allied powers. Under "shadow war" (an essentially metaphorical concept) we understand the sum total of all irregular forms of warfare—from the procurement and evaluation of secret intelligence, through the mobilization of guerrillas and resistance movements, to deception, propaganda, and psychological warfare.

Setting up the American secret intelligence service, COI, in June of 1941, establishing the OSS in June 1942, and dissolving the OSS in September 1945 were events that both reflected and influenced general political and institutional trends. Without Roosevelt's initiative to coordinate the intelligence function, without the fear of a Nazi "fifth column," without the Pearl Harbor-induced insight into the U.S. government's lack of preparedness, without the dynamic expansion of the OSS and its belief in successful subversive warfare, 1947 would hardly have produced the Central Intelligence Agency (CIA), which would go on to conduct a new shadow war, this time under cold war conditions.

BETWEEN 1941 and 1945 America's wartime secret intelligence service was led by William Joseph Donovan (1883–1959), in civilian life a successful Wall Street lawyer and Catholic Republican of Irish descent. Donovan, who had

earned the nickname "Wild Bill" as the daring leader of the 165th Infantry Regiment in the First World War, could justly claim to be the highest decorated officer in American history.[5] But his wish to take part in the Second World War
as a general, or at least as Secretary of War, was never fulfilled.[6]

The military career that he started in the New York National Guard and finished with the deployment of covert operations against the Soviet Union could
serve as a parable for some of the twentieth century's crucial developments. By
the time America declared war in December 1941, the World War hero Donovan, who in 1939 was still ostentatiously promulgating the ethos of the soldier
(that "in an age of bullies we cannot afford to be a sissy"[7]), let himself be persuaded (not least of all by the British) that espionage, sabotage, and subversion
were alternative and effective forms of warfare.

This study—thematically situated within a range of topics that spans the
analysis of enemy actions, the investigation of unconventional secret intelligence methods, and postwar political planning—attempts to offer an overview
of the projects, operations, and visions of the COI and OSS.

Numerous written documents are available for the study of America's secret
intelligence service during the Second World War. In the case of the OSS (in
contrast to the secret intelligence services of the Soviet and British allies, whose
files remain almost entirely under lock and key), it is the wealth of classical evidence, not its paucity, that makes things difficult for the researcher. The OSS
files—stored by the tens of thousands in gray boxes and preserved on microfilm
(sometimes scantily catalogued)[8]—represent, as Bradley F. Smith euphorically
assessed the matter in 1991, "the first time in the life of the planet" when "a
nearly complete body of records produced by an intelligence organization . . .
has been placed in the public and scholarly domain."[9] This means that about
90 percent of the secret intelligence documents for the Second World War are
available (only the non-American documents, along with biographical dossiers,
remain closed off), in contrast to the State Department, where less than 10 percent of the documents from the same period have been kept.[10]

It is self-evident that well over a mile of OSS material had to be supplemented by unpublished records and files from military and Presidential
archives and documents from private collections. An additional source used for
the first time in this study is the *Interview Collection* of the OSS Oral History
Project, which proved to be a thoroughly critical complement to the written
record, provided important subjective appraisals, and contributed significantly
to understanding internal bureaucratic processes.[11]

THIS STUDY is not the first portrayal of the OSS. As soon as the war was over,
a series of publications about the history of the American secret intelligence
service appeared. They were almost always written by former OSS employees

who put their memories and their own activities at the center. Glorified descriptions of secret operations and the aura of adventure shaped the presentation. The intelligence service's abrupt dissolution in 1945 only contributed to making the OSS's brief existence shine in an even brighter light. As the *Adventures, True Accounts*, and *Tales of the OSS* piled onto the American book market in the Fifties and Sixties, it was obvious even to the layperson that the authors' vivid imagination stimulated by marketing aspirations was substituting for a lack of historically reliable sources.[12]Furthermore, the pressure and distortions of the Cold War caused research to drift into ideologically motivated apologetics.[13]

Only with the release of the official "Secret War Report" in 1976 did OSS historiography reach a level that allowed the American secret intelligence service's real sphere of influence during the Second World War to be recognized and that inspired research questions pointing in new directions.[14] In the same year, too, the first group of OSS documents was released, initially by the State Department, and after 1980 by the CIA, so that a number of accomplished historians began to take interest in the new source material. From that time on, whoever worked mainly on the Second World War, the anti-Nazi resistance, or postwar American planning could hardly bypass these new documents. At a single stroke, scholarly discussion of the OSS became respectable.[15]

To list all the publications that resulted from the release of the CIA's massive backlog of files after 1980 would be to engage in a procedure as simple as it would be nonsensical, a detective's job with an investigative charm that has faded in the era of the internet. In addition, the narrow focus and technical character of most of the individual studies puts them beyond the pale of genuine scholarly discourse.[16] With regard to the Third Reich, historians have been active in three narrow, though productive, research fields. First of all, there was a research interest in the OSS Research and Analysis (R&A) division's political reports on Germany. Preoccupation with the R&A studies acquired a special fascination because this division of the OSS included several German émigré intellectuals—such as Felix Gilbert, Herbert Marcuse, Franz Leopold Neumann, and Otto Kirchheimer—who enjoyed high esteem and status on both sides of the Atlantic. Accordingly, the R&A analyses were read and interpreted as significant testimony to the political and intellectual history of the German emigration.[17]

The infiltration of OSS agents into the German Reich became a second favorite area of research; in this field American historians set the tone, especially since the agents smuggled into Germany beginning in 1944 were the first Americans who came into contact with Germans when the war was almost over. As pioneers with subversive missions, they formed the vanguard of the American occupation army in Germany and were regarded as forerunners of the teams of agents deployed against the Soviet Union during the cold war by the CIA and *Special Forces*.

Third and finally, another field of research emerged focusing on the evaluation of the German resistance against National Socialism, a focus leading primarily to the publication of source material.[18]

SINCE THE HIGH DEGREE of interconnectedness among information procurement, strategic planning, and subversive operations constituted perhaps the most prominent feature of America's secret intelligence service—unlike the British, the OSS did not strictly separate information from sabotage and psychological warfare—the following study attempts a comprehensive investigation including all the office's important functions. The shadow war against Hitler—not against Hitler personally, as a narrow interpretation of the book's title might suggest—cannot be reconstructed by discussing the operations of individual divisions, but only by looking at the sum total of the different activities, some isolated, some interrelated, in this far-flung secret intelligence apparatus. In addition to the Office's attempt at identifying the German Reich's political, economic, and moral weak points (and therefore, in a certain sense, its Achilles' heel), the central coordinates at which the work of the OSS aimed included putting feelers out to anti-Hitler elements, infiltrating spies and sabotage agents behind enemy lines, and implementing propaganda operations. In the following investigation, the entire spectrum of these activities comes into view.[19]

Special attention is given to the foreign outposts of the OSS in Bern and London as well as to their staff members' ideological orientation, dynamics, and imagination, which lent each one of these outposts a specific character. London planned the major projects for infiltrating agents into France and Germany and maintained close ties to trade union circles; Allen Dulles in Bern, by contrast, pursued a highly politically motivated, conservative intelligence strategy of strengthening anti-Hitler elements and putting out feelers to conservative circles. With the establishment of outposts in northern Africa and Europe during the course of the war, a net was drawn ever more tightly around the German Reich—from Cairo and Caserta to Bern and Wiesbaden-Biebrich (although the meshwork was occasionally torn when one of the spy rings got smashed). Describing the two most important OSS outposts helps do justice to the fact that the secret war against Hitler, while planned and directed from out of Washington, was implemented and conducted in Europe.

THIS PORTRAYAL OF the secret intelligence war essentially rests on a chronological framework, for the decisions, analyses, and projects undertaken by the OSS can be adequately portrayed and assessed only when projected against military and political developments. The simultaneity of all the different operations, however, demands that the chronological macro-frame be punctured at various points, that a prior historical setting or later impact be anticipated, so that thematic and chronological organizing principles interpenetrate or overlap each other.

Special consideration must be given to the "turning point of 1943," when the secret intelligence analysts not only reflected on strategic parallels to the First World War, but also developed ideological credos that, in a nutshell, anticipated the political controversies and constellations of the cold war. Both the conviction that the German Reich would sooner or later lose and Washington's worry about the founding of the National Committee for a Free Germany (the Nationalkomitee Freies Deutschland, or NKfD) in Moscow prompted the OSS analysts to contemplate historical options and the future political course of the United States at a critical historical juncture.[20]

The founding of the COI in June 1941 and the defeat of Germany in May 1945 provide two coordinates for this study's time frame. This line need only be drawn forward and backward to the extent that Donovan's July 1940 trip to England, in which the OSS director received a major impetus for his intelligence work, forms the thematic overture, while Allen Dulles's (chronologically somewhat indeterminate) attempt to influence postwar policy on Germany marks the end of the portrayal.

A MONOGRAPH about the shadow war against Hitler must, first and foremost, describe the projects and activities of the OSS. In order to sound out the secret intelligence service's political and institutional environment and sketch the organization's major outlines, the evaluations made by the OSS will be compared, wherever possible, with similar assessments from the State Department and Army and Navy intelligence services (G-2 and ONI). In addition, the British secret services' strategic discussions and assessments receive special consideration, to the extent that these can be reconstructed from American documents or are mentioned in official accounts.

Further, the analyses produced by the OSS research division R&A are repeatedly and deliberately compared and contrasted with assessments from other OSS divisions. This permits at least an occasional demonstration of whatever ideological orientation the R&A analyses betray, and of what role they played in the internal discourse of the OSS. In addition, at key junctures the question will be raised as to what information the researchers had at their disposal, what methods they applied to their evaluations, and to what extent the military estimates even approached reality. Finally, in the case of the *Economic Objectives Unit,* which was responsible for determining specific bombing targets, the problem of the intelligence material's military relevance comes into view.

An additional focus comes from the ideological tensions between Donovan's secret intelligence service and the Office of War Information (OWI), tensions that surfaced early in 1942 in the debate about the legitimacy and morality of subversive propaganda missions. Here one gets a glimpse into the much-discussed and fundamental question of whether "dark" operations were compatible with a democratic self-image habituated to transparency. Finally, attention is drawn to an organization only loosely associated with the OSS: the private secret intelligence service run by John Franklin Carter for President Roosevelt. This is done not only because scholarship has almost completely overlooked Carter's organization, and because an eminently conservative figure in the person of Hitler's former foreign press chief Ernst Hanfstaengl served as an informant for the American President, but also because the operation is suited to illuminating and analyzing Roosevelt's relationship to the world of secret intelligence, a relationship that has otherwise largely eluded historical reconstruction.

Unless it is going to abandon clarity and precision, the "wide lens perspective" adopted for this investigation (a perspective that attempts to depict the entire panorama of activities undertaken by different OSS divisions and outposts) must present individual episodes, analyses, and operations that can be viewed at a glance: the appraisal of the global situation as America entered the war, the peace feelers of the German-American negotiator Federico Stallforth, the role of political émigrés, Dulles's contact with the resistance against Hitler, the deployment of German prisoners of war as OSS agents, the use of American music in the war of radio subversion, and so on.

In this sense, the account offered here does not provide some kind of encyclopedic grand overview, but rather an arrangement of relevant scenes and perspectives. The basis for selecting cases is detailed knowledge of the documents. That familiarity with the documents offers insights into constellations and fields of operation previously unknown and typical in every case.[21]

Here, inevitably, the form of presentation has to accommodate its subject. To mention just a few examples: Donovan's trip to London demands vividness, the portrayal of Hanfstaengl's imprisonment atmosphere. The conflict between the OSS and OWI requires an ideologically conclusive interpretation. The account of Pearl Harbor has to catch up with the historiographical discourse. The evaluation of individual propaganda projects compels precise textual analysis.

THE FOLLOWING ACCOUNT strives to be, in the Nietzschean sense, "critical" rather than "antiquarian," and not to pile up a "bunch of indigestible stones of knowledge."[22] To be sure, it is unavoidable that the opening chapters begin with some facts about the historical place and structure of the OSS and that, alongside the secret intelligence services' activities, the office's most important institutional and organizational changes also be discussed in the course of the presentation. Furthermore, the evaluation of intelligence will be accorded more attention than intelligence procurement. This will aid in the attempt to counter the clichés created by journalists and novelists about the glamorous culture of the secret intelligence service, and to measure the aspirations of the actors against the success of their projects.

Finally, this is not just a matter of taking a look at the dramatic "highlights" of the OSS. Rather, it is also about critically illuminating America's shadow war in all its shadings.

I

The Setting

HISTORICAL PERSPECTIVES

The Place of the OSS in American History

For decades there were two versions of how the American secret service COI came into being—an American and a British version. The Americans characterized William Donovan as the "creator" of the COI, and his secret service as a genuinely American institution.[1] The British, by contrast, pushed William S. Stephenson (alias "Intrepid") onto center stage, the "quiet Canadian" who influenced Donovan on Churchill's behalf, got him to take a trip to England (1940), and "fed" him the idea of founding a secret service.[2] More interesting than the details of this dual historical tradition is the fact that, whether consciously or unconsciously, the organization's "British parentage" was simply suppressed on the American side.[3]

What may appear coincidental in the controversy about the origins of the COI—the coexistence of two traditions and the insistence on a national *American* secret service tradition—is, in fact, symptomatic of a fundamental tension that decisively shaped the institution of America's secret intelligence service. On the one hand, there was massive resentment in the U.S. against the "dirty business" of "snooping," since—according to Stimson's oft-cited remark—

"gentlemen do not read each others' mail." On the other hand, an attempt was made to prove that espionage was a national and indeed an honorable tradition.[4] For the one group, "secret intelligence" was, as it were, an 'imported curse' for which no provision had been made in any Constitutional clause; the others saw it as something inextricably bound up with American history.

It is anything but a coincidence that a whole series of OSS veterans, including two CIA directors along with William J. Donovan himself tried to demonstrate the close link between espionage and the origins of the American republic. William Casey even explained before a Senate committee that his first predecessor as Director of Central Intelligence was none other than the *pater patriae* of Mount Vernon.[5]

ESTABLISHING THE Coordinator of Information and the Office of Strategic Services was certainly not a matter of creation *ex nihilo*. Even during the War of Independence, Americans had obtained information about enemy troop movements by secret means and maintained a whole series of spy rings, of which the most famous, Paul Revere's "Mechanics," had been set up immediately after the Boston Tea Party, in December 1773. American agents observed British positions, conducted paramilitary subterfuge operations, and broke military codes. Just before the United States was founded, nearly all the modern espionage functions—from intelligence-gathering and decoding to sabotage and counter-intelligence—could be found in North America.[6]

Immediately after ratification of the U.S. Constitution, Congress granted George Washington the prerogative to spy as part of the executive power and, accordingly, approved the President's right to undocumented expenditures ("unvouchered funds") for purposes of espionage.[7] Washington and almost all of his successors in office—some more, others less—made use of this function.

While interest in secret intelligence waned in the first half of the nineteenth century, a national spying authority was established during the Civil War and in the era of Reconstruction. In 1863 the Northern states, who were using the modern technology of aerial reconnaissance with balloons, set up the Bureau of Military Information (BMI); and in the 1880s the Navy and Army founded their own, initially tiny, secret intelligence divisions—the Office of Naval Information (ONI) and Military Intelligence Division (MID).[8] The latter development simultaneously marked the "beginnings of professionalism" and seemed symptomatic, at least in hindsight, of the United States' rise to world power.[9]

Theodore Roosevelt had contributed only a little to building up American secret intelligence. The carrier of the big stick did not need a secret intelligence service for his subversive manipulations in Central America, which paved the way for building the Panama Canal. To be sure, his methods, which included support for rebels, foreshadowed those secret (*covert* or *special*) operations that were also to become a permanent component of subversive warmaking with the establishment of the OSS and CIA.[10]

There was an almost phenomenal growth in the intelligence bureaucracy in connection with the First World War, when the Military Intelligence Division (MID) formally became a division of the War Department, the State and War Departments established a code department, (the so-called *Black Chamber*), and the State Department, immediately after the war, set up a central department for coordinating all secret information.[11]

In the interwar period the military intelligence budget was cut every year until it reached rock bottom in 1937. The American public was first reawakened from a kind of Rip Van Winkle slumber in 1938, when the FBI tallied 634 spy cases instead of the usual 30 to 40, and when the secret intelligence and security authorities (from the FBI, through the State Department, to the Post Office and New York police) took a spectacular beating by letting fourteen German spies escape. Nevertheless, President Franklin Delano Roosevelt only started entertaining concrete thoughts about setting up a central secret intelligence service in early 1939, and it was to take another two years until, with the establishment of the Coordinator of Information (COI), he had a central government office created that was responsible for procuring secret information.[12]

There was a quite obviously cyclical character to the development of secret information-gathering services in the United States. Before and during wars, the institutions responsible for espionage and national security expanded; after a war, by contrast, funds were routinely and drastically cut back again.

Consequently, founding the COI, whose function consisted of getting and analyzing "all information and data, which may bear upon national security,"[13] was not seen as a revolutionary step, since in the same period there emerged a wide range of organizations—such as the Office of Civilian Defense, the Office of Facts and Figures and many others—that assumed some sort of responsibility for the national security of the United States. The establishment of these institutions primarily reflected the fact that the era of American isolationism was drawing to a close and that the United States was gradually getting ready for a potential military confrontation requiring the country to be equipped with solid information and intelligence.

THAT THE COI and its successor organization the OSS, in spite of their rather unspectacular origins, were each able to develop into a thoroughly new kind of institution between 1941 and 1945 may be attributed in no small measure to the fact that the war lasted so long, and that the budget of the COI/OSS soon surpassed anything that the Americans had ever been prepared to spend on intelligence in the past.[14]

In addition, it was the social and professional composition of the staff that lent the organization a thoroughly innovative tone. The low average age of OSS recruits and their lack of experience in secret intelligence each contributed to dilettantism and the special dynamic of Donovan's secret intelligence service. It was also unheard of to be hiring the squad of prominent professors and diplomats that left such an unmistakable imprint on the COI and OSS. That Donovan, in addition to procuring secret information, also turned guerrilla warfare into an important function of the OSS turned out to be quite decisive in establishing the new secret intelligence service as an organization that had very little in common with its predecessors.

The COI and OSS did not break with the historical traditions of secret intelligence in the U.S.. But since there had never been—and, moreover, never would be—a U.S. secret intelligence service whose missions were so vaguely defined, and which would develop its methods and determine its functions only in a struggle with its military opponents, the COI and OSS were to become a thoroughly unorthodox public authority. Its construction will now be more closely examined.

WITHIN THE SECRET INTELLIGENCE SERVICE

The Anatomy of the OSS

In the introduction to the OSS *War Report*, Anthony Cave Brown maintains that "the structure of the OSS was less complicated than it seemed on the charts. There was Donovan's office, the offices of the Assistant Directors, Special Assistants and Representatives, the Office of the Executive Officer, and the Secretariat. The Registry maintained the files, the Theater Officers kept a watchful but benevolent eye on the four areas into which OSS divided the world."[15] Brown's simplified characterization hardly does justice to the complex structure of the OSS. In reality it comprised a number of branches and sub-branches, divisions and subdivisions, sections and subsections subordinated partly to the director, partly to one of his deputy directors; Donovan's secret intelligence service was *de facto* subjected to permanent structural change, so that it requires a flow chart, and not a structural table, to represent the different functions of the OSS. Divisions were renamed as branches, offices were attached to new sections, some divisions only existed on paper, and even William Donovan was hardly the unrestricted boss of the intelligence service, since he was constantly being called to account before oversight boards and advisory committees—from the Planning Group (as liaison to the Joint Chiefs of Staff, JCS) to the Board of Review (as the internal auditor).[16]

Against this background, the following remarks about the organizational structure or "anatomy" of the OSS—which "dissect" the intelligence service into its "organs" and explain their functions—should be understood as an overview focusing on the most important divisions and their functions.[17]

THE TECHNICAL BACKBONE of the secret intelligence service was formed by the Communications Branch (CB) of the OSS, in charge of transmitting secret intelligence bulletins. The branch saw to it that news from agents in the field and from OSS outposts reached Washington. Members of the CB staff, of whom a high degree of expertise was expected, were adept not only at special theoretical fields like radio theory and decoding, but also at maintaining and repairing sensitive radio equipment. In the era of pre-transistor technology, the invention of the Strategic Services Transmitter-Receivers (SSTR-1) or OSS "suitcase radios" by the CB Division of the OSS was an enormous achievement that decisively enhanced the mobility of agents working with the resistance movements.[18]

When the staff of the Communications Branch devoted time to developing technical and electronic equipment, this occurred *en passant* as a rule. For the Research and Development Branch (R&D), by contrast, its main business was to invent, construct, and manufacture articles for spying, special weapons, and fake documents. R&D cooperated with the National Defense Research Committee (NDRC) and the Maryland Research Laboratory (MRL), two important national research institutions that placed their know-how on the development of special weapons at the disposal of the OSS. In addition to the OSS spy camera (a wide-lens apparatus, which did not need to be focused, went into mass production at Kodak on November 3, 1943), the R&D products most in demand were miniature bombs, time fuses, and revolvers with silencers. Occasionally, OSS agents coming from the Far East approached the R&D division and its manager, Dr. Stanley Platt Lovell, with exotic requests. Among the inventions R&D developed was an explosive with properties so similar to flour that it could actually be used to bake bread (codename "Aunt Jemima"). More serious requests came from the European war theater. Thus, OSS agents in France who were supposed to instruct the Maquisards in sabotage techniques learned from experience that the traditional British method for derailing trains—the "'one-meter' technique" whereby plastic explosives were placed at a distance of one meter alongside railway tracks—proved successful only half of the time. R&D, by contrast, developed a system allowing explosives to be placed *underneath* the tracks rather than alongside them, which destroyed them (at a 90 percent sucesss rate) for a length of 2.5 meters, while ripping a crater into the ground. The range of special instruments and weapons that R&D developed was enormous and, in many respects, outdid the notions evoked in James Bond movies about the creativity of the inventors and scientists working away in hidden laboratories.[19]

The Special Assistants Division (SAD) produced drugs—among others, the infamous truth drug TD and the suicide tablet L—and a camouflage division (CD) dealt exclusively with the development and production of camouflaged objects—for example, explosives that looked like coal, stones, or fertilizer, tin cans and artificial tree branches that functioned as "letter drops," as well as clothing for agents. "The enormity of such a task is indicated," summarized the author of the OSS War Report, "when it is realized that each agent had to be equipped with clothing sewn exactly as it would have been sewn if it were made in the local area for which he was destined; his eyeglasses, dental work, toothbrush, razor, brief case, travelling bag, shoes . . . had to be microscopically accurate."[20]

Just as important were the activities of the Censorship and Documentation Division (C&D), whose assignment was to forge such documents as identity cards, work permits, and driver's licenses. Thus, for example, the Maquisards in France were supplied by the OSS Operational Groups with documents that allowed them to undertake trips for their spy missions into Germany, Belgium, and the Netherlands. On the whole, the many useful and absurd R&D inventions (of which the latter were possibly in the majority) reflected the fact that the OSS as a whole represented nothing other than a giant laboratory operating on the principle of trial and error.

One division of an entirely different kind was Research and Analysis (R&A). Derided as "collection of librarians" by its detractors, it was cherished by its adulators as the "brains of the entire secret intelligence service" in a "towering position."[21] Even Colonel Richard Park, who was asked by the President at the start of 1945 to search for a handful of upright people in the OSS but then found almost nothing but devastating criticism for the intelligence service's global machinations, conceded that the Research and Intelligence Branch had "done an outstanding job" and deserved to be "salvaged."[22] The division, founded by James P. Baxter III, a history professor and president of Williams College, and headed after 1942 by Harvard historian William L. Langer, assembled a veritable pantheon of Ivy League academics and professionals. The fact that it was academics rather than diplomats and military men who played a central role in analyzing and evaluating intelligence was an innovation in the history of secret intelligence and became, to a certain extent, the trademark of the OSS.[23] R&A essentially produced three kinds of reports: regional studies that investigated the mineral resources, transportation, society, economy, and government of a given region (such as Normandy at the beginning of 1944 or Bavaria at the start of 1945); special studies on one or more specific regional factors (such as economics, politics, or geography); and studies on U.S. foreign policy. Within R&A there were four country groups: The German Reich came under the rubric Europe-Africa; in addition, there were divisions for the Near East, USSR, and Latin America.

The Central Information Division (CID) functioned as an information hub under the renowned journalist and Yale librarian Wilmarth Lewis, whose library comprised around 100,000 biographies relevant to intelligence-gathering along with a vast store of catalogue cards on almost every conceivable topic.[24] The incredible mass of information compiled, analyzed, and evaluated by the Research Division was, to a certain extent, the functional equivalent of the "enlightened" R&A maxim that identified "knowledge" with "power." In the age of total global war, according to R&A staff member Franz Neumann (who left his ideological imprint on the Central European Division), an explicitly "global" and "total" form of information procurement was also required.[25]

In contrast to the Research Division, which initially hired most of the employees working inside the OSS, the Foreign Nationalities Branch (FNB) merely consisted of a small but dynamic staff supported by university lecturers from Harvard, Princeton, Wisconsin, and California, and operated chiefly in cities with a high ethnic share of the population — Boston, Chicago, Cleveland, Detroit, Milwaukee, Pittsburgh, San Francisco, and Seattle. Founded in December 1941, the Foreign Nationalities Branch aimed at providing and analyzing news from abroad by way of "foreign nationality groups" in the U.S.[26] The concept of the FNB originated in the recognition that "the United States is a haven for a large number of politically important refugees" and that the more than 18 million American citizens born abroad and 5 million non-Americans constituted both a potential source of danger and a unique news pool that could be tapped for information purposes.[27] Unlike the FBI, the Foreign Nationalities Branch did not have a "policing function" but saw itself instead as a "fact-finding and fact-reporting organ." In contrast to the State Department, furthermore, the FNB was not authorized to formulate foreign policy goals or even to engage in foreign policy.[28] Beyond that, there was the especially explosive fact that the top man at the Foreign Nationalities Branch was DeWitt Clinton Poole, whose decidedly conservative and at times openly anti-Moscow remarks contrasted with the left-liberal spirit of the R&A research division.[29]

Another OSS division whose functions (like those of the FNB) partly overlapped with those of J. Edgar Hoover's FBI was the OSS Counterespionage Branch (X-2).[30] Its primary function was a passive one, to warn the OSS (and the other Allied intelligence services) against infiltration by enemy agents. At the same time, however, X-2 was involved in active operations where the objective was to carry out diversionary maneuvers or send double agents into the field.[31] The designation X-2 came from the English, whose secret service MI-5 had an XX Committee that specialized in getting German agents taken prisoner "turned" and then deploying them as double agents.[32]

While X-2's way of obtaining information was primarily motivated by defensive considerations, the work of the Secret Intelligence Branch (SI) served the "dynamic" goal of formulating policies; here members of the SI staff resorted principally to materials that could only be obtained through unofficial channels. Although Allen Dulles, the most acclaimed SI agent, characterized "intelligence" as "tradecraft," there were no official guidelines for espionage in the Office of Strategic Services. Espionage demanded a large measure of creativity and imagination, which prompted Charles Ameringer to distinguish between the "craft of intelligence" and the "art of espionage."[33] In its search for qualified agents and suitable cover organizations, the OSS was aided by the ethnic diversity of the American population. Thus, beginning in 1942, hundreds of Italians, French, Yugoslavs, and Greeks could be recruited and trained as secret agents, to be infiltrated later into assignments from out of Algiers, London, and Cairo. Mastery of the language was frequently the decisive factor in recruiting agents, which led to the curious case of a man like Robert Houlihan, who had learned ancient Greek in a Jesuit school, getting assigned to operations in Greece.[34] However much a whiff of romance and risk adhered to the activities of OSS spies, the day-to-day reality was often marked by long periods of inactivity.[35]

The job of the Reporting Board, Washington's coordinating office for Secret Intelligence, was to sound out agents' reliability and evaluate the information they provided according to criteria as objective as possible. In principle, both "source" and "information" were evaluated and classified according to a cleverly contrived system of letters and numbers.[36] The growing number of reports posed big problems for the SI evaluators. Although Whitney Shepardson, who had made a name for himself before the war as a diplomat, journalist, and businessman and then taken over management of the SI branch in 1943, issued an order upon assuming office that was meant to curb the quantity of reports in favor of quality, by November 1944 the SI Reporting Board had already evaluated about half a million individual pieces of information from just under 55,000 field reports.[37]

Among the subdivisions of the Secret Intelligence Branch, the Labor Section acquired special significance. In light of the traditional mistrust that workers and trade unions held against government officials and the military apparatus, the establishment of a branch intended to win the cooperation and support of Europe's organized resistance was a downright delicate business.

Since American unions were internally divided into rival factions, the deployment of trade unionists for a liaison with Europe's "labor underground" was not, *de facto*, practical. So it was something of a miracle for Arthur Goldberg, a Chicago attorney specializing in civil rights and labor questions, to have succeeded as early as 1942 in setting up a Labor Section capable of initiating contact with European trade unions and labor organizations and ultimately mobilizing tens of thousands of workers (whether directly or indirectly) to spy for the OSS.[38]

A semi-autonomous agency that cooperated with the Labor Section on a contractual basis was the Office of European Labor Research (OELR), set up by the former Social Democratic Reichstag deputy Toni Sender. Among other things, the OELR compiled a "Who's Who" of European labor leaders as well as numerous "Inside Reports," such as one on the morale of the German population and the Wehrmacht.[39]

In contrast to the agents of the SI branch, the Special Operations or SO agents were not spies but rather saboteurs, whose main goals were the physical subversion of the enemy by means of "covert action" and material, technical support for underground movements.

As a rule, SO agents were active in small groups of three or four people (such as the legendary Jedburgh teams in France) that offered the underground movements logistic and technical instruction and, in addition, attempted to coordinate the guerrillas' paramilitary with the Army's conventional operations.

The Morale Operations Branch of the OSS was essentially authorized "to incite and spread dissension, confusion, and disorder" in enemy territory and provoke subversive activities against the governments there. In addition to the "manipulation of individuals or groups," other methods considered for achieving these aims were primarily "the organization and conduct of secret ("black") propaganda to be disseminated" via radio, newspapers, pamphlets, photographs, or rumors.[40]

The morally indifferent undertone that clung to all the "morale operations" turned the division run by Oechsner into the OSS's most controversial branch. Even James Grafton Rogers, the chair of the OSS Planning Group, made disrespectful remarks about MO's activities and apostrophized the division's activities as "a silly performance."[41] William J. Donovan, however, saw in the MO agents' "dirty tricks" an especially important contribution toward infiltrating enemy lines and fomenting and encouraging resistance groups. He used every available opportunity to inform the President about the "unorthodox" and "creative" forms by which the OSS waged war.[42]

It was self-evident that the OSS should have its own division for training agents—the so-called Schools and Training Branch (S&T). Training had to be kept as secret as possible. As a rule, it took place in the prestigious Congressional Country Club outside Washington, D.C., in the Cacoctin Mountains, or at the so-called "Farm" near Baltimore. Since there were hardly any espionage or sabotage specialists in the U.S., initially British lecturers were "loaned out," or else OSS lecturers were sent to Great Britain for training.[43]

THE MOST CONSPICUOUS characteristic of the OSS was the variety of functions that it combined under a single roof. The Office of Strategic Services operated as a kind of polyp whose tentacles became active in the most diverse range of fields—even if not always with the kind of coordination required. In retrospect, OSS psychologists concluded, the Office of Strategic Services "undertook and carried out more different types of enterprises calling for more varied skills than any other single organization *of its size* in the history of our country."[44] Without a doubt, the fact that the OSS had integrated the country's scholarly intelligentsia into its operations contributed to the modernity of an office that made the slogan "Knowledge is power" one of its leading axioms.[45] Admittedly, there was even greater historical significance in the unusual overall structure of the OSS, which combined under one roof the acquisition of secret intelligence with the implementation of covert operations.[46] When one asks how it could happen that the OSS apparatus—viewed with hostility by several government offices, permanently reorganizing, hugely bureaucratic, with its numerous specialized fields and a plethora of functions both foreign and domestic—did not just collapse like a house of cards, one needs to be reminded, first of all, that every division and subdivision of the OSS developed its identity in the struggle against National Socialist Germany and Japan. OSS staff members "did what they did," as OSS analyst Alex Inkeles assessed the organization in retrospect, "because the United States was at war and they felt they had to join the war effort. . . . The enemy, especially Nazi Germany, was clearly bad and deeply hated by everybody during the Second World War."[47] Secondly, there was the character of William J. Donovan, which had a pronounced integrating effect. The Wall Street lawyer and World War hero was anything but a bureaucrat. He did not put any narrow limits on the organization but instead—with his pioneering spirit, adventurousness, and imagination—positively inspired and motivated the men and women on the OSS staff.

II

———— ⊗⊗⊗ ————

Donovan on the Offensive
and America's Path to War

THE FIFTH COLUMN AS A DANGER

William J. Donovan's Lessons for America

The speed with which Hitler's troops marched westward, overrunning France and reaching the English Channel within just two weeks in May 1940, enthralled and shocked the world. When, one month later, the French signed a cease-fire in a railway car at Compiègne, the military and political humiliation of Germany's age-old rival seemed complete. France, one of the world's strongest powers, had been forced to its knees by Germany within a period of one and a half months, in spite of British support. Hardly anyone could have imagined such a development.

The news of Hitler's offensive alarmed not only the British, whose newly appointed Prime Minister Winston Churchill preached stoic endurance with his forceful words that "We shall not surrender."[1] For the Americans, too, war moved conspicuously closer in 1940. With special programs adding up to billions of dollars, Franklin Delano Roosevelt vastly expanded defense expenditures in May and June of 1940. At the same time the President fortified the interventionist camp by appointing two prominent Republicans to the top of the War and Navy departments: Roosevelt transferred Henry Stimson, the former

Secretary of State, to the War Department and installed Frank Knox, the GOP's Vice Presidential candidate in 1936, as Navy Secretary.[2] Stimson, like Knox, did not leave the slightest doubt about his intention to back Britain to the hilt, and Secretary of State Cordell Hull shared the view of his fellow Cabinet members.

As these offices were filled, William J. Donovan came out empty-handed. The Wall Street lawyer, who (like Roosevelt) had studied law at Columbia University and (like Stimson and Knox) was a prominent east coast Republican, would have to wait one more year before he received a government post—to run the Coordinator of Information (COI) office. But before that appointment, Donovan was given special assignments that took him in and out of Washington.

In this regard, a three-week trip to Britain that Colonel Donovan undertook in July 1940 has a special significance. Frank Knox, a close confidant of Donovan—and perhaps the only member of the Cabinet constantly in touch with the Colonel—had set up the mission, Stimson had advocated it, and the President had given his assent without any reservations. In light of the debacle of the French defeat, Donovan was supposed to find out whether the island of Britain was up to the challenge of a German invasion. An opinion poll conducted in the U.S. had shown 82 percent of all Americans believing in an Anglo-French victory over Germany in 1939; by June 1940, however, the mood had massively reversed, and a majority of Americans were now convinced that Hitler would vanquish the French and the English.[3] In addition, the German troops' rapid invasion had occasioned all kinds of speculation. An influential minority of Americans—including Frank Knox—firmly believed that Hitler's Blitzkrieg victory was attributable not primarily to the Führer's military genius, but rather to the activities of a "fifth column." Since the Spanish Civil War, Europeans thought of a "fifth column" as a group of persons who—whether out of selfish reasons, pure corruption, or political dissatisfaction—were open to cooperating with enemy intelligence services.[4] In his capacity as the publisher of the *Chicago Daily News*, Navy Secretary Knox gave his friend Bill Donovan the assignment of writing a report on the fifth column. To this end Knox had Donovan travel in the company of one of the newspaper's most experienced journalists, Edgar Ansel Mowrer. Mowrer, the Chicago paper's France correspondent, had been able to get out of Paris just in time to avoid seeing the German troops invade the French capital and exchange the tricolor for the swastika.[5]

The journalist and the lawyer, as different as their personalities may have seemed at first glance (Mowrer was a brilliant conversationalist who tended to exaggerate, while Donovan had an unimpaired sense of duty and the reserved manner of a statesman) were united by common convictions and characteristics. Both had a deep aversion to totalitarianism, both had a weakness for secret intelligence, and both loved adventure.[6] In the 1930s Donovan had undertaken a journey on his own initiative to inspect firsthand the strategies and tactics of European dictatorships. During the war in Abyssinia the World War veteran moved about the battlefields of Africa, and during the Spanish Civil War he studied new weapons and equipment that the Axis powers were testing in their engagements on Iberian terrain.[7]

If the messages that Donovan the private citizen had been sending the British failed to reverberate in the corridors of Whitehall—at the end of 1935, for example, Donovan had predicted the *Duce's* victory—by the summer of 1940 the British government was making an effort to give the American guest, now traveling as "Roosevelt's emissary," a reception befitting his rank. Donovan was downright courted.

Within hours of his arrival in London he received an invitation to Buckingham Palace, where he was greeted by King George VI. In the course of the trip to England, the American government's "emissary" encountered numerous leading characters from the British secret service bureaucracy, including Sir Stuart Menzies (Codename "C"), the head of the intelligence service SIS (Secret Intelligence Service), Colin Gubbins, the manager of the research division of military intelligence, MI-R, and Admiral John Godfrey, the director of the Navy intelligence service. In addition, the British had arranged for Donovan to meet with a number of illustrious intellectuals, all of whom had a passionate (though partly obscure) interest in secret intelligence. Thus, Donovan visited Professor J.B.S. Haldane, a Marxist who experimented with floating mines, Valentine Williams, the author of horror and mystery novels (Williams, characteristically, was responsible for Britain's foreign propaganda), as well as George Orwell, who had put out several studies on the Germans' subversive radio propaganda toward the end of the 1930s. His London hosts showed Donovan the latest Spitfire airplanes, demonstrated the technical peculiarities of British radar equipment, and initiated him into the military secrets of coastal defense. In brief, they did everything to impress Donovan and to prove England's defense capabilities. The only thing the English kept from Donovan was the most secret of all secrets, ULTRA—the successful decoding of the German Enigma machine.[8]

In the meantime, Donovan's companion, Edgar Ansel Mowrer, had been concentrating on collecting material about fifth column activities in countries occupied by the Germans. This formed the basis for a series of newspaper articles he wrote, with William Donovan's support, that found their way into all the U.S. newspapers in the summer of 1940 by way of the *Associated Press*, *United Press*, and *International News Service*. At the end of September these essays appeared as a brochure entitled "Fifth Column Lessons for America."[9] To what extent William Donovan contributed to this writing cannot be reconstructed with any exactitude. The suggestive writing style, with its occasionally pathetic tone, and the profusion of dramatic exaggerations, point unmistakably to Mowrer himself. But there can be no doubt that Donovan had contributed a portion of the manuscript and discussed its theses with Mowrer.[10]

In their commentary Donovan and Mowrer primarily emphasized that Adolf Hitler's triumphs were unthinkable without the activity of German agents abroad and sympathizers in the occupied countries. This was how they explained the role of "an active minority of the Germans" in promoting "the destruction of Czechoslovakia." But Norway, too, where there were hardly any Germans, was a victim of German subversion. There was a special urgency to the warnings Donovan and Mowrer made about Germany's foreign propaganda. Hitler had quite frankly confessed that, in the future, revolutionary propaganda would take the place of artillery. Whoever keeps in mind "the deep German instinct for candor and self confession" could easily be able "to find in every country a propaganda machine" capable of doing fifth column's work. Donovan and Mowrer explained that the Germans will do best at exploiting fifth columns wherever patriotism or understanding of Nazi Germany and its methods were wanting. Thus, to be sure "the Slovaks, who suffered their bondage under Hungary, could be duped. But Czechs and the Poles could not." Donovan and Mowrer characterized what Hitler had accomplished in France as a masterpiece of Fifth Column work:

> Here everything that Hitler had promised came to pass with almost mathematical precision. He did not strike until he was in touch with certain important Frenchmen who were ready to treat with him. He needed but one swift blow. He terrified the soldiers by his noise-making engines, he demoralized the officers by the surprise and the power of his attacks, he bewildered the generals by the daring of his strategic conceptions, he troubled the entire population by his radio propaganda that insisted that France was being betrayed by the British and by the French "war-mongers." He spread horrible rumors through villages, issued fearsome reports by wireless, and then, when the population had congested the roads in their flight, machine-gunned them to heighten their panic.[11]

What Donovan and Mowrer wanted their American readers to envision was a panorama of horror. With a mixture of admiration and disgust they portrayed Hitler as a master of propaganda—more as a sly magician than as a competent general. Again and again they emphasized that it was not the strength or tactics of the German troops that was responsible for the Nazis' lighting rapid victory, but rather the many tricks performed by Hitler the conjurer and propaganda artist. Hitler—this was the bottom line for Donovan and Mowrer—could be beaten, and Great Britain could match "Nazi Germany" militarily. Not least of all, these assertions were directed against those skeptics from the ranks of the U.S. administration—such as Ambassador Joseph Kennedy, who tried to torpedo Mowrer's investigations—who openly took the position that Great Britain would never be able to withstand a German attack and that British defeat was imminent.[12]

The urgent question of how Hitler had "accomplished this" was answered laconically by Donovan and Mowrer: "By patient activity":

> For years his [Hitler's] agents in France had . . . patiently 'worked' the French leaders. When necessary, they are were assisted by beautiful women: the Baroness von Einem, the Princess von Hohenlohe and others of lesser brilliance. . . . They 'arranged' for the trips to Germany of authors like Alphonse de Chateaubriant and newspapermen like Jean Fontenoy, both of whom returned rabid Hitlerians.[13]

Pulling out all the stops on the register of rhetorical exaggeration, Donovan and Mowrer concluded:

> They [Hitler's agents] went everywhere, saw everybody, came to know everything, dipped into French politics through those scandalously venal French newspapers. To the weak and cynical they preached defeatism, to the unsuccessful, hatred of the Jew, to all the possibility of living on good terms with Germany, if only France would break relations with the abominable Bolsheviks.[14]

On the whole, the pamphlet explained, Hitler had spent not less than $200 million per annum for his fifth columns. The "immensity of this sum" was the Führer's secret of success. Nazi Germany was "not a government—not even a 'folkdom.'" "Nazi Germany," it said in the Donovan-Mowrer pamphlet, "is a conspiracy." No fewer than four million people were "conscious agents" for the foreign organization of the Nazi Party. The Nazi conspiracy's intended sphere of influence was "universal," "its aim world dominion."[15]

While the authors' appraisal of Hitler's plans for world domination got them close to the reality, $200 million expenditure they cited was pure invention. Donovan and Mowrer could have arrived at this sum only by assuming that organizations as different as the Gestapo, the Propaganda Ministry, the German Labor Front, military intelligence, the Foreign Ministry, as well as the embassies and consulates had special funds at their disposal for financing the fifth column. Donovan and Mowrer thereby suggested that the Nazi state had a central German organization coordinating spying and propaganda activities. $200 million, to be sure, seemed like "a lot of money"; still, when one considered that all the news organizations with their 30,000 employees could "claim credit for the ease of Hitler's many victories, it is obvious that the same result could hardly be obtained so cheaply in any other way."[16]

That the Nazis' fifth column was not just aiming at Europe was a point Donovan and Mowrer hammered home to their readers when they explained that Hitler was attempting to put the Americans in a position where they would have no choice but passive acquiescence to Great Britain's collapse. The Führer was even attempting to transform the United States into a "Nazi Gau" controlled by German-Americans. Americans, they wrote, were especially receptive to National Socialist propaganda.[17]

The "Fifth Column Pamphlet," which was widely disseminated throughout America in the early summer of 1940, simultaneously registered and promoted a reversal of the public mood that had taken hold in the United States during the first half of 1940. Shortly before the Donovan-Mowrer pamphlet was distributed, Edmond Taylor had published a book with the rousing title *Strategy of Terror*. This correspondent for the *Chicago Tribune*, who like Edgar Ansel Mowrer had been working in France until the war broke out, had startled the American public with his report that the Nazis had been conducting a "propaganda war" for several years in France, a "war of nerves" to which no reporter had done justice, and which posed a danger worldwide.[18] Seemingly *en passant*, President Roosevelt also took up the topic in one of his legendary fireside chats: "We know of other methods, new methods of attack. The Trojan horse. The fifth column that betrays a nation unprepared for treachery. Spies, saboteurs, and traitors are the actors in this new strategy."[19] In May and June of 1940 the American government was in no way prepared for a war, and even a year later Charles Lindbergh could correctly assert that the great majority of Americans did not want any military engagement.[20] Roosevelt's brief remark and the widely circulated series of articles by Donovan and Mowrer may have contributed to the gradual emergence in the U.S. of an awareness about how dangerously novel Hitler's war was. The American public did not have to buy every spectacular story that an Edmond Taylor or Edgar Ansel Mowrer asked them to believe. The fact that Donovan and Roosevelt proclaimed the same message, however, carried greater weight, and certainly had an impact on the American people.

After his return from London, William Donovan's primary interest lay in convincing the American government of England's strength. Even if it could not have escaped the World War veteran's notice that the English were hopeless underdogs compared to the Germans in many respects, such as the number of ground troops they had, he did everything he could to promote the U.S. government's confidence in the British defense capability. Donovan had a memorandum (prepared by Valentine William) sent to General Sherman

Miles of the Office of Military Intelligence saying that the English home front was in no way susceptible to Hitler's sabotage and propaganda. Unlike in France, the high standard of the British civil service and the English population's unanimity and morale guaranteed that these kinds of infringements did not stand a chance.[21] At the same time, William Donovan missed no opportunity to draw attention to the urgent British need for destroyers. At his law firm Donovan, Leisure, New, and Lumbard, he put a clever young attorney, James R. Withrow, to work reviewing the legality of transferring destroyers to Great Britain. The investigation lay the legal groundwork for the historic "destroyers for bases" deal that made it possible to deliver fifty old destroyers (of First World War vintage) to England, and so to shape the opening act in a more active U.S. foreign policy.[22]

In the summer of 1940 Donovan was not the only U.S. emissary to have flown to England in order to get prognoses about the course of the war in Europe, but no other person enjoyed as much trust on both sides of the Atlantic as the Wall Street lawyer, no one at that time had better ties both to the Roosevelt administration and to British military planners, and no one else was privileged enough to meet with the leading heads of the British intelligence agency and discuss their ideas about subversion and propaganda. Donovan's ties to British intelligence, foreordained him a year later, in July 1941, to assume the leadership of the COI.

Even without Donovan's mission, Roosevelt, Stimson, and Knox would have pushed for active support of Great Britain after Germany's lightning-paced occupation of France, and they would have tried to rouse the American public out of its isolationist daydreaming. Donovan's activities accelerated these developments; they did not trigger them. Yet the London episode had major significance for Donovan as the future architect of the American secret intelligence service. Without Donovan's belief in the importance of the fifth column it would be hard to understand why the OSS placed such an emphasis on analyzing enemy propaganda, strategies of psychological warfare, "Germany first," and monitoring ethnic groups in the U.S. The COI and the OSS were born of the conviction that propaganda and sabotage are effective forms of warfare capable of replacing some traditional troops. Because Donovan argued in his fifth column pamphlet that the Nazis' global espionage and propaganda network was an effective institution that laid the groundwork for military triumphs, he subtly suggested to the U.S. government that establishing a central espionage and propaganda authority would signify America's entry into the "struggle against Hitler without weapons."

Moreover, it was anything but a coincidence that Donovan placed the loudest proponents of the Fifth Column myth on the OSS staff, and that he assigned important tasks to Edmund Taylor, Edgar Ansel Mowrer and James R.

Withrow. The OSS would later apply the tactic of stupefaction and terror that Taylor had described in his *Strategy of Terror*; Taylor's book would indeed become recommended reading for staff at the COI and OSS.[23] Taylor had pleaded for rumor campaigns, radio operations, and the deployment of secret agents. It was Donovan's idea that Hitler should be beaten with his own subversive weapons.[24]

ON THE EVE OF CONFRONTATION

William J. Donovan as Director of Intelligence and the Origins of the COI

The months between the founding of the Coordinator of Information in June 1941 and Hitler's declaration of war in December 1941 were completely preoccupied with building the Coordinator of Information. William J. Donovan designed a secret intelligence service that would obtain and analyze every conceivable piece of information about the military adversary and identify the enemy's weak points. The German population and the Wehrmacht were supposed to be demoralized using the instruments of psychological warfare and guerrilla actions.

Donovan did not care about whether his intelligence staff's members were on the left or on the right politically, whether they were interventionists like himself or isolationists, as Carl Schorske (for example) was initially. What counted was that the new institution's "agents" possessed special talents in their fields. As R&A staff member Joseph Kaplan recalled, he "hired anybody whom he thought could do something to help the war effort that was different from what the military were doing."[25] A few COI recruits—especially clerical staff, secretaries, and engineers—were hired through inconspicuous newspaper announcements. Donovan kept taking refined security precautions, however, in order to prevent the public from learning more about the COI's employees and their work. According to FBI records, the measures he took included destroying all the staff lists prepared before November 1, 1941, since during those first few months of the COI he had recruited a number of Communists and "questionable types" of whom the press was not supposed to be aware.[26]

Recruiting researchers and analysts was a job the COI Director left to the President of Williams College, Dr. James Baxter, who within a few weeks had gathered around him a group of scholars capable of overshadowing any faculty from the best American university. For spying and sabotage projects, "Wild Bill" Donovan fell back on elite troops from the U.S. Army as well as on Communists—for example, veterans of the Spanish Civil War—who had made a reputation as anti-Nazis, whereas for the top positions he preferred to place captains of industry, company board chairmen, or diplomats. The latter practice led contemporaries to quip that the initials in OSS stood for "Oh So Social."[27]

The COI and OSS were, without a doubt, the intellectual creation of William J. Donovan. The "culture" of the secret intelligence service mirrored its director's conviction that hierarchical structures and narrow bureaucratic guidelines unnecessarily restricted the effectiveness and dynamism of the office. Donovan was a master of delegation. He respected his division chiefs' expertise, and for administrative execution he depended on his staff, especially on his deputy, Edward Buxton. In the words of Donovan's secretary Eloise Page, Buxton was "sort of like an uncle. . . . I thought he had good judgement. I'm not sure I thought he was the smartest person on earth. But I liked him." He was in charge when Donovan was away and Donovan was away a great deal. Donovan "loved to be in the thick of things. He loved to run operations and he had to have his finger in the pie, in the operational pie."[28]

There was hardly anyone on the OSS staff who did not get to see Donovan during the war. The Colonel, later promoted to Brigadier General, surfaced in North Africa and in Italy, in the Balkans, in Normandy, and in southern France, in England, and even in Germany toward the end. Frederick Burkhardt met him at a cocktail party in Algiers, David Crockett traveled with him in a Jeep through liberated Rome, Abram Flues discussed an OSS mission to Budapest with him in Yugoslavia. The World War I veteran always seemed to be at the front, always where the soldiers were staying. When Donovan showed up for a meeting in Algiers, August Heckscher (later an advisor to President Kennedy) reported, everything was "polished, for days ahead, for weeks ahead." When he entered Rome, according to Crockett, "the news spread like wildfire . . . and all the agents showed up" on the street.[29] Donovan was a "very dramatic . . . figure," as Heckscher affirmed, "and he certainly was responsible for the glamor that surrounded OSS but also for the high morale which I think was maintained."

Wherever he surfaced, the OSS director succeeded in creating the impression that he was especially interested in the operations or projects of the person to whom he was talking. In the OSS it was a well-kept secret at the time that, prior to these meetings, he not infrequently had somebody slip him a note about his interlocutor containing private and professional background information which Donovan then loved to use in order to baffle everyone with his phenomenal command of detailed knowledge or his know-how. In "his" secret intelligence service Donovan — unlike, say, Allen Dulles — hardly had any enemies. The lower-ranking staff, like Sherman Kent's secretary Charlotte Bowman, feared and respected him, but they regarded him as downright "loveable."[30]

That a man like H. Stuart Hughes developed a regular "aversion" to Colonel Donovan was an exception to the rule. Donovan wanted to parachute Hughes into Italy, which struck the historian not only as hair-raising and absurd, but also scared him to death. For Hughes and a few of his colleagues, "Wild Bill" stood not so much for daring as for a "certain wild style of administration and the sense that everything was chaotic. . . . There were no rules."[31] Hughes hit on a vital issue with his critique, but most of the OSS staff members were not bothered by their boss's lack of organizational talent. Thus, the future CIA director Richard Helms, who otherwise had little positive to say about the OSS, knew that there could be "no doubt about the fact that" Donovan "was a visionary." He had "the ability to make people enjoy working for him. . . . So, when Donovan started to put together the first Coordinator of Information and then expanded that into the OSS and so forth, people were willing to go to work for Donovan. They knew who he was. Here he was, a hero of the World War I, a Congressional Medal of Honor winner, a man of great courage and vision. His only shortcoming was that, being a lawyer, he was a bad organizer. But he managed to get people around him to put these things together."[32] Even Arthur Schlesinger, Jr., a convinced Democrat, conceded in hindsight that he "liked Donovan very much." He was "open-minded." "He listened to anything. He'd try anything. He was adventuresome. He was not a conventionalist. He had great personal charm." He was a Republican but, as Schlesinger emphasized, "a New York Republican," never particularly dogmatic. "He had run against [Herbert] Lehman . . . for governor, but Roosevelt liked him. He liked Roosevelt."[33]

On November 7, 1941, the President approved Donovan's first budgetary request. He had asked for $14.1 million; he was guaranteed $12.9 million, with the major share earmarked for international radio propaganda. The R&A researchers received a not-inconsiderable sum of $800,000. The largest single item was, however, reserved for information-gathering, for "counterespionage and secret activities."[34] Donovan dreamed of bringing the war in the Old World to a swift conclusion, if possible with minor losses.

Federico Stallforth's Peace Feeler

In the autumn of 1941, in the Washington headquarters of the Coordinator of Information, there was a strictly confidential conversation among General Donovan, his representative in Germany, William D. Whitney, and the businessman Federico Stallforth. On this occasion Stallforth presented a memorandum that set forth the conditions whereby a group of German generals indicated they were prepared to end the war.

Federico Stallforth, born in 1882 in Mexico as the son of the German consul there, was hardly an unknown quantity in either the United States or Germany. But although his political and economic activities on both sides of the Atlantic had been discussed at the highest political levels, Stallforth remained a dubious figure, whose intentions and goals require a painstaking effort to re-construct.[35]

It is clear that Stallforth, a former member of the Dawes Commission, had considerable wealth, which he had acquired representing the interests of several American oil, steel, and insurance conglomerates. His economic standing opened the door for him to first-class clubs in the U.S. and laid the foundation for his ties to the giants of American business and society.[36] Between July 1940 and April 1941 this German-American businessman had used his connections to government circles in Germany to persuade officials there that he could keep the U.S. out of the war.[37] In the Reich Stallforth was regarded as a potential peace negotiator who would be intervening entirely on behalf of National Socialist Germany.[38]

Doubts about Stallforth's loyalty first crystallized when the German ambassador to Washington, Dieckhoff, was solicited for a confidential opinion about Stallforth's personality and activities during a stay in Berlin. "Mr. Stallforth," his statement read, "is a typical 'promoter,' a project-maker. . . . I can only warn against getting involved with this very adroit but unreliable man, on whom the State Department has several files."[39]

The Reich government's attitude, however, did not prevent Stallforth from searching for new ways to negotiate peace. For this he turned to Ulrich von Hassell, on whom he had initially made a "very good impression,"[40] and to a group of military people who announced that, a group of German generals, "Falkenhausen, Halder, Stülpnagel," and maybe also Brauchitsch, could be won over to a peace initiative. They announced their agreement with the "eight points" of the Atlantic Charter, pleaded for a monarchy on the British model, and emphasized that they were making "these suggestions, not because of fear, but to save the white race from further destruction."[41] After Stallforth's peace feelers had been spurned in London—the Foreign Office called the businessman a "splendid intruder"[42]—the self-appointed diplomat turned to the Americans.

By the time that the proposals made by the German military opposition and submitted by Stallforth arrived, President Roosevelt had long since made up his mind to pursue a more aggressive foreign policy course. Between the beginning of 1940 and the late summer of 1941, the Roosevelt administration's expectations about the potential for making peace with Germany had changed along with the international situation. Whereas in early 1940 some hopes were still being pinned on peace negotiations with Hitler, by the summer of 1941 America would not have accepted any peace agreement that did not involve Hitler's fall from power.[43]

Stallforth had pinned his biggest hopes on Donovan, having told the German officers on whose behalf he was negotiating that he would be approaching Donovan, Wendell Willkie (who had been the Republican candidate for

President in 1940) and General Wood in the U.S., whereupon Donovan would offer assurances that Willkie and Wood would be cooperating with Roosevelt. And, in fact, the COI director promptly transmitted the German opposition's plans to the President, and there is some evidence indicating that Roosevelt initially gave Stallforth hope that the German proposals would be considered.[44] Between Stallforth's return to the United States in September and the German declaration of war after Pearl Harbor was attacked, the COI director kept Harry Hopkins and the President up to date on Stallforth's assessment of the domestic German situation, though without any indication that the White House had participated in the German opposition's plans. In contrast to Donovan, who showed interest both in Stallforth's peace plans and in his business deals—Stallforth had, among other things, founded a corporation intended to let the U.S. buy Axis ships docked in South America[45]—Roosevelt adopted a rather cool stance toward Stallforth's plans.

While the American businessman had emphasized to his contacts in Germany that he was pursuing a dual goal in his negotiations—stopping Hitler's war and preventing Roosevelt from entering the war—the talks he held with Donovan in October 1941 showed that Stallforth was really preoccupied with ending the war by using national-conservative circles within the German army. The businessman was firmly convinced that a revolt in Germany could only emanate from the Wehrmacht, and that this required an Anglo-American guarantee of "fair play." Concretely, he believed that "someone of the old regime, such as Hjalmar Schacht, the former president of the Reichsbank, could get together secretly with the Governor of the Bank of England, Montagu Norman, and someone from the United States" in order to instigate an army revolt against Hitler. Stallforth had apparently also negotiated with German diplomat Ulrich von Hassell along these lines. "Everyone in Germany," Stallforth explained, "is tired of the war; they are only afraid that the other side will not play fair if they make peace without Hitler."[46]

In order to drive home the necessity of concluding peace as soon as possible to Donovan, and thereby also to Roosevelt, Stallforth sketched a horrifying picture of a powerful German Reich that would expand in every direction "in case peace is not made and we should declare war." He had information that the Germans would try to invade the Iberian peninsula in the southwest and push through to Suez and the Caucasus in the east. They were planning to construct an "economic Empire" and "just sit tight and wait until the Western powers decide to make peace." Stallforth expressed the conviction that the Reich was economically in a more favorable position than the U.S. and Great Britain, and that the problems that America now needed to solve faded into insignificance compared to the difficulties of a protracted war.

Donovan saw no reason to doubt Stallforth's appraisal of the Reich's military and moral potency. In the context of COI projects that had analyzed nearly a quarter million private letters from Germany, the conclusion drawn in American secret intelligence by November 1941 was that the German population's mood was not yet broken and that a desperate belief in a happier utopian future prevailed. Furthermore, the COI analysis said, the mood had already reached its low point at the end of August or beginning of September.[47]

Whether Stallforth himself believed the assertion about German troop strength is uncertain. In any event, by describing this military power he hoped to prevent the Americans from intervening militarily and to move them toward concluding peace with the German opposition. At the same time he made it unmistakably clear, on October 13, 1941, that "if satisfactory peace under the leadership of the United States is not immediately effected there is only one proper course for the United States and that is to declare war immediately. This is the psychological moment for such entry." Nothing would prove more fateful than if one were to fail to show the world a United Front—not just militarily, but economically as well.[48]

Apparently Roosevelt wanted Stallforth's proposals subjected to further examination without according the affair all too great an urgency since the president delegated the files to Harry Hopkins. Hopkins, however, after reading the "Stallforth Papers," concluded that "under no circumstances, would I encourage this man to go to Germany." Hopkins wrote Donovan that "I . . . think you should be the unwisest man in the world to permit him [Stallforth] to carry out any negotiations with Germany. I should think the F.B.I. would have a fellow like this under the closest surveillance."[49] Nevertheless, instead of filing the matter away immediately after receiving the letter, Donovan wrote once more to Hopkins: "Surely you are supposing that the State Department has already allowed him [Stallforth] to negotiate in Germany. I want to talk to you about this." Although Donovan hoped for more from Stallforth's "coup" than the FBI or Hopkins, a fierce exchange of views could hardly have come about between Hopkins and Donovan in November 1941, especially since Hopkins was obtaining information via a personal friend, John A. Kingsbury, and passing it on to Donovan, who let some doubts crop up concerning Stallforth's pro-American orientation.[50] In any case, after Pearl Harbor, there was no longer any point in contemplating peace missions à la Stallforth.

In several respects, the Stallforth episode was a lesson for the Coordinator of Information. On the one hand, it demonstrated that there was an opposition to Hitler in the German Reich, and that the COI knew virtually nothing about this group. Although Donovan did not exhibit that much trust toward either Stallforth or the German military men—Donovan's liberal advisers in the research division regarded the German generals in particular as "aggressive and expansionist"[51] —the Stallforth reports at least offered a glance behind the scene of the National Socialist regime, illuminating in broad outline both the German population's mood and political disposition of the ruling strata. Secondly, it could be seen that official Washington had developed at most a limited interest in the German opposition's peace feelers. For the future, Donovan believed, this meant that America's secret intelligence service would take on the role of establishing contacts with the German opposition and sorting out the plausibility of their offers.

If a man like Stallforth, even before America's entry into the war, had already realized that America's intelligence agency was a suitable address for informal messages, this function became even more important after December 1941, when entry into the war fundamentally restricted Washington's room for maneuver. It would only take a few weeks until Donovan—at the start of February 1942—undertook preparations for the establishment of an intelligence outpost in Switzerland. From there he wanted both to get a clearer picture of the anti-Hitler opposition in Germany and about the Reich's real military and economic strength.[52]

Pearl Harbor

The shocking Japanese attack on Pearl Harbor and the German declaration of war on the United States ended all the debates about pacifism and intervention that had divided the country for months. After Pearl Harbor President Roosevelt got a clear mandate for America's total mobilization. Like the rest of the military and government administration, the Coordinator of Information could count on a considerable boost in his budget. It was no longer questioned that there was a need for secret information channels into enemy territory abroad, and suddenly, as James Grafton Rogers realized in retrospect, it was even regarded as "criminal to think of abandoning" the COI.[53]

Donovan's name was on the list of people summoned to the White House on December 7, 1941. At the time of the attack on Pearl Harbor he was in New York at a football game, at which he was paged via loudspeaker.[54] That the attack came as such a complete surprise can hardly be attributed to any failure on Donovan's part. Among other things, it was Roosevelt who had failed to make the newly created COI responsible for evaluating SIGINT or "signals intelligence." By November 1941 the President's personal lack of interest in decoding, a marked fascination with propaganda, and a habit of underestimating espionage in its classic forms had all contributed to the situation. In contrast to Churchill, Roosevelt needed the catastrophe of Pearl Harbor in order for him to grant code-breaking an adequate (although by no means prominent) priority.[55]

The hypothetical question of whether the Pearl Harbor disaster could have been prevented had Roosevelt entrusted the analysis of SIGINT to Donovan, however, must be answered in the negative. After decades during which scholarship on the history of secret intelligence had to contend with various conspiracy theories according to which Roosevelt (or Churchill) had secret information and deliberately pushed the U.S. into war, and after Roberta Wohlstetter had argued in her influential Pearl Harbor study that military intelligence had enough information to have avoided Pearl Harbor, there are now good reasons for looking into the likelihood that the Japanese attack could not have been predicted.[56] The diplomatic code that was successfully broken by the Americans included numerous references to other potential military targets in addition to the references to Pearl Harbor. On the other hand, the Navy code, which revealed the goal and timing of the Japanese attack, had only been partly broken by U.S. cryptographers; and it can hardly be assumed that William Donovan's COI—preoccupied with getting itself established and entrusted with a large number of assignments—could have cracked the Japanese code within a few short months.[57] This would have required not only a staff of qualified cryptographers, but also the insight that Japan was a potent and acutely dangerous aggressor at the end of 1941. Influenced by his British interlocutors, however, and reinforced by reports from Germany like those of Federico Stallforth, Donovan's attention was focused almost exclusively on the European theater of war and especially on the German Reich, whose military and economic potency he strongly overestimated.

Also contributing to this situation were the reports that the COI director obtained from the German embassy in Washington via one of his secret agents, Malcolm Lovell, the Secretary of the Quaker Service Council.[58] The emissary Dr. Hans Thomsen voluntarily supplied information about the strength of the Reich and military developments on all fronts. With regard to the Germans' retreat in the east, he explained with conviction that these were only serving the purpose of assuming a comfortable and secure position. One would soon see that Germany's retreat to these "intermediate lines" will lead to peace between Russia and Germany. Furthermore, on November 13 Thomsen had already allowed a report to trickle through saying that Germany will immediately follow the Japanese if Japan makes war on the USA. Donovan, to be sure, promptly passed this news on to Roosevelt; the latter, however, did not really know what to make of it.[59]

That Donovan should not only have seen in Hans Thomsen an appropriate informant on Germany, but also have so easily lent credibility to the pro-American statements of a German diplomat, would be demonstrated by a top secret coup for which Donovan tried to recruit the German emissary shortly before Pearl Harbor. According to Malcolm Lovell's testimony, the COI director offered the German diplomat the incredible sum of a million dollars if he would publicly distance himself from Hitler's government. Donovan's plan failed, however, and at the end of 1941 Thomsen boarded the *Drottningholm* and returned to Germany.[60]

In his farewell letter to Malcolm Lovell, the departing emissary prophesied, two days after the German declaration of war on the Americans, that the German Reich would "conclude a just peace with the USA" and "protect the proper aims of the United States" after the "occupation" was complete and a "United Europe" had been established. What Thomsen envisioned was a world divided into two spheres, one American and the other pan-European, in which the Germans and the Americans would set the tone.[61]

If Hans Thomsen's attitude showed how very remote he was from reality, Donovan's attempt to win him over to the American side was no less utopian.[62] The coup Donovan was planning demonstrated not only that the COI director completely misinterpreted the German diplomat's notorious peace statements, but also that he had pinned far too many hopes on the action's propaganda effect. The thoughts underlying the intended action anticipated a line that would become a trademark of the Coordinator of Information and of the Office of Strategic Services: They reflected Donovan's unbroken belief in the power of unconventional operations.

Donovan's fascination with bizarre projects was clearly on display immediately after Pearl Harbor. Within a few weeks he was recommending to Roosevelt an entire series of operations that seemed to outdo each other in absurdity and immaturity. Thus, for example, he raised the idea of destroying what remained of the Vichy French fleet in a surprise attack, in order to reap "moral and strategic" profit from this action; a month later he proposed carrying out an immediate attack on Hokkaido with the half-destroyed Pacific fleet and some commando units.[63]

Whether Donovan would really have carried out these actions may be doubted. More to the point, one gets the impression that the head of the secret intelligence service functioned as Roosevelt's "brainstormer" and "supplier of ideas" who envisioned his role as one of looking every which way into alternative warfare, with a view toward sorting out unconventional strategies and tactics.

THE COI AND THE NEW "WORLD PATTERN"

A few days after the catastrophe of Pearl Harbor, the head of the COI research division, James P. Baxter, summed things up:

"The magnitude of the Naval disaster at Pearl Harbor and the subsequent destruction of two British capital ships off Malaya have upset all previous plans for the prosecution of the war. These disasters have profound repercussions of a political, economic, psychological and strategic character. Simultaneously Japan has launched a surprise offensive on a broad front; pressure by Hitler has probably released the French fleet to Germany; Germany has pointedly announced a halt of military operations in Russia; France and Spain appear to be entering the war as Axis partners; Russia has failed to attack Japan; and Japan has not included Russia as an object of attack in her far flung plans. All these events fall into a new world pattern.[64]

Characteristically, almost all studies of the COI interpret Pearl Harbor's impact in a global as well as in a regional perspective. In this respect it is symptomatic that Baxter's analysis should have linked the destruction of the American fleet in Pearl Harbor to the destruction of British ships near Malaya, and that the basic issue seemed to be not "the ascendancy of Japan," but how "recent events have placed the Axis in a position of immediate ascendancy in the Far East." But how were the military, strategic, and economic implications of this ascendancy interpreted inside America's secret intelligence service? Where did the Coordinator of Information locate the nexus of international relations? And what prognoses did the COI make for the rest of the war?

Interestingly, the new constellation in the Pacific region was by no means what American intelligence analysts were portraying as a danger. To be sure, it was envisioned that the U.S. would be cut off from "vital strategic commodities" in the near future, especially from rubber, while Japan would simultaneously be gaining "access to vital, critical, and strategic materials," including oil. At the same time, the COI analysts had to consider that these developments would not have any immediate influence on the course of the war, since the U.S. would still be able to get by without raw materials from Asia for quite some time. A serious impact was seen, however, in the disruption of British communication and transportation links to the Far East, India, and "Free China."[65]

In addition to the impact of the new "world pattern" on the Pacific region, the "position of Russia" and the danger of "Russia's defection" were singled out for discussion. William Langer and his team of analysts proceeded from the assumption that Hitler, after being stopped in his advance against the Soviet Union, would seek to stabilize the Eastern Front in order to withdraw more troops and possibly try "matching the Japanese attack [on Pearl Harbor] by some spectacular success in another field."[66] Langer and his staff assumed that Hitler would "seek fresh laurels" in northern Africa, and to that extent they were certainly correct.[67] Their main attention, to be sure, was directed toward the German-Soviet relationship, since they saw an unequivocal danger in any potential settlement between Hitler and Stalin. In this context, a COI research group headed by Bruce Hopper, the analyst responsible for eastern Europe, came to the conclusion that there were at least five serious reasons weighing against any Soviet capitulation: First, the Russians were not prepared to accept the Ukraine as a "buffer state between Teuton and Slav." Secondly, they were afraid of the Soviet Union's possible dissolution into separate ethnic states. Thirdly, the loss of eastern Karelia would deprive the Russians of the "ice-free Port of Murmansk" (the "Finland factor"). Fourth, the mood and morale in the "Third Fatherland War" was so bitter and intensive that Stalin could hardly succeed in motivating the population to accept a peace dictated by the Nazis. Fifth and last of all, Stalin's hatred for Hitler fundamentally spoke against the Soviets making concessions.

After an exhaustive analysis and weighing of additional factors—from the tensions between Foreign Minister Ribbentrop and Air Marshall Göring to German ambitions in the Mediterranean region, from the role of Turkey to the meaning of "world revolution" as a central element of Soviet politics—Hopper predicted that the Soviet Union would under no circumstances accept a German peace offer and emphasized that the current conflict, from a long-term perspective, was a war "about the re-division of the earth," in the course of which "the friend of yesterday may be the foe of tomorrow, and vice versa." Concretely, he ventured prophesying that the Soviet Union would hold out in the West in order to "gain a breathing space for the winter," and that the Russians—at least for the foreseeable future—would honor the Neutrality Pact of April 1941 with Japan.[68] Hopper would be proven right about almost all the points of his tentative analysis.

Even a hypothetical settlement between the Reich and the Western Allies was something the COI analysts regarded as unrealistic in December 1941. It was assumed in the COI that Germany could offer the English more "attractive bait" for peace negotiations—"the retention of the Empire, with the exception of certain strategic provisions," "the creation of a Continental Europe of nominally independent states," as well as "favorable trade arrangements."[69] Nevertheless, it was believed that neither the British nor the Americans could be inclined toward a German peace offer. The COI analysts reached this conclusion after they had identified those groups in the British and American public who would welcome a German peace offer: defeatists, isolationists, and big business elements in Great Britain, defeatists, isolationists, company bosses, and Catholics in the U.S.[70] In weighing all the circumstances, however, the diagnosticians quickly came to the conclusion that neither Great Britain nor the United States would be interested in a hypothetical German peace offer.

Seen in their totality, the COI analyses of December 1941 are noteworthy for their high degree of predictive accuracy. They were nearly correct in their estimation of Hitler's interests in northern Africa, they prophesied that the Russo-Japanese neutrality pact would not be abrogated, foresaw that the Allies would not develop any serious interest in potential peace offers, and predicted that the end of the World War would bring about shifts in coalitions and new ideological frontlines.

In a report to Roosevelt Donovan picked up on the theme of how the "anxiety" that Pearl Harbor had triggered with respect to the Pacific dared not shift priorities in the appraisal of the global situation: "The Atlantic remains the decisive theater of war." If there were to be "an irremediable disaster," then it would be "the invasion and collapse of Britain." Roosevelt had explained in his fireside chat of December 9 that unity on all fronts was the most important goal.[71] In the COI this goal was interpreted even more radically: One had to stand at the side of the British and in the struggle against Hitler with all the powers at one's disposal. One might even "lose the battle in the Pacific and still win the war in the Atlantic."

In spite of the shock of Pearl Harbor, "Germany first" was and remained an immovable priority for William J. Donovan's secret intelligence work.[72]

Germany's Military and Economic Capabilities in the COI's Calculations, 1941

Just one day after Germany declared war on the U.S., a weighty COI paper on "The German Military and Economic Situation" was resting on the President's desk.[73] Drafts of the study had already been in circulation at the end of November, but the world events now coming to a head had accelerated the paper's completion.[74] Donovan, and even more so the President, wanted to be informed as quickly and reliably as possible about the Reich. The fact that the R&A paper was written by economists from the research division shaped the study's basic questions and character. In contrast to the historians and political scientists working for the COI, who were interested in political and strategic developments, the economists were chiefly concerned with documenting the material situation of the German armed forces and uncovering those weak points in the Wehrmacht's supplies, logistics, and morale that could cause a military collapse.

In the course of their analysis, the economists came to the conclusion that the German economic system, as a result of large-scale German operations in the east, was subject to multiple burdens. In addition to "pressure on overall warfighting strength" and "means of transport," there was a special problem in that the "utilization . . . of the railroads, industrial, and consumer durables intensified." In addition, the war had brought a number of "specifically German weaknesses" to light that ranged from the withdrawal of labor from agriculture and industry, through scarce provisions, the impending exhaustion of oil reserves, and depletion of metal resources, all the way to the population's battered morale. In spite of all the data that American intelligence had collected on the

German war economy, the COI analysts did not venture any concrete prognosis. They merely found fault with a "dilemma in timing" to which the German leadership was subjected: The military people had to decide if they should scale back their operations to a "defensive minimum" in order to "maximize preparations for the . . . offensive at the start of the year" or whether they should instead use the winter to withdraw to territories where they could improve their supply situation. Irrespective of whether they established strategic or economic priorities, it was to be expected "in the approaching months" that the German military operations would be continued "at a severely reduced level."[75]

The COI directed special attention to the German population's sinking mood. For the economists, "lower morale" was a factor that, much like "human losses" or "material losses," could indicate a weakening of the system as a whole and thereby point toward Germany's potential collapse. At the same time, however, it was emphasized that a decline in the public mood need not necessarily lead to a "collapse of morale." Should the pendulum of military fortune swing back fully against the Germans, one could expect Goebbels to reverse the official propaganda line and begin pushing a "last-ditch defense" instead of the "current defensive position." This kind of development could be expected, however, only if the Propaganda Ministry succeeded in inoculating into the Germans a belief that Allied victory would bring a catastrophe upon Germany that had to be avoided at all cost.[76]

Except in the context of "morale," the German leadership's political calculations remained virtually ignored, a circumstance that undoubtedly constituted a grave shortcoming in the COI's study. The economists from R&A viewed the German war economy as a "system" whose "input" and "output" could be regulated according to rational criteria and whose strategic and economic situation could be "manipulated," "maximized," or "minimized." The elementary insight that the war situation depended not only on objective economic factors, but also on the decisionmakers' political ambitions and ideological preferences, was not taken into consideration here.

The military and economic prognoses of December 1941 were, if not exactly Delphic, at least formulated so vaguely as to remain open to a variety of interpretations.[77] Whether Donovan's intelligence service overestimated or underestimated Germany's economic and military weaknesses in December 1941, therefore, is a question that cannot easily be answered. On the one hand, the estimates for the Reich's production and armaments figures assumed by the COI were set much too high. Thus, for example, COI analysts used the absurd figure of 24,000 German airplanes in June 1941 as a basis for their forecasts. In reality the Reich only had about 3,000 fighter planes and bombers at this time. Furthermore, they proceeded from the assumption of a monthly production quota of 1,000 to 1,700 tanks, a figure five times above the actual numbers.[78] On the other hand, these much too high estimates on armaments did not lead American intelligence to overestimate the German Reich's total strength. The COI foresaw that a military collapse was not to be expected in 1942, since the supply problems and bottlenecks for material were not all that far-reaching and could, in any event, be compensated for in many instances. At the same time it was speculated that the Reich's economic and military shortcomings would, for all practical purposes, be expressed in the long run. In the judgment of the COI, the German Reich was no unassailable giant, but rather a "war machine" with particular weaknesses.

IN THE WAKE of research by David Kahn, who investigated the U.S. perception of Japan and Germany in 1941 from a comparative perspective,[79] there has been a boost to the historiographical view of the Americans as having underestimated the Japanese while overestimating the Germans, and of how "racist prejudices and national arrogance contributed to this misjudgment."[80] "All this," according to Kahn, "was the *other* side of racism. America underrated the little yellow men of Japan, but overrated the blue-eyed blonds of Germany."[81] As fascinating as this thesis seems at first glance, it can hardly (as Kahn himself concedes) explain why, for example, even Great Britain and France overestimated the Reich's military strength.[82]

In the American Navy, racist prejudice may indeed have been the decisive factor behind underestimating the Japanese;[83] for the Coordinator of Intelligence, by contrast, there was neither a unified ideology (the COI staff had been working together for only a few weeks), nor were there indications of even the most subtle forms of racism. In the months after Pearl Harbor, when anti-Japanese hysteria became widespread in the United States, reaching a climax with the forced resettlement and internment of thousands of Americans on the west coast, Donovan's secret intelligence service played a relatively moderate role. COI staff member John Steinbeck made no small contribution to this moderate attitude when he insisted that the fundamental loyalty of Americans of Japanese descent should not be called into question.[84]

All in all, a pronounced sobriety characterized the COI studies of German military strength. That the COI started out with estimates of German armaments that were much too high may be attributed not least of all to its initial reliance on files from military intelligence and on British sources and informants like Thomsen and Stallforth, who overestimated the strength of the Reich.[85]

Assessing the Situation in the East

Approximately three months after the Barbarossa campaign, Germany's advance into the Soviet Union, had been brought to a standstill by the Soviet counteroffensive, the COI's research division submitted a monumental report subjecting the "German campaign of June 22 through December 6" to detailed critical examination.[86] The goals of the COI analysis were to assess Germany's need for provisions in the east, study its supply methods, and estimate their effects on German attacks against the Soviets.

In contrast to memoranda from other COI divisions, the research division's studies were not characterized by direct evaluation of incoming information. Instead, as a rule, they posed a question relevant to the immediate military situation and attempted to answer the question by drawing on all available documents. When no appropriate studies were available, the research division was not infrequently forced to create the missing information — using estimated values and approximate measures.[87] In the case of the Eastern front study, the COI staff cited the inadequacies of the basic data and the resulting inaccuracy of the estimations. Wherever possible, the study's authors resorted to what they called "reliable German information." The many gaps were filled on the basis of comparable U.S. figures, and if neither one of these possibilities availed itself, inquires were directed to Army specialists and to engineers and technicians, whose testimony served as the basis for estimates.[88] At the heart of the investigation was a critical analysis of the transportation modes and facilities that were securing the front with fresh supplies.[89]

Although motor vehicles also played a major role, the COI scholars came to the conclusion that railway capacity posed the biggest problem for the Wehrmacht. Bad weather conditions and great distances between the train stations and the front could, to be sure, have presented problems in individual cases; what was decisive, however, was getting sufficient quantities of supplies to the unloading stations. The COI study assumed that nine (later ten) independent main lines — in addition to half a dozen branch lines — would become available to the Wehrmacht as of mid-July: three (four, as of September) single-track lines, and six dual-track ones. It was clear that the Germans would have to reduce the Russian broad-gauge tracks to standard width, but it was surmised correctly that the work that needed to be done on the railroad lines was hardly leading to delays in the German advance. What was regarded as more serious, however, were the repairs that took place in the first weeks of occupation and the hindrances that emerged close to the front because of destruction through artillery or air bombardment.[90] In detailed analyses of each individual front's problem obtaining fresh supplies, the R&A scholars argued that the German supply problem had placed limits on the course of fighting, and that the Wehrmacht found itself compelled several times between June and December to insert intervals of rest in order to replenish materials and prepare for bigger attacks.[91]

On the whole, the COI study summed up, the Germans in early 1942 were far worse off than they had been in June 1941. The effectiveness of the initial German advance resulted from the surprise character of the attack. The German army in June 1941 was presumably in top condition as regards manpower, morale, and equipment. In early 1942, however, the situation was "vastly different." Severe losses during the Barbarossa campaign had "affected the best troops in disproportionate measure." Many soldiers who were not registered "on the casualty list" were—as a result of the devastation of winter—"in relatively poor mental and physical condition"; furthermore, equipment was deficient. The COI analysts did concede that they were not in any position "to estimate the *relative* strength of the German army," since they didn't have reliable figures for the Soviet side; nevertheless, all the evidence from April and May 1942 pointed toward the Germans not being adequately prepared for additional operations like those of June 1941. Inside American intelligence, there were special doubts as to whether a coordinated advance on all fronts was possible.[92]

ALTHOUGH THE Barbarossa campaign was a failure, Hitler (as is well known) planned in early 1942 to continue the campaign and announced in his guidelines of January 1942 that "the goal [remained] . . . unchanged . . . in the long run." At around the same time that the American intelligence staff was concluding its Russia study, the Führer—who in the meantime had dismissed Brauchitsch and assumed supreme command of the army himself—wanted to proceed step by step, capture Leningrad, and break through to the Caucasus, while simultaneously holding in reserve the central army group (Heeresgruppe Mitte).[93] When delays arose in the summer of 1942, the Wehrmacht high command retreated from the principle of staggered attacks and pursued a plan of simultaneous attack against all targets. Since coordination between different wings got lost owing to the branching out of different troops, and since the distance between deployment bases and the front came to 900 kilometers, the problem of fresh supplies assumed extraordinary dimensions and ultimately contributed decisively to the German forces' overexploitation and to Germany's defeat.[94]

The Coordinator of Information assumed that the Germans might be on the verge of implementing a major offensive toward the Caucasus relatively early. Nevertheless, R&A had predicted that, in all likelihood, the success of such an action would be compromised by inadequate preparations on the part of the Wehrmacht's northern (Herresgruppe Nord) and central army groups, as well as by overextended frontlines. In contrast to Hitler, who misjudged the actual conditions, the COI researchers in May 1942 appreciated that the German high command was in no position to seize the initiative on all fronts, and that the advance of the southern troops toward the Caucasus would lead to drastic problems of fresh supplies.

Without a doubt, American intelligence proved that it had a stronger sense of reality than the supreme commander of the German army, and this was the case even though the Germans in early 1942 had far more accurate data about their own army's strength and the distribution of their opponents' forces than did the Americans.[95]

Indeed, what is remarkable about the COI diagnoses is not the accuracy of their underlying information, but the reasonable conclusions they drew from data and information that was frequently inadequate. Whoever takes the trouble to examine the information about troop strength and the number of trucks and trains quickly comes to the conclusion that the COI had correct figures to start working with only in exceptional cases. Thus, for example, the number of soldiers participating in the Russia campaign, estimated at "5 million," was set far too high; in reality, only about 3 million Germans and half a million allied troops took part in the eastern campaign in the summer of 1941.[96] It seems even more astonishing that the COI study did not even consider two factors eminently important for the supply situation—namely, the disruption of transports by Soviet partisans and the deployment of horses. In the COI it was wrongly assumed that Soviet guerrillas were operating only on the front. In reality, however, the partisans were giving the Germans their biggest trouble in the occupied territories, so that the railroad network constantly had to be repaired and could be fully utilized only rarely.[97] As far as the transports were concerned, it was apparently not possible for the COI to imagine that a means of transportation as archaic as the horse-drawn wagon would play so important a role in the Russia campaign. In fact, however, the Germans deployed more than 600,000 horses (even 750,000, according to some estimates) in the Soviet Union, and there is no doubt that the supply situation would have broken down completely in several regions had it not been for the deployment of the wagons.[98]

Ironically, when the Coordinator of Information hit the nail on the head with his suspicion that railway was the weak link in the German transport chain, or when COI scholars made sharp-minded observations highlighting hard-to-solve transportation problems or the problem of the Germans' overextended frontlines, these insights could be attributed to the fact that R&A had only insufficient information and had overestimated the mobility and capacity of motor vehicles. Activities were ascribed to the latter that really could be performed by horses.

But how useful were the COI researchers' studies? Did the inadequacies they typically emphasized indicate that the reports American intelligence produced using social science methods could ultimately not be trusted? Did they not demonstrate that the scholars working for America's secret intelligence service were too far-removed from the object of their investigations?

If one compares the analyses of the COI with other memoranda circulating in Washington early in 1942, it is striking how most of those writing memos attributed greater importance to America's entry into the war for the situation in the east than did the Coordinator of Information. It is also striking how there was considerable speculation about the defection of Germany's allies, suggesting an ominous weakening of the Reich.[99] Since Germany needed oil, and

"Hitler's prestige a quick new triumph," Hitler would attempt pushing through to Baku via Turkey, declared one report circulating in all the high government offices and relying on British information. In reality, it made no sense in 1942 to talk of any acute danger to Germany from its allies' possible defection or from any food shortage threatening the home front—possibilities that prompted some memo writers to predict a "serious" development for 1942 should the German army in the east prove unable to "rearrange" itself completely.[100]

In contrast to the reports that reached Washington via American or British secret intelligence channels, the COI researchers' studies were characterized, almost without exception, by a narrow vantage point and by cautious judgments, which prevented R&A from interpreting the sum total of German weaknesses all too hastily as signs of a potential general crisis for the Reich. At the same time, the COI researchers' obsession with specifying concrete factors that might lead to the Reich's breakdown sharpened their view of complexity in the Reich's military and economic system. In the COI it was appreciated that concrete material weaknesses or shifts in mood would not immediately lead to Germany's breakdown, that it was possible to redirect and compensate for shortcomings in morale by using reserves or propaganda operations.

By no means did the political and military changes of December 1941—the U.S. entry into the war and the failure of the Barbarossa campaign—lead to exaggerated optimism within Donovan's secret intelligence service. The data that COI analysts had at their disposal were decidedly inadequate, since the Coordinator did not yet have its own foreign stations in Europe, and R&A had only limited participation in the secret flow of information. Nevertheless, the research division had uncovered the central weaknesses in the German military and supply apparatus and was completely correct about predicting that the Reich could not be forced to its knees in the immediate future. On the one hand, it was the COI analysts' methodical caution that was responsible for this rather accurate assessment. On the other hand, a fair amount of intuition and luck had come into play.

BETWEEN OPINION RESEARCH
AND COUNTERESPIONAGE

The Foreign Nationalities Branch and the Role of German Émigrés

In contrast to those groups in the American population that demanded rigorous surveillance and internment of "enemy aliens" after Pearl Harbor, William J. Donovan was enough of a realist to recognize that America's colossal émigré potential presented an opportunity as well as posing a threat.

In December 1941 approximately 5 million non-Americans lived in the U.S.; more than 18 million were born abroad, and an additional 23 million had at least one parent born abroad.[101] Since the political outlook of these groups was still determined by ties to the homeland, the Coordinator of Information wanted to study the different political currents found among foreign groups in the U.S. Where "direct observation is difficult or impossible, as often is in time of war, this indirect method of looking in a mirror in order to catch the lineaments of a foreign situation is indispensable."[102]

Furthermore, since Donovan had recognized the enormous opportunity that systematic inspection and evaluation of the foreign press offered his work at the Coordinator of Information office, he turned to the U.S. Attorney General on September 26, 1941 and offered him $50,000 to gather material on the foreign press.[103] The project, however, was never realized, since the COI quickly determined that the "readers" in the Department of Justice and FBI "were trained to scan only for items revealing subversive activities here" but "were not completely versed in the technique of appraising and analyzing political intelligence abroad." Accordingly, the need to have a well-functioning press service provided the initial stimulus for the establishment of a Foreign Nationalities Branch (FNB) in the COI.

An additional impetus came from the State Department in October. State had an interest in being informed about "'free'" movements" in the U.S.; there was no way, however, that these movements were going to be accorded "formal or informal recognition."[104] The COI director, who had a "vision of creating an organization that could fill gaps,"[105] appeared both enthusiastic and "ready to respond." He set up the Foreign Nationalities project, put DeWitt C. Poole and John C. Wiley, two career diplomats, at the head of the project, and explained to the State Department that the newly created secret intelligence section could immediately start functioning as an official drop-in center for political émigrés.[106]

Shortly afterward, Donovan formally requested approval from the President for the establishment of the Foreign Nationalities Branch (FNB). In his letter to Roosevelt he said that the FNB would be there to keep the State Department and other offices up to date "about foreign personalities" and political groups. Roosevelt agreed to the recommendation straightaway.[107]

However, the civil servant responsible for secret intelligence matters in the State Department, Adolf Berle, soon signaled that there would be conditions attached to his approval of this new department. He was not only afraid that the COI might come to overshadow the State Department in the course of the war but also feared too close a link "between the British and the COI." Finally, he even "thought, or pretended to think, that the Foreign Nationalities Branch was actually a cover for some kind of internal Gestapo—at least a potential one."[108]

Even though Berle's reservations were exaggerated, the FNB's activities—at least until the end of 1942—gave some indication that this department in the COI was not acting exclusively as an opinion research institute. It worked very closely with the FBI, and not infrequently its published reports were primarily preoccupied with individuals and their political behavior. This procedure was not compatible with the official mission of the FNB. At the end of 1942, therefore, FNB division chief Wiley would be recalled by the COI director and given a new position.[109]

German-Americans, Exile, and Propaganda

The first FNB report Donovan commissioned on "The German-American Population in the United States" was written by a journalist from an old German-American family, Frank Bohn, who chaired the German-American Congress for Democracy in New York.[110]

In his memoranda for the COI, Bohn warned forcefully against equating the immigrants of the nineteenth century with the German-Americans of later decades. Whereas the democratically minded "48ers" quickly Americanized, thus producing such illustrious descendents as Wendell Willkie, Edward Stettinius, Adolph Ochs, and Henry Morgenthau, from now on—because of the pro-German mentality of millions of Americans of German origin—a creeping danger for the U.S. lurked behind this ethnic group, one that might ultimately lead to military defeat. In contrast to earlier waves of immigrants, most German-Americans in the twentieth century journeyed to America not out of democratic conviction, but because of material incentives. These immigrants' lack of political consciousness was the "best way possible to help the enemy." Since Goebbels had been supplying the German-American press since 1933 with paid announcements, attractively written articles, and cartoons, the ground had been prepared for a kind of pro-German sentiment that might prove irreversible if not deliberately counteracted.

Frank Bohn's reports and memoranda, all of which reached the Coordinator of Information before Pearl Harbor, saw the main danger not in the Nazis' acts of subversion, but rather in the neutral attitude of German-Americans. In his work for the German American Congress for Democracy Bohn avoided stirring up inordinate anxieties about a fifth column; instead, he saw himself as an interventionist voice calling out from the desert of political apathy. Since German national character, in this view, was shaped by a pronounced tendency toward "emotionalism," German-Americans were easily seduced and Nazi propaganda took advantage of this realization.[111]

Frank Bohn told Donovan in the autumn of 1941 that propaganda against Hitler up to now had been wanting and ineffective and urgently needed to be expanded.[112] Bohn, who had worked during the First World War for the Committee on Public Information in France and Switzerland using propaganda to build up the republican anti-Kaiser faction, was convinced that propaganda in the Second World War could be more effective than it had been in the First.

His proposals were received with great interest by Donovan, Wiley, and Poole. As of early 1942, therefore, the two heads of the Foreign Nationalities Branch were requesting assistance from a circle of cooperative émigrés in order to work out effective propaganda strategies.[113]

IT BECOMES CLEAR just how unorthodox and thoroughly innovative the Foreign Nationalities Branch's efforts (their institutionalized "tapping" of foreign nationals as informants) were when one bears in mind the resentment toward émigrés that limited Washington's room for maneuver vis-à-vis foreign nationals and enemy aliens. Permanent obstacles or security checks were expected from the FBI whenever a government office wanted to cooperate with émigrés or even hire them; in the State Department, Adolf Berle represented the viewpoint that lively European discussions have their place on the other side of the water, and that the exiles should not get involved in American life and American politics.[114] The first head of the COI research division, James Baxter, had spoken out forcefully against hiring enemy aliens, and Franz Neumann, later in charge of the Central European Division at R&A—although himself an émigré—said confidentially in October 1942 that, while he was constantly being invited to talk to different groups in New York, he felt utter "disgust" about "accepting [the] invitations." He was, as one staff member of the Foreign Nationalities Branch put it, "absolutely opposed to using any exile groups for government work."[115] When the U.S. Attorney General's remarks in October 1942 gave rise to speculation about rescinding Germans' enemy alien status, the British Foreign Office smelled danger, and Foreign Secretary Anthony Eden made haste to point out quite explicitly that the British would view such a step not only as "dangerous," but also as "undesirable."[116] Whenever German political émigrés sought a close connection to the U.S. government, alarm bells went off at the Foreign Office, especially for the head of British propaganda in New York, John Wheeler-Bennett.

A weighty argument speaking against the American government recognizing the émigrés was the realization that it was unlikely (except in the rarest of cases) that exiles could count on support from their homeland's population after the war. Even John Wiley had to concede that the émigré "intellectuals had . . . no popularity and only a few contacts at home."[117] Whereas postwar political planning did represent a truly explosive field of operations for émigrés, there were no objections in principle to émigrés joining in the work of propaganda.[118]

Among the German exiles who offered the intelligence service their support for American propaganda work, one figure who stood out at the outset was the prominent leftist Catholic Dr. Werner Thormann, who had been responsible for French propaganda on Germany in Paris between September 1939 and June 1941 and was now working in the U.S. for the Council of Democracy.[119] Thormann, who received access to COI material, sharply criticized the dilettantish procedures of the intelligence service propagandists. Among other things, he expressed consternation at how quotes from English sources were retranslated and therefore frequently inexact. A "lack of precision" like this, together with "small psychological errors," made, in Thormann's opinion, "effective propaganda impossible." In addition, the German émigré, who had lived in Austria until the Anschluss, criticized the failure to keep the themes of propaganda up-to-date, a situation partly attributable to the intelligence service's exclusive reliance on American sources. Thormann was emphatic about rejecting the "Hollywood style" that characterized American productions abroad. It was important to broadcast reports that could undermine the effectiveness of "Axis propaganda" and, at the same time, shape public opinion.[120]

What Thormann meant by "Hollywood style" becomes clear when one looks at the clumsy, naïve propaganda directives drafted by some staff members of the Foreign Nationalities Branch, especially by the Foreign Information Service. Robert L. Reynolds, for example, a research assistant at the FNB, seriously believed that one could ward off Goebbels' propaganda with a "pro-German approach." One should simply make it clear to the Germans that they had "already demonstrated bravery" and therefore did not need "to continue with the destruction," that the war was really a "civil war" (against "German brethren abroad"), and that all "peaceful and peace-loving Germans could be assured of America's friendship." In the FNB, in contrast, there were other voices. A man like August Heckscher pushed for realistic propaganda that would both demolish the "specter" of Germany's complete destruction by the Allies but not convey "any false hopes."[121]

DONOVAN'S INITIATIVE to establish a Foreign Nationalities Branch proved, on the whole, to be a gain for America's secret intelligence service. One problem that emerged, however, was the way that the exiles, beginning around the end of 1941, were submitting an array of contradictory proposals on Germany's political future to the intelligence service. As appropriate as these reports and evaluations may have been, there was a great danger that they might cancel each other out whenever different émigré groups offered competing assessments (some positive, others negative) of the same people or of identical developments.

In addition, German émigrés were judged in completely different ways by different representatives of the intelligence service. DeWitt C. Poole, who in 1940 (when he was still head of the State Department's Russian Division) had openly warned against an all-embracing (nationalist and Communist) "anti-democratic revolution in Europe," feared a successive and global spread of Communist ideology, and therefore regarded the leftist exiles as dangerous.[122] On the other hand, the staff of the R&A research division—and, not least of all, their Germany expert, Dr. Walter Dorn—saw the German Communist Party as the "only serious émigré party."[123] Poole had some leftist exiles more or less criminally investigated, and he tried denouncing them, whereas R&A and the Labor Branch preferred working closely with the very same people, among them Paul Hagen.[124]

The materials that the Foreign Nationalities Branch collected during the course of the war about the German émigrés' political views were legion. It turned out to be a problem, however, that Donovan did not have the information gathered systematically evaluated. Thus, most of the information that the American secret intelligence service got from émigré circles remained "dead" material.

Against this background it is no wonder that President Roosevelt went his own way. While Donovan's secret intelligence service developed into the most important drop-in center for exiles over the course of the war, Roosevelt had tucked away his own "personal émigré" to analyze German propaganda. This man, who was completely cordoned off from the public while he lived in the capital, regularly conveyed his insights about Hitler and the Germans to the White House. He worked for John Franklin Carter's intelligence outfit, whose existence was known to just a few of Donovan's associates. Hardly a single American would learn during the war that the man in question, the émigré with the codename Dr. Sedgwick, was the former confidant of Hitler—Ernst "Putzi" Hanfstaengl.

EXCURSUS: FRANKLIN D. ROOSEVELT, JOHN FRANKLIN CARTER, AND ERNST "PUTZI" HANFSTAENGL

The Secret Carter Organization

Just four months before the Coordinator of Information was established, President Roosevelt had set up a small private secret intelligence service that was run by the journalist John Franklin Carter and ranked as one of the Roosevelt era's best kept secrets. Starting in the summer of 1942, the Carter organization kept in touch with Donovan by way of different channels and people; nevertheless, the agency did not show up in the budget of either the COI or OSS, but instead was paid out of the President's emergency fund.[125]

In order to guarantee the highest possible level of secrecy, Carter's staff did not have an official status to the outside world, nor was it even legitimated in an informal way by the White House. While this entailed some disadvantages—with respect to cooperation with the military and executive departments—it did make it easier to send agents abroad.[126]

Originally, the aim of Carter's organization had been to find out how stable European governments were and what kinds of political and social developments would have to be taken into account during the war. John Franklin Carter, who had worked for the State Department in the 1930s while making a (second) name for himself as an author of books and articles for *Vanity Fair* under the pseudonym Jay Franklin, seemed to be the right man for a job like this. The dynamic Carter had already caught Roosevelt's eye before he was first elected President, in January 1932 when FDR had him invited him to his country estate at Hyde Park, where the two discussed the possibility of future collaboration. A short time later Carter, now openly on assignment for the State Department, traveled to Europe, where he stopped at a number of metropolises—Paris, Rome, Vienna, Budapest, and Berlin—and got an introduction to recent political and social developments.[127] Quite by chance John Franklin Carter met Hanfstaengl in Munich where they discovered that their parents had known each other: Hanfstaengl's mother was born Katharine Sedgwick, Ellery Sedgwick was an old friend of Carter's father, and Theodore Sedgwick had been his predecessor at the pulpit in Williamstown, Massachusetts.[128] Hanfstaengl arranged for Carter to interview Hermann Göring, which was published in the *New York Times*;[129] barely a decade later, when Hanfstaengl left Germany and was held at an internment camp in Kingston, Ontario, the strange friendship between Carter and Hanfstaengl was renewed: Carter asked Hanfstaengl if he would be ready to work for the American government; the latter agreed and with the personal approval of Roosevelt became one of the key staff members in Carter's private intelligence service.[130]

The spectrum of projects implemented by Carter's organization, and often suggested by Roosevelt himself, was enormous. In 1941 the tiny secret intelligence service brought out a study about the loyalty of the Japanese in different parts of North America. At the start of 1942 an observer was sent to the Aleutian islands. In cooperation with engineers who had been residing in eastern Europe through 1940, Carter's organization collected information about oil deposits and conveyers there. From time to time, there were cooperative projects with Polish secret intelligence. And the prominent anthropologist Henry Field was placed at the head of a project on migration (the "M-Project"), since Roosevelt foresaw as early as 1942 that the relocation of millions of displaced persons would pose a global challenge to the postwar order.[131]

These undertakings, however, were rather modest in scope compared to the "S"-Project revolving around Ernst Hanfstaengl (alias Dr. Sedgwick).

The "S"-Project: Hanfstaengl in the Service of American Secret Intelligence

It makes sense to ask how it could happen that Franklin Delano Roosevelt—occasionally acting in the face of serious opposition from his British Alliance partners and the FBI—would end up employing this hardly uncontroversial ex-Nazi.[132] One of the keys to Roosevelt's interest in Hanfstaengl must have come from their time together at the Harvard Club, when "Putzi" would regularly entertain his fellow students by playing the piano.[133]

Born in Munich in 1887, Hanfstaengl enrolled at Harvard during the First World War before returning to Germany in 1921, and in the wake of the Munich putsch he became a close friend of Hitler, foreign press spokesman for the NSDAP, and Hitler's favorite pianist. His American heritage, which had turned him into a wanderer between the Old and New Worlds, presumably prevented Hanfstaengl from acquiring those "nasty psychopathological features" that "characterized the average Hitler hanger-on."[134] Nevertheless, throughout his entire life this supposed cosmopolitan sympathized with the ideas of the National Socialist movement. Even after he had fallen out of favor with Hitler in 1937 and fled to Great Britain via Switzerland, he made a futile effort (according to information from British officials) at reconciliation with the Führer.[135]

When Carter paid a call on Hanfstaengl in Canada, one of the things he brought the latter was a message from the President that must have been sympathetic toward the Germans, if not verbatim (according to Carter's recollection), then at least in tenor: "You can tell him [Hanfstaengl]," Roosevelt said in mid-1942, "that there's no reason on God's earth why the Germans shouldn't again become the kind of nation they were under Bismarck. Not militaristic. They were productive; they were peaceful; they were a great part of Europe. And that's the kind of Germany I would like to see. If he [Hanfstaengl] would like to work on that basis, fine."[136]

Immediately after Carter had seen to it that Hanfstaengl was delivered to the United States, he received a bitter letter from the British Embassy in Washington stating unambiguously that it had "considerable misgiving" about this enterprise and had only approved it because of the President's intervention. The British officials were explicit in emphasizing that they placed a high value on the strictest security measures and discretion. By no means could Hanfstaengl be allowed to leave the American army camp where he was being housed. Visits had to be regulated, controlled, and watched, and every conceivable measure had to be taken to prevent the public from ever knowing about the project: "I think," Sir Ronald J. Campbell, Charge d'Affaires at the British Embassy, wrote on June 23, 1942, "we all agree about the danger of confusing anybody's mind at this time into the belief that there are good and bad ex-Nazis!"[137]

In spite of the President's backing and the commitment of Sumner Welles, the question of how to guard Hanfstaengl after he had been delivered to the U.S. government proved to be a serious problem. In June 1942 Carter turned to the FBI, requesting that a cultivated "special agent" with a knowledge of German and a good general education be hired. The agent, it was said, did not have to be paid by the Bureau, since money had been authorized by the Board of Psychological Warfare. In the meantime, it was known inside the FBI that the special agent would be given the job of Putzi Hanfstaengl's surveillance. Since J. Edgar Hoover's people wanted to have as little as possible to do with Carter and Donovan—not to mention Hitler's former bosom buddy—Carter's request was rejected with that striking bureaucratic argument: "acute personnel shortage."[138] And so it happened that Hanfstaengl, after being extradited to America, was first accommodated at Fort Belvoir in Virginia, where U.S. Army soldiers guarded him. When rumors from the camp about a high-ranking Nazi living a pleasant life in Virginia threatened to start circulating outside, and when Hanfstaengl began making all kinds of enemies in the camp because of his arrogant demeanor and racist invective, the commander of Fort Belvoir requested that the Nazi prisoner be removed.[139]

Hanfstaengl was removed, and to Bush Hill, an old, out-of-the-way estate near Alexandria, Virginia, rented out under the name of the Federal Communications Commission (FCC).[140] In the half-decaying but feudal Bush Hill residence, "Nazi Prisoner No. 1" was now guarded by civilians. In addition (and presumably at the instigation of the British ambassador Lord Halifax), the Anglophile Henry Field was attached to the Hanfstaengl entourage as a go-between.[141]

Hanfstaengl's main activity for the U.S. government consisted in analyzing German radio broadcasts. For this purpose, John Franklin Carter had an extremely sensitive Hallicrafter receiving apparatus installed by the FCC, which allowed the most important radio broadcasts from Germany to be picked up at Bush Hill. "Dr. S." was not only supposed to summarize the news; he was also to identify the weak points in Germany's propaganda and make suggestions for the Americans' retaliatory psychological warfare against Nazi Germany.[142] To this end Hanfstaengl's daily routine was strictly regulated. In the morning he read and excerpted the relevant American daily newspapers. At times picked by Carter and the FCC he listened to news from Germany by short wave, and at noon he treated himself to a short pause frequently dedicated to reading Oswald Spengler or a biography of Frederick the Great. In the afternoon he prepared short memoranda concentrating on the essentials for his clients—Carter, Roosevelt, and Donovan.[143]

Analyses of Germany and Propaganda Plans

From the outset, the propagandists initiated into the "S" project were undoubtedly aware that Sedgwick-Hanfstaengl's studies, analyses, and commentaries were going to display a certain ideological coloration. During his incarceration on the British Isles, Hanfstaengl was asked if he would be ready to help destroy Germany. This POW VIP, however, had flatly refused. He would certainly help topple Hitler's government, but he would not assist in destroying his homeland.[144]

As late as the end of 1943, Jack Morgan, a State Department official who was granted frequent access to Hanfstaengl and conducted a number of interviews with him, expressed the conviction that Dr. Sedgwick was a Nazi in spirit. If the National Socialist party "had been of mind to tolerate any opposition whatever," in Morgan's opinion, "he [Hanfstaengl] would have liked to remain in Germany to play the rôle of 'loyal opposition.'" Hanfstaengl gave the foreign service officer the impression of always wanting to convince others that everything was hunky-dory in the Reich. Nevertheless, according to Morgan, the views espoused by Dr. S. provided highly interesting study material.[145]

For Hanfstaengl the Second World War was above all "a world civil-war"[146] in which the chief contestants were not so much the participating warring nations as they were two ideological factions. Looking at Germany, Hanfstaengl predicted the staging, as it were, of a Manichaean-like final battle between the Christian ideology of a "democratic commonwealth à la Niemöller" and Communist doctrine, for which he coined the formula "Stalin in Strassburg." Here the German commentator warned that even an Allied military victory over Nazi Germany was no guarantee of political stability. If it took too long for Germany to have a revolution, as Hanfstaengl ominously emphasized in the summer of 1943, a "metamorphosis from swastika to sickle and hammer" threatened to take place "in less time than certain experts seemed to believe." Secondly, Hanfstaengl did not leave any doubts as to how he envisioned an effective revolution in Germany: as a putsch of "the old Prussian Reichswehr Junker caste" around Hindenburg (!), Groener, and von Seeckt, who had "never really accepted the Austrian corporal [Hitler]" and his staff of expansionists. Third and last of all, Hanfstaengl urged the Americans to depart from the Casablanca formula of unconditional surrender. The "dissatisfied militarists in Germany" needed a message of hope from the West indicating that they "were not being thrown into the same pot with the actual Nazi 'war-breeding gangs' . . ."[147]

In his commentaries Hanfstaengl drew a fundamental distinction between the Hitler clique and its promoter Goebbels, on the one hand (Hanfstaengl had a special aversion to the Reich Propaganda Minister), and a conservative nationalistic circle of German generals, businessmen, and intellectuals, on the other. In addition to counting Hjalmar Schacht as a member of the latter group, Hanfstaengl made a point of including Ernst Jünger, whom he characterized as the "coming man in Germany," a "patriotic . . . person" feared by Hitler and "known to a very large number of under-cover, liberal anti-Nazis forces in Germany." [148] That assessments like this were less a reflection of social reality than of Hanfstaengl's affinity for certain conservative circles and for ambivalent (and, from time to time, anarchistic) ideals could not have escaped Roosevelt, especially since outside reviewers occasionally added comments to Sedgwick's memoranda in order to place Hanfstaengl's assessments in an objective light.

Quite apart from all this, it emerged during the course of the war that no other German living in the U.S. had Ernst Hanfstaengl's ability to analyze Hitler's psyche and distinguish between truth and lies in Goebbels' speeches. Jack Morgan was of the view that "Putzi is just as good a key to German policy as though we had daily access to one of the high officials of the German government."[149] And, indeed, Hanfstaengl kept hitting the nail on the head with his evaluations of National Socialist propaganda, for example, when he insisted that (for once) Goebbels' version of the Katyn massacre should be believed.[150]

ALONG WITH THE daily commentaries on Nazi radio programs he heard at Bush Hill, Ernst Hanfstaengl composed a highly regarded psychobiography of Adolf Hitler, whose utility was indirectly confirmed by way of psychologist Henry A. Murray's own studies[151]; Hanfstaengl also offered concrete suggestions for subversive radio propaganda operations against the Germans, proposals that were of special interest to his American clients. An especially telling example of Hanfstaengl's approach and of his clients' reactions was the proposal to stage a fake propaganda speech by Hitler, which he prepared late in the spring of 1944.[152]

For months Hanfstaengl had been emphasizing that it was a fundamental feature of National Socialist propaganda to stir up fear of the Soviets as "Asiatic Bolshevists" pushing westward, whereas the U.S. and Great Britain barely counted as enemies in the Nazi world view. If, accordingly, in the context of the upcoming invasion of France, one might succeed in getting a Hitler double (hired by the OSS) to broadcast a staged radio speech in which "the fake Hitler" would "state that his first duty is to defend European civilization from Asiatic Bolshevism" and push for a joint Anglo-American struggle on Germany's side, the Germans would welcome this as a plausible Hitler maneuver rather than see it as a trick. Specifically, Dr. Sedgwick suggested that the pseudo-Hitler being used as a mouthpiece by the Americans should instruct German troops and civilians to offer no more than a pretext of resistance against the Anglo-American armed forces. The "OSS Hitler" would explain that an agreement had been reached with England's and America's leaders to cooperate with the Germans, since the common goal of the Western civilization's major powers was to push back "the Jewish hordes of Asiatic Bolshevists from Europe." In addition, the fake Hitler was supposed to explain that the U.S. would be setting up air bases in Germany in order to recapture (!) Moscow, Leningrad, and Stalingrad. To the outside world, the whole thing had to look like a "coup of his [Hitler's] 'intuition.' " If the Americans' advance into Germany should succeed, American troops might, suddenly and unexpectedly, turn against the Reich. In light of the distress that could be expected among the population, the Americans would have an easy time in Germany. As strange as the plan seemed, if it were only implemented shrewdly enough, "either via a fake Hitler or through some other official-sounding set-up," it just might, as Hanfstaengl stressed, "save lives and time."[153]

When the propaganda plan was presented to the President, he asked Donovan and Under Secretary of State Edward Stettinius for their opinions. Since at least two weeks had passed between Hanfstaengl's drafting of the plan and the comments provided by the OSS and State Department,[154] the proposal did not arrive at the OSS until June 6, 1944, the day of the Normandy invasion.[155] By now, according to acting OSS director Edward Buxton (Donovan himself was in Normandy at the beginning of June), "the most opportune time for such a broadcast has passed." Moreover, he remarked: "A black radio program with a fake Hitler could be proven spurious too easily," and "if the enemy detected its source, he could employ the same basic propaganda against us to exploit an apparent divergence of interest between Russia and the U.S./U.K."[156]

Whereas Buxton's objections were directed more toward the project's technical feasibility, Edward Stettinius regarded the plan as delicate for political reasons. "We have carefully considered this proposal," he wrote to Roosevelt on June 7, 1944. "We feel that even if the scheme were feasible, which we think is doubtful, it would be impossible to convince the Soviet Government that it represented only psychological warfare. We believe that they [the Soviets], and many other people in Europe besides the Germans, would believe the suggested broadcast represented a secret policy of the United States and England. In our opinion, therefore, the proposal should not be considered seriously."[157]

In light of the plan's abstruse character, it is not so surprising that it was rejected in the end. One might rather ask why the President did not categorically reject it out of hand. Carter, above all, as head of Roosevelt's private secret intelligence service, had an attitude betraying a certain openness and predilection for risk that seemed bizarre and dangerous under the circumstances of America's alliance with the Soviet Union.

In addition to the official American reactions, the propaganda plan's ideological orientation is also of interest for the light it sheds on Hanfstaengl's political preferences and ambitions. If things had gone his way, his imagined joint undertaking by Germans and Americans against the Soviets would have taken place in reality. The propaganda plan he proposed came closest to this aim. Hanfstaengl's aversion to Hitler was profound, to be sure, especially since it was rooted in a feeling of personal humiliation; compared to the disgust he felt for Stalin, though, it was secondary. Hanfstaengl's future vision of a militarily powerful Germany as the stronghold of Christian-Occidental culture became less plausible with each passing day of the war. Therefore his fabrication was not only supposed to point out the potential dangers of Bolshevist expansionism; it was, above all, aimed at occupying Germany as soon as possible and therefore bringing about an end to the country's physical and cultural destruction. From Hanfstaengl's perspective, the possibility that the Soviets would see the plan as an affront must have been an added attraction.[158]

The End of the "S"-Project

The problem of Hanfstaengl's personal security kept coming to a head throughout the course of 1943. Not least of all, it was the high attrition rate of bodyguards and the impending danger of the press discovering Hanfstaengl's whereabouts that contributed to the problem.[159] Early in 1944, therefore, John Franklin Carter was asked by Roosevelt's secretary to bring in the FBI to provide security for Hanfstaengl's residence. Nevertheless, both Hoover and his boss, Attorney General Francis Biddle, raised objections with the President. Carter had come out in favor of a site in Washington; Biddle, by contrast, said: "That the only thing we can do is to order Hanfstaengl interned in Gloucester, New Jersey (near Philadelphia), where he will be available to Carter for consultation." The President, who attempted to mediate between the factions and had no interest in locking horns with either Hoover or Biddle, told Carter that he should not bring Hanfstaengl to Washington and that, instead of using the FBI, he should make one more attempt to approach the Army about guarding Hanfstaengl.[160]

Since Churchill, on behalf of the British, had spoken out against revoking Hanfstaengl's POW status (in Great Britain the former German foreign press chief was regarded as a prisoner of war, in contrast to the U.S., where he was treated as an enemy alien) it was only a matter of time before the English demanded the return of their VIP prisoner of war.[161] The British request was granted for two main reasons. First of all, at the end of June 1944 Edward Stettinius let Roosevelt know, "very confidentially, that the State Department really did not know what they were doing and that Mr. Carter receives $10,000 a month and the State Department does not feel that this work is of enough value to warrant spending that amount of money." Secondly, there was an acute danger toward the end of the summer of 1944 that British officials might publicly acknowledge the internment of prominent Nazis. Roosevelt's active role in the matter (as FDR had good reason to fear) might have triggered an avalanche and possibly cost him his job. In September, therefore, Hanfstaengl was taken to the Isle of Man along the northwest British coast, where he remained in touch with Carter and, indirectly, with the President as well.[162]

Hanfstaengl was, as he dramatically depicted in his memoirs, so frustrated about the extradition that he seriously toyed with thoughts of suicide. Until the end of August 1944 his bottom-line message to Washington was a warning about a Nazi "last ditch stand." The assassination attempt of July 1944 was, in his view, less an indicator of the Third Reich's collapse than a sign of weakness in a re-sistance that was not receiving any support from the Western powers. If the U.S. were to stick to the Casablanca formula, according to Hanfstaengl, there would be no possibility of peace in 1944: "Unconditional surrender" in his view, was "the last life-belt Hitler and Goebbels have."[163] Hanfstaengl was never able to comprehend that his proposals were not a practical option for Roosevelt, that a pro-German propaganda line and revocation of the Casablanca formula could drive a wedge into the alliance with the Russians.

It is hard to determine how seriously Roosevelt took the whole matter and how much importance was attached to Hanfstaengl's analyses in the President's calculations. In all probability, Roosevelt saw Hanfstaengl primarily as an ex-egete who, unlike anybody else, was able to help him appreciate the mental world of his National Socialist adversaries without obligating him in the slight-est. In addition, there was the fact that Roosevelt got enormous satisfaction from the comic aspects of the undertaking; "Operation Hanfstaengl" was a ven-ture he virtually staged: The President placed none other than Hanfstaengl's own son at Dr. Sedgwick's side in Fort Belvoir (young Egon was an American citizen and a soldier in the U.S. Army), and for Bush Hill he even provided the old entertainer from the Harvard Club with a Steinway concert piano.[164] "It was a picturesque and wildly funny affair," Carter explained in an interview whose publication he prohibited "until we are all dead."[165] In a certain way, the dedication that William Dodd, then U.S. ambassador in Berlin, had written to the President in a 1934 book of cartoon sketches, turned out to be self-confirming: "A bit of German humor must still be permitted," and "no other man who ever lived in the White House had more insight into human motiva-tion than Roosevelt." The subject of the volume Dodd was presenting to the

President was Ernst Hanfstaengl's "Hitler in der Karikatur der Welt" ("Hitler in Caricature the World Over.")[166]

The "staging" of the Sedgwick project, to be sure, did not just reflect President's sense of humor. Roosevelt's interest in the Sedgwick analyses and in Carter's secret intelligence service illustrated the very "active interest in HUMINT," in "human source intelligence," that was so characteristic of Roosevelt—quite in contrast to his successor Truman. Although the most important secret intelligence in the Second World War came to the U.S. by way of electronic eavesdropping on messages from enemy signals, via SIGINT or "signals intelligence," FDR mainly left their evaluation to the military. The fact that Roosevelt regularly met with John Franklin Carter and that he personally knew Hanfstaengl led him to lend Carter's little secret intelligence service more attention than it deserved.[167] While FDR hardly even developed an interest in MAGIC and ULTRA, and while the OSS analyses that reached his desk show signs of his having worked on them only in the rarest of cases, the President did take a personal interest in Carter's intelligence outfit.

THE COI IN CRISIS AND THE CREATION OF THE OSS

The fact that President Roosevelt maintained his own secret intelligence service, in the form of the Carter organization, was not the only reason for the latent crisis that gripped Donovan's intelligence outfit in early 1942. Whoever is aware of the COI's quite vague authority and jurisdiction, of its internal tensions (both ideological and organizational), and even of the dilettantism and conceptual shortcomings of the entire enterprise would almost have to be astonished at how the COI was able to survive America's entry into the war.

Half a year after the establishment of America's first centralized secret intelligence service, Pearl Harbor brought about the greatest intelligence debacle in American history, without any possibility that the Coordinator of Intelligence might have foreseen the catastrophe or been able to sound an alarm. The COI research division's staff, which was supposed to advise the President on political and strategic questions, was mocked by its colleagues in the Army, Navy, and foreign service as "Johnny-come-lately-professors."[168] The Foreign Nationalities Branch operated in the U.S. and therefore (it could be argued with some justification) on illegal terrain, since espionage activity in North and South America were reserved for other government organizations—primarily the FBI and Nelson Rockefeller's Coordinator of Inter-American Affairs (CIAA).[169] In Europe Donovan had not yet started the construction of foreign agent networks, not to mention the establishment of foreign outposts, and the largest "operation" as measured in budgetary terms—the creation of a War Theatre Building intended to keep the President up to date on the course of the war using the most modern media (such as overhead slide viewers, films, maps, and projectors)—was not taken seriously by anybody and eventually fell victim to Harry Hopkins' budget cuts.[170] The director of secret intelligence was under enormous pressure to succeed, and he really did have to be asked whether established institutions—especially the military intelligence services and the State Department—might not be more effective and professional at carrying out the tasks at hand. To top it all off, there was trench warfare inside the intelligence service, leading in June 1942 to the dissolution of the COI and ultimately to the establishment of a new secret intelligence service, the OSS.

The conflict had ideological roots and was chiefly played out between COI director William Donovan and one of his co-directors, the head of the Foreign Information Service (FIS), Robert Sherwood. For the work he was doing at the COI, Robert Sherwood, a playwright and President's speechwriter, had mainly recruited friends and former colleagues who shared his admiration for Roosevelt as well as for the liberal values and social policy goals of the New Deal.[171] In contrast to the heads of the other COI divisions—and, incidentally, also in contrast to Baxter, whose R&A division otherwise tended to attract "liberal" intellectuals—Sherwood was notorious for avoiding military people, diplomats, and those elite Wall Street and big business types with whom the Republican Donovan was more than happy to be surrounded. The result was that the Pulitzer Prize winner Sherwood gathered around himself a group of several hundred newspaper and radio people, directors, and authors operating in the "shirtsleeves" atmosphere of the FIS and developing clear aversions to the uniformed professionals.[172] In addition, they sketched out a propaganda concept that betrayed a decidedly idealistic orientation and portrayed the President as a symbol of an American idealism.

The differences between Donovan and Sherwood were also underscored by regional separation—Washington was the site of the COI headquarters, while the Foreign Information Service was in New York[173]—and widened into an open and unbridgeable gap when Robert Sherwood recognized that Donovan wanted to bind the COI to the military leadership, and when it occurred to Donovan that Sherwood's ideas about propaganda left no room for subversive operations.

For Donovan, propaganda was one element within the framework of a comprehensive program of psychological warfare that had "physical as well as moral functions." For example, the goal behind instigating a revolt or maneuvering anti-Nazi resistance would legitimate almost any kind of method. For the COI director, propaganda was a weapon like any other instrument that might serve to deceive and harass the enemy or, in some cases, even eliminate the adversary. Sherwood, on the other hand, saw "propaganda" as an instrument of democratic education. With respect to Germany, it was a matter of *"explaining Nazism in order to achieve a complete emotional and intellectual mobilization of the American people."*[174] Donovan wanted to wear down the enemy's morale; Sherwood, by contrast, wanted a world-wide proclamation of the "gospel" of the "American way of life" — as the "Voice of America" in the radio broadcasts of the FIC.[175] The two propaganda strategies were diametrically opposed and indeed incompatible.

To be sure, not all of the Foreign Information Service's staff members were obedient disciples of the Sherwood congregation. One exception was Edmond Taylor, who had been initiated into the ideology and technique of "black" propaganda, that is propaganda disavowing its origins, at the British propaganda center Woburn Abbey in Bedfordshire. The English had persuaded Taylor, like Donovan before him, that subversive propaganda could be a powerful weapon; and after he returned from Europe this journalist simply could not contain his sense of ridicule about Sherwood and the liberals surrounding him, since their idea of "psychological warfare [was] apparently nothing more than radio sermons about President Roosevelt and his recently proclaimed Four Freedoms."[176] Taylor's remark was by no means intended as just cheap polemics. This FIS employee did appreciate that the use of subversive propaganda was an issue touching on the very ethos of democracy. At the same time, however, he believed that an "open society" like America's absolutely had to be protected against the Nazis' aggressive propaganda attacks. In Taylor's view, however, this was only possible by taking over the opponent's psychological weapons. For him, "all methods [were] democratic" when it came to saving an endangered democracy.[177]

One of Taylor's early plans for subversive warfare proposed creating a decidedly amateurish radio station advertising on behalf of the National Socialist movement. The programs were to be transmitted from Canada in order to discredit American isolationists and pacifists by broadcasting the isolationists' remarks and publications in tandem with excerpts from speeches by Hitler and Mussolini. Taylor thereby hoped to force the Nazis and their "accomplices and sympathizers" in the U.S. into retreat. The thoroughly adventurous and (moreover) illegal proposal was never realized. Its major impact presumably came from the repugnance it elicited among those FIS employees who already suspected how dirty and tasteless the more subversive varieties of propaganda could be.[178]

As early as the end of 1941, tensions began showing up between Sherwood and Donovan in another area: when Donovan initiated the creation of a Psychoanalytic Field Unit (PFU) under the leadership of psychologist and psychoanalyst Walter C. Langer, the brother of Harvard historian William L.

Langer.[179] Walter Langer's objective was to define those fundamental concepts of a "psychology of Germany" that had "culminated in the Nazi regime." Toward this end the psychologist wanted to undertake a comprehensive psychoanalysis of Nazi ideology, as revealed in Nazi speeches and writings, National Socialist activities, or in individuals with "strong Nazi or fascist tendencies." In addition, he hoped to interpret the contemporary music, literature, film culture, and radio broadcasts of the Nazis in accordance with all the rules of the Freudian craft.[180] While Donovan and a small faction of the FIS were downright enthusiastic about Dr. Langer's Psychoanalytic Field Unit,[181] Sherwood appeared "alarmed" at how "psychoanalysts were getting mixed up in our work." He was "absolutely certain" "that the Organization of the Coordinator of Information [will become] a target of ridicule in government circles and the press," since "in the public mind" this was "almost as if we were to take advice from astrologers or palm-readers." Sherwood's criticism forced Walter Langer to submit his resignation on December 10, 1941, much to Donovan's regret.[182]

The completely different reactions of Donovan and Sherwood to Langer's project are symptomatic of the basic conflict in world views between the two COI protagonists. From Sherwood's perspective there were at least three central objections against continuing the Psychoanalytical Field Unit: First of all, to him Langer's goals were apparently too obscure. Sherwood valued political operations that were transparent. Donovan, by contrast, maintained that the business of secret intelligence required all kinds of "exotic" professions, even if their social acceptance was not always guaranteed. Circus performers were as much a part of the professional repertoire of the COI and OSS as psychoanalysts, football stars, safecrackers, and purse snatchers.[183] Secondly, Sherwood regarded the undertaking as un-American. He believed American values, institutions, and traditions needed to triumph and that the world had to be convinced of the righteousness of the American cause. And, thirdly, the head of the FIS was explicitly opposed to the experimental character of psychoanalysis.[184] What Sherwood saw as a disadvantage Donovan regarded as a virtue. The COI director believed that modern science's unorthodox reservoir of methods was the very thing a secret intelligence service needed to turn into an instrument.[185]

By early 1942, it had become apparent that Donovan and Sherwood could not work in one and the same institution. In a memorandum to President Roosevelt, Sherwood pointed out that it would be not right to have rabid anti-New Dealers or Roosevelt haters in the military or even in the OPM. He did not think, however, that someone like Donovan should participate in an undertaking that was to be an expression of President Roosevelt's own philosophy.[186] Sherwood proposed that FDR dissolve the secret intelligence service, expand the FIS into an autonomous agency, and nominate William Donovan for a position in the Army or Navy. Donovan, he said, would be overjoyed if the President would only disclose to him that his service would be of a special, secret, and possibly mysterious nature; this way, his personal prestige would remain undamaged.[187]

Sherwood's memorandum to President Roosevelt, which circulated in Washington for several weeks, not only reflected the wickedly mocking tone that had become widespread in discussions about the future of the COI; it also exposed, even if only as a set of malicious clichés, Donovan's military inclinations while demonstrating, finally, that the dispute between Donovan and Sherwood was no trivial matter. Both COI exponents had gotten involved in a tug-of-war where the stakes were all or nothing.[188]

That the Coordinator of Information—who was attacked not only from his own ranks, but also by the CIAA, FBI, Budget Bureau, State Department, JCS, and by the press[189]—was able to withstand the cross-fire of criticism for months was mostly due to Franklin Delano Roosevelt's organizational and working style. FDR believed that his hold on the reins of administrative power had to be tightest whenever he was trying to promote overlapping jurisdictions and, by implication, competition between government agencies. It was in this spirit that Roosevelt had once given Henry Morgenthau the advice to never let "the left hand know what the right hand is doing."[190]

On June 13, 1942, in a Solomonic judgment[191] reached after countless heated debates, Roosevelt issued Executive Order 9182, leading to the establishment of the Office of War Information (OWI), and a military order creating the Office of Strategic Services (OSS).[192] All the parties participating in the dispute were able to claim with some justification that they had won. Sherwood succeeded in transferring the Foreign Information Service almost unscathed into the Office of War Information, led by Elmer Davis, and thereby into a civilian institution representing Roosevelt's views.[193] Donovan was appointed director of a secret intelligence service that worked closely with the Joint Chiefs of Staff, thus fulfilling one of "Wild Bill's" wishes. In addition, he was able to credit himself with the victory of getting the COI's controversial spying and sabotage functions officially sanctioned in December 1942 as OSS functions.[194] Roosevelt himself, by merging several government offices (the OFF, OGR, FIS, and the information section of the OEM) had taken the wind out of the sails of those critics who found the atomized bureaucracy[195] of Washington information offices too expensive and confusing.

Splitting the FIS meant that the OSS staff shrank from around 1,900 to 1,100.[196] The real loss for Donovan was that "propaganda" was now officially a function of the Office of War Information[197]. To be sure, the new and old director of intelligence did not particularly care about keeping Americans and the world up to date about the success of the U.S. war effort (that was the main job of the OWI); under no circumstances, however, was Donovan prepared to let black propaganda be dropped as an instrument of subversive warfare. That the OSS would be the sole heir to its institutional predecessor's "dark" functions—sabotage, espionage counterespionage, guerrilla warfare, underground work in enemy territory abroad, and black propaganda—suited Donovan just fine. With the establishment of the OSS, the intelligence service director's interests focused more on finding ways to accelerate the collapse of Hitler's Germany. In order to achieve this goal, the first job was to determine how strong the German Reich was, to evaluate the Germans' morale, and to become informed about those economic and strategic weaknesses that might contribute to Germany's collapse.

III

1943: The Turning Point

STRATEGIES AND DISCOURSES

State Department Versus OSS: Initial Speculation
About a German Collapse, 1942

As 1942 began, German troops were gathering on the Eastern Front and German-Italian formations were assembling in northern Africa for new offensive maneuvers. Washington was speculating about a collapse of the German home front. What triggered the speculation was a memorandum by Assistant Secretary of State Adolf A. Berle about the prospects for a "Political Propaganda Campaign Directed Toward Germany." In it he explained that "the time is due (if not overdue) for an all-out political campaign to upset the Nazi Government in Germany. The conditions," it seemed to Berle, "appear favorable, and there is a very fair chance of a successful outcome. On the other hand, the risk is negligible."[1] For the lawyer and Harvard graduate, who had served as an intelligence officer in the U.S. Army during the First World War before joining the American delegation at the Paris peace conference, the parallels between the two world wars seemed self-evident.[2] He was especially fascinated by the fact that the political turning point of 1918 came *"not after but before* the defeat of the German armies in the field."[3] This insight was constantly prompting

Berle to sound out incoming intelligence reports for latent indicators of an imminent German collapse. Thus, as early as the summer of 1941, Berle believed
he recognized a series of positive signs indicating a potential collapse of the
Reich. By way of eavesdropping on radio traffic between Berlin and Tokyo,
(under the codename MAGIC), to which Berle, in contrast to Donovan, had
enjoyed access since the beginning of 1941, the Assistant Secretary ran across a
July 1941 message saying that there was no way the Germas would ever invade
Great Britain, that progress in the Russia campaign was certainly not meeting
German expectations, and that, from a German perspective, "losses of tanks,
airplanes, and material" were "quite large and replacements difficult."[4]

Since the same source had already announced Germany's Russia campaign
six months in advance, Berle had almost blind faith in the top secret MAGIC
reports.[5] Accordingly, he interpreted a series of radio messages that he read
early in 1942 as an "avenue" by which the Germans were "cautiously seeking"
to "open peace negotiations"—a peace feeler that was practically "itself in the
nature of a betrayal of the Japanese interest." In particular, Berle regarded it as
"fairly well established that one group of German generals has been actively
canvassing the possibility of a change of government," that "Germany is cautiously seeking some avenue by which she can open peace negotiations, and is
gradually adapting her propaganda to that end." The Undersecretary, to be
sure, conceded that "the German armies are successful in the military sense,"
yet he believed "that the underlying [political] situation appears to have dete-
riorated to a point where"—analogously to the situation in 1918—"defeat or disintegration seems almost certain unless peace is made."[6]

In order to discuss his ideas about a political propaganda campaign against
Hitler within a circle of competent conversation partners, Adolf Berle turned
on April 24, 1942 to Robert Sherwood, and a few days later he met with Sherwood, Deuel, Taylor, and Warburg in the State Department for a critique.[7] On
this occasion Berle revealed that he intended to publish a secret German document illustrating Germany's precarious situation, since "release of this document . . . would so undermine the German morale that the collapse would be
accelerated and that thereby a great number of lives, perhaps half a million,"
Berle speculated, "would be saved." In addition, he hoped that "a probable use
of gas and bacteriological warfare—perhaps against England—[would] be
avoided, and the Russians prevented from advancing into Germany perhaps to
the line of the Oder."[8] Interestingly, Berle was not prepared to offer more precise details about the German secret document.[9] He merely emphasized that
there could be no doubt about his source's authenticity, and he highlighted the
positive impact he expected to achieve from publishing this piece. The group
around Sherwood feared that the action would have a negative effect on the
home fronts in the U.S. and England, possibly "reducing public pressure for

the opening of a second front in Western Europe." Berle, by contrast, argued decisively that "the American people would fight harder if they thought victory was sure than if they were in doubt as to whether victory were possible."[10]

It was not by accident that Berle arrived at the thought of launching a large-scale propaganda campaign against Germany in April 1942. The Undersecretary had evidently been inspired by Joseph Stalin and Anthony Eden, who had recognized, as Berle put it, "the timeliness of a political attack." In fact, in a legendary daily command of February 23, 1942, Stalin had indicated that it was important to distinguish between the clique around Hitler and the German population.[11] Asked about Stalin's order in a Parliamentary debate, Eden had explained that while Great Britain objected to German rearmament, it also was interested in seeing to it that "Germany did not [become] a source of poison for its neighbors because of its economic collapse."[12] It was, above all, Stalin's remarks that were giving the German population a positive signal, and Berle hoped to initiate a specifically American variant of Stalin's command as a propaganda operation. As a historic model, Woodrow Wilson's "Flag Day Speech" was what Berle had in mind. In that famous speech Wilson had distinguished between the "German people," who "would be preserved" and "Kaiserism," which "would have to go."[13]

In order to encourage the Germans' optimism and the trust they placed in the U.S. government's actions, Berle felt that the propaganda should be based on the Atlantic Charter, which promised "the advantages of the post-war plans should be available to vanquished as well as victors." The propaganda "statement would have to call for something more than mere elimination of the present German Government." It would also have to call for "rigid and severe justice executed against Gestapo and S.S. units." Simultaneously, the element of religious freedom was to be emphasized, "appealing to Catholics and the Niemöller group."[14]

Allen Dulles analyzed the Berle memorandum one week after the talk between Sherwood's intelligence service delegation and Berle.[15] The "gentleman spy" (P. Grose), who at the time was heading the New York COI office and keeping closely in touch with both German émigrés and refugees from all the Nazi-occupied territories, found Berle's ideas "most interesting." He had second thoughts, however, about whether one could profitably play the trump card of a propaganda campaign more than once. In his estimation it "might be too soon to undertake this now." For "if Germany had initial successes in the Russian campaign," according to Dulles, "our propaganda drive might quickly be forgotten." Fundamental objections had also once been raised by Robert Lansing[16] against his uncle Woodrow Wilson's tactics. In between the two World Wars, however, Hitler had "dinned into their [the Germans'] consciousness a story, largely false, of the alleged deceit practised upon Germany before the last Armistice."

In addition, Dulles warned against pushing for an "immediate overthrow of the Nazi government." "I am not sure," Dulles wrote in his reply to Berle, "but that Hitler, once the myth of infallibility has been shattered—and it has already been strained by the Russia campaign—would not be something in the nature of an asset to us. When Hitler falls it should not come through a quiet coup d'etat but as the result of an open conflict between Nazi and military elements."[17]

The fact that Donovan was unhappy with both Berle's remarks and Sherwood's comments says something about the culture of America's wartime intelligence. Two and a half weeks after the State Department deemed the time for a propaganda campaign against Hitler "overdue," Donovan saw no need for quick action. Instead, he forwarded the "propaganda dossier" to R&A head Dr. Baxter, whom the intelligence director habitually entrusted with careful scrutiny of historical statements and assertions. In so doing, however, Donovan did not neglect to express his own view in one of those terse theses he often dictated to his secretary on the run.[18] To begin with, Donovan stated in objecting to Berle's position, it would be misleading to believe that a collapse of the German home front was imminent. Secondly, there were not enough signs of German weakness to justify the comparison between 1942 and 1918. Third of all, Donovan emphasized, it was not Allied (Wilsonian) propaganda that induced Germany's collapse, but rather Bolshevik propaganda. In brief, Donovan believed that a complete "military defeat of Germany is essential before we can begin to talk about a peace offensive on the part of the United Nations."[19]

Between Adolf Berle's initiative (on April 23) and the completion of an R&A commentary (on May 29) that was as well-founded as it was comprehensive— and largely as a result of optimistic war reports on the battle in the Coral Sea near Charkov—the U.S. was experiencing a kind of widespread optimism that was characterized by one Swedish correspondent as "victory panic" and that culminated in a euphoric *Newsweek* cover story presenting the prospect of an Allied victory in 1942 ("Chance for Victory in 1942 Causes Allied Hopes to Soar").[20]

The R&A report countered the optimistic picture of the military situation that Berle and the American press were drawing early in 1942 with a series of individual observations based on careful analysis and putting in a nutshell the available intelligence about the Reich's political and military situation. Thus, the research team headed by Baxter regarded the bombing campaign against Germany as "spectacular and 'newsworthy.'" Nevertheless, it was conceded that "this bombardment will have no major effect on the German war effort against Russia between now and the time when operations are curtailed by the winter," since it was not very efficient on technical grounds.[21]

R&A was similarly critical with regard to Germany's oil situation, which was held to be less precarious than American press reports had led the public to believe. In fact, oil production and consumption were in equilibrium; and even during the expensive autumn offensive the Germans had hardly been required to fall back on their oil reserves.[22] In addition, Baxter's research group warned against "optimistic estimates of German permanent casualties on the Russian front." While the British and other (American) sources had to sustain losses of up to 2.3 million, R&A had calculated—on the basis of projections and a methodologically refined, extremely careful evaluation of the local German press—that losses really amounted to 1.25 million[23]. After the war it emerged that the R&A figures were quite accurate—Germany's total losses on the Eastern Front amounted to about 1.16 million between June 1941 and April 1942.[24]

In addition, the R&A report emphasized that supposed disagreements between the Wehrmacht and the NSDAP were far from being as serious as Berle assumed they were; the Germans' nutritional situation was tolerable (no serious difficulties were expected before the end of the calendar year), and the belief that propaganda operations could induce "serious cracks . . . in the morale front" was characterized by R&A as mere illusion or "wishful thinking."[25] As far as recent German peace feelers were concerned, they were regarded in the research division as so much waste paper. Baxter's research group took the view that there were, in principle, "two kinds of peace feelers"—the "offer from desperation" and the feeler "arising from confidence." In the First World War, characteristically, the Germans confidently offered peace in December 1916, when the Axis powers found themselves in an extraordinarily strong position after the total defeat of Romania and the failure of the Brusilov offensive. By contrast, desperate offers like the Prince Sixtus affair and the Ludendorff initiative arose later. In any event the R&A study doubted that the Nazis' peace feelers could be compared with the peace feelers of 1918. An analogy was detected to the situation between the end of 1916 and the beginning of 1917, and as a matter of principle the intelligence analysts warned that peace feelers have considerable propaganda value in periods of strength: "If they are accepted, they open the way for the consolidation of German gains," and "if they are refused, they may at least spread the demoralizing conviction that Germany is in a notably weakened condition." In reality, however, the Nazis' power was stable, and neither in the occupied territories nor in Italy, France, or Norway could one detect unambiguous signs that "controlling authority (hence, Nazi influence)" was being undermined.

Finally, the study referred admonishingly to a point of view that was overlooked by contemporary reports from the State Department and military intelligence: Even if the *external* circumstances made a parallel to the First World War seem obvious in some respects, it had to be emphasized that the "propaganda-police environment of the Nazi state" was fundamentally different from the situation in the Kaiserreich. In the First World War, German propaganda was a pathetic failure when it came to projecting war aims: the Nazis, by contrast, had "built up a resplendent picture of the New Order and of the future."[26]

Toward the end, after the researchers from R&A had plucked off one rosy petal after another from Berle's optimistic "myth of German vulnerability through propaganda," they did concede that "a judicious use of propaganda can undoubtedly be effective in widening the fissures in the German home front." Nevertheless, this would require picking a strategic moment, which might arise (for example) if the Germans suffered significant defeats in Russia.[27]

The picture that Donovan's intelligence service constructed about the structure and strength of the Reich was far more differentiated and realistic than the State Department's picture of Germany. Neither Donovan, Dulles, nor the R&A researchers believed that anyone would have an easy time with Hitler, and even in June 1942 Baxter had a typical report prepared that discussed the political and military consequences of a potential Russian collapse.[28] Donovan wanted to believe in guerilla operations and black propaganda as miracle weapons in the fight against Hitler. That more open forms of propaganda could also have a decisive impact on the war was something that did not readily occur to him. To Donovan, an old military man, it was an unalterable tenet that armies were what decided wars. Dulles, in the context of an exchange of views with the State Department, developed the thesis that the way to force Germany to its knees was not to remove Hitler, but rather to broaden the gap between Hitler and the army. A few months later, however, as head of the OSS outpost in Bern and under the influence of reports on the resistance to Hitler, he would modify his position significantly.

In light of the intelligence service's massive doubts, it was not particularly surprising that Berle's initiative should have run aground, especially since Roosevelt was hardly open to persuasion that a political propaganda campaign against Germany might be useful early in 1942. Berle's initiative probably had its greatest impact, however, in a theoretical rather than practical way: As would be seen in 1943, the topic of the two World Wars' comparability, introduced by the State Department into the intelligence community's discussion, would significantly help shape the debates on how to end the war.

The Discussion About Strategic Priorities, 1943

At the end of 1942 military planners on both sides of the Atlantic had no clear ideas about which strategy to take in 1943 following the successful North Africa invasion. At no other time were Washington and London so intensively preoccupied with figuring out how to carry out the impending operations. Admiral King was set on actions directed against Japan, while General Marshall spoke out in favor of invading France. In the fall even Churchill was wavering between the "Mediterranean strategy" he was known to favor and opening of the second front he had promised Stalin for 1943. To be sure, the Prime Minister feared that Allied capacity would prove insufficient for a landing in France. He was especially worried by how the Americans had diverted significant resources away to the Pacific region, while U.S. forces being sent to Great Britain remained well below the troop strengths expected.[29]

At the turn of the year William J. Donovan was proceeding from the assumption that it was possible to conduct an all-out war *either* in the Pacific *or* in Europe. To put it another way: For the OSS Director, the question was whether the Allies should concentrate their war effort on Japan or scale back their operations in Asia and deploy all their forces in Europe. *Tertium non datur.* Here Donovan was interested in determining how the military strength and morale of the Germans and Japanese could be estimated, which bombing strategy should be followed, and whether the Middle East should be penetrated (in addition to bases in north Africa) for the sake of rushing to the aid of the Soviets who were fighting the Germans at Stalingrad. The debate on strategy—to which the OSS Board of Analysts contributed in addition to Brigadier General Bonner F. Fellers from the military intelligence service G-2—extended from December 1942 through the end of January 1943. Since OSS internal correspondence contains revealing information about how the global situation was evaluated at this important turning point in the war, the following section will focus more sharply on the core judgments and arguments of this detailed discourse within the intelligence community.

The discussion was triggered by Donovan's memo of November 26, 1942, in which he asked the research division for a "study which would disclose the factors (political, economic and psychological) that must be considered in determining which front—European or Pacific—should be stabilized and which attacked."[30]

In order to get the most comprehensive possible picture of the Allies' strategic options, William Langer arranged for a whole series of conferences in which the Board of Analysts—the commission, made up of prominent professors and high-ranking Army and Navy experts, that shaped opinions for the OSS Director and was sometimes irreverently dubbed the "do-nothing aristocracy" by the OSS staff—would carry out a thorough discussion of the "Strategic Problem of 1943."[31] The result was a comprehensive study chaired by career diplomat John C. Wiley, who, along with DeWitt C. Poole, had run the Foreign Nationalities Branch through the end of 1942 and been appointed to the Board of Analysts at the beginning of 1943.[32]

The argumentation and results of the Wiley study may be quickly summarized:[33] "Hypothesis I," which proceeded from the assumption of a concentration of forces in Japan and simultaneous stabilization of the European situation, was based on a fear articulated by Charles Remer, the head of the R&A division on the Far East, that Japan could become extremely expansionary within one or two years and "almost impregnable," and that the Allies of the U.S. would be "too exhausted" after defeating Germany "to aid us in subduing Japan."[34] In opposition to Remer's argument, the other members of the commission held that, while Japan did indeed have large stocks of raw materials at its disposal, these could only be used in small amounts owing to a relatively limited production capacity in shipbuilding and airplane manufacture. As far as the political sphere was concerned, the Board of Analysts opined that China would not conclude a peace agreement with Japan under any circumstances, that Russia would remain on the defensive, and that Great Britain would support the U.S. against Japan even *after* Hitler's defeat.

Psychological warfare was not something one wanted to pursue in Asia at the beginning of 1943 because, as Wiley put it, Asians are "culturally remote from us" and "almost inaccessible to effective propaganda";[35] and from a military perspective the OSS was not expecting "that Japan will undertake to make further conquests of vital importance."[36]

The alternative "Hypothesis II," which proceeded from the notion of a concentration of forces in Europe, was also based on the assumption that National Socialist Germany was "our chief enemy" that "ideologically" presented "a menace" to the American system, that relaxing the war effort against Hitler would lead German soldiers to return to industry, and that this would undermine relations with Britain as well as precipitate a dangerous Soviet defeat or defection. For John C. Wiley and the OSS Board of Analysts, it was obvious at the start of 1943 that the burden on Russia and the heavy demands placed on Great Britain in the past had already been so enormous that "the chances of ultimate success will depend more and more on the size of the American contribution." Even in the field of psychological warfare, everything spoke in favor of a concentration of forces against Hitler, since "the subjected nations of Europe have with us a common cultural heritage. We can speak to them," Wiley explained, "and they listen. If they are disappointed, they will soon become useless, and we shall have lost a valuable asset."[37]

As far as the military aspects were concerned, Wiley's view was that the U.S. was already so deeply involved in Europe that the margin between minimum and maximum deployment was "not great." In each case one would have to give Russia material support and supply the English with food and military equipment. Furthermore, the Africa expedition represented a "large investment." As Wiley put it: "Unless we are content to see our Army in North Africa in a sense interned, we must use that area not as a seat but as a springboard." If, in addition to all this, one also took into account that distances across the Atlantic were much shorter than transport routes across the Pacific, there would be no doubt that forces would have to be concentrated on Germany in 1943. Wiley and his colleagues in the OSS Board of Analysts expressed the hope for a "successful opening of a second land front in Europe in 1943." Furthermore, they believed there was the possibility of a "complete expulsion of the enemy from North Africa" and a "chance of knocking Italy out of the war."[38]

Donovan emphasized that public opinion in the U.S. and England demanded a total concentration of forces against Europe. The Americans would accept a "Germany first" strategy as long as the situation in Japan was contained. By contrast, British morale threatened to break should the Allies move against Japan first.[39] While the OSS Director proposed minor revisions to the Wiley study, he asked Brigadier General Bonner F. Fellers, who assisted the OSS as an advisor, for an appraisal of the strategic situation.[40]

Bonner Frank Fellers, who knew the Mediterranean region firsthand as former military attaché in Cairo and was held in high esteem by General Marshall as a "very valuable observer" (though also as a terrible strategist!), held the view that the United States should intervene in the Middle East as leader of an international corps deploying a large fleet of bombers.[41] This thoroughly unconventional proposal rested on Fellers' estimation of the British, of whose military leadership he had an extraordinarily low opinion. For Fellers, the "Middle East," which he characterized as the "most important piece of land in the world," was not adequately secured against Hitler militarily. He speculated that the Germans, once they broke out of Europe, would select the Middle East as a "logical objective." Everything had to be done to keep Hitler in Europe, to bomb him from every direction, and to undertake a systematic effort to eliminate the threat of submarines.[42]

Concretely, Fellers proposed that "by midsummer of 1943 the United Nations should have established a series of strategic and impregnable bases from French Morocco to the Caspian," since Hitler's southern flank would extend from the Pyrenees to the Caucasus, and his eastern front would reach from Murmansk to the Caucasus. If one could close the circle around Hitler, he would be forced to distribute his divisions along a front 6,000 miles long. The Allies would then need only "to locate these weak spots, amass superior forces against enemy weaknesses and strike." Along with the fear that the Red Army, lacking support, might be dealt a devastating blow from bombers, Fellers' "encirclement strategy" also offered some advantages with regard to the supply situation. Thus, he assumed that Hitler, if he could be kept in Europe, would only be able to continue the war for two years at most, while the Allies were in exactly the opposite position: They could secure fuel supplies in the Middle East and were therefore in a position to provide serious relief for their Atlantic transportation fleet.[43]

Fellers, who in January 1943 was just getting acquainted with the military constellation in the Far East (at the time he was on MacArthur's staff), was convinced that a large-scale deceptive maneuver could be used in the Orient. "The possibilities" for pretending to Hitler that the focus of Allied war efforts had been shifted from Europe to Japan were, in his view, "almost fantastic."[44] When one considers that Fellers' cable traffic from Cairo to Washington had been decoded by the Germans barely a year earlier, giving Rommel an important military advantage, the Brigadier General's proposal is not entirely without a certain irony. Fellers obviously wished to strike back with the same means the defender had used so effectively to mislead the Americans.[45]

After Fellers had introduced his proposals into the discussion, Donovan, who valued a lively exchange of ideas among the different intelligence authorities, saw to it that Fellers and Wiley offered professional opinions on each other's memoranda, and that R&A experts also got involved in the discussion.[46] Interestingly, Fellers' study and his commentary on the Wiley memorandum set off heavy criticism within R&A. To begin with, the R&A economists under Emile Despres severely challenged the assessment, based on military intelligence data, of the Germans' supposedly precarious nutritional situation. In the OSS it had been calculated that current diet restricted neither the fighting capability of German troops nor the productivity of industrial workers.[47] Secondly, the OSS did not see any danger of a German military breakthrough in the Middle East, since the British had adequately extended their armed forces there in 1942, according to an R&A estimate. Finally, the economists in the OSS research division favored a buildup of bases in the Middle East, since North Africa offered the best opportunities for an offensive. And, fourthly, R&A rejected the systematic bombing of the Ploesti refineries in Romania for a variety of technical reasons.[48]

In spite of the emphatic way the OSS protested against advancing into the Orient and concentrating forces toward the Far East, the most conspicuous trademark of the advice provided by the OSS was its openness (or, to put it another way, its indecisiveness) regarding concrete military operations. When one considers how strongly George Marshall pleaded in January 1943 (partly on the basis of OSS documents) for the quickest possible invasion of western Europe, and with what determination the British pleaded for additional operations in the Mediterranean region, it seems baffling that the OSS Board of Analysts should have favored both an invasion of Italy and a second land front in 1943 without appreciating the fundamental conflict between these two aims.[49] This appears all the more astonishing when one bears in mind that the OSS was not underestimating the strength of the Reich; on the contrary, it had more realistic data than the military intelligence service G-2. The apparent underlying paradox can only be explained by the fact that the OSS was still not anticipating a German collapse at the start of 1943 and had a primary interest in concentrating all its military efforts on Hitler as the "chief enemy."

In the meantime, decisions about Allied strategy were made at a high level and entirely without consulting Donovan. While John Wiley, William Langer, and Emile Depres were talking to Bonner Fellers, well into the last week of January, about individual questions such as the effectiveness of bombing Romanian oil facilities,[50] President Roosevelt—between January 14–23, 1943, at the Casablanca conference, and against the advice of General Marshall—swung over to Britain's strategy, which envisioned a northward advance into Sicily and Sardinia.[51] Had Donovan been asked to advise Roosevelt toward the end of 1942 and been presented with the alternative Mediterranean strategy versus an invasion across the English Channel, the OSS would surely have been able to give the President concrete information to help him make a decision. But it did not come to that.

The fact that Roosevelt did not consult his secret intelligence service chief at the end of 1942 demonstrates that the President placed less trust in the OSS, which was actually established in order to handle strategic problems, than he did in his own instincts. Against the background of the decisions that were made in January 1943 in Anfa, a suburb of Casablanca, the strategic discussions going on within the OSS look like playing with sandcastles. Only indirectly did they make a contribution to the Casablanca delegation's discussions, and they did not contribute to the President's decisionmaking. As the events of January 1943 were to prove, Franklin Delano Roosevelt did not seem to have all that much interest in his secret intelligence service as an authority on strategy or political consulting.

LESSONS FROM MOSCOW AND THE OSS' ANSWER

The National Committee for a Free Germany and the Beginnings of the Crisis Between the Allies

No political event triggered as much insecurity within the staff of the OSS than the Moscow-sponsored "Union of Anti-Fascist Forces" for the "Free Germany" movement. On July 12 and 13, 1943, Wehrmacht prisoners of war and Communist émigrés—including Wilhelm Pieck, Walter Ulbricht, and Erich Weinert—had founded the National Committee for a Free Germany (Nationalkomitee Freies Deutschland, or NKFD), which resorted to the heavily symbolic black, white, and red flag of the Kaiserreich as a way of appealing to Germans' patriotic feeling and tried to induce a quick end to the war by stirring up opposition to Hitler and stoking the Germans' desire for peace.[52] Allen Dulles had already prophesized on February 23 that the officers taken prisoner in Stalingrad would develop a revolutionary movement and cooperate with the Russians. At that time, nobody at Washington headquarters was paying attention. After a proclamation of the German "political refugees" and prisoners of war was published in July, though, it was immediately suspected that the manifesto's publication was an initiative launched by Stalin to help implement the Soviet Union's psychological, military, and political goals. On the same day that the program of the NKFD[53] was published in the American press, the chairman of the OSS Planning Group, James Grafton Rogers, openly expressed his alarm about the "peace program" of the "Free Germans." In a circular letter distributed to all the important secret intelligence offices, he reported that the Planning Group had accorded "critical importance" to developments in the Soviet capital and had asked OSS listening posts in Bern, Stockholm, Cairo, and Istanbul to "report promptly" on reactions in Europe and especially in the Reich.[54]

At the same time Rogers used all his resources to obtain an appraisal of the Soviet-German initiative from political émigrés living in the U.S. Only a few days later a memorandum drawn up by the planning group around Poole[55] was made available. The memo not only anticipated basically the conceivable interpretations that the Western Allies would go on to develop concerning the Free Germany Committee; it also reflected the range of opinions among politically prominent exiles.[56]

By any measure, it is astonishing how little time it required for the tiny Foreign Nationalities Branch around Poole to get spokespersons for the different political émigré groups into action. From Count Coudenhove-Kalergi to Milan Hodza, from Raoul Aglion to Julius Deutsch, from Henry Ehrmann to Stoyan Gavrilovich, from Gerhart Seger through Albert Grzesinki and Greta Beigel to Hans Simons, everyone offered a personal judgment for the record.[57] The charm of these commentaries derived not least of all from the way that some émigrés (to the U.S.) talked about other "émigrés" (in the Soviet Union) and from how their remarks, often enough, came out sounding emotional and clichéd.[58] Common to all the remarks was the assumption that "psychological warfare" was "in some degree" an explanation for the NKFD. In addition, many commentators believed that the organization "fits into a pattern which had been transpiring for a long time past" and was "the logical culmination of a propaganda pattern which Russia has long directed toward Germany." It was just as obvious that pan-European champion Coudenhove-Kalergi would interpret the NKFD as a potential instrument for Russian expansionism as it was that Czech exile Milan Hodza would fear a German-Russian rapprochement.[59]

To be sure, a majority of these prominent exiles had their doubts about whether the Free German movement could ever "rally wide support in Germany." The educator Reinhold Schairer, who had been prominent in the youth movement,[60] did not see this move in Moscow's chess game as some kind of psychological warfare but rather as a "practical program" whereby the

Wehrmacht, the churches, industry, and the landed estate owners could be lured into an act of "professed repentance."[61] In contrast to Schairer, former Social Democratic Reichstag deputy Gerhard Seger interpreted the NKFD not so much as a menacing authority but more as an indicator that the Kremlin felt excluded from the circle of Western Allies and wanted to push the U.S. and Great Britain toward closer cooperation in the future. "Moscow," according to Seger, "was probably displeased by the Roosevelt-Churchill appeal to the Italian people without Russian participation."[62]

In spite of the disparities among the émigrés' different assessments and the wide range of speculation about the NKFD, a spectrum of views supplemented by voices from the State Department and Great Britain, Poole concluded his memorandum to the OSS Planning Group with an assessment that betrayed no uncertainty. Poole underscored how the "New Germany" manifesto needed to be "taken very seriously" and stressed that the establishment of the NKFD "cannot be dismissed as a simple maneuver of psychological warfare; still less as Communist propaganda." In the National Committee's Moscow declaration Poole saw an appeal, clothed in bourgeois language, that was directed at the German population and might lead to a puppet government in which Moscow pulled the strings of conservative figureheads like Pastor Niemöller, Field Marshall von Brauchitsch, and Hjalmar Schacht. Poole's fears led him to take at face value almost all rumors pointing in this direction.[64]

Although several informants from the Foreign Nationalities Branch doubted that Moscow had arranged the action by remote control, the FNB's boss explained that the establishment of the NKFD was merely another step in a Soviet program that had started around the end of 1942. Furthermore, for Poole the National Committee stood in a long line of diplomatic history going back to Bismarck's reinsurance policy vis-à-vis Russia and to the Rapallo treaty, which (incidentally) was concluded just at the time Poole was working in the U.S. embassy in Moscow.[65]

Even before America's entry into the war, the head of the Foreign Nationalities Branch had feared that the "antidemocratic revolution" in Europe might spread out like a tumor into the world at large.[66] For this diplomat, the establishment of the NKFD summoned up all those negative visions of rapprochement between the Germans and the Russians that in the past had prompted his call for "democracy [to] turn militant again" if it were going to "survive" and prevent a global ideological crisis.[67] For Poole, the establishment of the Free Germany Committee signified arrival at a prominent crossroad; it was a "symptom in the general pathology" currently troubling the world.[68]

WHILE POOLE SAW the formation of the Free German Committee as the beginning of an ideological struggle flaring up to continue beyond the war's end, and for which the Soviet Union was well-prepared while the West had nothing to offer but "laissez faire," the scholars of R&A evaluated the situation more calmly. For R&A the inter-Allied crisis emerging with the formation of the Free Germany Committee was not a move in the Soviet political chess game arranged by remote control and with questionable intentions, but rather a result of poor communication between Churchill and Roosevelt, on the one hand, and Stalin, on the other. If the Atlantic Charter of August 1941 already represented one unilaterally promulgated program, by July 1943 the Americans and the British were issuing a whole series of programmatic statements and appeals, again without Soviet participation: Shortly after landing in Sicily on July 10 (Operation HUSKY), an Allied military government had been set up on occupied territory in Sicily, and on July 16 Roosevelt and Churchill appealed to the Italian people, urging them to topple the Fascist regime and surrender. It was immediately thereafter, according to R&A, that the Soviet Union announced the formation of the National Committee over the radio and broadcast its manifesto.[69]

The R&A researchers emphasized that political relations among the three Allies could no longer remain in the "present state of vague and uncertain equilibrium between agreement and disagreement." The biggest danger was seen in how the rifts among Washington, London, and Moscow could be easily exploited by Goebbels or even lead to a separate peace. From that perspective, five days after the Moscow manifesto became public, the analysts in the research division advised against starting a Western counter-project to the Free Germany Committee, since this would simply create more tension with Moscow. It was more important to work with the Russians on developing a "positive and workable common policy respecting Germany," both in order to counter the Nazi plot to drive a wedge between the Allies and in order to prevent the Soviet Union from mobilizing a strong anti-Nazi faction and thereby keep the "good Germans" for themselves.[70]

In R&A, to be sure, there was more interest in diplomatic relations than in the social policy implications of the Moscow manifesto. At the beginning of August, therefore, the German population's expected reaction to the Free Germany Manifesto was the centerpiece of an R&A special study.[71] Methodologically, the OSS researchers proceeded by trying carefully to analyze and investigate the manifesto for its (manifest or latent) elements of appeal, for how individual social groups and forces in the Reich would likely react to the NKFD's "propaganda crusade." Here they determined that there were numerous parallels "at first sight" between the content of the Moscow manifesto and the Weimar constitution of 1919.[72] It was conceded, however, according to OSS prisoner of war surveys, that appealing to democratic memories could hardly have an impact in Germany. The older generation, it was said, understood nothing about democracy, and the younger generation presumably had stronger memories of the "impotence and failure of the Weimar Republic."[73]

R&A interpreters believed that the real significance of the NKFD manifesto derived from its linking democratic elements with an appeal to the Germans' longing for "national survival" and "independence." The NKFD was addressing the fundamental declaration it promulgated from Moscow to all social strata—from workers, through the middle class and officer corps, to "leftist" Nazis. While OSS researchers surely recognized that such a collection of divergent interest groups was not suitable as the basis for a future democratic government in Germany, they were nevertheless taken in by the illusion that the manifesto showed enough revolutionary implications to revitalize the old leftist anti-Nazi opposition of German workers and the remnants of the KPD.

In R&A at the beginning of August 1943, it was believed that the NKFD presumably deserved to be accorded greater significance than the Weimar constitution, that the segments of the population capable of being mobilized constituted an effective force for toppling the Nazi regime, and that National Bolshevism exerted a strong "attraction on youth and intellectuals." By contrast, the danger that the "German masses" could be driven into the "Bolshevik camp" by the NKFD appeal and the chance of revolution was regarded as downright small. Instead, it was believed (or hoped) that the National Committee's summons would promote that ideological strand of "democratic socialism" that in R&A's view dominated the so-called "German underground movement." R&A regarded the societal effects predicted for the Moscow manifesto with 'critical sympathy.' One wanted—especially in Herbert Marcuse's circles[74]—a social revolution in Germany and was apparently certain that Social Democracy rather than Bolshevism would win the day as long as the Allies succeeded in suppressing fears of the Reich's "dismemberment" and of the German population's "enslavement."

Marcuse and his staff did not want to admit that the political Left in Germany had long since ceased to represent an organized force and that the mobilization of KPD and SPD functionaries via the Moscow summons was completely illusory in the summer of 1943.[75] In a letter to the Foreign Office from August 3, the German Security Service chief Ernst Kaltenbrunner had characterized the National Committee as a "play thought up, staged, and skillfully mounted as propaganda by émigrés," and aside from the "usual reports about the distribution of flyers and leaflets" he could apparently not ascertain "any immediate impact" of the NKFD's creation on the German population. There could be no talk of reactivating the kind of worker opposition on which the R&A was hedging its bets.[76]

The NKFD manifesto was thoroughly discussed inside the OSS Planning Group as well, and on August 6 James Grafton Rogers submitted a memorandum to the Joint Chiefs of Staff (JCS) about the Moscow manifesto's meaning. Within two weeks after the appearance of the NKFD program, therefore, intensive debates had unfolded at all levels of the OSS—from FNB interviewers through R&A analysts to members of the Planning Group—about the ominous text of the "German refugees and prisoners." Interestingly, on August 6 it was not yet clear to the Planning Group which interpretation of the manifesto they would be submitting to George Marshall.

In the end the Planning Group decided to devote their entire memorandum to the JCS to interpreting those tensions arising from the manifesto that had implications for the Western Allies' relationship with the Soviets.[77] Here the planning team arrived at the conclusion, as anxious as it was crass, that "present Soviet policy towards post-war political development in Germany, as reflected in the manifesto, is dangerous in its implications. The manifesto, while undoubtedly aiming at the overthrow of the Hitler government, at the same time contemplates the setting up within Germany of a government favorable to Moscow. This might result in a communistic Germany. . . . Further, success of the manifesto might bring about a breakdown of [military] resistance, in which event Russia, with forces on the field, would be in a position to arrange a peace and a German government to its liking." Rogers let the Joint Chiefs see that he regarded "an examination of America's political position with respect to the manifesto as warranted." According to Rogers' warning, "complete political unity does not exist between the Soviet Union and the other United Nations, and political differences rising out of the manifesto may lead to a dangerous situation between these countries."[78]

Although the Planning Group was acquainted with the judgment of Alexander Werth, the Moscow correspondent of the *Sunday Times*,[79] and had also been informed about the Moscow leadership's official evaluation of the NKFD, the Soviet version was neither much noticed nor believed. Werth had conceded that the NKFD had "obviously met with the consent of and by arrangement with the Soviet authorities"; beyond that, however, there was "absolutely no indication that the Soviet government is committed to any point in the manifesto." Werth also claimed "that, juridically, the Free German Committee has no more status, in the Russian view, than various emigre groupings in Britain and the U.S., such as the people around Rauschning, Hanfstaengl, and Strasser."[80] For James Grafton Rogers and his colleagues in the Planning Group—and especially for John Wiley and Hugh R. Wilson—the establishment of the NKFD and the publication of the Moscow manifesto became something like the road to Damascus. Rogers, Wiley, and Wilson formed an influential faction in the OSS that began issuing increasingly emphatic warnings after the summer of 1943 about how postwar Russia was poised to be a dangerous victor at the future time or place in which the Allies' former enemies now under "bar-

barian rule"—Germany and Japan—would be out of the picture. A development like this had to be countered in the West by a political change of course or by Western-oriented psychological warfare.[81]

In a broader sense, the analyses of the NKFD led to a politicization of the OSS and to the intensification of a latent conflict with Marshall and the JCS. The OSS Planning Group had, as Rogers pointedly and accurately stressed in retrospect, "a deep interest in the political ramifications of the war" that was frankly not shared by the Joint Chiefs, since the latter were trying "to win the war by use of force" but did not view "the results of victory or defeat" as their business.[82]

Interestingly, in August 1943 it was the conservative faction of the OSS that succeeded in warning Washington's military and political leadership against a supposedly aggressive Soviet Union, while the voices of R&A committed to balance and cooperation with the Soviet Union faded away without any detectable, resonance.[83] A certain paradox resulted from the rebuff given to James Grafton Rogers (both by the JCS and by President Roosevelt) when he proposed a change of course—namely, revising the policy of "unconditional surrender"—in the fall of 1943. The Joint Chiefs did not see themselves as responsible for political questions, and in a private talk with Rogers Roosevelt took the view that "we were not sure enough of winning the war to risk any weakening of Russia's enthusiasm for the conquest of Germany." "After a victory," however, "he [Roosevelt] felt he could control Stalin—'Uncle Joe' ".[84]

Under the impression that the OSS Planning Group was completely powerless when it came to political questions, Rogers was led toward a deep-seated sense of resignation, which prompted him to quit his post in America's secret intelligence service in January 1944, only a few months after the establishment of the NKFD.[85]

Secret Intelligence Initiatives for Mobilizing German Émigrés

Even before the manifesto of the NKFD had been dispatched and publicized, and before the American public had been informed about the Moscow initiative, two OSS staff members meeting in Washington, Irving H. Sherman and Hugh R. Wilson, were setting their sights on a "Committee for German Freedom" (or "Committee for German Liberation"), a group inspired and promoted by the OSS. Irving Sherman, a New York banker who worked for the OSS office on Manhattan's Fifth Avenue, where he headed the SI division's German and Swiss Desk and maintained superb connections both to German émigrés and opponents of the Nazis, discovered in Hugh R. Wilson a conversation partner who was more interested in politically mobilizing the German émigrés than any other member of the OSS. As a long-time envoy to Switzerland

(1927–1937) and U.S. envoy in Germany (1938–1939), Wilson had forged ties to German politicians, many of whom had emigrated to Switzerland and the United States after 1933.[86]

Should it have been possible for the OSS to organize German political émigrés so that they could exert political influence on Nazi Germany? When he proposed establishing a Free German Committee, an idea that reached the OSS Planning Group via Hugh Wilson at the beginning of August, Irving Sherman proceeded from the basic realization that the German mind, shaped by "methodical orderliness," could be enticed only by logical arguments. "The German" was therefore "not easily converted to disloyalty to his government." National Socialist Germany, Sherman emphasized, was accepted by the Germans not least of all because it had been "'legally' constituted" and created a legalistic framework for its frequently extreme or absurd measures. So long as things were going well, Sherman believed, radical behavior could not be expected from the Germans. Since war fortunes had taken a turn against the Germans in the summer of 1943, however, a favorable opportunity arose for the establishment of an émigré-run authority to "save" the German Reich. Sherman regretted that the Russians had just achieved fulfillment of a very similar idea. In order to avoid any possible conceptual confusion with the Moscow organization, he proposed a different nomenclature: The émigrés' association should not be called "*Committee* for German Liberation," as originally planned, but the "Save Germany *Group*" or "Restorierung des Vaterlandes Gruppe" (or RVG—literally, "Restoration of the Fatherland Group"). Sherman hoped to gain the broadest possible following of potential regime opponents or defeatists by having the RVG made up of "the outstanding representatives in each particular category of German society"

The list of potential delegates, of whom eight to ten were meant to function as Committee representatives, included writers like Oskar Maria Graf and Thomas Mann, prominent Catholics like Carl Spiecker and Annette Kolb, émigré politicians, diplomats, and jurists like Hermann Rauschning, Wilhelm Sollmann, Max Brauer, Freiherr Wolfgang von und zu Putlitz, Hans Simons, Horst Baerensprung, and Kurt Riezler.[87] The Western *Deutschlandkomitee* was supposed to operate from behind enemy lines out of a region bordering Germany, from where it would tell Germans that the end of the war was imminent but that "there is still time now to save countless lives." In deliberate appeals, the population would be summoned to distance itself from the Nazi regime, whereby declared opponents of the Nazis might secure a "deserved place" for themselves in postwar Germany. Beyond that, the Wehrmacht was to be challenged—with appeals to its "tradition" and general sense of "obligation"—to take up armed resistance against Hitler.[88]

Thereafter, Siegfried Aufhäuser, Max Brauer, and Rudolf Katz—three members of the Social Democratic executive from the German Labor Delegation (GLD) closely identified with the more conservative wing of the party's movement-in-exile—approached Berle and asked him to assist in organizing an international conference of German exiles who would then go on to organize a permanent "Council of Free Democratic Germans." The plan was to establish a committee "to lead the fight against Nazism and to prepare the rebuilding of democratic Germany." The GLD explained that the Moscow National Committee had met with no resonance at all among German workers. Workers were not only interested in putting an end to Hitler's rule, but also in uprooting German "militarism and feudalism." In its communication with Berle the GLD stressed how ten years of Hitler's dictatorship made it necessary to consolidate democratic forces "from the bottom up" and how the principle of local self-government had to be introduced as quickly as possible after the war.

The OSS told Aufhäuser and his fellow Social Democrats that the State Department was going to impose restrictions on all initiatives undertaken by émigrés. The group therefore conceded from the outset that it was not their desire to set up a government in exile or "in any way hamper any war action." Another concession was voluntarily granting the U.S. authorities a right of censorship. Since the work of a "Council of Free Democratic Germans" could be effectively achieved only if the United Nations and "especially the United States" offered "a certain moral assistance," and since organizing a major international conference required making travel and visa arrangements, concrete assistance from the State Department was indispensable. The list of émigrés that Aufhäuser and his friends wanted to bring together from different regions in the U.S., as well as from England, Sweden, and Switzerland, was impressive at first glance. Social Democrats like Hans Vogel and Erich Ollenhauer, Fritz Tarno and Kurt Heinig, Otto Braun and Wilhelm Hoegner would be invited along with representatives of democratic, bourgeois, and Catholic circles, such as the former Reichskanzler Heinrich Brüning, Joseph Wirth, Gottfried Treviranus, Oscar Meyer, Arnold Brecht, and Erich Koch-Weser.[89] As soon as its first conference had been announced, however, the GLD hit on the questionable idea of forming a special invitation committee that would exclude all the Social Democrats who had fallen out of favor with them—especially the members of the "Renewal" ("Neu Beginnen") group. It could have been predicted that this kind of "undemocratic behavior" would lead to tensions within the Social Democratic émigré community.[90]

While the GLD's request lay on Berle's desk for more than four weeks as unfinished business, German émigré circles in different parts of the country put out announcements in which they defined their attitude toward the Moscow National Committee. The first resolution of exiles about the NKFD came from the ranks of prominent writers, artists, and scholars in Hollywood. Thomas and Heinrich Mann, Lion Feuchtwanger, Bruno Frank, Bertolt Brecht, Berthold Viertel, Hans Reichenbach, and Ludwig Marcuse signed a political summons to different exile groups in the U.S. in which they "welcomed . . . the demonstration by German prisoners of war in the Soviet Union" and called for distinguishing "sharply" between "the Hitler regime . . . on the one hand and the German people on the other."[91] Together with Hermann Budzislawski and Carl Zuckmayer, Dorothy Thompson drafted her own text[92] oriented around Eisenhower's declaration to the Italian people and highlighting the declaration's American provenance.[93] The émigrés in exile on the California coast, however, could not identify with Thompson's version. And so it kept going. One after another, Toni Sender, Herbert Weichmann, and Albert Grzesinski formulated their own programmatic manifestos (the last of these, it is hardly surprising, penned in a decidedly anti-Soviet style), but the more declarations got sent out, the clearer it became that the German émigrés would never be able to unite around a common political position on the NFKD.[94]

In addition, it became obvious that there was a seemingly fundamental ideological rift (overlaid by personal aversions) between the socialists from the "Renewal" ("Neu Beginnen") group supported by Dorothy Thompson and the conservative German Worker Delegation. When the German Worker Delegation was founded in 1938, it claimed to represent the Social Democratic party in the U.S.; owing to the rapidly growing political influence of Paul Hagen and his "Neu Beginnen" group (who succeeded in winning over three out of five members of the SPD's original party executive to his side), and also owing to a lack of political openness on the part of the GLD, the latter increasingly strayed offsides.[95] While Aufhäuser, Brauer, and Katz tried to create a representation for exiles led by old-guard Social Democrats with backing from Washington, Hagen attempted to form a common front of all German democrats in exile. The plan was to organize a mass meeting of the Free Germans in the U.S. on the occasion of the Free World Congress in New York in the autumn of 1943.[96] Since the German workers' delegation refused to take part in a conference bringing together all the exile groups, the initiative's success was in jeopardy.

In the meantime, good prospects for the different German exiles' projects had also dimmed for other reasons, related to the process of political decision-making in Washington. For one, the State Department rejected the German Labor Delegation's request for support in organizing its planned international conference. While Berle, to be sure, declared that the "sincerity" of the GLD with respect to their democratic goals was "evident," he made it clear that nothing had changed since December 1941 in the State Department guidelines on recognizing exile leaders and representatives of émigrés. The American government granted "no official recognition" to movements and conferences like the one proposed by Aufhäuser, but it did allow all these groups "to lay their case before American public opinion."[97] Berle offered by way of justification for his position the fact that there was no realistic information on "the degree of support" that the exile leaders had in their own countries. Therefore one could only speculate or entertain suspicions about such support. Decisions about how to use the free movements could not be made by the U.S. government; they rested with each national population.[98] Furthermore, in the meantime a report from the Psychological Warfare Staff (PWS) had come out opposing Irving Sherman's proposed Restoration of the Fatherland Group (RVG) for three reasons. First of all, it was said, an initiative like that was in the province of the Office of War Information (OWI) and not the OSS. Secondly, there was the danger that the RVG might be viewed as a counter-committee to the NKFD. And, third, the State Department had still not given the green light for the "more liberal use of Germans" by the OWI.[99]

The OSS, however, did not give up. Various individuals were trying to intervene, on all fronts and behind the scenes, in order to pave the way toward establishing a body that might, after all, represent Germans in exile, and perhaps even form a government in exile. A contact of Donovan's approached Julius Deutsch and told him that the American government did indeed have an interest in designating a common front and assembly for German exiles. Poole turned to Berle and asked him to revise his position on the German Workers Delegation. The Planning Group decided (in spite of the Psychological Warfare Staff's negative decision) to continue its discussion about the "Restoration of the Fatherland Group," and Irving Sherman supplied Rogers with a number of arguments meant to defuse the Psychological Warfare Staff's objections.[100] But what kinds of arrangements could really be made for the exiles?

Poole won a victory when he persuaded Adolf Berle about the importance of supporting the German Labor Delegation. It proved helpful to the head of the FNB that he had once been a State Department colleague of Berle and that both of them shared the same political outlook. On the basis of this "coincidence," Berle signaled that it "would be well to give diplomatic refugees of the type of those in the German Labor Delegation help within reasonable limits." In order to prevent other exile groups from feeling discriminated against, however, the State Department would not officially show up as a sponsor of the GLD; instead, the OSS would "use its own facilities in order to help the German Labor Delegation."[101] When one takes into account that Berle and his people were being flooded with all manner of obscure political proposals from German émigrés— including those from such strange personalities as Dr. Proewig, Baron von Sodens' personal physician[102] — and when one also looks at how inflexible the State Department's position on German émigrés had been over the years, it could be seen as a respectable accomplishment just to have gotten Berle to the point where he played along with accepting the OSS initiative to back the GLD.

The OSS' ability to act was, however, not limited only by outside forces. The ideological rift that cut across the entire German émigré community, proved equally problematic. Poole, Emmy Rado, and Irving Sherman, who belonged to the intelligence service's conservative wing, leaned toward the German émigré group around Brauer and Aufhäuser, whereas the R&A staff (and especially Dr. Walther Dorn) denied the conservative Social Democrats any political import and instead favored leftist socialists and the "Neu Beginnen" ("Renewal") group.[103]

For a brief time at the end of October it looked as if the different factions — both in the OSS and among the political émigrés from Germany — would be able to agree on joint representation for the German exiles, if only Thomas Mann were to assume its leadership. But when the OSS Foreign Nationalities Branch let it be known that Paul Hagen was behind the proposal for Thomas Mann's presidency — Hagen had indiscreetly told an FNB staff member that he wanted to *"wrap up"* the Nobel Prize laureate "into a German committee" — this immediately triggered a high-level alarm.[104] Rado, Poole, and Sherman pulled out all the stops to frustrate Hagen's plan, since (it was said) Hagen had "now stolen a march" on all the participants "and formed a Committee under the ostensible leadership of Thomas Mann."[105]

Over the next several days Poole operated behind the scenes, as reported to Berle in a "confidential" letter on November 10. He instructed Berle to prevent Thomas Mann from taking on the presidency of any German committee and to put off action on founding a body representing Germans in exile to a later date.[106] And so it happened that Thomas Mann, who insisted on getting official recognition from the State Department, took himself out of the running for the chairmanship of a group representing German exiles.

Among the German exiles convened for a joint "émigré front" in New York, Mann's withdrawal — which entered the annals of exile history under the slogan "Mann Overboard" — triggered a real shock.[107] Nobody there knew that the OSS had thwarted unity among the various forces representing Germans in exile. Among many émigrés, speechlessness turned into pure antipathy toward Mann when the doyen of German writers addressed the assembled émigrés and — quite in the spirit of a Rex Stout, Emil Ludwig, or Friedrich Wilhelm Foerster — conjured up the vision of a 50-year occupation of Germany. Mann also entertained the idea of a 30-year quarantine for German children, since they would otherwise be certain to infect the morality of Allied children.[108]

For some émigrés, Mann may have been the hope for representing all the exiles jointly. At the very least, the question now arose as to whether it was possible for the émigrés to develop political guidelines or proposals for postwar Germany if they were not even capable of smoothing over tensions in their own ranks.

Not by a long shot, to be sure, had all émigrés decided to throw in the towel now that Mann had withdrawn, even if the different German exile initiatives had even less reason to hope for support from American government circles after early 1944 than before. Thus, for example, the Council for a Democratic

Germany, which was chaired by the German Theologian Paul Tillich, had to struggle against the prejudice—launched by Brüning and taken up by Poole and Sherman—that the Council was really an organ of the Soviet Union.[109] The émigrés Hans Speyer and Gerhard Colm, who worked for the U.S. government, said in early 1944 that "even the most carefully chosen publication from the most united group of émigrés today would accomplish the opposite of . . . what it intended."[110]

It is one of the ironies of OSS history that America's secret intelligence service, which in the summer of 1943 was the only high government or military office pushing for the establishment of a representative body for Germans in exile, ultimately contributed toward blocking them from issuing a joint declaration. Had Poole and Berle, who were, after all, quite close to each other, been pulling together, then Thomas Mann might have been motivated to assume the chairmanship of a German committee. To be sure, in light of Roosevelt's inflexible position and the fractiousness of the German émigrés, it is reasonable to ask whether this thin-skinned writer might not have resigned at a later date anyway.

Not least of all, the fall 1943 episode shows how certain circles in the OSS— above all, Poole (in the Foreign Nationalities Branch), Irving Sherman (in the New York SI branch), and Hugh Wilson and James G. Rogers (in the Planning Group)—were trying to use the OSS not solely as an intelligence service per se, but also as an instrument to implement their own political ideas. Their efforts at intervention sprang from a general fear of what political consequences of the Second World War might be. In this context Poole, the self-appointed spokesman for the conservative OSS faction, spoke about an "incalculable metamorphosis" taking place at this moment. He was certain that the Soviet Union had prepared its own groups not only for Poland and Germany, but presumably also for every other country on the European continent, and he feared that a German government-in-exile in the U.S.—with left-socialists like Paul Hagen pulling wires behind the scenes—might lay the foundations for a Communist postwar Germany.[111] The job of the secret intelligence service, according to Poole, was more than that of keeping émigrés in the U.S. under observation. Beyond that, he was also trying to keep the émigrés in check and manipulate them politically.

GERMANY AND THE GERMANS

The Mood of the Germans as Assessed by the OSS

Throughout 1943, as expectations of the Reich's collapse grew stronger, Donovan's intelligence service became preoccupied with the question of the morale of Germany's population. To be sure, the OSS had been steadily gathering information about the German public mood during the first year and a half of the war. Nevertheless, news from the Reich was still trickling in sparingly throughout 1942. In March 1942, after the first major study conducted by the research department's Psychology Division (PD) had concluded that the Germans' attitude demonstrated widespread support for the regime "in word and deed," the R&A division shifted its attention to other priorities.[112]

In addition to the OSS, the State Department, military intelligence, and the FBI were making a special effort to collect, evaluate, and disseminate intelligence about German morale. The most obvious hallmarks of the 1942 reports were the disparities among individual sources of uneven reliability. Whereas it was possible to obtain well-founded information from Germany via diplomatic channels and from journalists before Pearl Harbor, after December 1941 the intelligence service had to switch to other means, such as intercepting enemy communications. The OSS specialized in interrogating émigrés and analyzing letters that were sent from Germany to, say, sailors jailed in South America or prisoners of war in Jamaica or Australia. In addition, the SI branch evaluated news from Polish secret intelligence, while the research division resorted to the German press, pamphlets by German émigrés, and the German Life-History Archive at Harvard University, which contained valuable information about the socioeconomic makeup and mentality of specific German population groups. The FBI reports, which were frequently not sent to the OSS, but only to the State Department and to Army and Navy intelligence, came mostly from anonymous informants whose identity and reliability not even Hoover's people could vouch for. Thus, for example, it was possible for an FBI memorandum circulating around Washington in May 1942 to describe the morale of German troops as downright low and to prophesize Hitler's fall. While this report also contained some realistic estimates, and although its informant apparently kept in touch with the German opposition to Hitler (he announced that Goerdeler would be assuming civilian leadership in the Reich once Hitler had been eliminated), three weeks later another FBI memorandum made the rounds that was practically dripping with absurd assertions and fictitious news. Everywhere throughout the Reich, it was argued, secret organizations opposing the Nazis were being formed. In June and July of 1942, the memo said, more than 40,000 Germans making negative remarks about Hitler had been arrested. Furthermore, the public mood was so bad that one could count on the Nazi regime collapsing in the winter of 1942.[113]

All of the secret intelligence services encountered the problem that the individual reports they were getting could claim to be valid only for a specific time and place. How, for example, was one to assess a report arriving from an informant in the German state of Württemberg and claiming that the population there was blocking the deportation of Jews in August and September 1942 because most of the Gestapo agents and SS people were Prussians and there was no tolerance in this part of Germany for the kind of Prussian arrogance, violence, and brutality familiar from history. Should one have concurred with the observer's judgment that southwest Germany might witness a "revolution against Hitler and the Nazis" at any time.[114] And what conclusion could be drawn from those fragments of information coming from the Polish secret intelligence services who were reporting about worker uprisings that had been suppressed or who hinted that the German population in some places no longer gave the "Heil Hitler" salute as a greeting?[115]

Unlike the OSS, America's military and Navy intelligence services had already acquired thousands of reports and data about the morale of the Germans at an early stage. What was missing, however, were analyses with predictive value. Material and information was collected, stored, and archived, but any conclusions drawn by the researchers in G-2 and ONI ended up sounding downright trivial. Thus, for example, in a key report from December 1942 military intelligence arrived at the perplexingly vague insight that German morale overall has decreased. If anyone even ventured to make a prediction, then the military and naval intelligence staff would proceed from the assumption that German morale was likely to turn defeatist through the early part of 1943, since any German hopes for some kind of success in Russia would have been reversed.[116]

Interestingly, very similar reports were coming in from Great Britain. Thus, London was assuming in March 1943 that Goebbels would have a hard time maintaining the public mood he wanted, since he had staked his all-or-nothing propaganda on "total victory" and was now unable to fulfill his grandiose promises. In addition, it was said that the German government, in light of the low public morale, would be prepared to make a "considerable . . . sacrifice" to the Anglo-American Allies if the latter, in return, would "build a wall against the Russians."[117]

By the start of 1943, as the view gradually began to prevail in both London's and Washington's intelligence services that the Germans' morale had become so weak that the Reich's collapse was just a matter of time, the OSS was vehemently against jumping to conclusions of this sort, and it protested that there was nothing inevitable about the erosion of the Nazi regime. The most succinct expression of this view came from a memorandum about "German Morale after Tunisia" that Franz Neumann had written.[118] In his study, the head of R&A's Central European Division simply relied on sources that were accessible to the general public; a commentator from G-2 was therefore right to wonder why this OSS report was stamped "secret."[119] What was new, however, about Neumann's analysis was its underlying postulate that the reports about the public mood and other dispatches from the Reich essentially had to be interpreted against the backdrop of the Hitler regime's totalitarian character. Neumann and his crew emphasized that individual expressions of feeling were far from being an indicator that the Reich lacked stability, since social controls, sanctions, and acts of terror prevented the National Socialist state from having a "public opinion" in the customary democratic sense.[120] The Nazi state, in the view of the R&A researchers, was to be compared to the "model of an army" (Franz Neumann) or to a "conveyer belt" (Herbert Marcuse) that promoted Nazis and non-Nazis in the same manner and allowed no scope for individual action.[121]

If the OSS analysts found little reason for euphoria from diminished German morale in the wake of Stalingrad and Tunisia, it found equally little reason to think that the Italian crisis and surrender (for which the OSS had been working, using radio and leaflets, since 1942) would have any lasting impact on the German home front.[122] The OSS did concede that faith in a German final victory had "considerably diminished" after Mussolini's fall; at the same time, however, it was asserted that German propaganda had succeeded in playing down the significance of the Italian collapse and demonstrating that the Allied demand for unconditional surrender was unacceptable. Furthermore, the Italian example showed that the end of a totalitarian regime would not necessarily trigger that social revolution on which the German "underground movement" (as Marcuse called it) pinned its hopes.[123] Indeed, it was in the autumn of 1943 that the head of the American 'Dogwood' spy ring in Istanbul, Alfred Schwarz, received several reports implying that the population's low morale, apparent everywhere throughout the Reich, would not necessarily be converted into revolutionary energy, but might instead result in bitterness, in slogans urging the population to hold out, and in warnings against the "enemies of the German people." The Germans, it was said, could not understand why the industries producing raw material were not being bombed, and why, instead, attacks were being flown on German residential areas.[124]

When, at the end of 1943, the OSS reviewed the events of the past year and evaluated the reports it had been receiving from the Reich, it arrived at the hardly optimistic conclusion that the Germans' fighting strength and productive capacity, both on the battlefront and home front, were not showing any decline worth mentioning. Morale, to be sure, continued to be bad, but it had leveled off to a certain steady state. The army leadership was still the only social group that could shake things up. Under the impact of the conferences at Moscow and Teheran, where the Allies had agreed on a united course of action, however, the German military would not possibly have any reason for overthrowing the regime. Himmler's terror machine had taken over the last key positions in the administration, and no action could be expected from the political opposition on the left, especially since the absence of any positive conception of psychological warfare complicated this task.[125]

A German Parallel: 1918 and 1943

Adolf Hitler's obvious interest in the events of 1918 was known to be based on a kind of trauma that never entirely left the former frontline soldier and that, even during the Second World War, made him afraid of a "stab-in-the-back" by domestic enemies even more than he feared military defeat.[126] For Churchill and the British, the First World War was inscribed in memory not only as a nightmare of blood and death, but also as a struggle that simply would not end. It took four years for the most powerful countries in the world to wrestle Germany to the ground, and then only for two decades. In September 1939 the British war cabinet had announced that the current conflict would take at least three years, while the Undersecretary in the Foreign Office lapsed into laconic pessimism when he explained that the British would "have to lose the war for four years" before they could win a decisive victory.[127] For Roosevelt the catastrophe of the First World War stood, not least of all, for Woodrow Wilson's soft propaganda line, which had proved disastrous. This also prompted him, in a manner of speaking, to stand Wilsonian principles on their head. He deceived the American public into thinking that the concept of "unconditional surrender" was something that just suddenly occurred to him at a press conference, just slipping off the tip of his tongue. In fact, however, the formula was the outcome of thoroughgoing reflection and calculation on the part of the President. Robert E. Sherwood, Roosevelt's speechwriter and close friend, noted after the war: "What Roosevelt was saying was that there would be no negotiated peace, no compromise with the Nazism and with the Fascism, no 'escape clauses,' provided by another Fourteen Points which could lead to another Hitler. (The ghost of Woodrow Wilson was again at his shoulder.)"[128] For the decisionmakers in Berlin, London, and Washington, the example of the First World War formed a frame of reference repeatedly used to measure both the present and the outcome anticipated for the Second World War.

From early 1943 onward, the Office of Strategic Services was intensely preoccupied with the question of the extent to which the end of the First World War could serve as a pattern for Nazi Germany's potential collapse. The New York OSS office had a collection of reports to which eyewitnesses of the collapse and revolution of 1918–19 had contributed, and many an émigré concerned about Germany's future had warned the Americans that the Communists had played their propaganda card well back then.[129] But was it really propaganda and social unrest that had brought about the demise of the Kaiserreich? Or were other factors at work? If one could only understand the collapse of 1918 properly, the R&A researchers argued, this could assume enormous importance "in developing an action plan which will shorten the war."[130]

When it compared the economic and military situation of 1918 to what it was facing early in 1943, the OSS arrived at a dual conclusion. First of all, National Socialist Germany was economically in a better position than the Hohenzollern empire. In contrast to how things were during the First World War, Germans in the Second World War occupied a far more extensive "territory to exploit," were able to fall back on larger stocks of strategic materials, and were also able (as a result of technological developments) to manufacture a number of urgently required goods synthetically. Secondly, though, the situation looked much less positive where military strength was concerned: In absolute numbers, Germany in March 1943 had 400,000 fewer men who could be recruited into the army compared to March 1918, and the contrast with its opponent's resources hardly made the situation in 1943 any rosier. From all these observations, the OSS concluded that Nazi Germany had enough supplies of men and material for a much broader offensive, which, however, would lead to a more rapid decline of the German position in case the offensive were stopped.[131]

In the summer of 1943, after a few members of the OSS research division staff had pored over the voluminous German documents concerning the breakdown of the old regime in 1918, they believed they had found the key to Germany's rapid collapse at the end of the First World War in the German "realization of the inevitability of defeat." At the beginning of 1918 the German army still had a decent fighting spirit; it had been the best-trained army in the world with the most progressive military doctrine. After the recognition that victory was unattainable, however, there was a rapid decline in morale and many desertions. In 1942 and 1943 OSS surveys of Wehrmacht soldiers taken prisoner in northern Africa had demonstrated that the expectation of a victory against Russia was the most important factor for the troops' stamina and high morale. With increasing problems at the Eastern Front, therefore, it was predictable that the Wehrmacht's fighting spirit would subside. To be sure — and here is where the OSS critique of Roosevelt's political course came in — "unconditional surrender" was not a goal for which a German could be enthusiastic. The formula (according to the OSS analysis) did not offer an alternative to holding out, but was instead compatible with National Socialist propaganda being drummed into the Germans and saying that the Allies wanted to exterminate Germany as a nation. What was needed was a "positive goal for Germany" that could distract the Germans from their fear and encourage soldiers and civilians alike to rebel against their leaders and bring the war to an end. As the OSS analysts summed it up in August 1943, if one were successful in straightening out the Germans' hopes, it might be possible to "shorten the war by six months"[132]

Late in the summer of 1943, the British also ordered their secret intelligence staffs to make comparisons between the patterns and events of 1918 and 1943. In contrast to the Americans, who evaluated published German documents on the First World War, the English analyzed the Great War as it was reflected in their own intelligence files. In so doing, they conceded that their country had been "very wide off the mark" when it came to "the Allied estimate of Germany's power and will to continue the struggle" during the First World War. The reason for this flagrant miscalculation was that the British had let themselves be blinded by the enemy's apparent military strength, while they failed to take into consideration the political and military indicators of a German collapse.[133]

A comparative study of the documents for 1918 and 1943 led the British war cabinet's secret intelligence staff to conclude that there were "many striking similarities." Then as now, it had "become increasingly difficult to disguise the true state of affairs from the country as a whole." Even if the food situation in 1943 was not as serious as in 1918, "heavy casualties, particularly on the Russian Front, and the shattering effect of Allied air raids have produced a similar, and perhaps even greater, sense of hopelessness and loss of morale." Although the political situation in Nazi Germany could not be compared with that of 1918 — after all, it was conceded, "the Nazi regime has had ten years in which to destroy all trace of democratic ideas and institutions" — London believed that the comparison with 1918 was appropriate and instructive enough to be used as a foil for evaluating the present. While intelligence services, as a rule, tend to produce pessimistic diagnoses (so that they cannot be accused of ignorance in case of a catastrophe), the British in 1943 were afraid that they might fail — for the second time in 25 years — to make a prompt diagnosis of Germany's collapse. Therefore they lapsed into the other extreme and cast far too optimistic a light on their evaluation of the situation. The British secret intelligence services played up the parallels between 1918 and 1943, and they warned against overestimating military factors while neglecting economics and morale.[134]

It was hardly surprising that Washington did not agree with the British appraisal of the situation. The research division in particular (acting entirely in the spirit of Franz Neumann's *Behemoth*, "a kind of bible for people working on Nazi Germany"[135]) — had repeatedly campaigned for recognizing the striking difference between the "military dictatorship of the last war" and the totalitarian "Nazi dictatorship" as an argument for the noncomparability of the societal situation[136]. In contrast to the Kaiserreich, there were no longer any "voluntary organizations" in the Nazi state, and "any attempt to form them or express discontent" was "met with ruthless terror." Furthermore, the attitudes and motivations of the different social classes could not be compared with those of the First World War, something that was attributable to the different character of the opposing coalitions. Thus, the U.S. and England strove primarily to put an end to Germany's drive to become a world power, whereas the Soviet Union aimed at more long-term goals regarding Germany's economic and social reconstruction. The Russians had "nothing to fear and everything to gain from the fullest possible development of a radical popular movement." The R&A researchers—especially Herbert Marcuse, who wrote the studies on the collapse of Germany along with Felix Gilbert and Franz Neumann—chided those circles in Great Britain and the U.S. who continued to show themselves hostile to or fearful of popular forces. These Anglo-American voices were thereby insinuating that the Western Allies could encourage and strengthen the Reich's democratic forces if they would place greater trust in the possibility of a popular uprising in Germany. R&A did not, however, venture to make a more concrete prediction about how the Second World War would actually end. Rather, the research division developed a wealth of different collapse scenarios discussing what a likely end would look like under different political, social, and military conditions.[137]

There can be no doubt that the Americans in 1943 had come up with a more realistic, more critical appraisal of the parallels to the events of 1918 than had their allies on the other side of the Atlantic. To be sure, there was widespread agreement that the Allies were not going to support the conservative opposition of officers and big industrialists to the extent of letting them escape the consequences of defeat; with respect to the timing of the regime's anticipated collapse, however, the American diagnoses proved better than the British ones. Why was this so?

To begin with—and not least of all owing to the sharp-sighted comments of a Franz Neumann, who placed the political system of National Socialist domination at the center of his analyses—the U.S. developed a sensitivity to the historical uniqueness of the Nazi regime that was occasionally lacking among the British. In addition, the English (not only in their secret service staffs, but also in the government and Foreign Office) tended, much more than the Americans did, to equate the Kaiserreich with the Third Reich and Prussianism with Hitlerism, as when Anthony Eden saw the "old false gods" at work both in 1914 and 1939, gods that needed to be destroyed, or when Sir Robert Vansittart warned that there was a "real" militaristic-Prussian Germany whose essence was contained inside whatever "accidental" Germany happened to be there.[138] Third and last of all, London overestimated the significance of bombing attacks and their effects on the morale of the German population, for it was precisely in the air war that the English saw the biggest difference between how the First and Second World Wars were conducted and the most important technological progress that had been achieved in the interwar period.

IDEOLOGY AND ECONOMY IN THE BOMBING WAR

Theories and Experiences

The experience of the First World War and the memory of the traumatic stalemate in the trenches along the Western front motivated a number of interwar theorists who saw aerial war as a simple way out of the fatal and deep-seated traditions of land and sea wars. The Zeppelin, which in Germany was played up as a kind of mythical miracle weapon, became perhaps the most impressive symbol for a newfangled way of waging war from the air, a method that seemed to demand fewer men and material than conventional forms of military conflict.[139] Whoever possessed military aircraft, so ran the doctrine of the air war prophets, was capable of defeating the enemy at lighting speed, since the opponent would not be in a position to undertake effective protective measures: Ultimately, trenches and blockades would be unable to counteract attacks from the air.

Independently of each other, Sir Hugh Trenchard in Great Britain and Giulio Douhet in Italy became advocates of an influential war theory whose premise was that aerial attacks would inevitably force any opponent to surrender. Trenchard, the first head of the RAF after the "Great War," held the view that civilian morale in working-class urban neighborhoods was especially vulnerable, and that bombing cities would result in a trail of frustration, social exhaustion, uprisings, and revolution. Giulio Douhet even believed that the capability to conduct strategic aerial warfare could pave the way for Italy to acquire Great Power status.

In the U.S., the lecturers at the Air Corps Tactical School at Maxwell Field, who dominated the American discourse on aerial theory, placed far greater value on the analysis and vulnerability of economic infrastructure than was done in Europe. The Maxwell Field analysts were especially strong proponents of the view that precise bombing attacks against transport routes, oil refineries, or above-ground power lines could have a cumulative effect and bring the industrial system to the point of collapse. Their concentration on precision bombing not only reflected the kind of fascination with newfangled technological concepts that generally exercised Americans; it also derived from an isolationist sentiment and apathy against all things military that shaped American domestic politics in the 1930s. A theory that would have turned the opposing side's population into a military goal, claimed aerial war historian Williamson Murray, would have thoroughly undermined the attractiveness of "air power" in Congress.[140]

While, beginning in 1942, the Americans first aerial missions were against critical industries in Europe with the aim (as in the attacks targeting ball bearing factories) of destroying the fabric of German industry at especially sensitive spots, the British—under the notorious command of Air Marshall Sir Arthur Harris—had fixed on the strategy of carpet bombing. The story of "Bomber" Harris has already been told many times; it is among the most controversial chapters of the Second World War and need not be recounted in detail here.[141] Suffice it to recall that Harris assumed command of aerial operations at a time when the British Bomber Command was in great difficulty. British bomber pilots had enormous problems navigating approaches to nighttime targets, and not infrequently they found it completely impossible to make out major cities from the air. In this precarious situation—a situation characterized by cynical escalations, and in which the Luftwaffe was flying missions against England that it called "Baedecker Raids"—Harris, with complete backing from the Prime Minister, championed an aggressive course that openly aimed at the so-called "de-housing" of the Germans. Since Harris also clung stubbornly to the theory of carpet bombing in the war years to follow, by which time the Bomber Command had already proven its capacity for precision bombing (as in the aerial attacks on the Eder valley dam and Möhne levee in May 1943), American and English versions of aerial war planning were developing in ways that drifted widely apart.[142] If the American side wanted to fly precision attacks against European targets, they needed an institution of their own capable of identifying information about potential targets independently of the British secret services. In 1943 this realization led the OSS to set up the Enemy Objectives Unit (EOU) at the American embassy on 40 Berkeley Square in London.[143]

The Enemy Objectives Unit (EOU)

Since the concepts for an American air war crystallized only quite gradually, at first the Air Force's intelligence staff (A-2) had only vague ideas and sporadic bits of information concerning bombing targets in Europe. Until about mid-1942 the chief planner of A-2, Colonel Richard D'Oyly Hughes—a former British army officer who had settled in St. Louis after a long stay in India and had become an American citizen—still had to rely on British information for the American air war.[144] As time went by, the British maps and target descriptions seemed increasingly inadequate to Hughes. Ultimately, it was the mutually contrasting aerial doctrines in Great Britain and the U.S. that prompted the head of the USSTAF to create an independent American intelligence and planning unit. While the British had become convinced by 1942 that bombing continental targets was not possible by day, the U.S. Air Force (which had—literally—been "given wings" by the technology of the "Flying Fortresses" and "Norden bombsights") came to believe that daytime attacks could be accomplished. Therefore when Hughes, who was stationed in London, approached John G. Winant and General Eisenhower about creating a strategic "target intelligence," he was referred to Donovan. Apparently no other institution within the U.S. war bureaucracy was ready, willing, and able to undertake this task. The OSS, which saw itself as a "flexible agency" (William Donovan) and "gap filler" (Charles Kindleberger), quickly recruited a group of scholars who became engaged in the analysis of potential bombing targets.[145]

It was no accident that the staff of the semiautonomous OSS unit, which cooperated closely with the United States Strategic Air Force (USSAF) but was never incorporated into it, consisted almost exclusively of economists. The EOU team's professional orientation reflected the unit's main goal, which lay in weakening the German economy through deliberately chosen strategic bombing attacks. The troop—initially led by Chandler Morse, and which soon included such illustrious and remarkable figures as Walt W. Rostow, Charles Poor Kindleberger, Carl Kaysen, and William Salant—had the assignment of developing criteria to select industrial "targets." In other words, the OSS economists were concerned with determining why a specific target within a so-called "system" should be attacked, and with finding out if the target was large enough and the technical (bomber) capacities adequate for a "surgical" precision attack. The strategy that Chandler Morse and Charles Kindleberger had in mind was therefore clearly opposed to British air war practice, which had no clearly defined concept of the opponent's "collapse." The British rule was instead to carry out simultaneous attacks against cities and sporadic strikes against precise targets, and then to speculate about whether any kind of success, be it economic or political, surrender or collapse, had been achieved. The scholars in the OSS believed in the existence of "panacea targets" (A. Harris) or those whose bombardment would do the maximum amount of damage; more than that, they had faith in their ability to identify these panacea targets mathematically.[146]

Since the Enemy Objective Unit's special duties took shape only gradually, the OSS economists had to deal with the way the U.S. Air Force was also expanding its operations in the European war theater just one step at a time. While this protracted development stood in the way of effective aerial warfare, it gave the Enemy Objective Unit staff one single advantage: namely, that by February 1944, when the American Airforce had reached its "full strength and capabilities," the EOU would also have a "well-disciplined air doctrine."

The small OSS unit was by no means the only force that had worked out a strategic concept for the Western Allies' bombing attacks: As of the winter of 1942, Morse's group was cooperating very closely with the United States Strategic Air Force (Colonel Hughes), the British Air Staff (Air Commander Bufton and Group Captain Morley), British Air Intelligence (and its liaison officer Colonel Kingmann Douglass), as well as with the Ministry of Economic Warfare (O.L. Lawrence). The strategic decisions that were made were the outcome of discussions among these authorities and their representatives. There was no Allied "air war discourse" in which the EOU was not a participant.

In concrete terms, the work done by this group of OSS economists—who were housed in London's U.S. embassy, paid by America's secret intelligence service, working for the U.S. Air Force, and who enjoyed a relatively high degree of autonomy as they developed a legendary team spirit within this institutional triangle—was distinguished in two ways from the work being done by the other air war planning groups. To begin with, the EOU was the only organization at the European war theater that had specialized exclusively in "target thinking" and in providing specific kinds of information about potential targets ("target intelligence"). The British MEW, to be sure, continually analyzed the incoming flow of information about Germany's economic situation in general, but the question of what damage could be inflicted on individual objects faded into the background. Analogously, the British Air Ministry (or AM) collected every kind of information that could be obtained, but the "target aspect" did not receive special consideration in the AM either.[147]

Since the EOU staff was preoccupied with specific "enemy objects," it based its work on the sober and often meticulous analysis of fragments of information. As Kindleberger recalled in his book, the group had to resort to all kinds of possible information, including news material, aerial pictures, or interrogations of prisoners of war. Delivery numbers from the joysticks of airplanes that were obtained from Polish sources, for example, revealed how many planes of a particular type were being produced. When it was not possible to get hold of the information sought via incoming reports, the attempt was made to obtain the missing intelligence by detective research. Thus, for example, early in 1943 Kindleberger and his team discovered by analyzing a plane wreck that the Focke-Wulf factory had been moved from Bremen to Marienburg (the inscription 'Focke-Wulf Bremen' had been replaced by 'Focke-Wulf Marienburg' on an airplane compass).[148] Constant reading of intelligence reports, meticulous analysis of details about targets (from the size and proportions of bridges to the designations for ball bearing types) formed the basis for all of the interpretations, be they ever so abstract, and occasionally proved advantageous compared to the British method, which frequently relied only on information intercepted by the ULTRA intelligence unit.[149]

Formulating theories was, in a certain sense, the second trademark of the Enemy Objectives Unit. The OSS economists really did attempt to develop a kind of "general theory of strategic air bombardment" that was supposed to function as an antidote to "getting lost" in details. Here the OSS economists developed an elaborate code featuring concepts like "target system," "interdiction," "cushion," "depth," "pattern of consumption," and "pipeline." In the Enemy Objectives Unit production plants were viewed not just as individual plants, but as elements within a "system" that observed and rigorously took into account the complexity and interdependence of the modern industrial economic system — such as the dependence of the steel industry on coal and the dependence of the coal industry on steel.[150]

In addition, the manpower factor played a significant role. In order for bombing raids to influence the enemy's "fighting capacity," the attack had to exert "depth" as part of its impact on the target industry. Depending on how great the "distance" was between the industrial plant under attack and military operations, and depending on whether the industry had reserves or substitute products at its disposal, a greater or smaller depth could be achieved. The capacity to absorb or recoil from a depth effect was designated as a "cushion" by the EOU economists. The cushion factor was relevant when one considers that bombing raids could inflict serious damage without diminishing the enemy's fighting capacity in general. It was at least conceivable that workers on the home front, prisoners of war, or foreign workers could be recruited to repair the damage.[151]

At the beginning of the war, intelligence and operations were strictly separated from each other. Contact between the Ministry of Economic Warfare in London and the bomber operations was the only, even if informal, tie between these two separate spheres. With the establishment of the EOU in London, the link between intelligence and operations became an institution.

From Casablanca to POINTBLANK

At the Casablanca conference, Churchill, Roosevelt, and their military chiefs agreed for the first time on a joint concept for the Allied bombing offensive. In the directive, which marked the start of a new era in the air war against Germany, addressed to the commanders of the British and American air forces on January 21, 1943, it said: "Your primary object will be the progressive destruction and dislocation of the German military, industrial and economic system, and the undermining of the morale of the German people to a point where their capacity for armed resistance is fatally weakened." And "within that general concept," the directive continued, five "objectives" were listed in order of priority:

a) German submarine (U-boat) shipyards
b) the German aircraft industry
c) the transportation system
d) oil facilities
e) other targets of the enemy war industry.[152]

The Casablanca directive, which at first glance looked like a concrete plan, was really a collection of vague guidelines. The introductory declaration was notable for its vagueness; even the list of priority targets was seen as variable—all depending on the "strategic situation."[153] No sooner had the directive been issued than a discussion started to take place within the EOU and among its London partner organizations that would eventually lead to a reversal of priorities. The OSS economists came out strongly in favor of drastically reducing attacks on submarine shipyards and for provisionally postponing the targeting of the transportation system and of oil facilities. Only in the aircraft industry—and especially in the category of single-motor fighter planes—did the scholars at the Enemy Objectives Unit find a target worthy of attack. While the OSS estimated that it would be more effective to combat U-boats on the high seas than in shipyards during the early part of 1943, and while the transportation system and oil industry embraced "literally hundreds of targets" that would vastly overtax the capacity of the Anglo-American air forces, it seemed like an obvious goal to concentrate on German fighter planes.

The OSS was not the only institution that saw bombing German fighter planes as a priority. Early in 1943 the military situation had become so critical that the necessity of attacking the fighter planes had become almost inevitable, and so it met with broad approval. Neither the British bombing raids on the Ruhr region (in the autumn of 1942 and the spring of 1943) nor the daytime American attacks against specific targets in southern Germany had achieved any sweeping success. The hoped-for Sisyphus effect of a German industry driven to despair by its factories' destruction failed to materialize. On the contrary: The attacks flown against the Ruhr region led only temporarily to the industry's debilitation, since the damage was absorbed within a matter of weeks and then gave way to a steady increase in production. In addition, losses on the Allied side were assuming thoroughly alarming proportions. During a single daytime attack on Stuttgart, for example, 45 of 338 American airplanes were shot down; and during the U.S. Air Force's attack on the ball bearing industry in Schweinfurt in October 1943 only 231 of 291 airplanes returned. In spite of the Allied air forces' growing strength, the prospects for destroying the enemy economy became worse, all the more so if they did not succeed in reducing the stock of fighter planes.[154]

In the early summer of 1943 Allied bomber commanders drew the appropriate conclusion by coming out with a new plan—POINTBLANK—that declared destruction of German fighter planes as the highest priority. In the directive of the Combined Bomber Offensive it said: "The Germans, recognizing the vulnerability of their vital industries, are rapidly increasing the strength of their fighter defenses. . . . *If the growth of the German fighter strength is not arrested quickly, it may become literally impossible to carry out the destruction planned and thus to create the conditions necessary for the ultimate decisive action by our combined forces on the Continent*. . . . Hence the successful prosecution of the air offensive against the principal objectives is dependent upon a prior (or simultaneous) offensive against the German fighter strength."[155]

POINTBLANK reflected, almost uninterruptedly, the OSS economists' basic thinking in May and June 1943. For weeks the Enemy Objectives Unit had been providing the analytic groundwork for the new Allied strategy, and it had also significantly influenced the final version of the pioneering directive.[156]

Interestingly, it was not as a result of analyzing the increasingly critical military situation that the London staff of the OSS had become convinced of the need to decimate German fighter strength; rather, this was the outcome of a complex military-economic calculation that took into account strategic factors and military industry sales as well as the structure of Germany's aircraft industry, not to mention the vulnerability and recovery time for specific factory facilities. From the perspective of the OSS, the attack against airplane production was a task that would primarily "reduce the cost and increase the efficiency of the bombardment program in this [the European] theatre."[157] Of special relevance was the central consideration—characterized as the EOU "party line"—that reducing fighter strength would seem to promise a maximum impact for relatively little effort. The danger that production might be increased from 550 single-motor fighter planes per month to 1,200 airplanes played as much of a role in the economists' calculation as the high "turnover," which, the OSS estimated, led to a complete replacement of the airplane stock within two and a half months, making attacks particularly worthwhile. "Because of high operational wastage," it said in a memorandum summarizing the analysis, it was possible that "fighter airplane strength striking power . . . can be affected by attacks on production more drastically and more immediately than for any other item of military equipment."[158]

When in July 1943 the Eighth Air Force's primary mission became bombing those "targets" that the OSS experts had been proposing, it represented a major success for Kindleberger and his team. In the end there was an entire series of factors—not least of which was the "laborious salesmanship" of Colonel Hughes, who pushed the proposals on precision bombing through the "Whitehall maze"—that led to POINTBLANK's realization. Nevertheless, the OSS analyses deserved a great deal of credit for the trend in enemy fighter plane production, which, after rising to nearly 1,000 per month in the course of 1943, were then forced back to a quota of 250 by the end of February 1944.[159] Although it should be assumed that the OSS economists' analytic rationale was not fully understood in all its complexity by the Air Ministry or Anglo-American bomber command, the British and American chiefs of staff adopted at least partially the objectives formulated by the EOU. This had a great deal to do with the fact that the "targets" proposed by the economists also appeared to be appropriate objectives from a military perspective. In 1944, however, there was one sensational conflict between the London OSS team and the British Air Staff, a dispute that reflected in almost classical fashion the differences in outlook between the American scholars and their British counterparts.

Tensions with the British and the Philosophy of the EOU

The protagonists of the duel that was carried out on an ideological and military-bureaucratic level were the Enemy Objectives Unit of the OSS and, on the British side, Solly (later Lord) Zuckerman. The Englishman was working as the scientific advisor to Air Marshal Tedder, the deputy supreme commander of the Allied air forces, whom Zuckerman had already impressed during the campaigns in North Africa and Italy. The "one-man-brain-trust," [160] as Walt Rostow called him, not entirely without irony, was originally a biologist and had earned his spurs with an analysis of primate sexual and social behavior, a career trajectory reflected in the title of his autobiography "From Apes to Warlord."[161] His ethnological studies had won Zuckerman a position as an Oxford don, lecturing on anatomy, and, with the outbreak of the war, a research position in the Ministry of Home Security, where, among other things, he dealt with the psychological effects of the German bombing attacks on Birmingham and Hull until, starting at the end of 1942 and in close cooperation with the British air force staff, he analyzed and calculated the effects of Allied bombing operations against Axis targets.

The controversy between Zuckerman and the EOU, between Tedder and Spaatz, between the British and the Americans, which erupted in January 1944 and dragged on for several weeks, was provoked by the question of which targets one could most effectively set for Allied bombers. After the targets proposed by the Theatre Intelligence Section of the military intelligence service G-2 had quickly proved how unsatisfactory they were, Zuckerman drafted a memo, which called for French and Belgian switchyards or marshalling yards to be bombed on a grand scale and in a manner analogous to the attacks being made on Sicilian and Italian train stations.[162] When the Zuckerman plan was submitted to the EOU analysts, they immediately saw serious reasons to oppose it. To begin with, from the perspective of the OSS economists in January 1944, the Italian model seemed to have lost its canonical status, since, even in the Italian war theater, departures were being made from the concept of bombing marshalling yards, while in the meantime experiments were being made with systematic raids against bridge systems ("Operation Strangle"). Secondly, it was "evident," as the OSS insisted, that Zuckerman's draft was not supported either by the target specialists from the Air Ministry and War Office or by O.E. Lawrence in the Ministry of Economic Warfare.[163]

Viewed superficially, it seems as if the OSS scholars and their Oxford colleague Zuckerman were having a heated debate over trivialities. How did it get to the point where a controversy about bombing marshalling yards or bridges at the beginning of 1944 was capable of making such big waves?[164] Each one of the participants' memoirs, which as a whole contradict each other on several points, describes just one part of the story. One key to understanding the British-American duel, however, is provided by a passage in Kindleberger's autobiography, where there is the laconic remark: "The debate over marshalling yards versus bridges went on through the early spring of 1944. It became partly entangled in the strategic issue of bombing oil plants, since the U.S. Air Force partly argued that if it could restrict its operations to bridges, it would have substantial forces available for attacks on oil."[165] What Kindleberger described as something that was "partly" a goal of the U.S. Air Force corresponded in reality to the "party line" of the Enemy Objectives Unit, whose program was not characterized by dogmatic persistence but rather by a genuine dynamic. While the head of the U.S. Strategic Air Force in Europe, Carl Spaatz, was at first primarily interested in the transport system (and thereby, at least potentially, in Zuckerman's plan), and while the British had developed a fundamental aversion against the oil targets in 1943—Arthur Harris characterized the English and American oil experts disrespectfully as "oily boys"—the U.S. economists, beginning in early 1944, chiefly favored a paradigm shift toward oil. In order to implement their goal, the EOU not only had to fight against British resentment, but they also had to convince Spaatz of the absurdity of Zuckerman's proposal, since costly raids against marshalling yards—in contrast to the raids on bridges—were incompatible with a systematic attack against enemy oil facilities.[166]

Until the start of 1944 the OSS had decided against a massive bombing of oil refineries and synthetic oil facilities, since the "target system" (with its 50 to 60 individual targets) seemed to lie beyond the Air Force's capacity. After the stock of German fighter planes had been so thoroughly decimated that a large-scale air attack against the Reich seemed feasible, however, the team of London scholars working for American intelligence came out in favor of bombing oil facilities. In a cogent prognosis from February 1944, Captain Barnett, the oil expert at London's OSS headquarters, took the view that no other target system promised greater success with regard to accelerating German defeat than oil, while Kindleberger and his staff, especially Robert Rosa, composed a series of memoranda against bombing the marshalling yards.[167]

At the end of February the OSS team had prepared a comprehensive memorandum conceived as an alternative to Zuckerman's plan. At its heart was a long paragraph dedicated to the "evaluation of the current enemy strategic situation."[168] There it said: "It is our view that the German government and the German High Command are prepared to continue to accept the drain of 'manpower' losses in Russia, Italy, and the Balkans, and to bear the weight of our air attack on German cities and industries in one hope; that of defeating operation Overlord and producing dissension among Britain, the United States, and Russia. What Germany expects to gain from such a success is not clear, but the O.K.W. may believe that separate peace with Russia might be salvaged or that the United States would shift attention to the Far East." The view in the OSS was that, under current circumstances, the Allied air forces "can pound German armaments production and German cities," though without inducing that symbolic turnaround—"reproducing Pantelleria"—of the kind that the collapse of Italy had introduced.[169]

In contrast to the Enemy Objectives Unit, numerous influential Britons—including Harris, Tedder, and Zuckerman—held the view that the German population's morale could be broken by a hail of bombs against military and civilian targets.[170] In the EOU's February memorandum, by contrast, it said: "Morale" is "not a useful target system. Panic, war weariness and fear of impoverishment . . . is not likely to speed disintegration of Nazi controls."[171] While the behavioral researcher Zuckerman was interested in the effect of bombing on morale, among other things, the team of economists around Charles Kindleberger concentrated exclusively on the "cost-benefit effect" and measurable damage that bombing raids would cause within the "system of the German war economy." In this spirit, the Enemy Objectives Unit proposed in their February memorandum the following objectives for targets: "i) the completion of Pointblank . . . ii) tactical support if absolutely required; iii) the completion of attack on oil which alone among the remaining target systems offers the opportunity . . . of bringing the German war effort to a close."[172]

Although both the R&A War Diary and EOU veterans after the war maintained that their ideological dispute with the British in 1944 was all about the alternatives of bombing bridges versus marshalling yards, in the EOU's February memorandum, which was designed as an alternative to Zuckerman's plan, there was characteristically no mention of bridges. More to the point, it was the "attack on oil," which was hidden in the memorandum as its third and final point, that really constituted the chief interest of the OSS analysts. When the EOU plan was submitted to Carl Spaatz on March 5, 1944, the General immediately recognized that he was now dealing de facto with an "oil plan." This notwithstanding, after a lengthy discussion that lasted into the early morning hours of March 6, he let himself be persuaded that it was worthwhile to defend the EOU plan's merits at the highest level.[173]

What went on in the American and British air force staffs and ministries over the following three weeks completely evaded any control by the scholars working in the London headquarters of the OSS. On March 25, 1944, when Eisenhower was in the Air Ministry and had to reach an historic decision about the Allies' future air war strategy, Tedder and Spaatz confronted each other. Tedder, entirely in line with Zuckerman, supported systematic attacks against railway installations; Spaatz argued that the raids on oil would yield the biggest strategic utility. Although even some British officers had reservations about the efficiency of the Tedder plan, Eisenhower ultimately came out in favor of strategic attacks against marshalling yards and miscellaneous transportation facilities, that is, in favor of a conservative line that seemed to promise more immediate success for the Overlord operation than the oil attacks proposed by the EOU. Eisenhower's main reason for his decision was that the oil plan would most likely have taken four or five months to show concrete results.[174] Unsuprisingly, the staff of the Enemy Objectives Unit reacted in a depressed way to Eisenhower's choice. Walt Rostow noted cryptically in his diary: "A tragic and also historic day. We are defeated. Bet 2 d[ollars] they [oil targets] will be attacked—even if too late."[175]

Rostow would soon be proven right, at least with the first part of his prognosis. At the beginning of April, the Fifteenth Air Force flew raids not only against the railroad facilities of Ploesti, but also against the oil refineries there; in mid-May facilities for manufacturing synthetic oil (including the one in Leuna) were bombed; throughout June oil became a priority of the air attacks against Germany. In addition, in the context of preparations for Overlord, attacks against Belgian and French railway bridges were also soon taking place. After the Ninth Air Force had proved unexpectedly successful in demolishing the bridge over the Seine near Vernon at the beginning of May, the British General Trafford Leigh-Mallory gave the order to begin destroying the bridges over the Albert Channel and Meuse river. At around the same time, the Allied armed forces' supreme command registered alarm at how the bombing attacks against railroad facilities were causing only a few minor delays. The Germans were repairing their marshalling yards with remarkable efficiency or simply redirecting the train traffic. Even if they could not be completely destroyed, the bridges were unusable for a long time to come. As soon as they were repaired, the bridges were immediately attacked by Allied bombers again. Shortly before the run-up to Operation Overlord, British and American bombers attacked all the bridges along the Seine in a kind of last-minute action. On D-Day, as a result of the Allied air attacks, the Seine was no longer passable for railway traffic.[176]

Had things gone according to the wishes or economic calculations of the Enemy Objectives Unit (and they were often the same),[177] the Western Allies would for starters have dispensed with the bombing of the French marshalling yards and instead attacked additional bridge systems; secondly, the oil plan would not have been done piecemeal but rather systematically and at an earlier time.

In retrospect the target systems proposed by the OSS analysts—bridges and oil facilities—proved to be extraordinarily efficient objectives. It was not even contested that the air attacks proposed by Zuckerman had some impact, in that they reduced the stock of locomotives and prevented craftsmen and mechanics from getting around to such tasks as extending the Atlantikwall. The Eighth U.S. Air Force, meanwhile, recognized that the Enemy Objectives Unit had a major share of responsibility for the success of Overlord and wished to have Kindleberger and Rostow decorated for their outstanding achievements in July 1944.[178] Looking at the Allied oil strategy, Albert Speer explained in his memoirs that the May attacks of the American Eighth Air Force against oil facilities in central and eastern Europe signified "a new era in the air war" and "the end of German armaments production."[179] And even Arthur Harris conceded shortly before the end of the war that he had initially misestimated the Operation's potential: "In the spring of 1944," as he put it in his memoirs, "the Americans began a series of attacks against German synthetic oil plants. . . . At the time, I was altogether opposed to this further diversion, which, as I saw it, would only prolong the respite which the German industrial cities had gained from the use of the bombers in a tactical role; . . . In the event, of course, the offensive against oil was a complete success . . . but I still don't think that it was *reasonable*, at that time, to expect that the campaign would succeed; what the Allied strategists did was to bet on an outsider, and it happened to win the race."[180]

From the perspective of the OSS analysts, common sense dictated betting on oil and bridges. In the military-economic target theory they developed, they saw a kind of "profit guarantee" or at least a formula for increasing "profitable opportunities." For the first time in history, scholars had developed concrete formulas allowing them to specify optimal target objectives and enemy weak points, not just by intuition and a certain amount of guesswork, but by making concrete calculations. This makes it possible to understand why the debate between the OSS and the British analysts was so heated. Kindleberger and his staff believed that they had calculated optimal targets with almost mathematical precision. They reproached the British for having a plan that refrained from using cost-benefit calculation. The OSS was proud of the EOU economists in its London think tank. After the war the historian Arthur Schlesinger Jr., who worked as a liaison between R&A and SI, explained, perhaps not entirely without a certain self-irony, that the "historians and political scientists seemed a bunch of dilettantes . . . next to the economists, with their brilliant fusion of analytical and quantitative techniques and their intimate involvement in military operations,"[181] and the Harvard historian and OSS veteran Franklin Ford saw the identification of appropriate targets for the Allied bombers as one of the most important aspects of OSS activity for the course of the Second World War.[182]

It would be absurd to assume that the EOU used their calculations to discover the German war economy's Achilles' heel. There was no strategic miracle target whose bombardment could have forced the German Reich to its knees with whatever means the Allied air forces had at their disposal; and when Soviet troops overran Romanian and Polish oil fields in the summer and autumn of 1944, this undoubtedly had more of an impact on oil production than the air operations carried out by the Allies.[183] The tiny EOU staff's activities were, nonetheless, of lasting importance. Both the bombardment of the bridges along the Seine and the focus on the oil targets contributed in a major way toward obstructing the German war effort. In addition, the philosophy of the OSS economists had a more subtle impact, in that it created the ideological foundation for an economically efficient bombing strategy that commands attention to this day.[184]

IV

Bern: The Big Window Onto the Fascist World

ALLEN DULLES AND THE ESTABLISHMENT
OF THE OSS OUTPOST IN BERN

On November 8, 1942, the same day that the Allies landed in North Africa, and on which the Germans countered by occupying the south of France and sealing off the border to neutral Switzerland, Allen Welsh Dulles made it across the border near Annemasse using a special pass, just in time to move into the chancellery building of the Belgian legation in the old city of Bern (the legendary Herrengasse 23) and into two other buildings in Dufourstrasse 24 and 26.[1] The official title for the barely fifty-year-old man with the rimless glasses, moustache, and obligatory pipe was Special Assistant to the American Minister (Leland Harrison) in Bern, yet only a few days after Dulles' arrival the Swiss press was calling him the "personal representative of President Roosevelt." In reality Dulles, who had taken over as manager of the OSS office in New York after a Wall Street career as an international law attorney, was the new boss of the OSS outpost in Bern.[2]

Donovan had the management of the London OSS headquarters in mind for his New York staffer, but Dulles insisted on being delegated to Bern, presumably because he had gotten to know Switzerland on two previous missions. During the First World War he had been secretary to the legation in Bern, where he had recruited Yugoslav and Czech dissidents to create a spy network in Austria; during the interwar period he had traveled frequently to Switzerland for international conferences on arms reduction. The success of that espionage enterprise had evidently led him to the conclusion that Switzerland was eminently suited to be a listening post and spy station against "the fascist world."[3] The memories Dulles had as he assumed his position in Bern must not have been entirely unlike those of the writer and dramatist W. Somerset Maugham, who had been stationed in Switzerland as a British secret agent and had described the Swiss Confederation as a showplace with "every sort of intrigue," where agents from secret services romped around and spies, revolutionaries, and agitators frequented the hotels.[4]

During the Second World War, the atmosphere in Switzerland was not shaped by that mood of revolutionary renewal that had dominated political, artistic, and literary circles during the First World War; as a result the foothold established by various secret intelligence services was that much firmer in places like Zurich, Geneva, Bern, Lucerne, and Basle. Thus, the Soviets maintained a spy ring (named "Lucy") that operated for years out of Lucerne in order to supply Moscow with intelligence.[5] By way of Roger Masson, the Swiss intelligence service had a secret line to secret intelligence chief Walter Schellenberg in Berlin;[6] and since 1936 the British had stationed an SIS agent, the head of the organization "Z," Claude Dansey, in Zurich.[7]

The Americans sent their own delegation of agents to Bern much later, and certainly with greater hesitation, than the other Great Powers. The first to arrive was Charles B. Dyar, who (for the first time in American history) was stationed at the U.S. legation under cover as a finance attaché.[8] He was followed in August 1942 by Fred J. Stalder, responsible for counterespionage, and in October by the petroleum attaché Fred Loofbourow, whose job was to track down factories for synthetic gasoline production and engage in atomic espionage (AZUSA); on November 12 Max Shoop, who was supposed to establish contact with the French maquis, arrived.[9]

In spite of Switzerland's neutral status, it was not all that easy for the Allied secret intelligence services to operate inside the Alpine republic. The intelligence services' activity was constrained by the extraordinary severity of tough Swiss censors. Problems were also posed by the presence of about 150,000 Germans, 40,000 of whom the OSS regarded as National Socialist sympathizers, and at least 1,500 as active Nazis.[10] In addition, for both technical and political reasons it was difficult to send secret messages from Switzerland to the U.S. The telephone lines ran through a commercial Swiss telephone company and were encoded immediately before they reached the airwaves. The Swiss government therefore knew all about the content of Dulles' telephone conversations, and the OSS head occasionally used his nightly telephone calls to keep the Swiss authorities informed, unofficially and indirectly, about certain events.[11]

The Germans were in no position to crack the OSS code; however, since the Bern head of the OSS was also using the State Department code, which the Germans were able to decipher for a while (the Nazis had just infiltrated one of their spies, Jacob Fürst, into the legation), it soon emerged that cabling highly confidential intelligence from neutral Switzerland to the United States might be downright dangerous. Among other things, Italian Foreign Minister Count Galeazzo Ciano's removal from office was attributable to a telegram transmitted by the State Department in which Dulles had indicated knowledge about the possibility of Mussolini's removal six months before Pietro Badoglio's coup.[12]

In contrast to the widespread notion that Allen Dulles had conjured up a network of agents out of thin air within a matter of weeks, the legendary "spymaster" was able, upon his arrival in Bern, to rely on an abundant number of contacts whose names are still, in part, kept under wraps by the CIA.[13] Dulles first found backing from Leland Harrison, the U.S. envoy in Bern, as well as from Sam E. Woods, who ran the American general consulate in Zurich and maintained close ties to a Berlin opponent of the Nazis by the name of Erwin Respondek ("Ralph").[14] "Ralph" routinely supplied the American diplomats with reports about the political situation in France and Germany; and, directly or indirectly between 1941 and 1945, Harrison was in touch with persons as diverse as Hjalmar Schacht, Eduard Schulte, Jules Sauerwein, Grégoire Gafencu, and Prince Max von Hohenlohe-Langenburg.[15] Along with Harrison and Woods, Dulles cooperated closely with Brigadier General Barnwell Legge, the American military attaché in Switzerland, as well as with Gerald Mayer from the Office of War Information.[16]

The person who turned out to be Allen Dulles' most important informant, to the point of becoming his right-hand man, was Gero von Schulze-Gaevernitz, whose father had been in touch with the Bern OSS head since the First World War. Repelled by the Nazis, the young professor's and politician's son, who had traveled to the Soviet Union in the 1920s and found a job after university at the banking house of Morgan Livermore in New York, applied for American citizenship before settling near Ascona, Switzerland in 1938. As the brother-in-law of German industrialist Edmund Stinnes, von Schulze-Gaevernitz maintained excellent contacts with German industrial, banking, and diplomatic circles, which provided him with a good reason to commute back and forth between Switzerland and Germany.[17]

Once the war broke out, Gaevernitz began to earn a living selling dollar bills to the security-conscious Swiss in exchange for checks, which proved to be a profitable business.[18] Still, his real interest was in the "struggle against Hitler," in which he hoped to participate "somehow and sometime."[19] In addition to Gaevernitz ("476"), Dulles had close, and quite intimate ties to Mary Bancroft, an eccentric member of American high society married to a Swiss.[20] Dulles put

Bancroft in touch with Hans Bernd Gisevius, whose book manuscripts she translated into English, while also establishing a link between Dulles and the psychoanalyst Carl Gustav Jung.[21]

Hans Bernd Gisevius, who worked as a counterintelligence agent under cover of being a vice-consul in the German consulate in Zurich, was perhaps the most dubious character. Yet Dulles had complete confidence in Gisevius (alias "Luber" or "512") after the former Gestapo man had drawn his attention to an American code cracked by counterintelligence and then began to inform him about a group of conspirators inside Germany.[22]

In telegrams to David Bruce and William J. Donovan, Dulles emphasized that C.G. Jung's "opinions on the reactions of German leaders, especially Hitler in view of his psychopathic characteristics, should not be disregarded." Dulles was particularly struck by Jung's insight that Hitler would "take recourse in any desperate measures up to the end," and that, "he does not exclude the possibility of a desperate moment." According to the Basle psychologist, the "magical power" the Führer possessed, in contrast to other Nazis, was based on how Hitler appealed to the unconscious, while Göring was the kind of character Germans could see right through and analyze.[23]

On the whole, Dulles' contacts represented a truly curious collection of agents, made up of counterintelligence spies, psychologists, and journalists who offered the OSS chief their appraisals of National Socialist Germany.[24] Although he was "bored to death" by the émigrés, he also maintained ties to political exiles in Switzerland.[25] The fact that Dulles (in contrast to his colleagues in the British secret service) seemed to have his ears open to anyone offering advice, no matter how obscure, constituted the special risk, but also the charm, of the OSS operation in Bern. Among the anti-Hitler German resistance circles, news of Dulles' arrival in the Swiss capital awakened hopes that, as would later become apparent, could hardly be fulfilled. Donovan, meanwhile, quickly realized that the information showing up at Washington headquarters "from Hitler's doorstep" was, as a rule, more reliable than the intelligence arriving in the U.S. via other channels. He therefore saw to it that all the important cables from Bern went immediately to the White House.

Within three weeks of his arrival in Switzerland, Allen Dulles sent a comprehensive telegram to the OSS headquarters in London and Washington in which he described the political situation in Italy, Germany, and the Balkans and submitted proposals for the development of a program for psychological warfare. Dulles' prescription for Germany was that—wholly independently of whatever policy the Allies might adopt toward Germany in the end—it was important *today* to convince the Germans that there was "hope [even] in defeat" and that the "innocent [would be] protected" and the guilty, by contrast, punished by law. The time would come, Dulles prophesized, when German opponents of the Nazis, in spite of their negative memories of Wilson's Fourteen Points, would see America's promises as their "only hope." At the moment one had to do everything possible to shake up the common soldiers' belief that there could be a final victory, and thereby to trigger mass desertions.[26]

Dulles saw initial signs of rifts in the Germans' morale in the upshot of Stalingrad, which had shattered the myth of Hitler's "infallibility and invincibility." The Bern spy chief, however, deprived all those Allied observers expecting an imminent end to the Third Reich of a goodly portion of their hopes by predicting that Germany, even without undertaking any military changes on the Eastern Front, would hold out for at least "a year or 18 months." According to the Bern OSS chief (whose reports were noted with interest by Roosevelt), neither current economic circumstances nor people's morale pointed toward Germany's "rapid collapse" heading toward the new year 1943.

Psychological and Military Warfare

Allen Dulles' arrival in Bern came precisely at a time when the sources for Admiral Wilhelm Canaris' secret intelligence service (*Abwehr*), which during the first two years of the war had supplied detailed intelligence on the defense of Switzerland, were gradually running dry, and when members of the anti-Hitler opposition were gathering around Hans Oster, as German counterintelligence intensified its search for contacts among Germany's military adversaries.[27] In this situation, counterintelligence officer Hans Bernd Gisevius became Dulles' most important informant about what was happening in the Reich. On January 13, 1943 Dulles cabled the following to Washington about his first meeting with the then 38-year-old special commander of counterintelligence: "In Zurich I saw a friend [Hans Bernd Gisevius] of "474" [Willem Visser t'Hooft] and "476" [Gero von Schulze-Gaevernitz] on Sunday, a German who is a friend of Niemüller [Martin Niemöller] and who is thought to be working closely with Schacht. He said that it is very important that encouragement be offered to the effect that negotiation with the United Nations for a durable peace could be instituted if the Nazi leaders were eliminated by the group resisting them. If this were not done, he said, chaos and revolution would ensue since Hitler would take up Bolshevism rather than give in to the western powers. He added that his friends did not want to risk their lives unless there is some hope of success for the movement."[28]

In the brief meeting—which Dulles did not take all too seriously in January 1943, since in his "personal opinion there has as yet been no serious organization of the movement"—a number of themes were sounded that would reverberate louder and louder as July 20, 1944 approached. The opposition in the Reich was no mass movement; instead, it consisted of different circles in counterintelligence, politics, business, and the churches. It implored the Americans, under the impact of the Soviets' rapid march westward, to abandon their intransigent attitude toward the German anti-Hitler opposition and suggested that, if the Americans did not come around to its position, the alternative would be chaos, revolution, and Bolshevism.

Although it was Dulles' view, ever since he took up his post in Bern, that eliminating Hitler would accelerate the Reich's collapse (early in 1942, by contrast, he was instead placing all his bets on broadening the gap between the NSDAP and the military[29]), in light of an initiative from Adam von Trott zu Solz he declared that apart from a *complete military victory* of the Allies the anti-Hitler groups should not expect encouragement from the Americans or negotiations of any kind.[30]

While this declaration showed that Dulles was anticipating the unconditional surrender formula that Roosevelt would be coining ten days later in Casablanca, his efforts over the next two years were, paradoxically, completely in line with a carefully launched revision in the official course of American policy. Dulles found a serious drawback, initially, in the American and British neglect of psychological, as opposed to military, warfare. When Roosevelt and Churchill met in Quebec in August 1943 to consult with each other about future military operations in the Balkans and about opening a second front in France, Dulles tried to get involved in the debate by asking Washington: "To vitalize our psychological warfare, can we not do something during or after the Quebec conference, in the way of appealing to the masses in the Axis countries." In order to avoid the impression that he was trying to soften the political principles of Casablanca, Dulles explicitly emphasized that he knew that the Casablanca Directive "must not and will not be altered." At the same time, however, he drew attention to how the Axis propagandists had perverted the President's message and created the impression that military defeat would spell the end of an ordered and respectable life in Germany and—as Ignazio Silone had emphasized[31]—in Italy as well.

Germany's population, according to Dulles, had to be inoculated by Allied propaganda into appreciating that the end of the war would mean the end of the bombing raids and the end of the Gestapo, and that Germany's reconstruction would result in the establishment of basic democratic rights and stability in social and economic affairs. In an usually optimistic diagnosis for Dulles, he added: "we *can* crack Germany and end the war this year. . . . Germany is a fighter who was knocked down a couple of times. She can go forward for several more rounds if we let her get her breath. If we hit her with the hardest military and political punch we have, we can bring about the collapse."[32]

What Dulles understood by "political punch[es]" was made clear, among other things, by the so-called "Free" Reports that were composed by a Swiss mechanic. For two months this author had traveled through Germany, and afterwards he declared that the Germans would not give up until they were "forced to their knees." Apart from a victory, Dulles believed, this goal might also be reached by means of propaganda if one forced the population into a defeatist attitude, confronted the public with the real situation, and destroyed any hope for a partial German victory.[33]

What at first looked like a contradiction—insisting on a quick and radical knockout of Germany and on a positive outlook for the postwar period—was the very pattern of propaganda and action on which Dulles pinned his hopes after 1943. From now on, all of the activities he developed with regard to the "gentle encouragement" of the anti-Hitler resistance came dangerously close to a risky balancing act. On the one hand, Dulles made contact with the anti-Hitler groups, who sent their emissaries to Switzerland. On the other hand, he made it clear to the resistance that the U.S. government would not accept an overthrow of the Nazi regime without a military defeat. On the one hand, he made a distinction between the "good Germans" and the "bad Germans"; on the other hand, he was not able to promise the "good Germans" official backing if they could not opt for eliminating Hitler.

To be sure, vis-à-vis his own government Dulles tried to create the impression that he regarded Casablanca's stipulations as non-negotiable, yet he missed no opportunity to persuade both Donovan and the President that there was something dubious about their political course of action. If Dulles had already attempted to intervene politically before (in August in Quebec), by the end of October he was repeating his bottom line position when he explained: "The Moscow conference will not be 100 per cent successful unless some common basis is found for an appeal to the German people by the U.S., Britain, and Russia. So far, U.S. and British slogans have been limited to unconditional surrender and the destruction of Prussian militarism, creating the impression that the Western powers seek the total destruction of the German people."[34]

As is well known, Dulles' suggestion for a joint declaration by the Western Allies and Russia played no role at the Moscow conference. There, the Americans, the British, and the Soviets agreed (not least of all because of a concern for dispelling, or at least muting, Russian mistrust of the Western Allies) that they would avoid even a hint of any separate peace or go-it-alone policy on the part of the West. Here one could see how little influence the OSS had on shaping American foreign policy.

While a man like James Grafton Rogers, who interpreted the lack of Allied cooperation primarily as a threat to world peace by the Soviet Union, withdrew from the OSS in frustration,[35] Dulles believed that the internal German opposition (or the "German underground," as he called it after the war) could contribute both to toppling the Hitler regime and to stabilizing postwar German society. This conviction became the mainspring of his contacts with the anti-Hitler conspirators, on whom he regularly reported back to Washington.

In November 1943 Dulles explained in a telegram sent to Donovan that there were "75 per cent or more Germans opposed to the Nazi regime." Among these, however, there were "only 2 groups who could possibly initiate practical action": On the one hand there were the generals who could remove Hitler and the Nazi regime by military force, and on the other hand there were the unions, who could use sabotage to help slow down the war effort. Under these circumstances, according to Dulles, it was the job of the OSS to attempt "teaching sabotage to workmen and encouraging action by hesitating generals."[36]

Opportunists and Conspirators

During his first year in Bern Dulles cabled Washington a mere fragment of what he knew about Hitler's opponents inside the Reich. This was attributable to the Bern OSS chief's doubts about the strength and effectiveness of the anti-Hitler movement; as well as to his awareness that the smallest leak would be disastrous and that nobody in Washington would be served by telegraphing details.[37] In addition, it was not always easy to make reliable judgments about the intentions of agents and informers arriving from Germany.

For example, the case of Prince Maximilian Egon zu Hohenlohe, who had been in touch with Leland Harrison since 1939 and would contact Dulles on several occasions starting in early 1943, was a case Dulles handled less confidentially than he did the matter of the July 20 conspirators.[38] Hohenlohe was one of the Third Reich's most dubious figures. As the descendent of a royal family, this voluntary expatriate prince enjoyed citizenship rights in the principality of Liechtenstein. On his numerous travels, which not infrequently took him to the Iberian peninsula (his wife owned lands and property in Spain, and in Mexico as well), the princely visitor would usually make a stop in Bern, where he presented himself as a spokesman for the interests of the resistance and as a stern critic of the NSDAP. In fact, however, Hohenlohe maintained close ties to the German Security Service (the *Sicherheitsdienst,* or SD), was in touch with Göring and civil servants at the Foreign Office, and sympathized with Wilhelm Frick, Hitler's thoroughly loyal Interior Minister.[39] What motivated Dulles to get involved with a character as suspicious as this?

When the Soviets exploited ties to Hohenlohe after the war for propaganda purposes and accused Dulles of anti-Semitism and of seeking a separate peace on the basis of three sets of conversational minutes from 1943 (the so-called "Bulls-Paul" conversations),[40] Allen Dulles, who in the meantime had risen to become director of the CIA, must have asked himself whether his contact with Hohenlohe had been worth all the trouble now that it had been dragged into the cold war.[41] Between 1943 and 1945, however, Hohenlohe's reports did provide a glimpse into the mood of the German population and behind the scenes of Berlin politics, a view that Dulles undoubtedly found indispensable. Dulles was just as aware as Leland Harrison that the Prince's efforts were closely tied to his aim of maintaining his extensive properties in the Sudetenland. In a telegram to "Argus" (Colonel Hohenthal from the Madrid OSS), Dulles called the Prince an "opportunist" and added that he did not believe Hohenlohe "ever was a Nazi." The Liechtensteiner "undoubtedly . . . developed Nazi . . . ties in order to protect his property in Bohemia," but to the OSS he was of "some use from the intelligence angle." In any event, there was no other informant who maintained direct contact with Himmler and officials of the Foreign Office like Henke and Steengracht, Reinhard Spitzy and Erich Kordt.

Hohenlohe's reporting was strongly colored by anti-Communism, and as of the fall of 1943 (after the bomb attacks on Hamburg and the fall of Mussolini) his messages were pervaded by a pessimism that overshadowed his former belief in the "power, if not invincibility" of the Germans. Even the prospect of Hitler's "new weapon" (Hohenlohe was reporting as early as August 1943 that serial production of a the new weapon had already commenced) had the prince questioning whether the circles inside Germany to whom he was close would be able to achieve their political goals. Should the opportunity present itself, Hohenlohe suggested, the OSS should attempt to engage Theo Kordt, an employee of the Bern legation, as a peace negotiator between the Americans and the Germans.[42] But this prospect would never present itself; and it is doubtful that the OSS would ever have gotten involved with the contacts Hohenlohe was arranging. It was symptomatic of Dulles' general openness to the widest variety of groups within National Socialist Germany that he should have maintained his contact with an opportunist like Hohenlohe throughout the war. As far as Dulles was concerned, all ties were appropriate from the standpoint of information procurement.

In Bern there was an awareness that contacts with German negotiators might be tricks the Gestapo was using to flush out and expose Hitler's opponents. There was ultimately no certainty about the authenticity of any one of the peace feelers.[43] Some of the approaches made by self-proclaimed opposition circles from inside the Reich were rebuffed by Dulles' agents at a very preliminary stage. One example was the attempt of a group around Major Steltzer, who proclaimed the formation of a military government under Rommel in August 1943.[44]

It would take until January 1944 for Dulles to become completely convinced that a major resistance organization existed inside the Reich, with members representing military and government circles. Up until that point Dulles had received so much information from the Reich that he no longer harbored any doubts about the readiness of the so-called "Breakers," those who were attempting to "break" Nazi rule, to go into action.[45] In 1943 the main transmission line for contact between the resistance circle inside Germany and the OSS in Bern mainly was via Hans Bernd Gisevius, but starting in early 1944 this was primarily taken over by Berlin businessman Eduard Waetjen (alias "Görter"), who (like Gisevius) worked for counterintelligence at the German General Consulate in Zurich. Dulles had enormous faith in Waetjen, who had studied law and maintained ties abroad via his American mother as well as through a father who worked for an American investment bank. In August 1942 "Eddy" Waetjen was still convinced that he would "fight to the end for Germany's existence." Shortly before he had met with Franz von Papen in Ankara and discussed the possibility of a separate peace with the U.S.: It must be possible, said Waetjen's proposal at the time, assuming that Germany's independence would be guaranteed and its leading role in Europe recognized, to send somebody to Washington to work out a negotiable peace on the basis of a German evacuation of all European countries with the "probable" exception of the Protectorate. This would let the U.S. declare that it had won the war.[46]

While Waetjen's hopes for a German final victory were increasingly coming to naught, this hardly made him give up on his notion of making peace with the Western powers. The establishment of the OSS outpost in Bern prompted Waetjen, whose sister was married to Sterling Rockefeller, to try contacting "Roosevelt's emissary" in the Swiss capital. Although the Gestapo knew about Waetjen's contacts with the resistance group around Count Helmuth James von Moltke, the Waetjen files remained unnoticed owing to an unusual accident on the part of one of Himmler's snatchers. Early in 1944, owing to an escape as ingenious as it was hair-raising (a plan to support a Muslim rebellion in Afghanistan), the thirty-seven-year-old counterintelligence agent (who was a friend of German intelligence agent Hans Oster) succeeded in sending his wife, children, and mother abroad, so that he did not have to worry about his relatives in case he was taken prisoner.

Waetjen was now the one who would inform Dulles about the "Breakers," a group that apparently brought together three different outlooks—evolutionary, revolutionary, and military. Although Dulles knew that they were primarily a conservative and thoroughly bourgeois group, the first reports about the Breakers he would issue stressed how the movement favored comprehensive changes in society, tended toward the left, and envisioned putting the "socialist leader Leuschner," the former Social Democratic Interior Minister of Hesse, at the head of a civilian interim government.[47]

Dulles himself must have regarded a government headed by Colonel-General Beck and Carl Goerdeler as Chancellor as acceptable. After all, Beck had been discussed within the OSS as the "German Badoglio" ever since August 1943.[48] Furthermore, Otto Braun, the former Prussian premier living in exile in Switzerland, had pressed Dulles to appreciate that a wartime Hitler needed to be removed by the *bourgeoisie* in order to prevent a repetition of the "onus of 1918" (that is, of the "stab in the back" legend, which had been a burden on the Social Democrats throughout the interwar period).[49] Vis-à-vis OSS headquarters, however, the chief agent in Bern tried (at least initially) to create the impression that a decidedly conservative and military movement would not be able to count on Washington's support. Nevertheless, the answer to Dulles' twofold query—about what offers he could actually make to the resistance movement and what policy the OSS was going to pursue with respect to the Breakers—turned out to be anything but encouraging. On February 2 the Washington head of the SI, Whitney Sheperdson, warned that Adolf Berle had again expressed his extreme aversion to any step that could help Germany sow discord among the Allies. If one recalls that Shepardson, who had been a friend of Dulles since the Paris peace negotiations, maintained a lively interest in the German resistance and was even a close friend of von Moltke, one gets a better sense of Shepardson's attitude: To be sure, Shepardson could not have been happy when he reported that the OSS's "room for maneuver" was "extremely constrained."[50] His message, meanwhile, made it very clear that the Breakers' initiative could not expect to get American backing if it was premised on separate negotiations with the West. Although, from this perspective, the German opposition's peace feelers were inauspicious—the Breakers were unwavering about their demand to negotiate directly and exclusively with the Western Allies[51] after the collapse of the Nazi regime—Dulles kept up his contacts with the conspirators throughout the following weeks.

Dulles' activities were so thoroughly and fundamentally handicapped by the political restrictions coming out of Washington and the conditions laid down by the Breaker group that he started running up against the limits of what was "permissible" as early as his first tentative explorations with Waetjen and Gisevius. In addition to the unconditional surrender formula, which restricted Dulles' scope for action as a matter of principle, Donovan informed him that nobody wanted to replace the Nazi regime with a military regime.[52] In spite of the large amount of information that the Bern outpost received between January and July 1944 via the Breakers,[53] Dulles could not predict with any certainty what kind of government would emerge from a putsch. He felt skeptical, above all, about the determination of the military and the capacity of the civilian resistance to carry out a coup and install a working government.

Since April 1943 Dulles had been afraid that Himmler would gradually get rid of the "Organization C"—the group in the Armed Forces Intelligence around Canaris.[54] The arrests of individual members of counterintelligence, of whose fate Dulles was continually kept abreast, led him to suspect that the

Gestapo had learned about the anti-Hitler conspiracy and was waiting to take drastic measures "when the situation had matured further."[55] An additional obstacle standing in the way of his arrangement with the Breakers was the "old predicament" that the conspirators were always either wanting to surrender to the East or to the West but could "never perceive the third alternative of capitulating to both at the same moment."[56]

Dulles told Washington he understood the problem that would arise for U.S. relations with the Soviets as a result of executing any plan in which a German opposition participated. Nevertheless, he wanted to exploit the activities of the group in order to undermine morale at the highest levels of the Wehrmacht.[57] Therefore he left the OSS in Washington in the dark about details of his talks with the emissaries of the German resistance, and even deliberately misinformed his superiors on a number of matters. Despite the protestations he telegraphed to Washington about adhering strictly to the narrow diplomatic authorizations within which the OSS was permitted to operate, Dulles signaled to the negotiators from the German resistance that he was the man in charge of Germany's political reconstruction, a message that must have reinforced the group around Beck and Goerdeler in their readiness to take action.[58] In order to prevent the British and the Soviets from criticizing and undermining this connection, "extreme discretion" was maintained.[59] Neither the SIS nor the SOE was initiated into the "Breakers" material. After the failure of the Hitler assassination plot, when OSS central headquarters in Washington decided to transmit a portion of the Breakers information to the British, Donovan himself saw to it the Soviets would not find out about Dulles' contacts either through British or State Department channels.[60]

Since all the efforts of the Breakers to obtain assurances from the Western Allies came to naught, the circles around Beck, Goerdeler, and Stauffenberg ultimately took action knowing that they had to move ahead on their own. On July 12 Dulles was alerted by Theodor Strünck to the "possibility that a dramatic event may take place up north"; three days later the news arrived that the "Bearcat" group around Berlin police chief Count Helldorf was also cooperating with the Breakers.[61] While the British secret service at the time of the assassination attempt expressed the view that there were "no indications" that the German military opposition was ever going to assume power, the OSS was quite prepared for the coup attempt of July 20, 1944.[62]

On the evening of Colonel von Stauffenberg's attempt to assassinate Hitler, Dulles got in touch with Donovan by radiophone. The tone of his message was sober: "The attempt on Hitler's life is, of course, the outstanding item of news this evening. . . . The man seems to have a charmed life, but possibly an all-wise Providence is saving him so that he may himself see the complete wreckage of the Germany he has led to destruction. . . . I presume you all have the news we have on this—we haven't very much except the names of the various generals and admirals who were wounded."[63]

A few days later, and in contrast to the radio message of July 20—which was intended not just for American listeners, but also meant to reach a Swiss and German audience (Dulles knew that the Swiss were eavesdropping on his radiophone messages)—Dulles cabled a top secret message to London and OSS headquarters in Washington, which was then forwarded to the White House within a matter of hours.[64] In this message Dulles proceeded from the assumption that the fate of the uprising had not yet been decided, and that in all likelihood everything would depend on whether the "Heimatheer" ("Home Army") would follow Himmler or look for direction from its old leaders, some of whom were involved in the conspiracy. Dulles characterized the report that the "Breakers do not control any adequate radio" as the "most discouraging feature"; nevertheless, he hoped that the opposition, which apparently "was not stamped out at once," might "be able to hold out in any part of *Germany*." In case that should happen, he proposed four measures that, in a nutshell, reflected the political and operational notions of Allen Dulles and to some extent also the ideology of the OSS: (1) Roosevelt should send a message to the German people in order to clear up any misunderstandings raised by the demand for unconditional surrender; (2) Berchtesgaden (where Dulles—mistakenly—suspected Hitler of hiding out) should be massively bombarded in order to disrupt communications inside the Reich; (3) any German cities that would line up on the side of the opposition would be spared, while Nazi strongholds and Gestapo centers would be mercilessly bombed; (4) propaganda leaflets should be dropped over the entire territory of the Reich.

Even before it was clear that the putsch had failed, Dulles (in cooperation with London OSS chief David Bruce, U.S. Ambassador Winant, and General Thomas J. Betts) succeeded in initiating the leaflet campaign. When the collapse of the coup undertaking became fully evident over the course of July 22, however, it dashed OSS hopes for any miraculous shortening of the war using a combination of targeted bombing and political propaganda.[65]

While Donovan was excited by the reports reaching Bern about the composition of the Breaker group and its goals, the assassination attempt did not meet with much of an official response from Washington. Franklin Ford, the historian working in the OSS research division and the man who would later write up a comprehensive "field report" about the political implications of July 20, recalled that on the day of the anti-Hitler putsch there was no great rush in the Washington OSS to undertake any kind of initiative.[66]

From German émigré circles in Stockholm, there were voices saying that the assassination attempt was merely something staged by Hitler.[67] Even the psychologist Walter C. Langer held the view that the incident had been arranged by Hitler so that his "miraculous escape from death" would "strength-en the myth that Hitler is under the protection of Divine Providence." The "technique for staging events of this kind" in order to eliminate domestic op-position was something that Langer, pointing to the Reichstag fire of February 1933, regarded as "not uncommon."[68] R&A also drew a negative portrait of the conspirators' group: In a study from July 27, 1944, they mockingly characterized the Breakers as a circle of "bankrupt generals, nationalist intellectuals, and (possible) nationalistic Socialist Democrats and civil servants" hoping to sell the West on going up against the Soviet Union.[69]

Dulles' information about the July 20 plot and the composition of the con-spirators' group may indeed have been sensational. No other Western country had as clear a picture of the preparations and goals of the conspirators and of what would befall them after the assassination attempt. With his prognoses about what was likely to happen next inside the Reich, however, Dulles was wide off the mark. Dulles' view on the day right after the coup was that the next assault on Hitler's life would be attempted by Communists (presumably with backing from soldiers, foreign workers, and prisoners of war),[70] and thereafter he was increasingly inclined toward the thesis that things were heading toward a fateful, last-minute clash between an eastern and a western faction of the German resistance. He even believed that Stauffenberg had planned to make peace with the Soviets if the putsch had been successful.[71] This interpretation (which was confirmed by Hans Bernd Gisevius as well as by Father Leiber in the Vatican) fit into the pattern of Dulles' preconceived perceptions about So-viet hegemonic aims and a Central Europe threatened by Communist expan-sion. The fear that "many Germans appear to believe that a Bolshevized Ger-many would facilitate an understanding with USSR" was so far-fetched that one may reasonably assume Dulles was taken by assessments and misinforma-tion from German circles who had an interest in establishing a bulwark against the Soviet Union.[72]

The German V Weapons and the Attack on Peenemünde

At the same time that news about the activities of the Breakers group was stir-ring up hopes about the Reich's collapse among Dulles and his staff, reports were arriving in Bern about that secret "miracle weapon" to which Hitler had already ominously alluded long ago. Although the English and the Americans had known for quite some time that Germany was experimenting with armed missiles, and although they had concrete indications that one of the research centers was located in the fishing village of Peenemünde on the island of Use-dom (southwest of Bornholm), Allied circles had initially taken little notice of these reports. This would change, however, in early 1943, when the Allies learned from different channels that German engineers were close to achieving a breakthrough in missile technology. Among other things, there was the March 1943 discovery by the British (on the basis of a conversation between two generals imprisoned in Tunisia) that these inklings of rocket construction were more than empty rumors.[73]

Only a month before, early in February 1943, German industrialist Walter Bovari (who had been given the code number 490 in his OSS telegrams) had warned Dulles that one of his factories was manufacturing a small machine part designated for the production of a secret weapon, of which little more was known than that it had to do with an aerial apparatus having the form of a flying torpedo. The research was being conducted by a scientist named Buchwald, "either in Darmstadt or Dortmund." Although the information seemed imprecise and the businessman Bovari had no technical background whatsoever, Dulles immediately gave the Bovari material his highest priority.

The manner in which the businessman got information about the German secret weapon left Dulles suspecting that the intelligence was sensitive and authentic, and that "490" had to be protected. For a second time in the same month, Bovari arrived in Bern to say that Hitler's secret weapon was an unmanned tank. It could be steered by remote control and filled with explosives so that it would blow up on contact with enemy tanks.[74] Both messages were typical for the kind of material that would be arriving in Bern over the next several months. Since most of the information was hearsay, and since the Germans also used disinformation techniques, the ever-growing stream of intelligence was a mixture of true and false, trivial and important, fallacious and misleading. In reality, the kind of remote control device reported by "490" was being produced for aircraft rather than for tanks. The real name of the scientist "Buchwald" was Professor Theodor Buchhold. He was not in charge of the entire rocket program but worked instead with the Darmstadt-based Wagner company—on developing accelerometers.[75] In order to obtain a consistent picture of the progress being made in German missile research and production, leading U.S. experts in the field of rocket technology were consulted to interpret the material.

After the war Major General Walter Dornberger, who had been in charge of developing long-distance weapons for the Reich, wondered why the Western Allies had not already bombed the experimental stations in Peenemünde on the Baltic by the end of 1942. The answer is simple: Neither Great Britain nor the United States had any concrete notion about the latest developments in missile technology. And even in January and March of 1943, when the first aerial photos of Dornberger's research station—with three triangularly shaped launching platforms, several large buildings, and a machine shop—were evaluated by the aerial experts of the Royal Air Force under Constance Babington-Smith, the

British scientists did not know any more about this strange facility's most likely use than generations of archaeologists have known about the use of Stonehenge.[76] In fact, the German engineers had a year-long lead on the development of so-called remote control weapons, of which in the end only the V weapons (from the German *Vergeltungswaffen*—meaning "retaliatory weapons") would become known to the general public.[77]

One thing helping to confuse the Allies was the fact that Peenemünde was the site for the manufacture of two weapons types totally different in construction and performance—the smaller V-1, a monoplane 8 meters long with an average speed of 545 kilometers per hour, and the larger V-2, more than 15 meters long, a long-range rocket that could be fired from a vertical position and (at 1,400 meters per second) could reach speeds almost ten times higher. While the V-1 was cheap to manufacture, easy to transport, and required only a little fuel, the V-2 rocket was downright expensive and technically delicate; in addition, the rockets burned up enormous amounts of alcohol and liquid oxygen, which Germany in 1943 was barely capable of producing in sufficient quantity. All these drawbacks, nevertheless, seemed outweighed by the precise remote control and enormous altitude that the V-2 rockets were able to achieve, and which were the features that turned them into such horrible weapons of surprise. The real and hard to exaggerate danger about the V-1 was that it could be fired against Great Britain in large numbers, so that the English could not construct an adequate aerial defense. There was no protection against the wide-range V-2 rockets with their built-in gyroscopic compasses and enormous climbing elevation, not to mention their accuracy.[78]

Compared to the reports at the disposal of the British secret intelligence service SIS by the end of June 1943,[79] just a little information was available to the OSS, and only some of this was estimated to be highly reliable. On May 29, 1943, Hans Bernd Gisevius had indicated to Allen Dulles that the Germans were experimenting with a remote control projectile that the military hoped they could use to bomb London. Less than four weeks later he reported that the Germans were manufacturing a small rocket approximately 60 cm. in diameter, 3 meters long, and weighing 2000 kg. The explosions required to propel the turbines were made under high pressure using a saltpeter solution and oil; the assembly and experimental station was located in Pomerania between Greifswald and Swinemünde, the tube was manufactured in Mühlheim on the Ruhr, and experimental launches with deviations measured at one percent took place with missiles heading in the direction of Danzig. Gisevius also reported that mass production of the rockets was expected for September or October, and that a much larger model was already in an experimental stage.[80]

Within four days Gisevius' report was forwarded to all the important OSS departments in Washington and New York, to David Bruce in London, and to

Army, Navy, and Air force intelligence. The technical details that Dulles' informant transmitted were for the most part either wrong or imprecise, but it was alarming enough to have learned that Peenemünde was the site for manufacturing rockets that could be deployed within a matter of months. Since Gisevius' information was regarded as proven and reliable, the report was given the highest priority.[81]

On August 17, 1943 the British inflicted an aerial assault, preceded by a successful diversionary maneuver, on the experimental missile station in Peenemünde. The impact was devastating: 130 scientists, including Dr. Thiel, in charge of rocket design, and 600 foreign workers who had previously sent important information about Peenemünde abroad, fell victim to the bombing, while 41 out of 600 British airplanes were shot down. The production of weapons of destruction was delayed by several weeks, if not months.[82]

Naturally, the question arises as to what part the intelligence gathered by the OSS played in the decision to bomb Peenemünde in August. In this context there is a conspicuous contrast between British historiography, which gives no indication of an American contribution, and the OSS literature, which suggests (though essentially without any proof) that the intelligence coming out of the Bern OSS station had an influence on the decision to bomb Peenemünde.[83] The official British account explicitly emphasizes that the English asked their Alliance partners in Washington and Moscow for intelligence material on German missile development during the summer of 1943, but that the American reply contained nothing that the British did not already know—with the only distinction being that the U.S. authorities linked the use of gas to the secret weapon.[84]

Did the intelligence that the OSS had at its disposal really contain no news? What role did the OSS material play in the British calculation? So long as the archives of the British secret service remain closed, these questions cannot be definitively answered. It is certain that the material at the disposal of the OSS suggested bombing Peenemünde, but also that Donovan's secret intelligence service did not explicitly push for such an action. Gisevius' message of June 24 saying that two different rockets were going to be manufactured in Peenemünde gave the Allies their first indication that the Germans were working on two projects simultaneously. This seemingly trivial insight was of central importance for the evaluation of the material, since it shed light on intelligence reports that otherwise seemed contradictory and inconsistent. British official historian Hinsley had maintained that the English first learned on July 25, 1943—and from diplomatic missions abroad—that the Germans were working on two different weapons systems.[85] According to this account, the English would not have been given a look at the OSS materials. Normally, the SI material that David Bruce received in London was immediately and routinely forwarded to the British SIS. A cable from February 1944, however, draws attention to this time period as one of tension with British intelligence; "Broadway" or MI-6, had not forwarded the missile information to the Americans.[86] From this angle, the possibility should not entirely be ruled out that the British and Americans were going their separate ways on this very question—the procurement and evaluation of technical and technological information—at least in the final phase of the war.

Paradoxically, when Peenemünde was bombed on August 17, 1943, British intelligence experts and the military—in spite of the numerous, often outstanding reports they received—were unable to obtain a clear picture of what the experimental facility in Peenemünde was being used for, whereas the meager but relatively clear material the OSS was getting apparently played no role in the decision to bomb the technical installations on the Baltic. Ultimately, it was the impossibility of ruling out any acute danger emanating from Peenemünde that proved to be the decisive factor in favor of military intervention there.

It should also be noted that the Americans working for the OSS in Washington and New York were groping about in the dark. While Washington's Secret Intelligence Branch had correctly evaluated the quality of the reports Bern was sending on the V weapons, elsewhere confusion reigned about the individual pieces of information that had arrived during the first half of 1943. The head of the R&D Branch, Stanley Lovell, assumed that an atom bomb was being manufactured in Peenemünde after an OSS telegram had reported that "heavy water" had been shipped there. He pushed to have the facility bombed and, well after the end of the war, he continued to believe that the "Peenemünde Raid" had delayed the development of the German atomic bomb and forced the Germans to use the more orthodox V-1 and V-2 rockets.[87] Even the Survey of Foreign Experts, the scholarly team of exiles and refugees that had been serving as a liaison between the Board of Economic Warfare (later the Foreign Economic Administration) and the OSS,[88] contributed little toward clearing up the mystery of the rockets. In June 1943 the Survey interviewed a series of German exiles who were familiar with Usedom island and the immediate vicinity of Peenemünde, but nobody had actually visited the region since 1937.[89]

Finally, beginning in the summer, OSS information from the Balkans led to the false assumption that important parts for the V-2 rockets were being manufactured in Auschwitz. From the reports it is hard to tell where this error came from. Were the informants, who were cooperating with the Dogwood-Cereus spy ring, possibly trying to alert the OSS not only to how Auschwitz in Upper Silesia had become the most important war arsenal for the Axis in the entire region, but also to how this site had turned into a labor and extermination camp with tens of thousands of foreign workers and political prisoners who were being guarded "by 2200 SS men"?[90] Although the OSS posts in London and Bern were constantly receiving reports keeping Donovan's secret intelligence service abreast of the progress being made in V-2 production, the real produc-

tion site—the concentration camp Dora-Mittelbau, an underground factory
north of Nordhausen in the Harz region—remained concealed until the end
of the war.[91]

As early as the beginning of September, Eduard Schulte, the German industrialist who broke the silence "about the Holocaust," had warned that "the rocket bomb must be taken very seriously." In Schulte's view, the bomb attack on
Peenemünde had merely delayed production by one or two months, and he emphasized an important part of production facilities had not been destroyed by
the RAF attack.[92] For Dulles these warnings from Schulte were reason enough
to persist in asking his informants—especially "493" (Frederick Loofbourow),
"512" (Hans Bernd Gisevius), "513" (a Polish informant), "643" (Schulte), and
"680" (Josef Joham)[93]—about how the development of the German V weapons
was proceeding. By September 15, 1943, the first reports had arrived concerning
a third German weapon that would later be called the V-3; at the same time,
Dulles' informants were reporting about the production of V-2 parts at the Rax
factory in Vienna (Wiener Neustadt) and in the Zeppelin works in
Friedrichshafen. Joham was the first to report that the V-2 rockets were known
as "A-4" in Germany, that Dr. Otto Ambros from IG-Farben in Ludwigshafen
was responsible for the chemical aspects of rocket development, and that the
missiles directed against Great Britain might possibly be ready to deploy within
five months, in February 1944.[94]

In December Dulles' associate stationed in Zurich, Loofbourow, provided
the OSS with lots of technical details about speed, range, and specific experiments with the V-2, information that had been supplied to Loofbourow by a
German electronics expert. It was in this context that the name of Professor
Wernher von Braun first cropped up. Loofbourow's informant emphasized that
Hitler's original target date for the deployment of the rockets (November 30,
1943) could not be kept because, among other reasons, there were problems
with the V-2 rockets' electrical ignition.[95]

In the course of 1944 it became increasingly important to identify the
launching ramps or "ski sites" for the V rockets, which were located behind the
coast of Dieppe, Boulogne, and Calais.[96] Although the Bern OSS outpost sent
intelligence cables about the V weapons to Washington non-stop, there was a
steady decline in the importance of Bern's HUMINT compared to other methods of reconnaissance. Information resulting from aerial photographic reconnaissance (especially after July 1944) and from tapping Germany's signal traffic
via ULTRA now proved decisive in helping the British and Americans identify
and then bomb the most important V weapons installations. Also helping to
weaken the German position was the fact that the Luftwaffe had been substan-
tially decimated during the last year of the war, so that defending the home
front proved increasingly difficult.[97] In addition, America's successful air raids

on oil facilities in northern Germany and a shortage of German pilots reduced the V weapons' launching quota.[98]

The mood in Germany suddenly changed when, just a few days after the successful Allied landing in Normandy, the first V-warheads were fired at southern England in June 1944. Early in 1944 an OSS research group around Rhoda Metraux and Hanna Krebs had determined (from having read thousands of letters to German prisoners of war in America) that Germans from all levels of society were hoping the war would end soon.[99] All at once, after the bombardment of southern England and London, there was a surge in the mood barometer, "enthusiasm," "jubilation," and vigorous "feelings of revenge." The propagandists had skillfully suggested to the German population that V is to be viewed as an abbreviation for *Vergeltung* (retaliation).[100] Accordingly, at the end of 1944 Dulles reported, on the basis of Swiss correspondents' reports from Berlin, that German morale had been dramatically lifted by the first reports about the secret weapon. Nevertheless, he believed that this "injection" would only last a little while and that German morale would sooner or later sink back to a level even lower than before as soon as the population recognized that the secret weapon was not showing any concrete results.[101] According to reports from working class circles (the "German friends of '328' ")[102] only a few Germans were still hoping "that the new weapon would give Germany a chance." Most believed that the Allies would develop countermeasures, and that this would make the German situation even more hopeless.[103] The friends of "328" were right. "The surge in morale that the new V weapon helped stimulate" was really, as German historian Marlis Steinert had figured out, "only of very short duration."[104]

On September 8, 1944, the first V-2 rockets were launched against Great Britain. Donovan, who only recently had visited French resistance groups in Geneva and Lyon, was in the Savoy Bar in London.[105] The impact of the 2,500 rockets that were about to be fired at London over the next few months was devastating. Nevertheless, the Allied secret intelligence services had helped make it possible to arrive at a close-to-realistic assessment of the V rockets' destructive potential, and this also meant that the English population was not entirely unprepared for the terror inflicted by the V-2. The OSS also knew all about how the destructive power of these new weapons was viewed by the Foreign Office in Berlin. For these insights American intelligence owed a debt of gratitude to a certain "George Wood," who had been routinely smuggling material from Berlin to Bern since 1943.[106]

The Wood Story

As a follow-up to Allen Dulles' stopover in New York on November 1944, William S. Stephenson, the Director of British Security Co-Ordination in New York wrote in a "top secret and personal" letter transmitted by "safe hand" to

William Donovan: "Dear Bill. The visit of your capable representative in Switzerland [Dulles] reminds me that I recently had the opportunity" to look at the "WOOD" cable traffic. "This is undoubtedly one of the biggest Secret Intelligence triumphs of this war."[107] Stephenson's evaluation from the autumn of 1944 stood in sharp contrast to the assessment made about "George Wood" by the English in August 1943. At that time Colonel Cartwright from the British legation in Bern had warned Allen Dulles about a German "chap" who was unquestionably going to turn to the OSS as well and who could offer nothing of any relevance to the Allies.[108] In contrast to the British, Dulles took an interest in the German emissary, especially since he had been introduced through the intervention of Ernesto Kocherthaler (a Spaniard born in Germany), whom Dulles regarded as an absolutely reliable contact.[109] What Kocherthaler valued about Fritz Kolbe, alias "George Wood," was his realistic assessment of the war situation. In contrast to the group around Major Steltzer and Field Marshall Rommel, who had turned to Kocherthaler the very same week about the group's plan to overthrow the Hitler regime, Kolbe-"Wood" was evidently not interested in driving a wedge between the Western Allies and the Soviet Union. Instead, this member of the Foreign Office staff was pushing for close cooperation between Americans and Soviets, cooperation he saw as being in the joint interest of the Russians and the Germans.[110] His resolve to pass along a series of top secret documents, to which he had access as a staff associate of Ambassador Karl Ritter in Berlin, was strengthened by a conversation with Prelate Schreiber, who had explicitly released him from his oath to Hitler.[111] Kolbe was a Prussian civil servant not inclined toward political escapades; in his youth he had belonged to the *Wandervögel* (Germany's romantic back-to-nature youth movement, literally "migratory birds"), had been stationed in Madrid and Capetown when the war broke out, and had a Swiss wife (his second) he hoped to divorce, since his girlfriend in Berlin was expecting a child. So he did not come to Bern looking for personal advantage, but rather as an idealist who had long since detached himself from the Nazi regime and was working toward Hitler's overthrow and a quick end to the war.

Kolbe refused to accept money for his information, but could Dulles trust him?[112] In addition to a series of telegrams that Kolbe submitted to his Bern interlocutors Gerald Mayer and Allen Dulles (Dulles was using the code name Douglas at their first conversation), the information presented by this peculiar guest from Berlin included intelligence about damage from a bombing raid on Ploesti and a meeting scheduled between German and Japanese submarines. From memory he sketched an outline of the Führer's headquarters in Rastenburg and warned the Americans that the Germans had deciphered several codes—something Dulles had already learned from Gisevius.[113] Although both the material and Kocherthaler's recommendation spoke in favor of the informant, Dulles treated Kolbe (who, as a colleague of

Ritter, the liaison between the Foreign Office and the Wehrmacht Supreme Command, got to see extremely sensitive reports and papers) with extreme caution. As of August 1943, Kolbe would only be called "Wood," "George," or "George Wood" in cable traffic from the OSS in Bern. He received the code numbers "674" and "803." His information was called "kappa," and the "kappa secrets" were handled as if they were more secret than the top secrets. In his first telegram about "Wood," Dulles emphasized that the highest security precautions should be taken in this case.[114]

In the months that followed, Dr. Kocherthaler in Switzerland received copies of telegrams from the Foreign Office as well as letters and postcards from Wood that must have led every intelligence insider to suspect that this intelligence source was either a genuine gold mine or a large-scale diversionary maneuver by the Germans. At any rate, there was a danger that the Foreign Office would let the Americans receive well-known text material in order to feed it into America's communications traffic and thereby crack the code system. After Dulles had received the first big batch of German documents from Kolbe, he cabled an unusually cryptic message to London and Washington: When deciphered, Donovan's message to "105" (Bruce) and "109" (Donovan) went approximately as follows: "674" (Fritz Kolbe) had left the OSS copies of outgoing and incoming telegrams from Alpha (the Foreign Office in Berlin) that were also of major interest to Zulu (the British). Dulles explained that because he could no longer be certain that Beta (the Bern communication channels) were not being tapped and deciphered, transmitting the material would take a lot of time. A portion of the information would therefore be forwarded to "521" (the British secret service MI-6 in Switzerland).

Dulles, following Gamma (a cross-examination), had been completely persuaded that Delta (the material from Kolbe) was authentic and valuable.[115] In fact, the intelligence that was arriving at the Bern OSS outpost all at once from "674" was unprecedented in its diversity, currency, and explosiveness. In September 1943 Wood reported about the damage that the bombing raids had inflicted on the Schweinfurt ball bearing factory, and he proposed additional targets for air raids; he passed on the schedule for the special train that went from Berlin to Hitler's headquarters in Rastenburg and paraphrased an order of the Führer for punishing Italian renegades. At the end of December he reported on the biggest weak link in German aircraft production, in condensers. The same message contained a list of firms that manufactured them.

Kolbe let the Americans know what ideas the Nazis had about the disposition of British troops in southern England, and in December 1943 he reported that Sükrü Saracoglu ("Harem") wanted to keep Turkey ("Yellow") neutral.[116] The most baffling material included information revealing that the Foreign Office knew all about the policy of the Allies. In one case the Germans found out from a French general what kind of postwar goals Stalin had in mind for Europe,[117] and several reports made it clear that the Nazi leadership was also keeping abreast of Allied war conference outcomes.

As early as November 1 Hitler had ordered that all the fortifications on the entire Western front, including Norway's and Denmark's, be extended as quickly as possible, since he believed that the Soviets would soon be pushing for the opening of a second front. On February 10 the Foreign Office had learned that Stalin, at the Teheran conference, had insisted on invading the Continent soon, but that the position of Roosevelt and Churchill, as well as differences among Spaatz, Harris, and Leigh-Mallory, meant that an invasion could not be expected any earlier than sometime between April and June 1944. It was no surprise that the Foreign Office already knew in mid-December about the content of the Pope's Easter message; von Weizsäcker was well known for keeping the Germans accurately informed about what happened at the Papal palace in Rome.[118] But what was the source from which the German Foreign Office had learned about the differences of opinion within the Allied military and about what happened at the war conferences? An answer emerged for the first time on November 4, 1943 in a telegram sent from Ankara by von Papen, in which he drew attention to an agent named Cicero, who was supplying the Germans with highly confidential British material.[119]

Elyesa Bazna alias Cicero—later the protagonist in the movie *Five Fingers*, which starred James Mason—worked as a butler for the British ambassador Knatchbull-Hugessen, whose document safe he routinely plundered.[120] Dulles immediately informed the British secret service about the leak in Ankara. Nevertheless, it would take weeks before the English reacted to this spectacular piece of news.[121] On January 25 they requested more Wood material, and as late as February 29, 1944 they were urgently asking for the exact time of Papen's November 3 cable.[122] The material given by "674" seemed too good to be true. Even stranger (comically so), the Gestapo had the same view about Operation Cicero. Just like the English, the Germans believed the pilfered material must have been part of a diversionary plan. Nobody wanted to be caught in an exposed position and fall into a trap set by the other side.[123] Even in January a high-ranking British intelligence official, Colonel McCormack, who (along with Kim Philby) was responsible for reviewing the Wood material, explained that he was rather inclined to regard the documents as inauthentic.

At around the same time an initial summary of the most important reports, designated the "Boston Series," went to President Roosevelt and the State, War, and Navy departments. It was conceivable, Donovan's lieutenant Edward Buxton wrote the President on January 10, 1944, that contact with Wood represented "the first significant" intelligence breakthrough into a German office exercising authority. At the same time, however, he drew attention to the fact that both the OSS and its British sister organization still had to examine the authenticity of the source and the material. Shortly afterward, there was a period of several weeks during which it was almost completely forbidden to forward the material to the President and the War and Navy secretaries, since McCormack exercised a veto on security grounds.[124] On December 29, Dulles had already staked his reputation on the authenticity of the documents.[125] As late as March 24, 1944, all the Wood dispatches still carried a special stamp saying that they were "not confirmed," and it was not until April 20 that OSS headquarters in Washington (and especially X-2) uttered its last suspicion that the entire affair was "a kind of trap." The "200 extremely valuable Easter eggs" (codename "Kapril"), as Dulles called them, ultimately proved decisive in getting Washington to recognize that the damage these reports might do to German interests was all out of proportion to any potential value they might have for any intelligence diversion.[126] In the meantime, however, no less than eight months had slipped by since Kolbe's first encounter with Dulles and Gerhard Mayer in Bern.[127]

The "Kapril" material from Easter 1944 was so extensive that the OSS leadership in Washington had no time to inspect it in detail. Therefore Dulles summarized the 400-page dossier in a memorandum that was ultimately forwarded to President Roosevelt as well. In the memo, Dulles graphically painted his impression of an "ominous decline and final collapse" of the Reich. Into a "tormented General Headquarters" [the Wehrmacht Supreme Command or OKW] and a "half-moribund Foreign Office," Dulles wrote, "flow the lamentations of a large number of diplomatic missions." It was "a scene" in which distraught secret agents and diplomats did their utmost to cope with the defeatism and desertion of "totally defiant satellites" and allies and obstinate neutrals. The "era of secret diplomacy under Canaris and the champagne salesman" [Rippentrop] was coming to an end. In Hungary a senile Miklós Horthy was playing the same role as Pétain. In Sofia the Bulgarians were outfoxing the Nazis with all kinds of games and absconding to Turkey on pleasure trips. Reports were reaching Bucharest of Russians on the heels of plundering German troops. In brief: The telegrams coming out of the Foreign Office were reflecting the last twitches of a Nazi diplomacy going into decay. Dulles expected the reader to be "tossed from one emotion into another, from tears to laughter." The intelligence reports were showing "the Germans in their final swan song of brutality" against peoples who had been so irrevocably and unsympathetically ensnared by the Gestapo for half a decade.[128]

Dulles' description of the political situation was unusually emotional, and it was so rhetorically overcharged that those at OSS central headquarters had doubts about the accuracy of this picture of a collapsing Nazi regime. Dulles felt compelled, therefore, to defend his report. It was not just the Foreign Office telegrams and a lengthy conversation with "Wood," Dulles told Washington, that had prompted his sketch of German decline; this view was also corroborated by reports from "Gorter" (Waetjen) and "512" (Gisevius), as well as by general background information to which he had access in Bern. By no means should his impressions be toned down, Dulles' defense continued. To be sure, he did not want to create the impression that the "Nazi army" was facing immediate collapse. The German military was still not ready "to tear open" the Western front for the Allies, but as soon as the "fourth front" was opened in the West,[129] it would presumably only be a matter of months before Germany's collapse could be expected.[130]

For the Americans, this insight into the chaos of the Reich's institutions confirmed the impression that Germany's downfall was inevitable, and it also enlivened hopes for a speedy victory. The decision to go through with the attempt at a landing in Normandy, however, was not influenced by the awareness of what was going on inside the Reich politically and militarily.

What was the significance of the "Wood" material for the course of the war? Everything seems to indicate that Fritz Kolbe had been putting his life in jeopardy for months, while the Allies were not extracting the kind of profit from his intimate reports that corresponded to the personal risks he was taking. As of the end of 1943, the dispatches about the damage being inflicted by Allied bombers were sent (without source attribution) to the military authorities, and these must have played a certain role (however modest) in evaluating the air raids. But by the middle of 1944, Wood's proposals from December 1943 advocating the bombing of essential factory facilities were still unimplemented. In mid-May of 1944, Dulles asked Washington why the Siemens condenser factories in Gera were not being bombed, and why the factory facilities in Leuna that Kolbe mentioned had not been bombed; why not Poelitz, and why not Eberswalde?[131]

Only the OSS in Chungking toward the end of the war seems to have found great value in the Kappa reports, since they offered authentic insight into the attitude of the Japanese government as well as reliable military information.[132] In Washington and London, however, the German telegrams were treated for months on end as "museum pieces" without any operational value.[133] Richard Helms, who later became CIA Director and worked closely with Dulles at the OSS in Wiesbaden after the war, must have come very close to the historical truth in his assessment of the Wood episode's significance when he made this skeptical remark to an interviewer: "You can take that wonderful job that Allen Dulles did with Kolbe." It was, Helms said, "so long before people were prepared to believe that this was on the level, that this was really" a case where "telegrams came from the German Foreign Office." The "war was almost over by the time this debate . . . about those documents was resolved."[134]

Well into the final weeks of the war, Kolbe was supplying the OSS with photographs of diplomatic messages from the Foreign Office. He reported about V-weapons, peace feelers, and the Volkssturm (People's Army), about transportation problems in the Reich and the supposed Nazi redoubt in the Alps.[135] For Dulles Kolbe put together a list of Foreign Office staff with a note about each one's reliability. Months later one of Kolbe's proteges happened upon an OSS list containing recommendations for filling ministerial posts in postwar Germany. Kolbe's name, however, would not be on the list.[136] Shortly before the end of the war, the OSS launched an attempt to bring the German chargé d'affaires in Bern, Otto Köcher, over to the Allied side; this failed, and it also brought both Kolbe and Köcher into conflict with the Swiss authorities.[137] From then on, Kolbe's star began to decline. Although he was lucky enough to survive a terrible auto accident in Berlin, and although Dulles, Frederick Stalder, and Richard Helms provided the former German agent with a considerable sum of Swiss francs and dollars to start a future in the U.S., Kolbe was not able to get established in America.[138]

TWO DECADES after the war, Allen Dulles characterized the OSS outpost in Bern as the "big window" onto the fascist world.[139] While the OSS spy did not have an opportunity to travel to Germany, he was able—by surveying events indirectly from the parapet built for him by Fritz Kolbe, Hans Bernd Gisevius, and Eduard Waetjen—to create an accurate picture of events inside the Reich. Furthermore, he had a network of agents willing to take risks, "almost without exception Communists and leftist groups," who crossed the border into Germany by way of France and across Alsace.[140] Dulles' informants also included a number of Rhine boatmen who kept him up-to-date about the Germans' morale and who warned him against placing excessive hope in any uprising by workers or foreign laborers in the Reich.[141] From "474," Willem A. Visser t'Hooft, the general secretary of the World Council of Churches then under construction in Geneva, Dulles learned that tens of thousands of Jews were being rounded up, deported, and killed,[142] and Eduard Schulte brought him the outrageous news about the systematic gassing of Jews.[143] Between 1943 and 1945 Dulles tried using money that he received from private persons or trade unions to bring individual Jews to freedom. He secured visas, helped smuggle people out, and obtained secure addresses, so long as this did not impinge on the business of espionage.[144] He did not, however, protest against the Holocaust.

In July 1946 President Truman awarded the OSS leader the Medal of Merit for his accomplishments at the OSS in Bern. In his tribute the President highlighted the "courage" and "wisdom" of the American secret intelligence chief. Although he had been constantly watched by enemy agents, Dulles had been able to "fulfill his duties in a manner reflecting the utmost credit on himself and his country."[145] In addition to the usual rhetorical hyperbole, the President's tribute suggested, among other things, that Dulles had been the first to discover the German testing laboratory in Peenemünde. From now on the future CIA Director would be surrounded by an ever growing number of legends that would congeal into the myth of the "super-spy" and hold back on all the misadventures — including the infiltration of the OSS outpost by SD agents and Soviet informants.[146] The tiny OSS outpost in Bern had undoubtedly collected a profuse amount of reliable intelligence from the Reich, surpassing anything gathered from the other OSS outposts.[147] Without the intelligence from Bern, Washington would have found out little about tensions and rivalries within the narrow circle of leaders around Hitler, Himmler, Goebbels, Borman, and Göring; without Allen Dulles the American interest in the resistance to National Socialism would have presumably been completely extinguished, and without the work of Bern's OSS director it would hardly have been possible to expand the number of secret intelligence outposts in Europe so rapidly.

The reason for Dulles' success did not primarily lie in the OSS chief's genius. That informants from the Foreign Office and German counterintelligence were willing to put their lives at risk and to smuggle messages to the enemy abroad was, not least of all, a result of desolation in the Third Reich, whose physical and moral deterioration made "defection" to the enemy appear opportune.

V

Media War and Black Propaganda

THE DIFFICULT BEGINNINGS OF
THE OSS MORALE OPERATIONS

The Morale Operations Branch of the OSS (MO), which was responsible for
"subverting the morale of America's enemies," began its career inauspiciously
in January 1943, with a staff that had to be accommodated initially in a win-
dowless basement at the OSS building in Washington and was then forced to
move more than four times within a single year. This beginning is indicative of
the value placed on this new branch of Donovan's intelligence service in its
first year. Since MO was founded later than the major divisions of the OSS, and
since therefore it was often only able to recruit second-class staff, a strange
working climate developed that one MO staffer characterized in retrospect as
"neurotic" and shaped by "inferiority complexes." Furthermore, the metier of
"propagandists" was regarded as thoroughly disreputable in the United States—
much more so than in Great Britain or Nazi Germany. This contributed to an
atmosphere in which neither SI, SO, nor the military—all of whom were supposed to cooperate closely with the Morale Operations Branch—respected
MO's work.[1]

After the COI was split into the OSS and OWI, the Office of War Information assumed an important position within the American government apparatus.

Frederick Oechsner, the head of the MO division,[2] ran into additional obstacles when an April 1943 directive from the Joint Chiefs of Staff deleted the original reference to the OSS's propaganda function, an action that completely sealed the OWI's divorce from the OSS.[3] Would MO even be able to pursue its line of work if it was denied the right to conduct propaganda activities? Was "propaganda equated with propaganda," as OWI head Elmer Davis insisted, or did black propaganda and black radio operations fall within the job description of the OSS?[4] When the first MO agents were deployed in the field in north Africa, these questions became moot, since the three local staff members of Oechner's branch did not have facilities that would have allowed them to undertake covert radio operations or to smuggle subversive literature behind enemy lines and since the prevailing atmosphere did not allow MO to operate independently of the military.[5]

In 1943 the MO Branch essentially restricted itself to gathering material to plant rumors and to think up leaflets intended to wear down enemy morale.[6] The first major project went to Harvard University psychiatrist Dr. Walter Langer,[7] who (between January and October 1943, on the basis of interviews with such people as Princess von Hohenlohe, Ernst Hanfstaengl, Otto Strasser, and Heinrich Brüning) produced a psychological profile of Hitler that was intended to serve as the foundation for a subversive rumor campaign. Langer's work dragged on until early 1944, since the London MO outpost did not really know what to do with the "Hitler biography" and immediately requested a shorter, "spiced-up" version of the extensive manuscript.

The idea behind this MO initiative was to destroy Hitler's image and generate a belief among the German public that some personal misfortune had befallen the Führer. For months on end, MO launched rumors into neutral countries anticipating speeches that Hitler was about to give—such as on the anniversary of the founding of the SA or of the Munich Beer Hall Putsch of 1923. Since the Führer did not show up at these talks as expected, correspondents speculated about whether Hitler's absence was attributable to his unstable mental condition, to his taking flight, or even to his death. On December 29, 1944 Goebbels felt compelled to present the rumors about Hitler's illness as products of his Propaganda Ministry. He himself had passed on these rumors to the press in neutral countries, Goebbels explained in a clever countermove, in order to shake the Allies out of their smug complacency.

Before the first projects emerged from Langer's study, Washington had drafted a number of different rumor campaigns that were at the heart of MO's work in 1943.[8] For theoretical instruction, the project staff was able to avail itself of notes that psychology professors G. W. Allport and H. A. Murray had written up for their courses at Harvard.[9] Since only a few of the MO staff knew much about Germany, Italy, or their satellites, the rumor operations were mainly characterized by daring imagination and a lack of realism. Once a project had been developed, it first had to get past the OSS Planning Group's censors, who exercised their veto in half the cases, either because the operations seemed too destructive or because they touched on themes—such as news about the Vatican or reports about a negotiated peace—that were excluded on principle from the domain of rumors.[10]

Among the projects immediately okayed in the summer of 1943 by OSS Planning chief James Grafton Rogers was a brochure that the OSS conceived as the Nazi regime's official sex education pamphlet, supposedly issued by the "Reichsgesundheitsführer" (the "Reich Health Führer" and State Secretary in the Reich Interior Ministry) and deliberately manufactured using the kind of font and paper employed in Germany for official information about venereal disease.[11] The pamphlet, whose content was changed several times in August and September 1943 (at first Dolan found it "too long" and "too 'technical' even for [krautheads]"[12]) stressed how many citizens would lose their ability to procreate as a result of special shocks from enemy air attacks that would impair the functioning of their nervous systems. One might avoid this, however, by strictly following certain medical advice. The main thing was to "attempt sexual relations as soon after the air-raid as possible, preferably within 24 hours." In addition, it was deemed highly advisable to stay away from work for at least three to nine days. Party functionaries were instructed to authorize special leaves for this purpose.[13] The aim of this action was to intensify the already virulent fear of air attacks and develop a procedure for inducing civilians to take leaves of absence.[14]

In September the first 25 copies of the pamphlet were sent off to Italy, and shortly thereafter they were forwarded to Arthur Goldberg from the OSS Labor Branch, who saw to it that they were circulated in Europe via the underground channels of the transport workers union.[15] It can no longer be ascertained whether the pamphlet ever reached its intended recipients or had any impact on German troops worth mentioning. What is clear is that the survival rate for most of the rumors that the MO attempted to spread in 1943 was unusually small, since there were not enough distribution channels and Oechner's branch was dependent for distribution upon the good will of SI and SO agents.

The OSS outpost in Stockholm, meanwhile, refused to decode the excessively lengthy MO telegrams it was getting from Washington, and Colonel Eddy in Algiers let the MO material wander directly into the wastepaper basket, while Allen Dulles was carrying out his own MO operations independently of Washington. Only the rumors that reached London had a good chance of being distributed, since Oechsner was mainly stationed in the British capital during 1943 and because the English supported their American colleagues' operations—in word, and occasionally in deed.[16]

After eight months the Morale Operations Branch had so little to show for itself that the Planning Group appointed a commission under Major Shor to determine why the department had failed. Shor, a former newspaper man who approached MO with considerable goodwill, noted in his final report of August 20, 1943 that the branch was ruled by "confusion" about its tasks and that Frederick Oechsner's longstanding absence was proving to be a fundamental problem. He recommended continuing the division's work and recruiting qualified new staff—especially nationally and internationally renowned business people—to carry out operations in the field. Another recommendation was to transfer the planning of operations to a higher body. The Morale Operations Division, according to Shor, needed to become an autonomous division and operate independently of SO. Once the war was over, there would no longer be any bridges to blow up; MO's work, on the other hand, could be continued and would ultimately pay off as an investment in America's future.[17]

FROM THE HAMILTON PLAN TO OPERATION SAUERKRAUT

In September 1943 the MO Branch began to think about how it might be able to guide the resistance to Hitler inside Germany by means of subversive propaganda. Psychologist Dr. James Hamilton was convinced that the job of organizing a German underground should receive the "highest priority" among projected OSS operations. A plan named after him wagered on mobilizing an anti-Hitler opposition animated by rumors. Hamilton proposed insinuating to the Germans that there were small circles of resisters throughout the Reich who had signed a document attesting to their membership in an opposition. In Hamilton's view, signing this document would have a ritual as well as a practical significance: It would strengthen the feeling of belonging to an opposition group and, once the war was over, serve as proof that the signatories had been "partners in victory." Hamilton proposed a design of three overlapping circles as the group's identifying symbol, and, in order to prevent Nazi opportunists from passing themselves off after the war as members of the "Resistance Fraternity . . . or . . . Hamburg Movement," the membership oath was to be undertaken on a dated postcard using a coded message.[18] While the initial phase of the "Fraternity Project" was supposed to be devoted entirely to undermining enemy morale in successive stages and to building up isolated resistance groups by means of black propaganda leaflets, in a later phase the aim was to cooperate with political opposition leaders and trade unions (both in Germany and abroad) and to carry out concrete actions, such as sabotage and strikes.

Essentially, the Hamilton Plan had three overriding goals. First of all, MO hoped that mobilizing anti-Hitler resistance in the Reich would induce an early end to the war and thereby lessen the toll in human life that an Allied invasion was expected to take. Secondly, by using leafleting slogans and manifestos prepared by the OSS, MO wanted to insinuate to the Germans that the formula of "unconditional surrender" (a formula from which MO subliminally distanced itself) was not the equivalent of "national suicide," but rather that this pointed the way toward Germany's "political and social rehabilitation." Third and finally, Hamilton and his team wanted to develop a Western psychological warfare initiative that could serve as a counterpart to the Moscow Declaration of the NKFD (the National Committee for a Free Germany).[19]

The Hamilton Plan, in any event, would never be realized, since the MO Planning Staff, the decisionmaking body set up by Major Shor, had fundamental criticisms of the project. The Planning Staff's Germany experts believed that the target group of defeatist Germans was "not worth" mobilizing, since there was hardly any expectation of follow-up activities, and also believed that MO's proposal would do more to damage the Reich's real opposition than the OSS might find acceptable. The ideology underlying the Hamilton Plan was symptomatic of the prevailing belief, widespread in MO Branch circles, that it was possible to guide the Germans' activities by means of propaganda and that the war could be miraculously shortened.[20] The Planning Staff, by contrast, proposed penetrating Germany at some later time and using subversive radio stations or infiltrating MO agents into the Reich.[21] Although the planning body's objections were based on the entirely accurate realization that there was no active resistance in Germany so far (except on a very small scale), and that the resistance cells run by the OSS on remote control had the slimmest prospects for surviving in light of rigorous Gestapo surveillance, the Planning Staff's explanations were also shaped by wishful thinking. It would take more than a year until the first MO agents could be infiltrated into Germany. Before that happened, however, "Operation Sauerkraut" was implemented, a project that could be characterized in many respects as innovative.[22]

Paradoxically, the failure of the July 20 plot led to a kind of boom for the Morale Operations Branch of the OSS. The news about the attempted assassination of Hitler spread like wildfire and affected the OSS. When Allen Dulles found out that Hitler had survived and been spared by an "all-wise Providence," his report was a mixture of bewilderment, cynicism, and disappointment.[23] For him, the assassination's failure must have meant, in the very first place, cutting off his relationship with the Breakers, with whom he had been in touch since 1943, and on whom he had pinned a few political hopes. Meanwhile, for the staff of MO, which had not been maintaining any personal contacts with the German opposition, the assassination attempt signified hope. The coup, regardless of whether it was successful or not, showed them that there was a German opposition to Hitler inside the Reich that was both willing and able to take action. Now the entire world could see that the foundations of Hitler's rule had been shaken, that the Führer was apparently no longer able to keep his hands on all the reins of power and the opposition under control. Four days after the assassination attempt, Donovan explained in a memorandum to the President that never before had Allied propaganda gotten such a favorable opportunity to strike at the heart of the Nazis' war effort.[24]

Even before the news reached the President, some staff members of the Morale Operations Branch in Italy had seized the initiative and started a project that took aim behind enemy lines—using new, and not entirely risk-free, methods. Shaken up by the news of the July 20 assassination attempt, members of Company D, a small OSS MO unit under the command of the Fifth Army and stationed in Tuscany not far from Siena, were discussing the impact of the coup on the soldiers' morale. For this colorful collection of characters, which included one woman in uniform, Barbara Lauwers, there was no doubt at all that the assassination attempt offered an unparalleled opportunity for a psychological attack on the Wehrmacht's morale, if only it were possible to smuggle propaganda material behind enemy lines.[25] Distributing subversive material by air (Operation Cornflake) had proven ineffective for a variety of reasons. To begin with, there were hardly any airplanes available for MO actions. Secondly, it was notoriously easy for enemy units to observe material being dropped off, or for the leaflets to end up in the wrong hands. Third and last of all, it was not easy to determine what kinds of impact and what reactions the subversive writings would have on the German soldiers.

The plan that Company D hatched on the night of July 21, 1944 was surprisingly simple and seemed to solve all outstanding problems at a single stroke: As agents for the covert actions, it would not be OSS or military people who would be recruited, but rather German prisoners of war—an idea concocted by the philosopher Frederick Burkhardt and the Austrian aristocrat Oliver von Schneditz (alias Oliver Rockhill), two R&A agents working in Italy.[26] It did not take long to come up with a name for the new OSS project. "We wanted to give [the operation] a title name which would be very German and at the same time understandable widely. I think it was Eddie's [Edward Linder's] idea, how about Sauerkraut? The Germans are called Krauts anyway. Sauerkraut seemed absolutely appropriate for the operation."[27]

Just a day after the failed assassination attempt on Hitler, in the Italian city of Aversa, William Dewart, Jr. and Barbara Lauwers interviewed a whole string of German prisoners of war who had made an impression on the camp commandant as opponents of the Nazis. The Germans who were recruited as Sauerkraut agents in the days and weeks to come were all distinguished by strong hostility toward Hitler. Almost without exception, they had surrendered within just a few weeks of their arrival in Italy. Some, like the Viennese insurance agent Hans Peter Klein, had fought on the side of the partisans; many had

lost family members in aerial attacks or in concentration camps, and a few—
like the young German illustrator Willi Haseneier—had been demoted as a result of their "dishonorable" conduct in the Wehrmacht.[28] Although not all the
agents were counting on getting preferential treatment from the Americans,
some certainly did express the hope of emigrating after the war to the United
States (where, incidentally, Haseneier would achieve world fame in Hollywood
under the name Will Williams).[29]

Equipped with false identity papers, weapons, Swiss Army watches, Italian
money, and stacks of MO propaganda, the first three Sauerkraut teams were already making their way behind enemy lines as early as July 25. Within two days,
the "temporary OSS agents" had finished a crash course on dealing with explosives and been given their cover stories. Their assignment was now to penetrate enemy territory by night, distribute the black propaganda material, and,
where possible, return with news about the reactions of Wehrmacht soldiers
and about military facilities.[30]

Between July and October, Sauerkraut teams were deployed three times near
Prato, Pistoia, and Bologna. Interviews with returning agents gave the impression that it was not all that difficult to move around behind enemy lines. The
agents succeeded in depositing propaganda material in trucks, warehouses, la-
trines, and unguarded ambulances—and, in some cases, even in tanks. Starting
in September 1944, interviewers for the U.S. Army were frequently reporting that
American propaganda material had fallen into the hands of German soldiers. A
large proportion of the Wehrmacht soldiers regarded the leaflets and newspapers
as products of a genuine anti-Hitler movement, and on September 13 G-2 even
reported that Field Marshall Kesselring was forced to deny explicitly some of the
rumors launched by MO. Making out military facilities constituted another
achievement of Operation Sauerkraut. Sauerkraut agents discovered the Fourth
Paratroop Division, found the site of German "Tiger" tanks, and determined
where infantry divisions were staying. In his concluding report to William
Donovan, Colonel Kenneth Mann, who had led the MO Branch since May
1944,[31] reported that Operation Sauerkraut had been a complete success and
that those skeptics who had warned that the German prisoners of war would simply dispose of their propaganda material were proven wrong.[32]

Barbara Lauwers recalls that "actually there was no security." The sixteen
German prisoners of war recruited for "Sauerkraut I" sat down with two OSS
agents on the loading space of a truck. "The sixteen guys could have overpow-
ered those two MPs very easily, sixteen against two, even though these two MPs
had guns." The agents, however, proved "eager to cooperate." At first glance it
even seemed a risky idea "to send a female [Barbara Lauwers] into a camp
which housed thousands of prisoners of war . . . Anything could have happened."[33] It can no longer be determined how great the danger of a Sauerkraut

rebellion really was. What is clear, however, is that defeatism had become widespread among the Wehrmacht soldiers, especially those deployed in Italy, and that the assassination attempt of July 20 made it abundantly clear to these soldiers that the German Reich was not going to last much longer.

Apart from that, the Sauerkraut action was not as successful as it was portrayed in retrospect by MO leader Kenneth Mann and his staff. The OSS counterspies feared that one of the sixteen prisoners of war operating as Sauerkraut agents in July was really a double agent (the man in question, along with his two comrades, had to be sent back to Aversa), one of the teams did not succeed initially in penetrating behind enemy lines during the night, because the Wehrmacht was shooting off flares, and, to top it all off, there was an exchange of fire between Sauerkraut agents and a member of the U.S. Army, resulting in the death of the solider and magnifying already latent tensions between the OSS and the Army.[34] The third deployment of Sauerkraut agents, too, did not exactly go according to plan: The team with the codename MARIE got caught in a shootout with members of the SS who had been watching how the "Sauerkrauts" had been hanging anti-Nazi propaganda on trees near Sibano.

It cannot be confirmed whether it was really this incident that had triggered those rumors about fights between the SS and the Wehrmacht that were being peddled around for the next several weeks. The MO Branch, however, immediately used the event as the occasion for starting a rumor campaign intended to drive a wedge between SS and Wehrmacht divisions in northern Italy.[35] From a legal perspective, not least of all, the Sauerkraut project was particularly problematic, since it was a violation of the Geneva Convention and Rules of Land Warfare to recruit POWs. They could neither be deployed for activities with a direct relationship to military operations nor recruited for dangerous activities or operations requiring stationing near the front. Barbara Lauwers, who had a law doctorate, was just as aware of the international war law violation as was the OSS leadership, who had originally proposed hiding the operation from the Joint Chiefs of Staff, since they were afraid of Marshall's veto. At the end of 1944, however, the planning staff of the Allied Armed Forces headquarters reported that they had no objections to deploying prisoners of war on an unconfirmed basis.[36] Since the Sauerkraut agents could not be officially recruited, it was also not possible to compensate them officially for their secret intelligence work. To be sure, here and there the MO staff found unorthodox ways to remunerate their German helpers.[37]

In contrast to the English, who characterized their experience with German prisoners of war as unsatisfactory—Robin Brook explained that it was hardly worthwhile experimenting with the Germans[38]—the OSS continued working together with German prisoners of war until April 1945. The "Sauerkrauts" and their successors who worked for the SI Branch, however, got little out of these dangerous missions once their operations were over because—and in spite of fierce protests from the Morale Operations Branch—they immediately had to return to the American POW camps without receiving even a modicum of official recognition.[39]

BLANKENHORN'S SOLDIERS-COUNCILS PROJECT AND THE "NEUES DEUTSCHLAND" UNDERGROUND MOVEMENT

Among the staff members of the Morale Operations Branch, Heber Blankenhorn stood out for two reasons. A bit older than the average staff member of MO, he was also an experienced veteran of the First World War who in 1918 had developed and implemented subversive leafleting operations in France. A publication entitled *Adventures in Propaganda* (Boston: Houghton Mifflin, 1919), gave his letters from the field (the subtitle was *Letters from an Intelligence Officer in France*) a widespread circulation and allowed the American public to see the kinds of opportunities that psychological warfare had to offer under conditions of modern warfare.[40] Donovan had recruited Blankenhorn for the OSS from the War Department at the end of 1942 and given him a leadership position in which "the pioneer" (as Blankenhorn was occasionally called in the OSS) was responsible for leafleting propaganda and psychological warfare.[41]

In the First World War Blankenhorn had gotten the impression that the soldiers councils formed in Germany in 1917 and 1918 represented a "natural growth within an army facing defeat." In opposition to the National Socialist version of history that characterized the formation of the soldiers councils as a "Bolshevist stab in the back," Blankenhorn emphasized how the councils were chiefly composed of non-Communists. The soldiers-council movement had sprung up spontaneously from the fertile soil of tattered army morale. Most of the soldiers councils had their origins in the mess hall committees that were tolerated in spite of the iron discipline that prevailed in the German army.

Early in 1944 Blankenhorn saw a historical parallel to the situation of the First World War. The G-2 veteran sincerely believed that a large-scale MO operation could provoke the formation of soldiers councils and thereby make a fundamental contribution toward toppling the Nazi regime. Blankenhorn saw the clearly sunken morale of the Wehrmacht as proof that a propitious moment had arrived for a similar kind of propaganda action. The prisoner of war surveys had shown that a considerably higher number of soldiers now regarded the war as a lost cause compared to 1943.[42] In addition, there were individual reports about the formation of soldiers councils in Italy, Norway, Germany, and especially France. Admittedly, a rekindling of soldiers committees was something Blankenhorn regarded as possible only in those units that had suffered a defeat. From OSS surveys in Italy it emerged that the order "to stand to the last man and the last cartridge" was particularly responsible for triggering discussions about surrender.[43]

Blankenhorn proceeded from the assumption that the goal of the soldiers-council movement in 1944 would have to be the same as in 1918. The soldiers councils would undermine trust in the German High Command, provoke disobedience toward the "last stand orders," incite individual groups to surrender, prepare the way for peace agitation, and "ultimately" summon "to mutiny" and "possibly . . . to insurrection." In Blankenhorn's view there were two schools of psychological warfare, a "manipulative" and an "insurrectionary" one. The project he conceived fell into the second category. The "manipulative approach" attempted to wear down the enemy (and ultimately drive him to confusion) by using forgeries, fraudulent orders, misleading documents, and rumors. The insurrectionary school, by contrast, rested on Churchill's definition equating psychological warfare with revolution: "The ambition" as Blankenhorn explained, "is to explode the enemy rather than bedevil him."[44] Early in 1944 those working in the Morale Operations Division were no longer as naïve as at the time when the Hamilton Plan was being developed. Blankenhorn knew very well that there was "no organized opposition within Germany." Nevertheless, he saw the steadily growing number of punishments by summary judgment, executions, concentration camps, and military jails as an indicator of potential unrest in the army.

Where France was concerned, Blankenhorn's project depended on distributing two types of leaflets, a task envisioned as the special responsibility of contacts in the French resistance, in addition to OSS agents. Leaflets of the first type were advertisements for soldiers councils; the second type, by contrast, had to do with a purported underground group entitled *Soldatenwacht*, ("Soldiers Watch"), whose logo was a hand with four fingers and whose slogan was "Home, to the Fourth Reich." The *Soldatenwacht* pretended to be reporting about the activities of existing soldiers groups, but it consciously dispensed with making any political evaluations.[45] Blankenhorn was able to recruit two surviving members of the soldiers councils of 1918 as writers to work either for MO or the OSS Labor Branch in London, and to distribute the pamphlets he got in touch with Captain Warisse, a member of the Commission of Prisoners of War (La Commission des Prisonniers de la Guerre), whose organization maintained ties not only to French POW camps but also to the Todt organization (in charge of Nazi construction work) and to railroad workers in France and Germany.

Early in 1944 some discussions took place involving the Psychological Warfare Division of the Supreme Headquarters for the Allied Expeditionary Force (PWD-SHAEF), Rae Smith of the MO in London, and Blankenhorn in which the question of cooperation with the French underground and the problem of the operation's political line were discussed. Smith from the London MO spoke out in favor of dumping the propaganda material out of airplanes and deploying OSS agents, while Blankenhorn insisted on cooperating with the French resistance. He reminded everybody that hired agents were to be trusted far less than the French and that even airplane pilots were known to report that their operations were completely successful when all they had really done was to fly a loop across the enemy border.

In the end, Blankenhorn had to make concessions to Smith, in return for which SHAEF quietly acquiesced to the risky operation. As far as the political direction of the soldiers committees was concerned, it was debated whether the soldiers committees were "essentially revolutionary" and whether the Allies even wanted to have an organization like this inside any enemy army. In interpreting the historical parallel, the representatives of the military and the OSS came to the unambiguous conclusion that the soldiers councils from the First World War had not really been revolutionary. They had been against the Kaiser and the General Staff and were republican, but they were by no means the "backbone of a Communist revolutionary movement." To be sure, there was a feeling that predictions about the Second World War would be much harder to make, and it was emphasized that one could not entirely rule out any "attempt to go Communist" in a "totally occupied and economically desperate Germany." Nevertheless, the *"probability* of the damage likely to enemy fighting capacity" would far outweigh the mere *"possibility* of ultimate political turns by Soldiers Committees."[46]

Although Blankenhorn had twelve leaflets drawn up, most of these drafts from the London OSS seem to have disappeared.[47] Ultimately, however, one of his brochures was published with an initial circulation of 10,000 copies and smuggled behind enemy lines. The text of this OSS black propaganda document was translated into German by Conrad Latour and Egon Jameson, who used language and diction closely following that of the OKW (the Supreme Wehrmacht Command — Oberkommando der Wehrmacht).[48]

The purported OKW paper was dated July 1944 and pretended to be a "secret command matter" (*Geheime Kommandosache*) as well as a "special issue of Reports for the Officer Corps" (*Sondernummer der Mitteilungen für das Offizierskorps*). The OSS intended for it to be read by enlisted men as well as officers. Under the title "Troop morale has to be raised" the eight-page paper — which could be distinguished from the regular "Reports" only by its handy pocket format, but not by its presentation or typography — stressed that the Führer's order to maintain position down "to the last man and the last bullet" was getting to the point where, with increasing frequency, it could no longer be executed literally. The paper cited a remark from Ludendorff, who (as was well known) took off to Sweden in 1918 and who, "as an old soldier" after the war, adjured each patriot's "damned duty" "to save oneself from . . . hopeless predicaments by flight and surrender." The supposed OKW paper added by way of commentary that the decision "to surrender or to hold out to the last man" should not be made by the individual soldiers, but only by the OKW. The paper explained "when and why officers had to save themselves" and reprinted "instructions about [the] treatment of soldiers groups," which really just served the purpose of showing German troops that committees like this existed and were capable of taking action. The soldiers councils, it said, were "only founded" "in order to mislead the troops toward disobedience." In light of the "altered military situation," however, it was the duty of the officer corps—"even under conditions of hopeless enemy superiority"—"to make up for the lack of weapons . . . by strengthening troop morale."[49] In conceiving this paper, Blankenhorn and his team placed great value on making sure that no enemy commander would be able to expose the brochure as Allied propaganda.

All the facts and allusions cited in the paper matched the reality German soldiers were facing and the range of their experience. As a result, the Germany experts of the PWD—and especially Colonel Kehm—were perplexed when told that the brochure had been fabricated by American intelligence. Between July and October 1944 tens of thousands of the fake "Reports for the Officers Corps" were smuggled into France by Mayor Lloyd's OSS unit, the Ninth Air Force. The Allies found them among captured German soldiers and in enemy positions they had overrun. G-2 sent reports about the paper to SHAEF, JCS telegrams mentioned the purported German document, a British correspondent at the front had the entire paper published in a British daily in September 1944, and the House of Commons was asked whether the Allies might not be able to exploit the purported OKW paper for propaganda purposes.[50]

From the perspective of the Morale Operations Branch, the Blankenhorn project was a success on which to build; early in 1945 the OSS hoped to carry on where it had left off the year before. David Williamson, the head of MO's European division, proposed reactivating the idea of soldiers councils and deploying German prisoners of war instead of American agents to distribute the leaflets. Meanwhile, the job of carrying on with the project was impeded by bureaucratic inertia within the Morale Operations Branch and by the numerous drafts required to get the PWD-SHAEF to approve new OSS projects.[51]

A PUBLICATION THAT got much wider circulation than the purported OKW Reports was the OSS newspaper published in Algiers and then later in Rome, "Das Neue Deutschland" (DND—"The New Germany"). It was distributed by Sauerkraut agents, among others, and presented itself as the periodical of an underground movement and secret peace party in Germany.[52] Eddie Lindner gave the paper the name "Das *Neue* Deutschland" after it had been brought to his attention that the name "Das *Freie* Deutschland" ("The *Free* Germany") was already taken by a Communist underground paper.[53]

The guiding principle for all contributions to "Neues Deutschland," whose circulation varied between 75,000 and more than a million, was their credibility. The goal was to avoid at all cost any hint of the texts' American origins. Therefore it was necessary that the Allied press was also taken in by the forgery.[54] It was not least of all for this reason that individual issues of the DND were subject to strict censorship by an editorial staff that included the renowned Chicago journalist and OSS staff member Wallace Deuel as well as Hans Speyer from the Office of War Information and James Riddleberger from the State Department.[55] In its biweekly editions, "Neues Deutschland" would sometimes goad toward sabotage, at other times toward desertion. Thus, for example, in one edition from October 1944 the paper urged its readers to "avoid induction into the 'Volkssturm' [Peoples Army] by calling in sick or by 'moving.'" The Neues Deutschland movement was prepared to "support vigorously those comrades who are hiding. . . . Food and money" had already "been prepared for this purpose." Where induction into the Volkssturm proved unavoidable, it was incumbent upon "every good German . . . to hide . . . the weapons he possessed . . . immediately in a secure place . . . in order to wipe out our murderers, the Gestapo, and the SS." The fictional Action Committee of the New Germany Movement, which had signed the October appeal, concluded its call to resistance with the pathos-ridden slogan: "The choice will be easy to make for every authentic German. Volkssturm [Peoples Army], yes . . . but *Volkssturm* [meaning, in this case: popular assault] *against the Party*!!"[56]

Not only did the Neues Deutschland movement have its own maxim — "The future belongs to those who are getting ready for it!" — printed on the paper's masthead; it also had its own signature tune, with lyrics and music composed by Eddie Lindner. The new *Deutschlandlied* (Song of Germany) was a march whose score appeared as a leaflet supplement to some issues. In a simple, catchy tune the song invoked Germany's phoenix-like rebirth from out of the ashes of the Third Reich. Coincidentally, the OSS text displays certain similarities with what would later be the national anthem of the German Democratic Republic:

> *Out of the ruins there blooms new verve.*
> *A new life shall again arise!*
> *New Germany we'll all now serve;*
> *the Third Reich, this is its demise!*
> *No class struggle!*
> *No racist hate!*
> *No Führer, no monarch!*
>
> *New Germany served by free humanity;*
> *New Germany lasting an eternity!*[57]

IT WAS CLEAR to everyone in the Morale Operations Branch that the place where the newspapers were going to be found would play a decisive role in covering up their Allied provenance. Nevertheless, quite a few pamphlets were dumped or launched behind enemy lines with so-called "leaflet bombs," developed by the OSS itself, which must have aroused suspicions among the population.[58] A complicated yet effective variation was the distribution of DND copies within the framework of "Operation Cornflake," whereby OSS material was addressed, packed into postal sacks, and dumped in the vicinity of trains that had been shot to pieces in order to create the impression that the sacks needed to be forwarded. In this way the underground paper reached a number of German households courtesy of the Deutsche Reichspost. A million copies with the misleading inscription "This fell into Allied hands when Paris was taken" had already been dumped over Vienna in the summer of 1944.[59]

In the OSS's own internal (and self-serving) evaluation, which admittedly has to be assessed with caution, "Das Neue Deutschland" ranked high on the list of MO triumphs. Between the summer of 1944 and early 1945 the OSS really did succeed in distributing millions of DND copies to the German population. Some of the prisoners of war who were surveyed even took it upon themselves to become active freedom fighters in the DND movement. They had apparently responded to the editors' calls to action and established their own resistance cells. Out of the more than 3,000 cooperating German prisoners of war surveyed by MO agents in May and June 1945, 44.9 percent declared that they had heard about "Neues Deutschland," 14% had apparently read it, and only one regarded the paper as covert Allied propaganda.[60] No comparable statistics are available for the civilian population. Nevertheless, it may be assumed that the paper's distribution inside the territory of the Reich was significantly lower than at the front in Italy, France, Austria, or in Hungary.

In the last weeks of the war, in the context of Operation "Anne," a subversive radio station established in Luxembourg City under the name "1212" single-mindedly continued spreading the series of rumors about the existence of a Neues Deutschland movement. A distinguishing feature of Radio 1212, which introduced its regular programming with a Rhenish folk song, was its quite objective reporting about events on the Western front, although the Soviet advance in the east (a highly ominous event for western Germany's population) was deliberately portrayed in gloomy tones. In addition to current news about bombing damage, which German propaganda was notorious for suppressing, Radio 1212 reported routinely on the Neues Deutschland movement, which was apparently represented in every major German city. Toward the end of the war listeners were encouraged to erase the second, fourth, and fifth letters of the Nazi party initials NSDAP so that nothing was left over except the monogram ND, for Neues Deutschland. Throughout Germany these radio instructions, concocted and implemented by the OSS and Operation "Annie" in cooperation with the OWI and American Army, found wide resonance. The Morale Operations Branch interpreted this as a success and claimed to have contributed toward eroding German morale and stimulating anti-Nazi resistance.[61] In April 1945 the German Reich really did lie in rubble and ashes, and the Germans were demoralized in any event. A genuine German resistance was out of the question.

OSS RADIO WAR: JOKER AND MATCHBOX

"Annie" was just one of several radio operations that the OSS carried out during the Second World War. Even before Pearl Harbor William J. Donovan sent a memorandum to President Roosevelt, expressing his opinion that radio was "the most powerful weapon of psychological warfare." It would take several years, however, until the OSS could participate in the subversive radio war against Hitler without technical assistance from the British.[62] The most important initial operation was an action that MO organized in cooperation with the OWI, "Italo Balbo," whose conception became the model for several operations to follow. Curiously, the idea for the subversive radio station was based on Oliver Garrett's Hollywood film script entitled *Underground. Underground* was the fictional story of a young German chemist who belonged to the anti-Hitler resistance, operated a "freedom station," and got his brother, a convinced Nazi, to join the underground.

"Radio Balbo" claimed to be the mouthpiece for a real underground movement in southern Italy. Its name was derived from a radio station operated out of Tunisia by a fascist who had belonged to the quadrumvirate around Mussolini in 1922 but fell out of his good graces within a year and shortly thereafter perished in an airplane accident under suspicious circumstances.[63] To the Italians the name Italo Balbo had a heroic ring with the unmistakable connotation of a certain anti-Duce element. The station went into operation at the end of June 1943—two weeks before the Allied invasion of Sicily under General Eisenhower—and broadcast subversive speeches and dialogues through July 25. The station mixed facts with fictitious news and sent Italy a profusion of MO rumors ostensibly reporting about the Balbo movement, which proved especially confusing to Allied war reporters and prompted Oliver Garrett to make the exaggerated remark that Radio Balbo had played a decisive role in Mussolini's decline.[64]

Radio Balbo became the model for "Operation Joker," which, just a few weeks after July 20, 1944, resurrected one of the assassination attempt's leading conspirators, General Ludwig Beck, via a BBC transmitter. In contrast to

Balbo, who merely lent his name to the fictitious underground movement from beyond the grave, Operation Joker suggested that the legendary General Beck was really still alive. In this way the Americans stirred up a rumor that was already circulating—for the second time—in the summer of 1944. In the first instance, which was in 1938 after Beck's resignation as chief of the General Staff, the Nazis had said that Beck had committed suicide. Now the OSS was spreading the legend of the general's reemergence. To this end a POW with the rank of major who was being held prisoner in the English town of Brondsbury supplied the general's voice, while four other German prisoners of war transmitted the radio addresses prepared for "Beck" by the MO. "Beck's" speeches, which were deliberately broadcast at a psychologically propitious time, after the fall of Aachen, contrasted the military know-how of the German General Staff with the bungling of a Führer driven by sick impulses. The fake general, who kept coming back to Clausewitz's book *On War* throughout his speeches, pushed his rhetoric to the point of sarcasm when he used quotes from Hitler's *Mein Kampf* in order to summon his listeners to rise up against Hitler: For as long as the regime was abusing its power, it was not just the right of each individual, but also a duty, to rebel against the Nazi regime.

"Beck," to be sure, hardly had an opportunity to address the German people, for the station was destroyed by the Nazis as early as the second broadcast. Speculative reports about the state of the military opposition in Nazi Germany appeared on the front pages of English and Swedish papers, and in American and French newspapers as well. Thus, Germany's war adversaries ended up being misled, while inside Hitler's Germany the costly enterprise fizzled out in the airwaves after only a brief transmission.[65]

That the OSS Morale Operations Branch was not able to implement all of its projects for psychological warfare was demonstrated by the case of Operation Matchbox, which was conceived by the OSS at the end of 1944 and foundered on a British veto. This projected radio series ostensibly emerged from leading circles within the Wehrmacht, German industry, and politics, and it simulated tensions between two factions in the Reich—between the fatalistic and ruthless Nazis surrounding Himmler, on the one hand, and a group of realists who were patriotic but inclined toward peace, on the other. The fictitious opposition was supposedly going to be announcing its readiness to conduct peace negotiations with the Allies on the radio, which would thereby prompt vacillating leadership circles inside the Reich toward a display of solidarity. Although General Eisenhower, who was known to have a weakness for psychological warfare operations, came out strongly in favor of Matchbox, the British unambiguously rejected the project, since they feared that the Nazis could discover the operation and use it for their own propaganda. In brief, the British declared that "Matchbox" was too "easily flammable." The English did not want to play with fire. The fictitious peace offer seemed too risky to them, especially since it harbored a danger that the British as well as the Germans might be deceived about genuine peace prospects.[66]

OPERATION MUSAC: AMERICAN POP MUSIC IN THE WAR AGAINST HITLER

In July 1944 Rae Smith, the head of the London OSS division for Morale Operations, approached his colleagues in Washington with a strange request. He asked for the Washington office to "deliver a flow of recordings of American songs with German lyrics." The recordings recordings were intended for the Calais Soldiers Station (*Soldatensender Calais*—after Calais was taken, it called itself "Soldiers Station West" or *Soldatensender West*), which pretended that it was run by Germans inside France. In reality, however, the station, established in 1943, was located in the English town of Milton Bryant, where the British had set up a highly modern radio and communications center with professional recording studios during the war. In the middle of the facility, which had been camouflaged and secured, a powerful 600,000 watt transformer had been erected and nicknamed Aspidistra (or "shield lily"—after the then popular hit song "The Biggest Aspidistra in the World"). The metal monster was outfitted with a directional antenna and could easily broadcast to all of Central Europe from Milton Bryant.[67]

After the war the Allies found out that the "soldiers station" had struck a highly positive note with the German civilian population. Almost a quarter of all Germans who listened to foreign stations were, according to an Allied survey, familiar with the station of the British secret service. The fact that the reports from Milton Bryant always presented unvarnished information about the military failures of German troops—and that they often contained disparaging remarks and disrespectful revelations about the political views or private lives of leading Nazi politicians—prompted a few listeners to suspect that the soldiers station was operated by the British. In the British secret service's Psychological Warfare Branch (SO1), however, a high value was placed on having the soldiers station transmit only those news stories the listeners were going to regard as "probably true." In light of the extreme risks associated with listening to enemy stations in Nazi Germany—in a number of cases the "misdemeanor" was prosecuted as treason and therefore punished with the death penalty—listening to the station represented a relatively safe alternative to the BBC or Voice of America, especially since the National Socialists did little to counteract the legend of the broadcasts' German origin.[68]

Since the beginning of 1944 the English were becoming increasingly worried that it might not be possible to keep the German troops to whom "Radio

Calais" was primarily addressed sufficiently entertained. There was no shortage of news programs, but not enough popular music. Under these circumstances the British turned to their colleagues in the London OSS. "The problem," as one OSS staff member recalled, "was to produce on a large scale the best that American popular music had to offer, and to create German lyrics which would hold the enemy's attention"[69] Rae Smith cabled Washington a whole list of names to be considered for choosing a "lyricist and gag man"; in addition, he suggested getting the Paul Kolner Agency in Hollywood and Columbia Records in New York involved. The lists that Smith forwarded to Washington included the names of several prominent exiles from German or Austrian cultural life, most notably Max Ophüls, Bruno Engler, Joseph Than, Willy Trenk-Trebitsch, Fritz Blocki, Max Willenz, Willy Wolff, Edward Schellhorn, Kurt Weill, and Frederick Hollaender. At intelligence headquarters in Washington, however, they gradually found out that most of the persons mentioned were not available on such short notice, and that people like Weill and Hollaender also did not seem suitable: In the end, after all, what the London operation needed was librettists, not composers.[70]

The Americans regarded the German émigré Bertolt Brecht as the most suitable candidate. Brecht, who had been Weill's librettist in Germany was said to have been the Weimar era's best satiric writer for the German stage. The only thing that gave the Washington OSS propaganda department pause was Brecht's "communist leanings." He had been a member of the German Communist Party, which made it hard to hire him formally. Even had the Morale Operations Branch been prepared to opt for Brecht (and had Brecht been prepared to work for it), he would have had to have been hired though the OSS Office of Security, run by Weston Howland, a well-known Boston textile manufacturer. Until early 1944 Howland had strictly prohibited hiring persons who had previously maintained ties to Communist organizations. As the war went on, however, the OSS security chief adopted a more liberal attitude, and news of Howland's change of course leaked out just at the time when the OSS was discussing whether to recruit Brecht.

In April 1944 OSS Major Graham Aldis reported that the Security Office "appears willing now to pass qualified persons suspected of previous communist affiliations."[71] This news prompted Samuel Scrivener from Washington's Morale Operations Branch to gather more information about Brecht. The Brecht dossier, which had originally consisted of a brief note by psychologist Walter Langer, kept growing day by day. "Bert (Berthold) Brecht," it said in an internal OSS memorandum received by Samuel Scrivener on May 17, 1944, had "recently moved away from the party." He was criticizing Stalin and the foreign policy of the Soviet Union because of the dissolution of the Comintern and the recognition of the Badoglio regime. Therefore Brecht was getting closer to a Trotskyist position. "Although Brecht [was] without a doubt one of the best contemporary German lyricists and authors," the OSS regarded him as suitable for propaganda work only under certain conditions. His influence on the "broad German masses" was limited. In spite of his "political sympathies for 'the people,'" his texts were "too avant-garde" to be understood by the little guy. Brecht's fans were intellectuals and Bohemians. The "man on the street," all the while, knew "little or hardly anything about Brecht."[72]

If some staff members of the MO Branch already had latent reservations about a Communist like Brecht, the May 17 memorandum questioned Brecht's usefulness in a more fundamental way. After all, Brecht's criticism of Stalin was directed not only against the most important ally of the United States, but simultaneously at the pragmatic principles behind America's Italy policy. In addition, linking Brecht with the German "intelligentsia"—when influencing frontline soldiers and the little guy was at stake—proved decisive in getting the OSS to start looking around for another candidate to fill the post of propaganda poet. Brecht himself, who in early 1944 was in Hollywood on the staff of the European Film Fund,[73] presumably never heard about the discussions being conducted in New York and Washington intelligence circles concerning his personality. Whether he might have been persuaded to cooperate with America's secret intelligence service will probably remain a mystery forever.[74]

Although the search for a German-speaking lyricist was pursued with great urgency in the early part of 1944, it took several weeks before the OSS was able to recruit a suitable person for the Soldiers Station project. In one case the OSS Office of Security was making things difficult, another time it proved impossible to persuade the candidate favored by the MO Branch to take the job, and in a third case the director of the MO propaganda school blocked the appointment since the potential coworker did not seem suitable for the position on account of his temperament.[75] Ultimately Lothar Metzl, a native Viennese cabaret writer and playwright, was recruited. The young writer, who had been living in New York since 1938 and serving in the army as a private first class since 1943, was an unknown commodity in the United States. In the Vienna of 1934, by contrast, where the 28-year-old doctor of law had abandoned his career as an attorney to become a writer, Metzl was well known. Metzl had made a name for himself there as co-founder of the legendary satirical cabaret *Literatur am Naschmarkt* and as an opera arranger before he fled Vienna in 1938, initially for Prague and later to the United States.[76]

The young Austrian writer had caught the attention of the OSS propaganda division quite early.[77] In particular, the clear diction, penetrating speech, and subtle humor of Metzl's texts met with praise. In addition, the OSS was impressed by the productivity this cabaret artist had demonstrated in the thirties. As an author of OSS propaganda texts, Metzl was expected to crank out high-quality texts in assembly-line fashion for $80 a week. No fewer than thirty texts a month were required for the OSS propaganda project, which Washington gave the codename "Musac."[78]

For insiders the word "Musac," an abbreviation for "musical action," evoked the name of the Muzak Record Company, a New York firm in whose studios some of the recordings for the Soldiers Station were supposed to be produced. It was understood that the action was subject to the strictest rules of secrecy. As a cover, the OSS was represented by a dummy corporation; this outfit, in turn, worked together with the J. Walter Thompson advertising agency. Interestingly, the entire leadership of the London Morale Operations Branch staff—from Rae Smith, through his delegate George Dibert, to the head of the London outpost of Musac, Ira Ashley—was recruited from the ranks of the Thompson Agency. J. Walter Thompson understood his company's support for the project as a contribution to the national war effort. Therefore his agency put one of his program directors, Lester O'Keefe, along with coworkers William Griffin and Walter O'Meara at the disposal of the OSS. In addition, Thompson engaged an orchestra, musicians, and directors, and rented suitable studio space.[79]

In contrast to Lothar Metzl, who was on the payroll of the OSS, the musicians were never to learn that they were actually working for American intelligence instead of a commercial music producer.[80] Hiring the musicians required tact. On the one hand, negotiations with the Musician's Union could never afford to reveal the true character of the operation; on the other hand, the budget for "Musac" was tight.[81] Notwithstanding these restrictions, the Thompson Agency was able to recruit NBC's Irving Miller as musical director and assemble an orchestra varying in size from eight to fourteen musicians and leaving little to be desired artistically.[82] When it came to choosing the singers, there was a large pool of German-speaking émigrés to draw on. The composer and musician Carroll Gibbons was flown in to New York from London to assess potential artists; in the end, only the best of these were hired. They included stars like Marlene Dietrich and her daughter Maria Manton, as well as Herta Glatz from the Vienna Opera. In addition, Greta Keller once a star of the German recording industry was recruited, as were Jarmila Novotna and Grete Stueckgold, two talented singers from the New York Metropolitan Opera, Vilma Kurer, "a personality singer of night club type" was meant to sing most of the sexually suggestive songs being presented. Also recruited were Daisy (Desi) Halban, who had made her reputation as a soprano, and Sig Arno, a comedian who in 1944 had landed a big hit in the Broadway production "Song of Norway."[83]

As soon as chances for the project's approval looked good and Lothar Metzl had composed enough texts to guarantee keeping to a schedule, it was possible to get started producing popular music for the OSS. Beginning on July 7, 1944, the illustrious Musac Crew met at least once a week. Each time, production had to take place within three hours—or within six hours in case there was a double session. The sessions demanded total involvement from all the participants, outstanding preparation, and a high degree of concentration. It was owing to the resourcefulness of Irving Miller and his successor Allen Roth that old musical and instrumental arrangements could be used whenever the OSS budget did not allow for any new ones. Recordings were sent off to London starting in early July, and the reaction of the Anglo-American team at the Soldiers Station was enthusiastic. "Metzl' lyrics splendid" was the spontaneous wording of the telegram from London. It was because of Musac that twelve hours of broadcast time (from 8 P.M. to 8:00 A.M.) could be secured to fill out an entertainment program that was as attractive as it was intelligent.[84]

Even before the first Musac productions were launched, it was clear that the entertainment being produced by the OSS had to be fundamentally distinguished from that of the Office of War Information (OWI). In a cable from June 1944 the London MO outpost explained: "OWI LIKES AMERICAN VOICES AND ACCENTS, OURS MUST HAVE FOREIGN CHARACTER. . . . WE CANNOT HAVE AMERICAN ACCENT BUT TYPICAL AMERICAN ARRANGEMENTS ARE IN ORDER. FOR EXAMPLE, HARRY JAMES WITH GOOD GERMAN LYRIC, AND PURE AUSTRIAN OR NORTH GERMAN VOICE." These instructions did not reflect any aesthetic preferences; rather, they were a necessary precondition for camouflaging Musac. Using identical voices and arrangements in the American entertainment programs would have blown the cover of the OSS operation.[85]

The Musac team did not have a hard time picking suitable American compositions. Within a short time they had accumulated so many scores—ranging musically from cowboy songs through Gershwin classics to Negro spirituals— that the supply would have lasted for several years. Problems of a technical nature arose, however, in connection with the texts. Since adjusting the character of the German language to American melodies takes some effort, only rarely was it possible simply to translate the original texts. Here Lothar Metzl made a virtue of necessity. For most of the songs he created new verses that fit the American rhythms while conforming to the German public's taste. Although he knew that the producers were mainly expecting pure entertainment from him, he mixed a whole series of propaganda texts into the batch of sentimental love songs, nostalgic ballads, and entertaining little songs that made up the bulk of Musac's production.

In retrospect Metzl conceded that he saw his assignment as a brilliant opportunity to write propaganda texts.[86] Here he applied a poetic technique that blurred the distinction between innocent rhymes and subversive verse. In one stanza of the American song "Hallelujah," for example, Metzl formulated an allusion to Hitler: "Satan's/ Running the government,/ So take a hint/ Throw him out!" (*Satan/ Fuehrt den Staat an,/ Nimm den Rat an/ Wirf ihn raus!*). In other songs Metzl played out the contrast between the unhappy present and the happy past. Thus, one of his sentimental ballads starts out: "In days gone-by/ We'd dream of bliss: / Our future was so bright, /And yet, how quickly / It was all over./ Things will be dark for some years to come." In order to muffle or destroy any remaining illusions listeners might have, the OSS lyricist went on to work in a death motif: "Dark is the night/ Just like life./ We glide into the night / Surrendering / To the dance tunes and the rhythm / Of the present / Yet far off in the rain lurks / Death."[87]

Of the barely forty Musac songs conceived as open propaganda, most lyrics were comical in nature, since the Musac players saw entertainment as "a strong weapon of psychological warfare." Thus, the topic for a number of witty songs was the unpleasantness and dangers of a soldier's life, while other songs adopted a mocking and chastising tone against the ever-growing gap between soldiers and officers. The most effective songs identified with German soldiers and adopted their perspective in order to strike out at the vulnerable points of Nazi rule and military leadership. A major aim here was to intensify the widespread mistrust that frontline soldiers had against party bosses and functionaries, who were generally regarded as corrupt, cowardly, and self-serving. One example of "comedy lyrics" was the text to "Ferdinand the Bull," recited in a characteristically impudent tone by the comedian Sig Arno:

> *When a-traveling you go*
> *But not a word you know*
> *Of the country's local lingo,*
> *You're bound to appear*
> *Like a gate-bashing steer,*
> *For the natives just say "no comprendo."*
> *The porter in the hotel*
> *And the bull out in the dell*
> *Double over in laughter spectacular.*
> *Still, the cultivated man*
> *Always learns what he can,*
> *So he tries to master the vernacular:*
>
> *Oh the Gau-*
> *Oh the Gau-*
> *The Gauleiter is suddenly going Hispanic.*
> *For the Gau-*
> *For the Gau-*
> *The Gauleiter can't overcome his panic.*

And the Gau-
Leiter's Frau
In a race packs her case,
For the whole menage
The entire baggage
Is disappearing to Madrid.
Ole!

Yes the Gau-
Yes the Gau-
The Gauleiter is learning some Japanese, too.
For the Gau-
Leiter Schlau
Suspects right now that Spanish will not get him through.
And the Gau-
Leiter's Frau
Bought a smart new kimono:
Should something happen to Franco.
Then they won't be va banquo,
And can move right on to Tokyo.
Banzai![88]

After the project had been launched and the $21,500 budget had been approved, the London recipients of the Musac lyrics became increasingly critical of Metzl's poetry. If at first they had uniformly praised his texts, they later criticized the excess of nostalgic themes and the often subversive character of some productions.[89] In the autumn of 1944 the London OSS hired its own, third-rate, lyricist, who produced about one song a week. Shortly thereafter the criticism directed against Metzl culminated in a letter from Lt. Commander Reichner to David Williamson in Washington: "The Metzl lyrics," the memo said, "have ranged from very good to poor—those in the latter category obviously because of rush. The difficulty with them is that they are not easily singable. Otherwise, our comment in general is: the simpler the lyric, the better for our purposes."[90]

Although Metzl issued a statement saying that he was grateful for Reichner's critique, he obviously felt unjustly attacked. In an office memorandum he defended himself to his New York boss Edward Cushing as follows: "When I set out to write lyrics for this operation, I was without guidance as to what was wanted. It was clear, however, that the songs were to be used for entertainment purposes, and with this in mind, I decided to devise lyrics which would amuse or move the listener and strike a responsive chord in his mind. . . . As the quality of my verses, I must admit that I have a style of my own. No writer worth a penny can do without self-expression. So I'm afraid my lyrics show that I don't quite belong with the lyricists of the 'June, Moon, Swoon' type."[91] Metzl refused to move away from his poetic principles, and those in charge of the Musac project—Rhoda Hirsch, Edward Cushing, and the gentlemen from the J. Walter Thompson —stood squarely behind their ghostwriter.

Nevertheless, the transatlantic discussion about the quality of Metzl's texts had made such waves that Edward Cushing decided to test the poetic and musical drawing power of the Musac tunes under the most authentic conditions possible. It so happened that the *New Yorker* magazine had just been reporting on how German POWs were entertaining themselves in American camps. Since that issue appeared, the American public had been informed that "some PW camps have small, spring-driven phonographs which were sent from Germany, and at some of the big ones the men have chipped in to buy more modern equipment." The OSS memo quoting the *New Yorker* article went on to emphasize: "*Shipment of German-made records arrive regularly.* About a third of these," it was reported, were "classical" music, while "the rest run to popular songs and bouncing waltzes."[92]

Cushing proposed smuggling in the records produced by the OSS under cover of phonograph deliveries from the German Red Cross, and Samuel Scrivener, who oversaw the technical implementation of the action, saw to it that the OSS records would be shaped and labeled so that they looked exactly like German products. After enough time had lapsed for the camp inmates to get used to the "new music," their musical preferences would be surveyed. To this end the Musac team had contrived a questionnaire meant to be presented to the POWs in the context of informal conversations not interrogations. The goal of the action was, among other things, to collect information on the listening habits of the German soldiers, sound out how well-acquainted the prisoners of war were with "enemy radio programs," and how important radio was "in . . . the actual realm of combat."[93] The outcome of the survey left no doubt about the success of Operation Musac: According to the OSS's internal evaluation, hundreds of German prisoners of war testified that the musical entertainment provided by the Anglo-American Soldiers Station was largely responsible for the station's high listener rating.[94]

The mentality and language of the soldiers constituted one moment to which the Musac production team needed to be attuned; the contemporary context and the current military situation were two other factors of nearly equal importance. Numerous Musac productions contained concrete allusions to current events. Even if they had some link to a particular time, the songs were kept so general that they could still be played for months afterward without losing any of their explosive power. One example was a song presented by Greta Keller, "I am like the Westwall" (*Ich bin wie der Westwall*), after the American melody "Come with me my Honey," which was recorded on September 28, 1944, two days after the First Army had attempted to overcome German resistance along the so-called Siegfried Line, the Westwall.

[Spoken] Now listen . . . No, don't! . . .
What's gotten into you?

Spare me your seductive art.
This is no way to win my heart.
Behave like a gentleman, or else you can can it.
Nibble at me, and you're biting at granite.

I am like the Westwall
and there's no way that I'm gonna fall.
I am like the Westwall.
Yes, I'm this way overall.
I've just one message, please:
Keep your hands off my knees.
I am like the Westwall –
you're eternally powerless vis-à-vis me.

And if we take in a picture show,
Leave me alone, or I just won't go.
Don't buy balcony seats for two,
Since I won't be there with you.

I am like etc.

And if it's more soldiers they want me to churn out—
I'm just a bad case of military burnout.
So give up, I'm keeping my poise till the day
This maiden can toss back her bridal bouquet.

[Spoken] What's gotten into you . . .
I am like [etc.]

[Spoken] How often do I really have to tell you
I am like the Westwall?[95]

The song's contemporary allusions had an explosive power deriving from a subtle irony that let the listener anticipate the virgin's seduction and, by implication, the invasion of the Americans. When the Westwall was no longer able to withstand the last phase of the Allied advance, even verses as seemingly harmless and witty as this, associating military events with flirtation, had to be downright irritating to the Soldiers Station's listeners. National Socialist propaganda about the "invulnerability" of the Siegfried Line now proved to be little more than an empty phrase, and to its audience the Westwall song left an extremely bitter aftertaste.

If the propaganda character of the lyrics was disguised at first, after February 1945 the directors of the Soldiers Station began mixing more and more songs with an unmistakably anti-Nazi message into their entertainment program. In order to foment annoyance with Hitler and his consorts, a distinction was deliberately drawn in the Musac songs between the war-weary masses of Germans and their Nazi leaders. Thus, a Musac production from February 1, 1945, entitled "In the Fourth Reich" (*Im Vierten Reich*)—a bitingly mocking song set to the melody of "Californ-i-ay"—severely took to task individual representatives of the Nazi ruling clique. At the same time, the text displayed solidarity with women, workers, and church people –the very social groups whose vexation and willingness to resist were particularly pronounced, according to the OSS research reports circulating in the Musac office:

> *There are many young poets*
> *and also old prophets*
> *who are prophesyin':*
> *Soon we'll see the old order dyin'*
> *between Oder and Rhine.*
> *Some seers already write*
> *they can now see the light*
> *of the dawn past the night,*
> *for they peer into a future that's bright,*
> *and they see (what a lovely surprise!)*
> *a better new Germany arise.*
> *Yes, in the Fourth Reich,*
> *peace comes to stay*
> *while the Führer moves away.*
> *Yes, in the Fourth Reich*
> *there'll be no Himmler to rant and to rail.*
> *Instead of guns we'll have butter*
> *And for every mother*
> *there will be this happy tale:*
> *In the lovely*
> *Fourth Reich*

We'll put Germany's seducers in jail.
And on May Day the street
is replete with the beat
of working class glee,
Singing: once more we're free
from this bloody tyranny.
Every pastor and priest
gets a new chance to feast
on freedom's sunshine,
and he donates the bread and the wine
without having hate
follow him into the shrine.
Yes, in the Fourth Reich
the Lord God comes to stay
while Goering moves away,
for the Fourth Reich
will be home to justice in time.
Once the Nazis are broken,
Germany will have awoken,
and be resurrected as well,
for in this lovely Fourth Reich,
there'll be no more Goebbels, that lying cheat,
no more radio spouting deceit,
no more of Hitler's tantrum shouts,
no more of Himmler's violent rubouts,
no more of Schirach's bossy grief,
no more of Ribbentrop, that thief,
no more Rosenberg panting,
or Ley's drunken ranting –
in the Fourth Reich
they all will just go straight to hell![96]

In November 1944, during the Musac working sessions, the team surrounding Lothar Metzl and Edward Cushing came up with the idea of recording a series of longer radio shows. These entertainment programs were called "The Lighting Stage" ("Die Blitzbuehne"). They were meant to be broadcast by the Soldiers Station, but primarily via radio stations at the front or behind enemy lines. In contrast to the Soldiers Station, which operated on AM or shortwave, these mobile radio stations could be flexibly deployed. The Lightning Stage's programs were conceived in such a way that the listeners were left completely in the dark about the origins of the broadcasts. The format combined elements of commercial American shows with the content and style of presentation characteristic of prewar German and Austrian cabaret.[97] The show presented itself as naïve improvisational theater staged before a public made up of Wehrmacht soldiers and officers. Coarse in tone and with an unvarnished style of humor, the artistic fanfare of this seemingly lighthearted vaudeville act was, in reality, meticulously and cleverly contrived. All the performances were variations on a single theme: defeat. The script for the Lightning Stage had been written by Lothar Metzl, the head of production was Edward Cushing, Lester O'Keefe was the director, Allen Roth musical director, and the players were comedians and singers like Sig Arno, John Hendrik, Herbert Berghof, and Lizzi Balla.

Lieutenant Colonel Stanley from military counterespionage took a set of three Musac variety shows along with him to Europe; starting on March 1945, the OSS Lighting Stage's songs and burlesques were beamed behind enemy lines by U.S. Army mobile radio stations.[98]

In February 1945 a German war reporter had noted that Wehrmacht soldiers were still listening to Allied radio stations, partly because they preferred the kind of music broadcast by the Allies. And, indeed, the musical landscape in Germany during the last years of the war was a picture of desolation.[99] A telegram from the OSS outpost in London had reported that "even Berlin" was passing off "Rhapsody in Blue" as a German melody ("by Hans Schmidt, born in Berlin").[100]

In the propaganda war against Hitler, OSS systematically exploited this vacuum in Germany's entertainment culture. Musac's trademark was not moral instruction, but rather "seductive art" (as in the Westwall song). The attractiveness of professional entertainment à la Hollywood became bait for the Soldiers Station's news program; the way that Musac's music, lyrics, and style of presentation aimed at undermining the morale of the German soldier turned the songs themselves into a refined weapon of psychological warfare.

There were no secret agents lurking behind Musac's actions, but rather trained actors from two key American domains: the advertising and entertainment industries. This was how Operation Musac made a genuinely American contribution to the shadow war against Hitler.

VI

Penetration of Germany

CONCEPTIONS

Until recently, scholarly research on American espionage has concentrated almost exclusively on the deployment of agents and on the personal fortunes of those approximately 200 OSS agents who infiltrated Germany, mostly by parachute, between September 1944 and May 1945 in order to procure military and political intelligence.[1] In this chapter, by contrast, the main subject for discussion will be the preconditions and the thinking that preceded those deployments. Why was it that infiltrating agents into Germany was a task carried out by the Americans rather than the British? Why was it the Labor Division that initiated the infiltration project? What consequences arose from this division's special interest in the project?

To approach each one of these questions is to invite reflection on the conceptions that formed the basis for secret OSS operations in Germany.

The Infiltration of Agents Into Germany in the British Calculation

In his study on Great Britain's attitude toward the European resistance, David Stafford alluded to one of the central paradoxes regarding the activities of the British secret intelligence service. Known as the Special Operations Executive

(SOE), it had been created in 1940. When one considers that its purpose was to mobilize a fifth column against the Nazis in Germany and Italy, it is astonishing how low the German Reich ranked on British military intelligence's list of priorities until D-Day. Stafford attempts to trace this apparent contradiction back to a series of primarily political factors. According to this British historian of the resistance, it was the weakness of the German resistance movement, but above all the Allied policy of demanding unconditional surrender from Germany and the mistrust that had grown in British intelligence circles as a result of the Venlo Incident (in which two British agents fell into an SD, or German Security Service, trap), that contributed to the SOE's hesitant attitude.

To be sure, Stafford's explanation—which subsequent scholarship keeps repeating—lists a catalogue of reasons for the overall British skepticism toward the German resistance. The question about British intelligence's more specific attitude in this one case, however, is still left unanswered.[2] Was the Foreign Office's evaluation identical with that of the British intelligence agencies? How did the British evaluate the chances for infiltrating Anglo-American agents onto the continent? Were there concrete plans for operations inside the Reich prior to the summer of 1944? To what extent did the OSS and SOE cooperate with each other? Why, in the end, was there no infiltration of Secret Intelligence Service (SIS) or SOE agents on a grand scale?

Interestingly, well into the early part of 1944 there were still those in the SIS who were toying with the idea of developing a joint British-American plan for the "penetration of Germany." By the end of June, however, the first rumors were already beginning to leak out signaling English lack of interest in a "German Sussex Plan," as the operation then envisioned was initially called. During several London conversations in which, among others, the head of the OSS-SI Germany department, Major Aubrey H. Harwood, participated—along with Harwood's opposite number, Major Galenne, and the SOE man responsible for western Europe, Robin (later Sir Robin) Brook—it was soon agreed that "Sussex" (the infiltration of British-American agents into France after 1944) and "German Sussex" (the infiltration of agents into Germany) had very little in common. While the Anglo-American Sussex teams were given a friendly reception in France by delegations from the French resistance (and also provided with secure addresses and, when necessary, secret hide-outs), it was impossible to count on comparable connections and contact addresses in Germany. In addition, it did not seem easy to find suitable agents who could move about safely in Germany in light of Gestapo controls. In spite of this, the British-American secret intelligence officials gathered around Galenne and Harwood came to the conclusion that ten teams should be infiltrated into Germany, each of which would be made up of an English or American observer and radio operator together with a German exile. German prisoners of war were not going to be recruited as agents, or at least not unless there was an extreme emergency.[3]

For the new project, just as in the case of Sussex, the British chose the name of a southern English county—"Kent." Yet while Sussex was lauded by the British and Americans as a model operation, Kent would never be realized. Since the British kept their reasons for scrapping the joint venture largely concealed, and since SIS and SOE documents are still classified as confidential, it requires a detective's approach to find out what factors shaped the climate of opinion on Broadway and Baker Street and what considerations preoccupied the British in the summer of 1944.

It is clear that the most important decisionmakers in the SOE, like those in the Foreign Office, had grave reservations about the German military resistance to Hitler which was often referred to as a "Prussian officers clique." Furthermore, nobody was wagering on finding opponents of the Nazis inside Germany who would be able to receive and support teams of SIS or SOE agents. Even decades after the end of the war, Brook expressed almost undisguisedly (at least by British standards) his indignation about the friendly attitude that the Bern OSS outpost took toward the "so-called resisters." Indeed, he was very skeptical about the "open house" that Dulles was keeping for the Widerstand. In the summer of 1944, nobody in the SOE was counting any longer on a revolution in Germany, nor did anyone in Baker Street have any interest in a conservative resistance à la Stauffenberg. The failure of the assassination attempt of July 20, which was such a severe blow to a man like Allen Dulles, merely confirmed for Brook and his staff the dangers lurking for British agents within the Reich's borders.[4]

For a while, the SIS and SOE toyed with the notion of recruiting prisoners of war on the spot; yet in mid-August 1943, just at the time the POW potential came to the attention of the OSS, the British finally decided to drop the idea. By its own folly, SIS thereby forfeited a productive source of agents, which could have been crucial capital.[5] Concern that the danger to agents might be too great (in France, it turned out, papers forged by SIS did not get past Gestapo controls[6]) and that no suitable group of people was available for recruitment purposes certainly helped to discourage implementation of Kent. Nevertheless, it is not entirely clear why the British were so much more pessimistic than the Americans. Was it perhaps, as the Canadian historian Nelson Brian McPherson speculates, the fear of no longer being *primus inter pares* that kept the British from endorsing Kent? An assumption like this presupposes that cooperation between the British and American secret intelligence services was primarily shaped by rivalry and competitive thinking, which cannot be unequivocally asserted in light of the positive relationship that had developed in the course of the successful Sussex operations.[7]

Everything seems to indicate, rather, that Britain's secret intelligence heads did not develop any special enthusiasm for the "penetration of Germany" because it hardly seemed promising to them. Whereas it was possible in France or in the Balkans to count on the support of the local resistance, deploying agents in Germany must have looked like an obstacle course to the British. In the west, the SIS and SOE had been concentrating all their energy on supporting the Normandy invasion and on organizing (with respectable results, and entirely in line with the ideology of a Hugh Dalton) the uprising of home-grown resistance movements; in the Reich this seemed not only impossible, but also unnecessary, since the British already had Ultra and were therefore in the know about German military operations. Finally, there was little more to be expected from secret agent missions than information about tactical or a few rare cases strategic military operations.

The rejection of the Kent plan, accordingly, was dictated by a pronounced sense of realism on the part of the British, who at that point, after years of operations in western and southern Europe, were within striking distance of occupying Germany and had nothing more they needed to prove.[8] By contrast, the situation looked quite different from the perspective of America's secret intelligence service.

American Secret Intelligence Plans for Operations in the German Reich

The fact that the OSS was thrown back on its own resources after the British rejected the Kent Plan did not cause the Americans to feel resigned; on the contrary, the rejection brought new energy into the discussions about the infiltration projects envisioned for Germany. Since SI and SO did not have access to Ultra material, infiltrating agents into the Reich assumed a higher priority within the OSS than it did within the English secret services. Early contacts with potential agents, building up a department capable of manufacturing forged Nazi documents, and the general dynamic that pushed the London OSS outpost toward rapid growth were all factors helping to remove any doubts within the OSS about its ability to infiltrate agents into the Reich sooner or later. At the outset, however, there was not only uncertainty about when the activities should commence, but also about which OSS division should take on the job of infiltration.

There was a strong case for having the Special Operations Branch, in charge of sabotage, assume management of the Penetration project. Even at the beginning of September Donovan was emphasizing (in a key report about the "Future of OSS Operations," which was sent to the President, among others) that it would be vital to pursue aggressive subversion behind enemy lines in the months to come. What the OSS had previously accomplished, for the most part, through training and organizing resistance movements, would have to be done with its own resources in the future.[9]

Stewart W. Hermann, a young, ambitious theologian who rapidly advanced to become head of the Central European Section (CES) as a result of his first-rate knowledge about Germany (until December 1941 he had occupied one of the American pastorial posts in Berlin), was enthusiastic about the idea of deploying OSS assault troops dedicated to clearing the way for the Allied armies by undertaking calculated acts of sabotage. The brutal terror of the Nazis and the attacks on the churches, which Hermann experienced up close during his time in Berlin, convinced this energetic Lutheran that the machinery of National Socialism had to be stopped as quickly, mercilessly, and at the same time with as little bloodshed as possible. While, in the long run, Stewart Hermann was calling for a "truly Christian politics of forgiveness," he saw his immediate goal was to conduct subversive OSS sabotage operations against the regime of the Antichrist Hitler.[10]

As far as the CES Division of the OSS was concerned, there was no lack of enthusiasm late that summer, 1944, but there was a shortage of manpower. The focus on the French theater of war and the shortage of German-speaking agents presented Hermann with a real handicap. In order to help alleviate the personnel shortage during the last months of the war, the theologian advocated using foreigners employed in Germany. These "foreign workers," who represented an impressive anti-Nazi potential in numerical terms, were to be used as a spearhead in the Allies' shadow war against Hitler. In addition, Hermann and his staff attempted to recruit a group of French Communists to the fight against the Gestapo. These were the members of the *Comité de l'Allemagne Libre pour l'Ouest* (CALPO). Yet before the Special Operations Branch had a chance to reorient itself, the department of the OSS in charge of intelligence procurement, the SI, had taken over leadership in matters pertaining to the infiltration of agents into Germany. Where activities inside the Reich were concerned, this meant that procuring information, not sabotage and subversion, would move to the forefront of the infiltration project.

The Post-Invasion Syndrome and the Significance of the OSS Labor Division for Operations in Germany

During the summer months of 1944, the military conditions in western Europe had been improving rapidly. In October the teams of agents sent into France were overrun by Allied troops. In view of the advancing troops, a kind of "victory fever" gripped the U.S., and politicians and lobbyists in the American capital were already starting to talk about dismantling the war organizations. Even Donovan's outfit was affected, and the OSS director not only saw himself forced to submit a smaller budget; at the same time he began to worry about the future of his organization. New assignments awaited some OSS protagonists in Europe (such as Bruce and Shepardson), others were deployed in Asia, and still others could not count on having their contracts extended beyond the end of year.[11]

General Eisenhower had hoped to win the war on French soil. Accordingly, the had concentrated all its forces there. Numerous agents with experience in France and a knowledge of French were at the disposal of the OSS; by contrast, there was a shortage of persons who knew anything about Germany.

The explosiveness of the situation is easier to understand if one remembers how much the invasion had been seen, both by Donovan and David Bruce (the head of the London OSS), as a "colossal gamble," a high-stakes game that, owing to this perception of enormous risk, received meticulous planning. Only on certain days during the month of June were all the conditions—moon, tide, light, sea, and weather—favorable enough to facilitate a successful invasion. Under the enormous pressure of circumstances, the OSS had pulled together all its available resources—and especially the potential of the researchers in R&A—in order to prepare and safeguard the dangerous amphibious invasion.[12]

William Casey, head of the SI with the OSS in London, recalled the period after the successful landing in Normandy, when the OSS had to reorient itself all at once: "All my activity, since I went to work with David Bruce . . . involved France and operations in France. Liaison with the forces in the South. It might be forces in the North and working with DeGaulle people and dropping agents into France . . . and the support of the French resistance. All of a sudden that was all over. . . . It wasn't worth a damn. We had a big organization. We knew how to drop people, we knew how to use radios, we had this ground air communications, we had practically no agents to descend into Germany." For the OSS in London, Germany was *terra incognita*.[13] Within a matter of weeks after the Normandy landing, a number of factors converged requiring new rules of the game for intelligence and calling for new prescriptions.

In this situation, in which it was not possible to have Washington conjure up more funds (nor additional agents), it fell to Arthur Goldberg, the Chicago son of Soviet immigrants from Prague (and years later appointed by President John Kennedy to the Supreme Court), to approach William Casey and inform him about the Germany contacts made by the OSS Labor Division. Although already established in 1942, Goldberg's division had been scraping out a living behind the scenes of the OSS bureaucracy through the autumn of 1944.[14] Most OSS staff, if they knew anything at all about the existence of the Labor Division, which was subordinated to the Secret Intelligence Branch, merely tolerated or ignored it. Many, however, were also opposed to Goldberg's ideas. In a country where, in Werner Sombart's classical formulation, there was "no socialism" (and where, for structural reasons, a socialist labor movement might even have been impossible), waves of mistrust hit especially hard and high against any government office that tried to count on the support of Europe's so-called "labor underground."

When the Office of Strategic Services tried to prepare agents to infiltrate Germany, it presumably had no other choice than to draw on the Labor Division's sources of information. For years Goldberg and his staff had maintained ties to trade unions in Europe and evaluated all the available information they could collect about the underground.

Interestingly, it was William Casey—who would later become a Cold Warrior and then "Reagan's Sword," as the President's CIA director[15]—who advocated using the Labor Division staff to plan the infiltration into Germany and the recruitment of agents, in spite of some staff members' socialist or even Communist background[16]: "We didn't have the connections, the resources, the communications, or the freedom of movement, anything," William Casey conceded in retrospect. "The only people thinking that way were the labor desk people. George Pratt, Carl LeBeau, Dick Watt, Joe Gould, [Lazare] Teper, [Henry] Sutton. . . . We had to turn to them to get the information about the controls, the rationing, how the hell to stay alive, how you document people at all, how to brief people. What cover stories would fly in Germany."[17] Here it is useful to take a look at the origins of the Labor Division and the role of the Austrian psychologist, Dr. Karl Frank—alias Paul Hagen—who had stimulated and significantly influenced the division's work.

EXCURSUS

Paul Hagen, the Origins of the OSS Labor Division, and the Trade Union Contacts of British Intelligence

Early in 1942, several months before the Coordinator of Information office was dissolved and transformed into the Office of Strategic Services, Paul Hagen approached the New York office of the COI run by Allen Dulles out of Rockefeller Center. He was not the only exile offering America's secret intelligence service his support. Other German-speaking exiles from across the entire political spectrum—from Baron Wolfgang zu Putlitz through Gottfried Treviranus and Heinrich Brüning to Albert Grzesinski and Ernst Fraenkel—offered their services to American intelligence, not always wholly altruistically. To be sure, it was primarily leftists who were soon to attract the suspicion of J. Edgar Hoover, and whose activities were to earn them the (intentionally disrespectful) designation "internationalist."[18] Paul Hagen was, without a doubt, one of the most notorious figures among the German-speaking émigrés. No other German exile was the subject of so many reports from American intelligence between 1941 and 1943 as was Hagen, no one else was met with so much mistrust, and no one polarized opinion as much.[19]

After the young psychologist had distinguished himself in the twenties, especially in Berlin, as a card-carrying Communist political firebrand, Karl Frank, as Hagen was then known, crossed over to the German Social Democratic Party (as early as 1930, according to his own account).[20] Shortly after the Austrian arrived in the United States, the American authorities learned that Hagen had served a jail term of several months in Germany in the mid-twenties, for kidnapping a Social Democrat in order to prevent the kidnap victim, named Schwartz, from making a speech on national radio favoring naval rearmament. Since arriving in America, Hagen was watched by the FBI and either interviewed or sounded out by the staff of the Foreign Nationalities Branch. Hagen was regarded as a potential agitator, as an unreliable fellow, and possibly as a Communist in disguise. It did not take long, however, before the Austrian—whose wealth of ideas and cool but cordial manners made a positive impression on many Americans—secured him a place in elegant New York society through his friend Ingrid Warburg.[21]

Early in April, Hagen turned to Allen Dulles with an elaborate proposal for American cooperation with the anti-Nazi underground movement. These remarks, which were soon circulating in several OSS departments, were closely related to the research Hagen had done for his book *Will Germany Crack?*(New York: Harper, 1942) and praised by the *New York Herald Tribune* as the "best book on Germany—present and future."[22] What fascinated the *Herald Tribune* reviewer was the fact that Hagen was able to point out weaknesses within the National Socialist regime at a time when Germany was scoring military triumphs in the east and in North Africa. Six months after America's entry into the war, Hagen boosted his American readers' morale by showing them that there was an opposition inside Hitler's Germany.[23] The fact that Hagen was an insider who had belonged to the German underground himself lent authenticity and weight to his remarks about an anti-Nazi opposition of intellectuals, peasants, and workers oriented around democratic goals.[24] In the memorandum he addressed to Dulles, Hagen emphasized that there was a virtually unnoticed anti-Nazi potential in Germany, which had significance for political warfare. He pointed out that U.S. armies had cooperated in the past with underground movements in Asia and South America.

From the outset Hagen tried using statistics and hard facts to remove the impression that the anti-Nazi potential in Germany was perhaps not big enough.[25] According to Hagen's sophisticated computations, supporting the workers' resistance was not only a moral duty, but also logical.

At the core of Hagen's comments was a catalogue containing proposals for concrete actions that he wanted U.S. intelligence to initiate as a way of supporting the organized underground: Initially, a special agency had to be established to keep careful records about the underground movements and to build up contacts—especially via Switzerland and Sweden. In the U.S. a research bureau should systematically evaluate all available German daily newspapers and publications and conduct interviews with prisoners of war. In addition, staff should be recruited for special "expeditions" entrusted with building ties to opponents of the Nazi regime in neutral countries and in South America. Here it made sense to turn primarily to trade unionists and Social Democrats. In a later phase, then, some thought could be given to recruiting antifascist prisoners of war for American intelligence and to infiltrating paratroop agents into Germany. Hagen saw a guarantee for the success of the action he proposed in the way that the secret intelligence staff would be made to feel not like go-betweens, but like the vanguard of a future anti-Nazi Germany.[26]

In a memorandum that Hagen now addressed directly to Goldberg instead of to Dulles, the Austrian stressed two factors that, in his view, favored the labor project's chances of success. To begin with, there were now six million foreign workers and so-called "volunteers" from all over Europe in National Socialist Germany, a development that opened up new opportunities for contacts to the workers movement in Germany; secondly, in the U.S., England, and neutral Europe, there were persons and groups with comprehensive knowledge about individual personalities in the underground.[27] According to Hagen's conception, carefully selected people should be infiltrated into Germany along all possible routes, with commandos or as paratroopers. Their main assignment should be to strengthen existing underground circles and construct new ones.[28]

A whole string of accusations and objections against both Hagen and the program he was proposing were articulated in the course of 1942. Thus, the rather more conservative forces in the OSS gathered around such figures as De-Witt C. Poole and Emmy Rado were afraid that Hagen was overshooting the mark and (despite his ostentatious protestations to the contrary) seeking a socialist or Communist revolution in Germany. In a memorandum that Rado forwarded to different staff members from the New York intelligence office, Hagen's group *Neu Beginnen* ("Renewal") was labeled as a "revolutionary force" that was really seeking a pan-German oligarchy—not a genuinely antifascist revolt of workers and dissidents, but rather a dictatorial regime. The aim of the envisioned "German Soviet government" would be to bring the balance of forces in Europe into a permanent disequilibrium in Germany's favor and to exclude the imperialist Western powers from the European concert.[29]

Not quite as alarming, but just as negative, was Albert Grzesinki's appraisal of Hagen. The former Prussian Interior Minister and Berlin chief of police had offered his services in support of the OSS at about the same time as Hagen. The impression that the Prussian made on the intelligence staff was that of a practical and knowledgeable man who, however, was frustrated because he had "nothing to do."[30]

In spite of several fundamental objections against Hagen and his "risky" proposals, there was an influential group within the OSS, first and foremost Donovan and Goldberg, who were fascinated by Hagen's unconventional ideas, so that the New York intelligence community soon turned away from the ideological obstacles to Hagen's plan and started discussing the question of how to put it into practice. The Germany expert at the OSS, Hugh R. Wilson, saw communications as a major problem. He asked Dulles to find out how to get around American censorship.[31] In addition, he admitted that he was just as impressed as Hagen by the necessity of cooperating with German workers and by the unique opportunity provided by presence of a hostile foreign army of millions of people right in the middle of Germany.

Nobody seems to have noticed that the Germany Hagen had come to know in the twenties and thirties could hardly be compared with counterparts from the Nazi Reich of 1942. In order to scrutinize Hagen's credibility as well as his plan's prospects for success, the OSS simply asked Hagen to name some witnesses to his illegal border crossings in the thirties, which it was not particularly hard for Hagen to do.[32]

Hagen's plan shaped the discourse within the SI division of the OSS for weeks on end; in June 1942 a Labor Section dealing with trade unions was actually established, initially as a subdivision of the SI Branch, under Arthur Goldberg's direction, and the Labor Section was almost totally oriented around Hagen's ideas: sending agents into neutral countries, collecting information from newspapers and radio, establishing contacts with trade unions, mobilizing the potential of foreign workers, infiltrating agents into Germany, in part by parachute. Hagen's agenda became a blueprint for the goals and work of the OSS Labor Division.[33]

For the Americans, Paul Hagen's plans were a novelty. The British, by contrast, long before any thought was given to establishing a labor desk in New York or Washington, had already been maintaining intelligence channels to European trade unions movements.

As early as 1940 a department D (as in "destruction") had been set up within the Secret Intelligence Service (SIS) to carry out operations directed at the Germans' weak spots. One of the centers for these actions was to be Scandinavia, especially since the British could count on efficient contacts with German exiles like Willy Brandt and August Enderle in Sweden, and also because there was support from J. H. Oldenbroek, the vice president of the Internation-

al Transport Workers Federation (ITF). The SIS department D's notorious shortage of money, Whitehall's suspicion, and the delicate implications of the sabotage project must certainly all have contributed toward scrapping the project.[34]

In Great Britain itself, there were only sporadic acts of cooperation between
the secret intelligence service and the émigré community. To be sure, Hugh Dalton, the MEW (Ministry of Economic Warfare) official in charge of intelligence
matters, had become personally involved in getting a number of leading SPD
members to come to London.[35] For Britain's secret war leadership, however, the
trade unionists and Social Democrats who had emigrated to England were used
in a limited capacity, above all in the field of radio propaganda.[36] In any event, as
an initiative undertaken by German exile Friedrich Stampfer in the winter of
1941/42 had already demonstrated, the participation of German exile organizations, as opposed to individual persons, was not really wanted in Great Britain.[37]

WHEN ARTHUR GOLDBERG arrived in London in September 1942 to set up
the first foreign outpost of the OSS Labor Division, he found a situation ideally
suited to his purpose in several respects. The workers' federations from six different occupied countries were maintaining their headquarters-in-exile in London, and five international industrial and craft unions had set up their secre-
tariats there. In no other city in the world were there more governments-in-exile,
and the neutral countries had also sent delegates from their labor associations.

On the British side, however, there was still no institution that could be
compared with the OSS Labor Division. "Only one man," it said in the OSS
War Report, "a protege of Ernest Bevin, was working full time on labor questions. Ostensibly, he was an adviser to PWE [Psychological Warfare Executive]
on labor questions; actually he was doing secret intelligence work for SOE in
this field. He was enthusiastic about the prospect of an OSS Labor Section office in London and endorsed the plans for cooperation with the continental
labor underground. He was convinced that if the American Government acted
in this field the British would follow suit—which they did."[38]

Goldberg's "Philosophy of the Underground" and the "Faust" Plan

When he started his job in London, Arthur Goldberg, who was enthusiastic
about Paul Hagen's plans, had envisioned an important role for the European
labor underground. At the beginning of 1943 he issued a statement saying that
"we are now entering upon a period of the war in which it becomes more important than ever to capitalize upon the forces of internal resistance behind
enemy lines." He talked about "elaborate plans and projects" for coordinating
resistance with the military invasion, and he prophesied that "the success of
these plans will mean much in the shortening of the war and in the lessening

of our casualties." At first, infiltrating agents into Germany was not one of the central issues for Goldberg. He thought it more important to build ties to underground organizations in the occupied countries. Although he described soliciting the trust and help of union organizations as a "difficult and arduous task" in light of the "traditional antipathy toward cooperating with governmental agencies," in February 1943 the London Labor Branch already had established contacts with the "labor underground" in all the occupied countries and provided "substantial help" in the form of money, materiel, or equipment for underground activities.[39]

A month after Goldberg's arrival in London, the first talks took place between the OSS and Hans Gottfurcht, the head of the National Group of German Trade Unionists in Great Britain (*Landesgruppe deutscher Gewerkschafter in Großbrittannien*), and around the same time Willi Eichler, the head of the International Socialist Militant League (the ISK or *Internationaler Sozialistischer Kampfbund*—characterized by the OSS as "extremely active" but "definitely anti-Marxist"), arranged a contact with the International Transport Workers Federation. Since, a short time later, Erich Ollenhauer got in touch with the U.S. embassy in Stockholm, soon there were also ties to Social Democratic exiles in Sweden.[40] The ability of Arthur Goldberg and his staff to gain a foothold as secret agents so quickly was attributable, above all, to their professional credo. Goldberg was chief counsel to the Congress of Industrial Organizations (CIO), and his successor, George O. Pratt, who in November had just assumed leadership of the London Labor Division, was counsel to the National Labor Relations Board (NLRB), a New Deal institution that was supposed to protect trade unions from attacks by big corporations. Wherever Arthur Goldberg appeared, he did so not as an agent of the U.S. military establishment, but as a representative of a labor institution. In that role he was much more unrestricted in carrying out political or psychological warfare operations than anybody in the U.S. military agencies.[41]

For the union lawyer Goldberg, the current war was not primarily a war between one military and another, but a "people's war" that, as such, also required a "people's secret intelligence service." Accordingly, Goldberg saw trade unions and workers organized worldwide as a "bulwark of resistance,' a subversive contingent for leading a "permanent sabotage and guerilla war" behind enemy lines. Not just the military, but the workers as well—especially the railroad engineers, sailors, dock workers, streetcar conductors, and truck drivers who had been organized in the International Transport Workers Federation—were actors in Goldberg's "intelligence service." They all had to be mobilized—for subversion, sabotage, and obtaining information about strategic, military, and political developments. "We cooperate with the ITF," Goldberg explained in a May 1943 memorandum prepared at Donovan's request, "and we use our institutions in order to penetrate the occupied and enemy countries of Europe." Among the transport workers, the railroad workers were of special importance. Many of them had assumed key positions in the enemy's transportation system, and were able to do more than just obtain and transmit information. As saboteurs they could be of immense help.

Goldberg emphasized that the prestige and popularity of America among the trade union groups in enemy and occupied areas was enormous. If European trade unionists only knew that they were in an alliance with the Americans, "effective resistance and cooperation with our military goals [will] quadruple."[42]

Planning for the infiltration of agents into Germany, codenamed "Faust," began in October 1943 and was put into practice a year later. The *trade union* division of the OSS was responsible for its planning. The agents recruited by Goldberg and his people were not only required to speak fluent German but were also expected to have "experience in underground activities in Germany" and contacts with "anti-Nazi groups." The Faust Plan's first goal was "contacting anti-Nazi groups, especially underground groups in Germany." In addition, these groups were to build networks of agents and obtain military, strategic, economic, and political intelligence.

In August 1944 there were no British plans for infiltrating agents into the Reich, and Goldberg and his people were the only ones among the Americans who had worked out and presented a plan to accomplish this. The Labor Division had recruited a number of "antifascist agents" and arranged for contact points in Germany. Here Goldberg was especially dependent on the assistance of CALPO, the Communist-oriented "Free Germany Committee for the West" (*Comité de l'Allemagne Libre pour l'Ouest*),[43] which put all its files at the disposal of the OSS and helped the Labor Division recruit the right kind of agents. On August 16 the Faust Plan was presented before the headquarters of the Allied armed forces. Three days later it was ratified by SHAEF.[44]

OPERATIONS

"Special Operations": Foreign Workers and CALPO Communists as "Trojan Horses"

While support for partisans and guerrillas in the German-occupied territories—especially in France, Yugoslavia, and Italy—played a fundamental role, the OSS had its hands tied when it came to subversive operations in the Reich. At the beginning of October 1944 the top-secret intelligence committee at SHAEF had stipulated that Allied prisoners of war should under no circumstances be recruited for war-like activities against the Germans. In addition, a

JCS resolution prohibited the OSS from supplying German and Austrian resistance groups with weapons. Although Donovan frequently pushed to have the OSS outposts in Bern and London send suggestions for "Special Operations" and suitable SO agents to Washington, this was not done. At the end of 1944, therefore, which group in the Reich could one have outfitted with weapons and incited toward a revolt? Who would have attempted an uprising?

The only legal gap that SHAEF left open for OSS guerilla activities in Germany was the million-large legion of foreign workers who, it was hoped, might be deployed as saboteurs and troublemakers. A second group was CALPO, the free German Movement in the West. While cooperation with the Free Germany Movement (*Bewegung Freies Deutschland*) was illegal, Donovan nevertheless decided to continue tacit cooperation with these left-leaning organizations.[45] CALPO agents were already working closely with the OSS as part of the French resistance, where they had proven to be courageous activists and guerrilla fighters.

Even as early as 1942, German émigrés had drawn the attention of American intelligence to the foreign worker potential in Germany. One of these émigrés, the journalist and economist Kurt Bloch, emphasized in a December 1942 memorandum that the foreign workers were number one on the list of opposition forces.[46] In September 1942 the Research and Analysis division was assuming that, while the OSS could certainly attempt to goad foreign workers into acts of sabotage, a more promising approach would be to mobilize a united front of German workers and foreign laborers. How the OSS researchers believed this utopia could be achieved remained unclear in the memoranda of R&A.[47] It was not until the summer of 1944 that the first plans for using foreign workers were realized. The most successful operation received the code name "Braddock." The idea came from Winston Churchill, who had been inspired by reading John Steinbeck's novel *The Moon is Down*[48] into proposing that simple incendiary weapons with instruction manuals for foreign workers be dropped into Germany. By way of preparation, the OSS and SOE started a joint propaganda campaign ("Trojan Horse") calling on foreign workers to engage in slowdowns on the job and sit-down strikes. On September 25, 1944, in the Frankfurt-Mainz region, the first 250,000 incendiary capsules were dropped into areas with high concentrations of foreign workers. That same day, numerous English radio stations broadcast an appeal by General Eisenhower in several languages calling on foreign workers to help weaken the German war industry and shorten the war through acts of sabotage. Some observers told the Swedish press that they had seen fires started by the capsules. The Reich Criminal Police also reacted nervously and viewed this as an occasion for enlightening its staff about the sabotage operations being run out of England.

Although Allen Dulles saw to it that a number of reports about subversive operations in the Reich were sent to OSS central headquarters at the end of

1944, he warned that there could be no talk of any unified resistance front (not even in its initial stages).[49] Regardless of this warning, SHAEF was convinced that foreign workers in Nazi Germany could be resorted to should the need arise. On January 22, 1945 OSS decided to make preparations for arming foreign workers with American weapons. Based on calculations from R&A and the British Ministry of Economic Warfare, it was assumed that between 7 and 8.5 million foreign workers resided in the Reich, of whom nearly 2 million, especially French and Polish workers, were ready to resist the Nazi regime. It was believed that a half a million could have been supplied with weapons from the air. The operation, planned down to the last detail, was never implemented. It may be assumed, however, that the OSS would have carried out this top-secret action had the Nazis undertaken a major massacre of the foreign workers. In light of the Gestapo's severe repressive measures, however, the project of a foreign workers' revolt against the Hitler regime was, de facto, an illusion.[50]

CALPO, from the OSS perspective, provided a better opportunity for implementing sabotage actions than the hard-to-reach foreign workers inside the Reich. Consisting of political refugees and deserters, these guerrillas participated, especially in southern and central France, in actions against the field gendarmerie and the Gestapo, published a number of underground newspapers (three of them—*Die Volksstimme, Die Wahrheit*, and the *Ruhr Echo*—in the Rhineland), maintained their own radio stations in Toulouse and Agen, and prepared comprehensive dossiers about Nazi war criminals.[51]

There was no doubt in the OSS that this western arm of the Moscow NKFD was a Communist organization. R&A characterized CALPO as a " 'national front' with the emphasis on the 'front' " and with a membership that was "90% Communist." As R&A was aware of the Communist label's negative connotations, they played the "national front" card for all it was worth.[52] Nevertheless, all of the OSS's divisions made an effort, at least initially, to cooperate with CALPO. R&A and X-2 were interested in the war crimes files of the NKFD-*Frankreich* (the French branch of the Free Germany National Committee). SI and the Labor Branch speculated about getting hold of a list of CALPO's "safe houses" and using its courier service into Switzerland. MO had an interest in the distribution apparatus for subversive propaganda writings, and SO hoped to recruit CALPO agents for coup de main actions in Germany. To objections like those raised by Arthur Schlesinger Jr., who as an R&A staff member had doubts about cooperating with CALPO Communists, Donovan, hoping to protect the OSS from CALPO infiltration, replied that CALPO should be used only until OSS was established in Germany.[53]

Cooperation between American intelligence and the CALPO paramilitary was not in line with legal regulations. Since decisionmakers in CALPO and the OSS were convinced that they had "much to gain and little to lose" from close cooperation, the two organizations arrived at an agreement to begin working together as of January 1945. The Free Germans provided the OSS with "safe addresses" for infiltrating agents into Germany, they let R&A microfilm all the CALPO files (with the exception of their membership lists), they let X-2 have their war criminal dossiers, and they offered the SI and SO 150 agents who would be trained and then examined by OSS counterespionage. In exchange, CALPO expected money, covers, and radio equipment, as well as transportation opportunities for its agents, of whom eight groups were already stationed in the greater Trier-Saarbrücken-Koblenz area in January. In addition, they used the American contacts in order to get CALPO members out of POW camps.[54]

The OSS gave every agent a $150 per week salary (not inconsiderable at the time) and a supplementary daily allowance of $5 for coup de main activities inside the Reich.[55] In France, CALPO paramilitary forces had killed a few dozen Gestapo agents and militia members, in addition to having carried out guerrilla activities against communications and transportation links, and Donovan was hoping that these activities could be continued inside the Reich.[56] Officially, the OSS denied its cooperation with the CALPO as such, claiming that it was only maintaining contacts with individual persons until the beginning of the occupation period. The last major SO project, which envisioned having about 100 agents from CALPO circles murder high-ranking Nazis and Gestapo workers (the plan was to liquidate high-ranking NSDAP members, members of the SS, SA, SD, Gestapo, and Kripo in the region north of the Nazi's Alpine redoubt), was never implemented, since even Donovan was afraid he might get his fingers burned with an action like this so close to the end of the war. Instead of getting rid of Nazi officers "ranked major or higher," the CALPO agents (22 of whom had gone through rigorous OSS training at the beginning of April) devoted their efforts to more limited sabotage projects and to a series of propaganda actions, mostly on their own accord. By January at the latest, it was common knowledge that CALPO was being financed by Moscow (among others) and receiving orders and materials from there. As of mid-April 1945, the OSS and CALPO were clearly disassociating themselves from each other. Compared to the actions that the Secret Intelligence Branch of the OSS planned and implemented, the operations of the SO were absolutely negligible. The SO had not been able to mobilize significant numbers of foreign workers, nor had CALPO's people reached the point where they could be deployed inside the Reich.[57]

Infiltrating SI Agents Into the Reich

Between September 1944 and April 1945 a total of 102 teams of agents from the SI Branch were infiltrated into Germany under the guidance of the OSS via England, Scandinavia, the Netherlands, France, and Switzerland. According to

OSS figures, losses were not nearly as great as had been feared; German border controls were far less effective than had been assumed.[58] All the agents had been furnished with cover stories that they carefully studied and rehearsed in POW camps before they were deployed in the field. The stories had been created by a 28-person special division of the OSS that was called the Bach Section, after the favorite composer of the department's leader, Lazare Teper. Teper, whose advisers included German exiles Erich Ollenhauer and Ludwig Rosenberg, gave the agents a completely new identity, while the C&D division of the OSS (in charge of forgeries) provided such essential documents as identification cards, military passports, discharge papers, or party membership cards.[59]

The first, and indeed one of the most successful, operations within the framework of the Faust Plan was the mission of OSS agent Jupp Kappius, alias Jack Smith, who was paradropped by the British to a site near Papenburg on the night of September 1–2, 1944 with the aim of helping to revive the trade union movement in the Ruhr region, Germany's industrial heartland. Together with his wife Änne, who (disguised as a Red Cross nurse) had already reached Germany by crossing the Swiss border in April, Kappius was weaving together an underground network whose fringes ran all the way to Ulm, Hamburg, and Berlin, as well as into trade union circles that had apparently participated in the July 20 conspiracy and had been lying low since then.[60] The OSS had assigned Kappius to foster resistance against the Nazi regime, carry out acts of sabotage in strategically important war plants, build up a network of agents, and use subversive operations to wear down German morale. To this end American intelligence had supplied him with a "waterproof cover" and a secure hide-out — a so-called safe address — in Bochum.[61]

When Kappius, who had once been a functionary of the International Socialist Militant League (the ISK or *Internationaler Sozialistischer Kampfbund*), arrived in Bochum, he found himself surrounded by like-minded comrades from the New Socialist Party (*Neue Sozialistische Partei*) who, in turn, had contacts in factories and public institutions. Within a matter of weeks, this OSS agent succeeded in forming a leadership group whose members included former supporters of the ISK, SPD, and SAP in Essen and Witten, as well as contacts in high places at the Deutsche Bank in Essen, the Reichsbahn railway, and the Stinnes and Krupp steel companies.

Although one Gestapo informer had temporarily penetrated the Kappius ring, the ISK underground movement largely remained intact. Problems were raised, however, by communications with trade unionists in remote cities and with OSS headquarters in London. "Downend" — as Kappius's mission was called in OSS code — could only contact London via courier, and an attempt to drop off a radio near Bochum was called off by the British SOE, which declared the site unsafe. Since the alternative proposed by SOE was located very close to an SS training camp, a radio link was never established. Even the weapons and explosives that Kappius ordered in order to blow up railroad lines and block Nazi leaders' escape routes would never be dropped off by the RAF. A modest triumph for Kappius's courageous mission came from the way his "underground circle" prevented a few Nazis' escape and prevented the destruction of food supply depots and factories in the last days of the war.

On April 9, 1945 the Americans flew Kappius back to England. Shortly before, he had been able to put some of his Bochum informants in touch with the military government. Instead of forming antifascist groups invested with regional police and executive powers in the tradition of the revolutionary council movement (as had been originally planned), the Bochum resistance made an arrangement with representatives of the military government and claimed them as a source of legitimation. There could be no talk about any political triumph on the part of Kappius's comrades. Although some of them served as informants for the Field Intelligence Service, Kappius's people gained no influence over politics in Bochum or over the makeup of the municipal administration there.[62]

It took more than two months for the Labor Branch in London to infiltrate their second agent— Anton Schrader (alias "Bobbie"), age 27, who had worked for Dutch intelligence. He was infiltrated into Holland near Meppel, as part of the TYL mission. In contrast to Jupp Kappius, "Bobbie" had a newfangled radio apparatus that the OSS had developed and given the name "Joan/Eleanor" (Joan and Eleanor were the girlfriends of the machine's two inventors), which allowed the agent to communicate by voice with an airplane pilot circling at a height of 10,000 meters. Since communication took place vertically and did not require a wired network connection, the danger of being tracked down during transmission was reduced to a minimum. Nevertheless, after keeping the OSS informed about German troop movements and bombing damage for several weeks, "Bobbie" was picked up by the Gestapo and not released for some time, so that from now on he was operating "under pressure." He did succeed, to be sure, in warning the OSS; he did not, however, carry out his assignment to establish an underground route for OSS agents from Holland to Germany, so that even William Casey admitted in retrospect that the mission was no great success.[63]

Even more disastrous was the outcome of the third OSS operation that began on January 30, 1945 in Stuttgart under the codename "Rubens": The team's radio apparatus was destroyed during the parachute jump, and both agents were arrested after they had succeeded in escaping into Switzerland. They had not been in touch with the OSS at any point.[64] The traditional radios (known as W/T) were, as one OSS associate, Robert Thompson, concisely conceded after the war, "a failure. It proved to be an entirely different matter to drop men and W/T equipment blind into Germany than to reception committees in France."[65] Even the Joan-Eleanor equipment had its drawbacks, as was demonstrated during the fourth operation of the London Labor Desk. This mission, codenamed "Hammer," was put into operation at the beginning of March 1945. Two Communists living in exile in Britain, Paul Land and Toni Ruh, were paradropped into Alt-Frieseck, fifty kilometers northwest of Berlin. Their mission was to establish contact with members of the Free Germany National Committee, recruit them for sabotage operations, and motivate them to organize an antifascist underground. Although the two OSS agents were able to get the information the OSS wanted about tank production in Berlin by using a BBC code, they were not able to send transmissions from the designated point of contact.

This risky deployment of agents did result in a few fruitful contacts on March 28. Land and Ruh reported that the Klingenberg power plant was operating at full capacity. They reported that the Berlin rapid transit network was the only mode of transportation that was still functioning, and that bombing the rapid transit lines might succeed in crippling traffic throughout the city. And they passed on the precise location of a freight train station as well as two armaments plants and requested weapons for sabotage operations. In March and April, in a Berlin that was almost completely destroyed, both OSS agents were able without much ado to move about freely, to procure food rations with cards forged by the OSS, to trade cigarettes for potatoes, and to converse with civilians and soldiers. The papers that the OSS forged for them—from military passes through discharge papers to identity cards—passed every inspection.[66]

Between September 1, 1944 and March 18, 1945, the Downend, Tyl, Rubens, and Hammer operations had infiltrated only four teams into the Reich from out of London, but after March 18 the number went up, reaching four teams a day. Whenever London had to be sent intelligence about military movements, the operations took the names of alcoholic beverages: (Martini was dropped off over Augsburg, Daiquiri in Aschaffenburg, Eggnog over Hanau, Cuba Libre landed in Göttingen, Manhattan in Chemnitz, Pink Lady in Erfurt, and Hot Punch in Passau). And operations were named after household tools whenever they were supposed to establish contact with members of the Free Germany National Committee (Chisel was infiltrated into Essen, Pickaxe to Landshut, Buzzsaw to Leipzig, Mallet to Berlin, and so on).[67]

At the same time, Gerhard van Arkel, the head of the Bern Labor Desk, succeeded in infiltrating a number of agents into the Reich across the Swiss-German border. In November van Arkel reported that underground work seemed to be getting easier day by day.[68] The number of Germans working for the OSS, as opponents of the Nazis "or for money or for both" was steadily on the rise. A pack of cigarettes now sufficed as a bribe, which had not been the case even two months ago. The Swiss, who, according to van Arkel, continued to make a lot of trouble, would soon have to realize where their real interests lie. The Soviet demarche had already resulted in a relaxing of controls, and the fact that the Swiss had a "ridiculous fear of the Communists" would help foster the work of the OSS. In December one Gestapo boss was already on the payroll of the OSS Labor Branch; and on Christmas Eve van Arkel was able to report that he had a man in Schaffhausen who could take care of unaccompanied safe border crossings.[69] Indeed, as of December 1944, the ability to penetrate the Reich or get behind enemy lines was no longer a major problem. The "Tourist Missions" that originated with Peter Viertel, the son of the writer Berthold Viertel, proved that German prisoners of war acting as OSS agents could be infiltrated 70 or 100 kilometers behind enemy lines almost without a hitch.[70] The agents were almost all "idealists" and opponents of the Nazis who were convinced that the war had been lost. For about a week at a time, they became "tourists in their own country" — in Baden Württemberg, Bavaria, and Austria. Most of them brought along intelligence about German military installations and troop movements. Their cover stories were produced on site, since they had access to large quantities of uniforms and papers.[71]

The fact that the deployments of OSS agents in Nazi Germany between February and May 1945 usually went swimmingly moved William Casey to portray the OSS missions as harmless operations. "The few agents we had placed inside Germany in 1944 without communications not only survived, but thrived," the future CIA director would write in his memoirs. "They established themselves, moved about, and found friends and helpers. The large number we dropped in 1945 did this more easily. They got jobs, . . . made friends, found housing. . . . The destruction of German city life dated back to 1943. Displaced persons moved through German cities with ease and freedom despite the Gestapo. The conclusion that we should have penetrated Germany earlier seems inescapable."[72] The legend about how easy it was to carry out the Faust Plan was transformed into the myth of the successful and heroic OSS mission. In a radio address on Labor Day 1945 William Donovan praised the OSS Labor Branch and the German and Austrian workers who, without uniforms and without glory, made important contributions to the Allied victory.[73]

Further scrutiny, however, shows that much of the reported success of these operations is a myth. There was a negligible amount of strategically relevant information to be exploited, and the flow of tactical information was more abundant; but the radio equipment's technical shortcomings often made communication impossible. In 1944 only a handful of agents could be used for infiltration, and in reality only a few teams of agents succeeded even once in establishing radio contact with OSS headquarters. Of 38 "successful missions," 27 were not in touch with London, either by courier or radio. A few lost their equipment, others their airplanes, and yet others ended up in jail.[74] Several agents were either tortured or shot, others went missing, and one of them managed to achieve the rank of major general in the GDR.[75]

In addition, there was the problem that the action's goals were as ambitious as they were diffuse. On the one hand, intelligence had to be procured; on the other hand, cadres had to be set up and an active resistance against the Nazi regime fomented. The possibility that a thoroughgoing promotion of resistance activity might also have spelled the end of wartime Germany's rudimentary worker and trade union circles was not something on which the hagiographic postwar portraits of the OSS bothered to reflect at all. Had the American agents posed a truly subversive danger to the Reich, the measures already introduced to counter this subversion by remote control would certainly have been intensified. Even a project like the organization of transportation strikes modeled after successful OSS operations in France was doomed to failure inside the Reich. Thus, for example, Agent "399" (Gerhard van Arkel) was still reporting in February 1945 that the high concentration of Gestapo informers was getting in the way of Reichsbahn railway strikes that had been planned.[76] Furthermore (van Arkel reported) the numerous foreigners working in transportation had no experience with strike techniques and union work. When Berliners declared a strike, workers in Hamburg could not be informed about it in time. The strike operations planned by the OSS for 1945 derived, in van Arkel's estimation, from "wishful thinking."[77]

Toward the end of the war, a whole series of agent teams were infiltrated into the so-called "redoubt" area in Bavaria and Austria. The most successful mission was that of the Greenup team, which landed in the Innsbruck region in February 1945 and prompted Gauleiter Hofer to make a famous radio address early in May that contributed to the "rescue" of that city, which was already surrounded by the Americans.[78] Via radio and courier, the agents transmitted important information to OSS quarters in Bern and London about the Alpine fortifications' suspected defense facilities. The individual reports had little fundamental influence, however, on the general perception of the redoubt by the OSS, since the reports arrived late and it took several days (and usually even weeks) to evaluate them.[79]

VII

Götterdämmerung: Between War and Peace

PHANTOM STRONGHOLD IN THE ALPS:
THE REDOUBT AS AN IDÉE FIXE?

At the beginning of the 1960s, when cold war tensions were at their height under the impact of the Berlin Wall's construction, the American historian Rodney Kennedy-Minott in his book *The Fortress That Never Was: The Myth of Hitler's Bavarian Stronghold* looked into the question of why the Soviets had gotten to occupy Berlin and Prague ahead of the Western Allies. For Minott there was no doubt that the diversion of Allied troops toward the south during the last six weeks of the war was a catastrophic move on Eisenhower's part that would seal the fate of Europe in the long run. The "political generals" from Britain wanted to take the German capital; by contrast, the Americans, who argued in military terms, concentrated their forces on Bavaria, since their intelligence services were taken in by the "myth of Hitler's Bavarian stronghold," as Kennedy-Minott stated in his subtitle. The sense of moral relief occasioned by the military victory in 1945, according to Kennedy-Minott, allowed the scope of America's mistake to be forgotten. In retrospect, however, it could be seen that Eisenhower's strategy had far-reaching consequences for the history of central and eastern Europe, and that there would no longer be any "small intelligence mistakes" in 'today's world.'[1]

The thesis that the American belief in the Alpine fortress was at the forefront of Eisenhower's military decisionmaking may be exaggerated; in any event, however, it does contain a kernel of truth. Along with the effort to end the war as quickly as possible and with a minimum of American casualties, the redoubt really had occupied a central role in the Supreme Allied Command's strategic calculation. After all, even in mid-April, just after the collapse of the Nazi regime, Eisenhower was still asking the Joint Chiefs of Staff not to proclaim victory, since "storming the citadels of Nazi resistance," as the General's pathetic formulation put it, might indeed require "deeds of stamina and heroism" that were comparable to the major battles of the war. The Allied victory over Europe should be declared only when key positions in the western Austrian redoubt had first been occupied.[2]

While military decisions at the highest levels have already been documented and analyzed by history scholars, to date no adequate explanation has been provided for the misevaluation of the redoubt by secret intelligence.[3] Why did intelligence circles believe in the existence of that mythical bulwark—the *Alpenfestung?*

Defense of the Alps and the Ideological Phantom of the "Nazi Underground"

Well into the last months of the war, curiously enough, the "redoubt" was not a term designating the Alpine bulwark planned by the Germans, but rather that gigantic home defense project that the Swiss had constructed between 1940 and 1942 under the direction of General Henri Guisan. The Swiss redoubt comprised the central cantons and was secured by three massive fortifications—Gotthard in the south, St. Moritz in the West, and Sargans in the east. Theoretically, the Swiss could have withdrawn into the country's interior in case of an attack by the Axis powers. However, as the feasibility of these defense installations was, of course, never tested, the redoubt's real value lay less in the actual physical fortifications than in the doctrine of military deterrence. During the Second World War, Germans associated the concept of the redoubt with the myth of Alpine invincibility; for the Swiss, the term came to acquire an expanded meaning (that would prevail well into the postwar period) as a metaphor for national autonomy effectively defended.[4]

Although Wehrmacht circles had been contemplating the establishment of a defensive line in the Alps since September 1943,[5] it was not until a year later that rumors about a German redoubt started to grow, and even then only quite gradually. In the summer of 1944 the Wehrmacht Supreme Command had been given the assignment of surveying southern positions in the Alps.[6] Independently of this development, and as a result of reports he was receiving from Germany, Allen Dulles in Bern was speculating that a number of leading Nazis were preparing to go underground there. "Most of these men until recently did not believe that Germany would be defeated," according to Dulles "Only now the actual situation has begun to dawn on them." For this reason, the "followers" of "Goebbels, Himmler, Bormann, Ley" had "begun to do what they can to create in Germany a state of confusion which will permit them to disappear at the proper time"[7]

A few weeks after Dulles's report had been forwarded to the Joint Chiefs of Staff, a comprehensive analysis by the OSS Research department on the political, social, and economic situation in southern Germany started making the rounds in Washington. In their summary the authors drew attention to how several government offices had been moved to southern Germany as a result of the Allied bombardments. In addition, the Germany experts at R&A anticipated that additional relocations of offices to southern Germany were likely in the course of the war.[8] A mass evacuation of troops, however, was not predicted; and there was no talk of any Alpine stronghold in the study.

At the end of 1944, the OSS in Washington had only a vague notion of what could be expected when the anticipated collapse of the Reich actually happened. The fragments of news arriving from London and Bern frequently contradicted each other. Sometimes there would be talk about increased German defense activities in the Alps and about the redoubt; at other times it was emphasized that there were no concrete plans for lines of defense—not even for the Rhine. Some evidence indicated that leading Nazis were preparing to change their identities and disappear at just the right time; other indicators pointed toward the conclusion that the Swedish government was ready to guarantee asylum to prominent Germans—perhaps not Hitler, Himmler, Goebbels, but possibly Goering as well as "Junkers," generals, and Germans from the upper crust. Finally, something that repeatedly kept coming up was the phantom of a Nazi underground or guerrilla war that might have to be taken into account after Germany officially surrendered.[9]

At most, it was with respect to the last point that a kind of consensus prevailed in American intelligence circles. Thus, in November 1944 a secret report of the Joint Intelligence Committee (JIC) on "Nazi Plans for Underground Resistance" was submitted to President Roosevelt and the country's highest civilian and military authorities.[10] The report assumed that the Second World War, analogous to the First, would produce a generation of postwar militants. It was to be expected that a Nazi resistance would be formed from among those groups within the NSDAP who had always been seeking world supremacy for Germany. Furthermore, one could count on the participation of those Germans who represented "militant authoritarianism" at home and "aggressive expansionism abroad": the Junkers, officers' associations, industrialists, and the dispossessed elements of the middle class.[11]

The authors of the JIC study, whose assessment obviously depended on the ideologically tinged evaluations of R&A, stressed the continuity of nationalism in German history and predicted that the Nazis would behave the same way at the end of this war as the German Nationalists had done after 1918. After all, the NSDAP had never made any secret of its admiration for the Freikorps, which was created after the First World War in order to torpedo the Allied occupation of the Rhine and to counteract German society's democratization. Following Germany's surrender, it was to be expected that the Nazi party would attempt to impair the Allied military government, discredit or extinguish cooperation with the Allies, conduct a guerrilla war, pursue acts of sabotage, and also push for a course of action permitting Germany's rapid remilitarization.[12] But since it was assumed that the presence of Allied troops and a policy of denazification would stand in the way of any voluntary military associations being formed, the true believers among the NSDAP membership (and especially in the SS) would, in all likelihood, go underground and put up vehement, fanatical resistance from their clandestine lairs.

According to the JIC study, the proclamation of a people's war and the stick-it-out slogans emanating from Goebbels' propaganda had to be seen as the overture to the kind of "unconditional resistance" one might expect from the Germans. The report of the Joint Intelligence Committee contained no explicit references to any Alpine stronghold. The study's aim was not to pinpoint where Nazi resistance might be located, but to sound out that resistance's social and historical dimensions. But precisely here lay one of the roots for misjudging the situation. The assumption that a kind of nationalism molded by incorrigibility and vanity would determine the Germans' behavior was one of the reasons for overestimating the Alpine stronghold. Influential circles in the American intelligence establishment were firmly convinced that the Nazis could certainly withstand a second military defeat like the one in 1918, but not a second national humiliation. Whoever thought this way was predisposed to regard the creation of an Alpine stronghold as possible; and whoever believed in this found enough evidence pointing in this direction.[13]

The Redoubt in the Calculation of the OSS

While the prospect of a Nazi underground was increasingly upsetting (as of December 1944), not only to the secret intelligence services, but also to the American public,[14] for the OSS the rumors had a positive side-effect, which William J. Donovan knew how to exploit systematically. After September 2, 1944, when the intelligence director had circulated an open appeal about how indispensable his organization was, he must have found it most opportune that Allen Dulles was reporting about the Nazis' underground plans at around the same time. The first reports about these kinds of developments were then forwarded to the White House and JCS with an explicit note saying that they were directly relevant to future OSS operations in Germany.[15]

Three months later, Donovan was able to report to the President that the OSS had set up a comprehensive "intelligence service" in Europe to collect both tactical and strategic information. In this context, "data on more than 50,000 suspects and [Nazi] underground personalities" had already been forwarded to SHAEF. Donovan used the opportunity to let the President understand that his intelligence agents could be meaningfully deployed, not least of all, "after the cessation of organized military resistance." "Our services," according to Dulles, "would be deployed for intelligence, counter-espionage, and countermeasures against enemy sabotage," and "in principle" the Joint Chiefs of Staff (JCS) had "already approved this proposal."[16] The underground plans of the Nazis and the associated threat to the postwar order gave the OSS a reason to exist beyond the end of the war.

In mid-February the "myth of the Alpine stronghold" was already so firmly established that Dulles declared: "It now seems generally accepted that a delayed defense fortress will lie in the Bavarian and Austrian Alps."[17] The Swiss press, above all, was constantly giving fresh impetus to rumors about the "German maquis plan" and a retreat into the mountains.[18] Several newspaper articles even contained maps of the Alpine fortress or reported that "substantial amounts of foodstuffs are being collected here, and that some underground factories are being prepared to supply arms required for mountain warfare." Dulles certainly recognized the fictitious character of a few reports; he thought it likely, however, that if "fanatical Nazis will fight it out to the bitter end, then something in the nature of a reduit is inevitable." The fact that "a critical analysis of reliable data received so far [March 3, 1945] does not indicate that the preparations have as yet progressed very far" did not mean the Alpine Fortress was a phantom; rather, he speculated that Hitler still did not understand the necessity of going underground. "The Germans have never been good in planning what they would do in the face of defeat," according to Dulles. "Their strength lay in planning for conquest . . . But when it came to preparing beforehand for the evacuation of Paris and Strasbourg, they failed dismally to think ahead of time or take even normal precautions."[19]

It would take until the end of March for Allen Dulles to declare explicitly "that the German reduit will be a less well-prepared affair than newspapers reports would lead us to believe." At this time, Dulles explained that "the lack of convincing evidence" had led him to this conviction. Furthermore, retreating to an Alpine fortress would be difficult to reconcile with the psychology of the Germans. "With their theories of the Superman," the Germans could hardly accept "that they are reduced to the status of guerilla fighters." In addition, "Hitler is not the type of man who, at this stage in his career, would be good at planning to play the role of Robin Hood."[20] In spite of this fundamental insight, Dulles was still irritated in early April by field reports indicating that the Germans were accelerating their activities to expand the redoubt and were stocking up on enough weapons and food to keep 25,000 men supplied for a year. During the last months of the war, Allen Dulles in particular kept being taken in by information that the German Security Service (SD) was feeding him via otherwise reliable Swiss and Austrian sources. At the same time, of course, Dulles was warning about newspaper reports exaggerating the extent of German preparations and the Alpine redoubt's territorial expansion.[21]

While Dulles usually cabled his information promptly to Washington and was not, as a rule, able to sound out individual reports for their veracity, the research division of the OSS in London developed an elaborate method and a catalogue of criteria meant to facilitate the separation of important military activities from incidental ones.[22] One of the biggest difficulties for R&A was evaluating the enormous mass of intelligence that naturally contained a wealth of irrelevant and unreliable information along with what was relevant. While the flow of information about the Alpine fortress was still slow-moving in the beginning of 1945, starting in February the R&A scholars in London and Washington were having to cope with a broad stream of ambiguous and contradictory news reports. Occasionally, the information seemed to indicate that the redoubt was a chimera. Not infrequently, however, the information was designed to instill fear into the addressees; this was the case, for example, when "very good sources" described a type of V weapon reportedly aimed at several large cities in central and western Europe from launchers inside the Alpine stronghold.[23] Curiously, as late as February and March 1945 the American scholars came to the vague conclusion that they would not be able to answer definitively the question of whether or not there will be a redoubt.[24] On the one hand, concrete proof was missing to verify the construction of any cohesive defense facility extending across a broad stretch of the Alpine region. On the other hand, the OSS analysts frequently noted how preparations seemed to be underway for circularly shaped or, in most cases, oblong fortification zones.[25]

The wealth of material and the methodological extravagance of the R&A reports occasionally led to a situation where the analyses were overtaken by real developments so that the interpretations were longer valid. Now and then, the OSS researchers made sections of their reports accessible to a restricted circle of interested readers. One of these, created in April 1945, dealt with the economic feasibility of the Alpine stronghold. It said that the "food is the main economic deficiency in the Alpine area under consideration." In meticulous detail, and taking into account dietetic factors, the economists and self-styled nutritionists from the OSS had calculated what kind of diet would be available to the inhabitants of western Austria under the conditions of a "fortress situation" and what kind of foodstuffs and fertilizers would have to be synthetically produced in order to supply the population adequately. Here the OSS scientists came to the conclusion that the nutritional situation was quite precarious and that a major share of foodstuffs would have to be imported. To the experts of the OSS research division, by contrast, it seemed relatively unproblematic — in spite of the general shortage of coal, steel, bauxite, and oil — to manufacture armaments in the redoubt. To be sure, they conceded, the loss of the industrial region to the east of the redoubt (along the Murz and Mur rivers) would seriously reduce the production capacity of Nazis entrenching themselves in the Alps.[26]

The notion that America's intelligence analysts in London since the start of 1945 were preoccupied (sometimes day and night) with the technical problems and feasibility of the Alpine fortress is not entirely without a certain irony, especially so when one considers that the few Nazi fanatics who still believed in a National Socialist heroes' fortress by early 1945 were barely interested in questions of how to plan and implement the development of the redoubt.

R&A left no stone unturned in its attempt to get at the Alpine mystery. In addition to reports from agents and the press, not to mention surveys of German POWs, the evaluation of aerial photographs played a key role since the beginning of 1945. Altogether, the photos seemed to imply that German activities in the Berchtesgaden countryside, in Vorarlberg, and in the Salzach, Iller, and Inn river valleys were serving storage rather than defense purposes, as the interpreters of the aerial photos almost unanimously agreed.[27] While the OSS researchers were nonetheless developing certain reservations about the results of their own diagnoses, their hesitancy may be attributed to two factors: On the one hand, some of the original prints were of poor quality. On the other hand, certain installations — such as camouflaged dugouts or tunnel entrances on steep cliffs — were hard to make out optically.

Above all, however, it was a combination of uncertainty and perfectionism that prevented the R&A scholars from making their own unambiguous assessments and from finally concluding their investigations into the supposed ultimate Nazi citadel. On March 20, 1945 it was finally acknowledged that there was no Alpine fortress, strictly speaking, although there were some scattered defense facilities, underground factories, and weapons depots, and that the Alpine region could not supply enough resources for the final battle of the war. No one dared, however, to rule out the possibility that a few fanatical Nazis might be ultimately lured (against all reason) toward the romantic appeal of the Alps and by the holiest of the Nazi shrines, the Obersalzberg. After the war, staff members of the R&A claimed that they had always regarded the Alpine stronghold as a fairy tale. So clear-cut an assessment, however, cannot be found anywhere in the documents.

The Alpine Fortress from the Perspective of British Intelligence

If one compares the methods and diagnoses of the British secret intelligence services—especially those of Military Intelligence (MI-14)—with those of the OSS, one is struck by how skeptical the English were, as a matter of principle, about almost all the reports they were getting from agents and the press. "Human Intelligence" (HUMINT) meant little to the British, while "photographic intelligence" (PHOTINT) played at best a secondary role. By contrast, SIGINT—"signal intelligence"—was regarded as reliable and almost sacrosanct by MI-14. Since mid-1944, Bletchley Park had been decoding signals indicating that the Germans intended to defend the Reich along the so-called "Blue line" at the southern foot of the Alps; there was not enough SIGINT evidence, however, to indicate that a redoubt was being organized.[28] At the beginning of February 1945 the British decoded reports about the evacuation of offices from Berlin. Parts of the Navy supreme command, so it said, would be evacuated to Wilhelmshaven, and radio stations for the security service and home defense would be set up in Nuremberg. There was still no such thing, however, as a concentrated migration toward Bavaria or Austria. Instead, government and military offices were being shifted to different regions of the Reich—toward central and southwestern Germany, to Thuringia and Weimar. To be sure, now and then the Secret Intelligence Service (SIS) delivered reports about " 'continued preparations' for a final stronghold in Austria and Bavaria." Since the SIS reports could not be corroborated by SIGINT, however, these dispatches were not given a high priority. Moreover, interviews with prisoners of war and deserters had shown that 90 percent of those surveyed had not yet heard about any redoubt.[29]

The British decoded the first (although indirect) reference hinting at the Alpine fortress on March 25, 1945 from German radio broadcasts: Five days earlier, Hitler had issued a directive ordering all substitute army training units to take up rear positions in both east and west. The British intelligence specialists, who had always taken a skeptical view of the redoubt hypothesis but never given up on it entirely, now suspected that these "'pure German'" Nazi units were possibly being reserved for a final battle in the national redoubt. While MI-14 dismissed as fantasies predictions that sixteen divisions were going to march toward Austria and that 600,000 people— including hostages—could survive for two years in the redoubt, by the end of March MI-14 did concede that it was entirely plausible that a fanatical elite of German militants might hold out in the Alpine bastion and fight to the end.[30]

Just then, General Eisenhower's staff decided to let the American armies press on against Bavaria in so that Hitler would be given "no opportunity" to set up a stronghold in the south of the Reich. The British were initially opposed because they saw Eisenhower's new plan as a violation of an agreement with the Soviets: The Alliance's chiefs of staff had originally agreed that British and American troops would advance north of the Rhine and push toward Berlin as quickly as possible. When Stalin accepted Eisenhower's plan on April 1, 1945, however, nothing stood in the way of the American march toward the Danube valley. There was no criticism of the new route on the part of the British intelligence establishment; for, indeed, both British and American intelligence experts agreed at the end of March that the Alpine region was supremely well-suited for guerrilla warfare and that—even if Austria's resources did not facilitate some final battle of mythical proportions—one should still attempt to prevent major troop contingents from forming in this impassible "stronghold terrain."[31]

The "Redoubt Psychosis" of the Americans and the Perspective of Gauleiter Hofer

After his arrest by the Americans, Franz Hofer, the Gauleiter of the Tyrol and Vorarlberg, asserted that the Americans, and not the Germans, had been the "fathers" of the redoubt concept. Since Hofer was in close contact with Innsbruck Security Service (SD) chief Gontard, and Gontard received insider reports from the American legation in Bern via a radio listening post in Bregenz and a spy named "Parker," the Gauleiter was informed about how the American diplomats in Bern were energetically discussing the question of an Alpine redoubt and keeping the State Department in Washington up to date about the discussions.[32]

In September 1944 the American legation was expecting that the frontlines of the Reich would collapse by mid-1945; Leland Harrison and his staff, however, feared that hostilities would be prolonged by six to eight months if the Germans should succeed in extending their Alpine defense positions northward. From the dispatches the Austrians heard through their electronic eavesdropping, it emerged that the Americans would hardly have risked a campaign against a truly fortified Austria; instead, they were ready at best to attempt a siege or cutoff of the Austrian redoubt.

These warnings emanating from Austria's neighbor must have been music to the ears of the Tyrolean Gauleiter. Franz Hofer, who by the autumn of 1944 could hardly have hoped any longer for a victory by Hitler, saw the concept of the Alpine redoubt being discussed by the Americans as a unique opportunity to preserve his Gau; after all, the American diplomats' paranoid attitude provided the best argument for completing the Alpine fort in Austria. No one could possibly have had his heart set on a buildup in the Alps as much as Hofer, since the defense facility would practically have transformed his Gau into a kind of Bastille. Little wonder that the most important man in the Tyrol-Vorarlberg region pulled every diplomatic string in an effort to get Hitler to build this kind of fortification. Hofer called the prospective facility *Alpen-Festung* ("Alpine Stronghold"). The concept was Hofer's original invention; yet it only took a few weeks for the word to become part of everyday German vocabulary (and, soon enough, in the international lexicon as well). The Austrian Gauleiter never really did understand that the word he coined was not going to lead to any concrete actions on the part of Hitler. Well into the postwar period, Hofer remained angry at Bormann, Jodl, and their associates for not having lobbied Hitler to build the Austrian bastion. Hofer was firmly convinced that expeditiously completing the Alpine defense project could have forced the Western Allies to the negotiating table. Had the "redoubt psychosis" of the Americans been systematically exploited, World War II might possibly have reached "a satisfactory conclusion."[33]

For Hitler, as for his closest advisers, the Alpine fortress was really not a priority. Unlike some of Hofer's opponents, the Führer would probably not have questioned his loyalty. The rumors from the last months of the war tarring Hofer (not entirely without reason) as a Tyrolean separatist who only wore his brown shirt for camouflage would not have prevented Hitler from reacting to Hofer's proposal. What made the Führer hesitate was his inability to plan withdrawals, together with panic at the very thought of defeat and its consequences. The fact that Hofer's vision at the end of 1944 could hardly have been completed (for lack of labor power and resources) took care of the rest.

When Hitler, on his fifty-sixth birthday (April 20, 1945), finally got around to ordering the execution of Hofer's plans, even the Führer himself must no longer have believed that the Alpine stronghold could be completed. His order was a last straw that, in the end, no one tried to grasp—not even Hofer.[34] But why was it that the Americans had not seen through this earlier?

Eisenhower, Marshall, Roosevelt

When the Supreme Allied Commander needed to make some concrete decisions about military strategy early in March 1945, there was still no consolidated intelligence picture of the Nazis' postwar plans. Eisenhower did not even get to see the rather cautiously argued studies made by R&A, since the OSS research division still had no concrete conclusions to show anyone at the beginning of March. Dulles's cables of February and March did not yield a consistent picture, and the impact of dispatches that appeared in both Swiss and American newspapers was, on the whole, alarming. Finally, an important step in the decisionmaking process was taken on March 10, 1945 with the release of a Joint Intelligence Committee study in which Eisenhower's intelligence advisers speculated that the Russians "will have invested or taken BERLIN and be continuing their advance towards LEIPZIG and PRAGUE" over the next several weeks. This would prevent "the Germans" from being able to "send a substantial number of divisions from the EAST to check our advance in the WEST."[35]

To be sure, the top-secret study assumed that within a short period of time Germany's military forces would no longer constitute an integrated unit and that German resistance would primarily be restricted to "SS, panzer, and parachute formations or guerilla groups"; at the same time, however, the team of Allied intelligence experts made it clear that the Germans were not about to suspend their resistance "so long as HITLER remains alive and a free agent." Above all, it was to be expected that military and administrative offices would be transferred to the Salzburg area. With this kind of action the Nazis would be trying to "prove to the younger generation that National Socialism and GERMANY never surrendered." In case southwestern Germany was "not rapidly occupied by the Allies, guerilla or dissident movements will gain ground and the Nazis may be able to put into effect some of their plans for establishing subversive organizations in GERMANY and other countries." By way of summary, therefore, the JIC study proposed "to undertake operations in southern GERMANY in order to overcome rapidly any organized resistance by the German armed forces or by guerilla movements which may have retreated to the inner zone and to this redoubt. It would be necessary as a first measure to occupy NUREMBERG, MUNICH and SALZBERG."[36]

At the end of March a certain skepticism had become widespread among the top military officers. Dwight D. Eisenhower and George C. Marshall, each on his own, had come to fear that Germany's anticipated surrender might not demarcate a clear-cut break between war and peace. To General Eisenhower, it seemed (on March 31): "The further this campaign progresses, the more probable it appears there will never be a clean cut military surrender. Our experience to date is even that when formations as small as a division are disrupted, their fragments continue to fight until surrendered." He went on to speculate: "Projecting this idea further, it would mean that eventually all the areas in which fragments of the German Army, particularly the Paratrooper, Panzer and SS elements may be located, will have to be taken by the application of or the threat of force. This would lead into a form of Guerilla Warfare which would require for its suppression a very large number of troops."[37]

Two days later, General Marshall presented the President with the dismal prospect that "Hitler and his principal Nazi subordinates" were likely to be "nominally exercising the powers of government" even after the collapse of the Reich.[38] To be sure, the Führer would only be able to transmit his propaganda via radio, but there was no way of counting on a surrender or abdication in the "last days of national catastrophe." For General Marshall there was no doubt that a highly pronounced sense of mission would motivate Hitler's behavior. The Führer was thoroughly conscious of how his place in world history depended closely on "the dignity of his exit." "Any cowardice, faltering, or negotiating with the Allies in the last hour would destroy the tragic myth he is seeking to create" among Germany's youth.

While the analysts in the OSS research division and the psychologists working for the OSS—Walter Langer at Harvard, for example, and Carl Gustav Jung in Zurich—had prophesied that Hitler would commit suicide in the face of a German defeat, the highest-ranking military officers took no notice of these predictions.[39] Instead, during the final weeks of the war, the President seemed more likely to be getting dispatches that credited the National Socialists with stamina. Although Eisenhower's prognoses were classified top secret, on April 5, 1945 President Roosevelt ordered that the prediction of a guerrilla war be immediately passed on to the press.[40] Conceivably, the President was so sure that the Nazis would hold out for a final battle that he wanted to prepare the American public for this gloomy reality. Possibly, however, he was also using the military prognosis to counteract a premature victory euphoria along the German frontline and at the home front in America.[41]

All in all, the role of the OSS with regard to the evaluation of the Alpine redoubt was not entirely commendable. In particular, the OSS telegrams in Bern, a few of which reached the White House, had caused more of a stir than was necessary. Between February and April 1945 it became evident that Bern's geographic proximity to the Reich and the good contacts that Dulles maintained with "reliable informants" tended to confuse rather than enlighten American intelligence about the supposedly legendary German fortress. It would certainly have been advantageous to the R&A staff in London had they been initiated into the Ultra secret. SIGINT proved to be a useful instrument for quickly unmasking a number of abstruse reports as preposterous. The reports written by British analysts were indeed more reliable and assured in their judgments than those of their Washington colleagues. The fact that the Americans had such a hard time distinguishing between fact and fiction was at least partly attributable to the way that the idea of the Alpine stronghold matched the image of the fanatical, nationalist Germans unwilling to be collectively humbled a second time after 1918. In addition, there was a lack of clarity in the German Reich (down to the very end) about whether the Alps should or should not be defended. Moreover, the German Security Service (SD) certainly did succeed in thoroughly deceiving the Allies with regard to the extent of Alpine defense facilities. This deceit, however, worked especially well on the press, which disseminated the myth throughout the U.S. and neutral countries.

At no time did the OSS fall into the chorus of Cassandras who were warning about a gruesomely bitter final struggle in the Alps or conjuring up some frightful fantasy about a formidable Nazi stronghold, although Donovan and his people did little to dispel comparable rumors. In the end, the Nazis' underground plans helped lend additional legitimacy to the activities of the OSS, which after 1945 was increasingly focused on collecting evidence against Nazi criminals.[42]

LAST-MINUTE PUTSCH

The Munich "Pheasant Hunt" and American Intelligence

In Munich on the night of April 27, 1945, the attention of the international press was riveted by a putsch in which the *Freiheitsaktion Bayern* ("Bavarian Freedom Action" — FAB), a resistance group made up of soldiers and civilians under the leadership of Captain Rupprecht Gerngroß attempted to take over the Bavarian Gauleiter and military command posts and to persuade General Ritter von Epp, the Bavarian Reich Governor (*Reichsstatthalter*), to issue a formal declaration of surrender.[43] Although the action was put down almost immediately, it was not without some impact. To the people of Munich and those branches of the Wehrmacht that found themselves in the middle of a chaotic retreat, the uprising signaled that morale on the home front had been broken and that determined resistance against the approaching American troops had become illusory; at the same time, the mutiny in Munich had led to an outrageous wave of murders by Nazi fanatics. While the events surrounding the putsch have already been described a number of times, scholarly research has almost completely ignored the secret intelligence dimension of the Munich events.[44] The OSS had not only been let in on the coup planned by the FAB; von Epp had also gotten in touch with American intelligence and submitted his plans for total surrender to the OSS. Finally, the information fed to the Morale Operations Branch from Bavaria via Gerngroß was used in such a way that the Branch was able to guide the resistance in Bavaria by means of subversive radio propaganda.[45]

The Peace Feelers of Ritter von Epp

About five weeks before the Munich putsch, OSS headquarters in Washington had received a cable from Bern in which Allen Dulles reported about the existence of a right-wing resistance group around General Ritter von Epp. A German diplomat by the name of Heinz Adolf Heintze, who was in touch with the

Foreign Office as well as with the Bavarian governor, had let the OSS know that Ritter von Epp was seeking cooperation with the Americans in light of the Third Reich's expected defeat. According to Heintze's report, von Epp wanted to put himself at the head of an anti-Hitler government and assume political power in Bavaria along with General Karl Kriebel from the OKW (Wehrmacht Supreme Command). By way of Cardinal von Faulhaber, who supported Ritter von Epp's initiative, the group had already attempted to get in touch with the Vatican. Since a Gestapo agent had ensconced himself in the Munich cardinal's entourage, however, this approach to the Vatican had not been feasible up to now.[46]

Whenever a telegram from Allen Dulles arrived, official Washington was used to almost anything. Nevertheless, this message about peace feelers from the Bavarian governor must have raised a lot of eyebrows. How could the dyed-in-the-wool National Socialist Franz Xavier Ritter von Epp, formerly a Freikorps leader and one of the oldest followers of Hitler, dare to put out peace feelers to America. Would Cardinal von Faulhaber, who was held in high regard in American intelligence circles, really make common cause with von Epp? What did the U.S. have to gain if it were to use this connection to Ritter von Epp?[47]

Dulles was aware of all these misgivings. As if to dispel them, his telegram emphasized that he had "full information about Epp's bad record." He would welcome it, however, if the information about Heintze and Kriebel could be sent his way. Furthermore, the OSS in Bern needed Washington's "views on question of policy [about] whether [we] should encourage even rascals" like von Epp, who were ready "to fight Hitler [and] Himmler in order [to] weaken [the] home front and in this case prejudice [the] possibility of [a] German reduit." Heintze, in any event, was returning from Bavaria within the week; in Bern he was regarded as reliable, since he apparently was a friend of Werner von Haeften, who had been executed following the assassination attempt of July 20.[48]

Before a reply could even arrive from Washington, Dulles saw to it that interest in Ritter von Epp's maneuver was not extinguished; he proposed to Donovan the theory that von Epp in Bavaria, Kaltenbrunner in Austria, and the "Sunrise" contacts of the OSS in Italy were all like chess players maneuvering their pieces in a similar kind of game.[49] It seemed to Dulles that this development offered the opportunity for checkmating "every effective organization of the Alpine stronghold." In addition, there was the interesting question as to whether Himmler might be pulling the strings behind all of these scenes, while making certain to distance himself from the recalcitrants.[50]

From now on Washington had good reason to be anxious about how the Bavarian episode might develop. More than that: The dispatches about Ritter von Epp were now routinely reaching the Joint Chiefs of Staff, the Secretary of State, and the White House.[51]

Only two days went by before Allen Dulles was able to provide more information about the Bavarian group, after his informant "476" (Schulze-Gaevernitz) had met with Heintze. According to the latest information, Ritter von Epp, "although he placed himself at the disposal of Nazis, remained [a] devout Catholic," a "Bavarian officer of [the] old school" who hoped "to spare Bavaria from becoming [a] battlefield." According to Schulze-Gaevernitz's investigations, as soon as central government control in Bavaria collapsed, Ritter von Epp intended to assume executive power (with the support of different Bavarian defense group commanders) and move against Himmler and the SS. The leading lights of the Catholic Church, including Cardinal Faulhaber, had been initiated into the planning.[52]

Allen Dulles was certainly aware that the group around Ritter von Epp represented "conservative right wing elements." Furthermore, he doubted whether the members of the Ritter von Epp Circle could summon up enough energy and determination to carry out their plans; nevertheless, he immediately took the first steps to "establish [a] clandestine line of communication to [the von Epp] group in order to follow developments."[53]

Dulles, who was well-known for his tendency to behave recklessly, treated the Munich operation like a game of chance. To his colleagues in the Paris outpost of the OSS, he called backing Ritter von Epp a "good gamble." One certainly could not predict whether the governor and his people might bring the "SS machine in Bavaria" to a standstill; in any event, however, one could count on obtaining useful military information. Therefore an agreement was reached with Paris to have a radio dispatcher (for security reasons, it had to be either an Austrian or a German) dropped off at a "safe house" in Gugelhof near Murnau in order to establish a link between OSS and Ritter von Epp.

In the meantime, there were more frequent dispatches about the conservative-reactionary makeup of the Bavarian group that included *Luftgau* (aerial district) commander Wolfgang Vorwald and SS Obergruppenführer (senior group commander) Benno Martin, in addition to General Karl Kriebel from Wehrkreis (defense district) VII in Nuremberg. As if to conceal the discredit within their own ranks, the group distanced itself from General Weissenberger in Nuremberg and SS Obergruppenführer Wilhelm Koppe in Munich. Weissenberger, so it was said, was an "ardent Nazi" who was expected to fight to the end, and in Koppe's case one was dealing with a "Nazi of the worst sort" who had committed many crimes in Poland as a member of Hans Frank's staff.[54]

It would be absurd to assume that Dulles was aiming for a genuine deal with the Bavarian governor or even intending to sponsor him in the postwar period in exchange for military information. Presumably Dulles believed that his hand held the most powerful trump cards in the game he was playing with Ritter von Epp. In the worst case the action would yield some intelligence material of military relevance, and in the best case Dulles might be able to enlist this reactionary Munich clique in the cause of ending the war against Hitler's Germany ahead of schedule.

In retrospect, however, it seems dubious whether Dulles and the OSS ended up as the winners in this case, since it would eventually become apparent that the Reich governor was neither able to offer any useful intelligence material nor ready for action. The reports that were arriving from Bavaria occasionally contained a kernel of truth, but some of them were simply fabricated out of whole cloth. Overall the material suggested that the Nazis were on the verge of expanding construction on the Alpine stronghold. Thus, for example, Dulles was informed that the Wehrmacht Supreme Command had been relocated to Bad Reichenhall and parts of the Foreign Office to Badgastein, that 6,000 soldiers were already residing in the Alpine stronghold at the beginning of April, and that several prominent hostages were being settled there. Since Dulles regarded the existence of the Nazi redoubt as entirely plausible, he promptly forwarded the Munich dispatches to Washington.[55] This is how it got to the point where Epp's alarming reports about the mythical Alpine stronghold reached Washington—along the quickest possible route from Bavaria, via Bern, to OSS central headquarters, the top-ranking military officers, and the President of the United States.[56]

The Munich Putsch of April 28

While Ritter von Epp did not participate in the planning leading to the April 28 putsch, the opposition figures around Captain Gerngroß cherished a hope that the Reich governor would support them. Even at the last minute, it was obvious that they wanted to have Ritter von Epp on their side. The coup's activities commenced on the cue "pheasant hunt" (*Fasanenjagd*). On the night of April 27–28, Captain Gerngroß, Lieutenant Leiling, and an American officer drove to Schornerhof near Starnberg, where General Ritter von Epp had set up staff quarters; they confronted the general with the "ghastly situation" in Munich and called on him to surrender, "end the chaos," and support the initiative of the FAB. For Ritter von Epp, as for his adjutant Major Caracciola, who had been initiated into the resistance plans, the confrontation came as a surprise.[57]

Ritter von Epp admitted to the putschists he had "something to make up for"; at the same time, he requested time to think it over. While the Interpreters' Company VII under the command of Captain Gerngroß seized control of the radio transmitter, Lieutenant Leiling drove Ritter von Epp to a meeting with the staff of Major Braun's tank division. Braun explained again to the governor that the FAB was all about avoiding additional bloodshed. Since the conspirators were not exactly household names, Ritter von Epp was asked to lend his own name to the enterprise, assume command of troops in those parts of Bavaria that were still unoccupied, and declare surrender. In the meantime, a division belonging to Major Braun's company had surprised the soldiers guarding the Erding radio transmitter, occupied the transmission facility, and broadcast the FAB's proclamation via Reich Radio Munich. The proclamation was made up of ten points, and heading the list were the "extermination of National Socialism's bloody tyranny," the "removal of militarism, which in its Prussian form has brought endless misery upon Germany," and a demand that the "German people . . . become a member of civilized humanity enjoying full and equal rights again."[58]

Although General Ritter von Epp must have accepted, by and large, the Freedom Action's vaguely formulated goals, after vacillating for quite some time, he ended up refusing to support the group around Captain Gerngroß.[59] To all appearances, the governor, who grew up in the traditions of the Bavarian military and nobility (he had been the last commander of the royal Bavarian infantry regiment), did not seem capable of transcending his own social and professional background. In particular, Point 2 of the putschists' freedom resolution, the "removal of militarism," went against the grain. Moreover, there was no doubt that Ritter von Epp lacked the courage to declare surrender without backing from some of his high-ranking party comrades. There is some evidence indicating that Ritter von Epp was trying to establish contact with General Gresler, Munich's military commander. Gresler could not be reached, however, and his second-in-command, General Maierhofer, thoroughly denounced the putschists as "Panzerschweine" (tank swine).[60]

Without decisive backing from Ritter von Epp, whom Gerngroß allowed to withdraw in a gesture as noble as it was naïve, the conspirators had a rough time of it. The fate of the rebellious troops, however, was sealed when Munich's Gauleiter Paul Giesler, to whom Ritter von Epp compliantly offered his services after his dismissal, used the Laibach radio station to address the people of Munich and declare that the uprising of the "shirkers" under "Captain Gernegroß" had been "defeated."[61]

While these events were taking place in Erding and Laibach, Munich remained comparatively quiet. For a few hours, there was a white flag hanging from the southern tower of the Frauenkirche;[62] but the city's administration did not fall into rebel hands. Only the building housing the newspaper *Neueste Müncher Nachrichten* was occupied by soldiers sporting armbands with the Bavarian flag. Just a few hours later, according to OSS reports, the rebels took off these white-and-blue armbands and were denying any link to the conspirators.[63] Most of the putschists succeeded in escaping the Munich Gauleiter's henchmen. Yet some rebels, including Major Caracciola, as well as several women and men who had responded to the Freedom Action's summons and were calling for resistance or surrender in Munich's suburbs, were killed as early as April 28 by Wehrmacht units or by the "Werewolf" under the command of the Nazi writer Zöberlein.[64]

While the military impact of the coup was practically nil, the action's impact on civilian morale was not inconsiderable. Word quickly got around that it was the Reich radio station in Munich, rather than London, that was summoning the people to end the Nazis' bloody tyranny, and to a number of Munich's residents the proclamation of the putschists demonstrated that the collapse of the Nazi regime (and, by implication, the start of a new political era) was drawing very near. In addition, the radio address directed against "Captain Gernegroß—[a] Gernegroß, of all people!" (Gauleiter Giesler was playing on the captain's surname, meaning "gladly large" or "wannabe bigshot") lacked the usual verve and persuasiveness. Instead of reinforcing belief in National Socialist rule, Giesler's address had a demoralizing effect. Above all, the name of the rebellious captain—Gerngroß—became a code word for regional anti-Nazi resistance and political renewal in Bavaria.

Immediately after the failure of the April 28 putsch, the OSS set about finding out why the opposition figures around Captain Gerngroß had placed their hopes on Ritter von Epp. How had the Reich governor's attitude been so misevaluated? Were there ties between Ritter von Epp and FAB? What had motivated the Bavarian aristocrat to establish contact with Dulles in Bern?

In their investigations, the American secret intelligence agents stumbled across the finding that, in addition to Major Caracciola, there were other persons from the hazy private circle and immediate professional environment around General Ritter von Epp who had participated in the coup of April 28. These people apparently knew that the general was in touch with Dulles and that he himself occasionally toyed with the idea of a "revolt from above" modeled after July 20, 1944. The Reich governor, it was said, had been in touch with several "high-ranking civil servants"—with Johannes Popitz, Ulrich von Hassell, and Hjalmar Schacht—who had been involved in the July 20 resistance movement.[65] Von Epp's associates portrayed their superior officer as a man who was increasingly disillusioned with the regime, who complained about being a mere figurehead, and who at 77 frequently longed to retire.

Moreover, Ritter von Epp (according to OSS inquiries) had taken up contact with General Gerd von Rundsted toward the end of the war in order to sound out the possibility of a joint civilian-military capitulation. After Gerd von Rundsted had been replaced by General Kesselring as Supreme Commander in the West, and after Kesselring indicated that he was not prepared to negotiate with the Bavarian governor about any surrender, von Epp considered the matter settled.[66] Some of his associates, however, pursued the capitulation idea further, especially when they realized that the American troops were rapidly drawing closer to Munich. Apparently they were seeking a fait accompli and therefore hoping they might be able to force the governor onto their side at the very last minute.[67]

Operation Capricorn: Simulated Resistance Under the Sign of the Zodiac

Several months before the April putsch attempt in Munich, and a few weeks before Ritter von Epp established contact with Allen Dulles, information about the existence of a potentially revolutionary group somewhere in Bavaria, probably in Munich, had poured into OSS central headquarters via the Bern outpost. A man whom the OSS had given the code name "Intact" had informed American intelligence that this group, while numerically small, was highly disciplined and made up partly of civilians, partly of specialized Wehrmacht units. The potential resistance fighters had not been among the conspirators of July 20, 1944, nor were they to be confused with the Munich student group that had been behind what was described as the failed revolt of 1943 (a reference to the activities of the "White Rose").[68]

At the OSS these vague bits of information fell into the hands of a man who (as Chief Intelligence Officer) had been entrusted with drawing up a subversive OSS radio program directed at the German public—Howard Becker. Becker, "a tall, slow-spoken, Gary Cooperish type," had taught at the University of Wisconsin in Madison as a sociology professor before he offered his services to the OSS.[69] It was important to him that the radio program he was devising for the OSS be thoroughly prepared.

At the heart of the Becker team's undertaking was the creation of a fictitious personality who could serve as a figure with whom potential opponents of the Nazis might identify. After a period of preparation lasting over two months, the OSS had created, so to speak, a "test-tube resistance fighter" who was given the name Hagedorn and who was distinguished by his decidedly anti-Nazi convictions. From an ideological point of view, Hagedorn was meant to represent the liberal and humanitarian tradition of the nineteenth century, coupled with a capacity for sober evaluation of the general situation. The aim of the Hagedorn radio addresses was to convince the population in the Munich area about the hopelessness of the military situation, to dissuade the Nazis from expanding construction of the Alpine stronghold, and to support potential resisters. The operation's code name was "Capricorn." As an emblem of hope and symbol of resistance, the zodiacal sign of the goat stood for mobility and survival under adverse conditions.[70]

Starting in mid-February 1945, the broadcasts devised for Operation Capricorn were transmitted over a period of nearly nine weeks. From a technical perspective, the OSS took advantage of the fact that a frequency used by the Germans had become available as a result of Allied bombing attacks. In order to achieve the greatest possible coherence with respect to ideology and language, all the Hagedorn radio addresses were composed by a single author, the German émigré Hans Rehfisch. Stephan Schnabel, a German-born actor at the Mercury Theatre, was recruited as Hagedorn's voice.

While Hagedorn was impressing upon his hearers that it was the duty of every German to rebel against Hitler, he simultaneously warned urgently against any second Warsaw or July 20. The moral duty of insurrection, according to Hagedorn, was beyond question; it was of the utmost importance, however, to wait for the right moment to rebel and to act only when the Allied armies had gotten close enough. In February Hagedorn warned that the time had "not yet come" for a revolutionary action. After 61 days, on April 27, 1945, the black propaganda radio broadcaster suspended its program with a notice that the American armed forces were in the process of occupying the station. He suggested to the listening audience that the right time for taking action had arrived. A few hours later Captain Gerngroß and his clique seized the initiative and started their "pheasant hunt."[71]

On June 15, 1945 three ringleaders of the FAB were interviewed in Munich by MO staff members Howard Becker, Edmund Reiss, and Rudi Weiß. In the course of the interview it emerged that their actions had been directly influenced by Hagedorn's radio broadcasts. In talking to the American agents they emphasized that the man who turned to the German people under the name "Hagedorn" was "a remarkable person" whom the Americans might well want to locate "in order to see of what service he can be in the new Germany." It had been difficult trying to get good reception on the wavelength where Hagedorn was holding his talks, "but he deeply influenced those who did hear him."[72] From the perspective of the MO Branch, Radio Capricorn was a complete success, since American intelligence succeeded at least partly in guiding the anti-Hitler resistance via the airwaves. Almost even more impressive was the fact that not a single German recognized the broadcasts' American provenance.[73]

In the wake of the putsch, the FAB became the gathering place for the nationalistically oriented anti-Hitler resistance in Bavaria. Gerngroß and his people used their notoriety in order to make a mark for themselves vis-à-vis the Americans as "the recognized leader[s] of *the* Bavarian resistance" and as "*the* anti-Nazi representatives of the people of Bavaria." The FAB provided the Americans with a draft constitution for the Free State of Bavaria and laid claim to the former parliamentary seats of the NSDAP and the DNVP. In its first *Field Intelligence Study*, the American secret intelligence service determined that the FAB wanted to establish an interim government on a Christian foundation that would push chiefly for strict maintenance of "law and order." At the same time, the OSS warned against treating the FAB as if it were essentially identical with the old Ritter von Epp circle, and it cautioned that the group increasingly represented a danger for military security. So it happened that the new political movement had already overplayed its hand in its first successful upsurge.[74]

GOOD AND BAD GERMANS

Allen Dulles as Promoter of Postwar German Politicians

During the war, nobody on the OSS staff developed as lively an interest in the political contours of postwar Germany as did Allen Dulles. By mid-1943 he had been deliberately exploiting his secret connections to Germany in order to scope out the political landscape. Central headquarters in Washington felt itself compelled to draw Dulles's attention toward the fact that the interest of OSS was completely "nonpolitical" and that its job was supporting the military, not promoting political doctrines.[75]

Dulles would regularly seek to promote two groups. On the one hand, there were the moderate circles who, according to Dulles, were especially concentrated in clerical circles, and on the other hand there was the anti-Hitler group of Breakers.

Early in 1944 Dulles struck a tone that suggested — in a manner now barely concealed — the urgency of postwar political involvement by the OSS: "For the purpose of averting political chaos in Germany which would promote the setting up of a Communist State," Dulles said, "we should give serious thought to whether or not, in the first stages of occupation, we should support those political groups, especially Centrum and Socialists[,] as a foundation for the establishment of a democratic government." In this context he attributed special importance to "the Catholic Centrum" as the "only closely knit Bourgeois element which is not linked up with Nazi ideology." The Protestants had been open to a "military Junker nationalism"; to be sure, there was "a good element represented in Bekenntnis Kirche [sic] which is prepared to support attempts by Catholics and Socialist to establish a Democratic system" after the war.[76] Dulles warned explicitly against drawing on schoolteachers to educate the German people; and in an unsolicited cable on February 15, 1944 he sent a list to Washington naming personalities — from Bishop Galen and Adolf Freudenberg to Otto Braun ("O.B."), Eduard Schulte, Wilhelm Abegg, and Willy Dreyfus — whom he regarded as "worthy of support" when it came to constructing a postwar German republic.[77]

To the OSS in Washington, Dulles apologetically explained that the prevailing opinion in Bern was that he, as Roosevelt's emissary, was responsible for the postwar order. Dulles said that he had never asserted this, but that he did believe the rumor provided a good cover for his activity as a secret agent and would therefore not do anything to clear up the misapprehension.[78] In reality, the closer the end of the war neared, the more the *opposite* impression cropped up—namely, that Dulles's secret agent activity was occasionally becoming a cover for *political* engagement on his part. William J. Donovan explicitly approved of having Dulles deal officially with postwar questions and, in the very same context, requested that Bern's "master spy" move his office to Germany "when Germany collapses, but prior to Allied occupation." "In all likelihood, the renascent anti-Nazi groups will look upon you as their first demi-official contact with America."[79]

In his assessment of potential leading personalities for postwar Germany, Dulles was partly influenced by the group around Hans Schönfeld, Willem Visser t'Hooft, his brother John Foster Dulles, that, together with Adam von Trott zu Solz, was counting on a renewal of Germany in the spirit of the ecumenical movement and that maintained ties to Bishop Bell in Chichester and Bishop Berggrav in Oslo; in part, he was also placing an almost blind faith in the assessments he was getting from his informants in German counterintelligence—Hans Bernd Gisevius and Eduard Waetjen.

Interestingly, Allen Dulles never gave up on his goal of promoting the anti-Nazi resistance, not even after the Stauffenberg assassination attempt had failed and the Gestapo had made short shrift of the July 20 conspirators. Dulles tried to do everything within his power to buttress (directly or indirectly) the groups associated with the Breakers as key political figures in a democratic postwar Germany. In no way did he take offense at the R&A department's characterization of the Breakers and their emissaries as rebels, palace revolutionaries, and bankrupt generals who simply could not be trusted.[80]

On August 6, 1945 Allen Dulles, now in Wiesbaden-Biebrich, sent a comprehensive list with nearly 200 names and the title "German Government Personnel" to the official in charge of the U.S. military government, Lieutenant Colonel Howard P. Jones. Dulles stressed how the basis for selecting candidates was information from German opposition circles, that they represented a cross-section of the German population, and that most of them had actively resisted National Socialism throughout the entire war.[81] As a rule, Dulles proposed candidates for positions like that of state secretary, and only a few were suggested for ministerial posts. On his list were names as disperate as Otto Heinz von der Gablenz from IG-Farben, a company manager who had been in touch with the Kreisau resistance Circle; Dr. Wilhelm Hoegner, whom Dulles had gotten to know in exile in Switzerland;[82] Fabian von Schlabrendorff, who had failed in an attempt to assassinate Hilter in 1943; and Hans Bernd Gisevius. For the "Health and Welfare Ministry" Allen Dulles was thinking mostly about Protestant theologian Otto Ohl, though next on the list were the surgeon and director of the Charité hospital, Ferdinand Sauerbruch, with whom Dulles had maintained contact during the war, as well as "his" man from German counterintelligence, Eduard Waetjen.[83]

Dulles had sixteen names on his list for the Justice Ministry, from Hans Anschütz to Wilhelm Zutt, all of whom were envisioned as candidates for a high-ranking civil service position, though not as ministers. In a telegram of August 11, 1945, furthermore, Dulles recommended Josef Müller, who had maintained a link between the military opposition and the Vatican, for Justice.[84] As labor minister Allen Dulles proposed Kurt Schumacher, and as his state secretary Otto Suhr; the remaining candidates—Joseph Simon and Adam Stegerwald—did not come under serious consideration in 1945 owing to their age. For the cultural portfolio the list included Dr. Eugen Gerstenmaier along with Theodor Heuss; in addition, Professor Constantin von Dietze from the "Freiburg Circle" was recommended, as was the Stuttgart State Librarian Wilhelm Hoffmann, who had been in touch with Adam von Trott.[85] Among the personalities envisioned for the finance, economics, food, agricultural, and industry portfolios, the names that kept cropping up were Hermann Abs, Hans Henckel-Donnersmarck, Wilhelm von Glasenapp, Hermann Hoepker-Aschoff, Werner von Simson, Andreas Hermes, Hans Schlange-Schoeningen, and Eduard Schulte, with Dulles being particularly adamant about recommending the latter for the post of industry minister.[86]

Dulles's political engagement took on an additional explosiveness because the Russians were working on their own "White Lists" for a German government in the Soviet Zone, and also because in the summer of 1945 Dulles was targeting the Soviets for spying—by Fritz Kolbe and Frederick Stalder. Among the personalities that Dulles had chosen for political office in the Soviet zone were Ferdinand Sauerbruch, whom Marshall Zhukov had proposed for the post of health minister on July 30, 1945.[87]

Especially conspicuous alongside the gallery of political personalities from the Weimar era was the large number of theologians: established churchmen like Otto Dibelius and Hans Lilje were on Dulles's list along with the Catholic theologians Karl Rahner, Friedrich Muckermann, and Harald Poelchau, as well as the Protestants Hellmuth Gollwitzer and Emil Fuchs.

There were at least two impulses that had motivated Dulles in compiling his list of "good Germans" or "crown jewels," as they were called in OSS jargon:[88] On the one hand, the Presbyterian minister's son believed that political stability in Germany could be best achieved by recruiting politicians from the churches and the moral environment of the July 20 conspiracy. On the other hand, he felt deeply obligated toward the victims of the Hitler assassination plot, with whom he had been in much closer contact (even if indirectly) than had any other Allied representative.

One consequence of this closeness to the conspirators, however, was that Dulles did not always assess his candidates with a properly critical attitude. Thus, for example, Hans Globke, who had worked on the juridical regulations connected to the persecution of the Jews, was one of Dulles's candidates for a future interior ministry. The OSS boss apparently believed—as, incidentally, did Adenauer, under whom Globke would later serve as state secretary—that the former administrative law expert in the National Socialist Interior Ministry had softened Hitler's anti-Jewish measures.[89]

In the OSS outpost at Biebrich, which had been set up in the sparkling wine factory (Henkel) of Ribbentrop's father-in-law, there were (as Franklin Ford, later Dean of the Harvard College of Arts and Sciences, recalled) recurrent controversies between Allen Dulles and the R&A staff with respect to the "crown jewels." "The atmosphere in Wiesbaden-Biebrich was one of some standoffishness about Allen Dulles because when he did have conferences, it was usually to tell us how we ought to be coming out about all this." Thus, for example, with respect to "a crown jewel . . . like Schlabrendorff," Dulles was "much more inclined to take him at his word about everything" than he was prepared to listen to what Franklin Ford and his R&A colleagues had to say. Even Gisevius, whom Dulles recommended for a civil service post in a future interior ministry, was viewed with great suspicion by R&A.[90] "My own impression," Franklin Ford summed up, was that Dulles "was so fascinated with these people who did, after all, make up the basis for any of the stuff that he sent from Switzerland, that there is a kind of loyalty that's created in secret operations of that kind, and he wanted them to have a fair shake from the Allies."[91]

Although Dulles, as a rule, was able to prevail against the objections of the youthful R&A staff, his involvement on behalf of the Germans who had kept him up to date throughout the war (about the anti-Hitler resistance, V-weapons, the Holocaust, and about political and military developments) turned out to be anything but successful. As of May 1945, the military administration and diplomatic circles set off a genuine wave of mistrust directed against Hans Schönfeld, Fritz Kolbe, Eduard Schulte, and Dulles's "Musketeers"—Gavernitz, Waetjen, and Gisevius. When the staff of the U.S. legation in Bern went through its files about "Nazi Underground Activities," they uncovered a plethora of records that linked Dulles's "good Germans" with Nazi machinations. For example, of Hans Schönfeld, the research director of the Ecumenical Council of Churches, who functioned as a contact to Adam von Trott zu Solz, memoranda turned up accusing the theologians of opportunism. Schönfeld, so it said, had participated in mysterious get-togethers in Geneva and enjoyed the trust, to a certain degree, of the public Nazi bureaucracy.[92] Fritz Kolbe had been compromised by his work anyway, so that Dulles was only able to support him financially.[93] Eduard Schulte, although never a member of the NSDAP, had nevertheless honored him, without his knowledge, with the title "World Business Leader" ("Weltwirtschaftsführer") in 1941.[94] Gavaernitz—a naturalized American, it should be noted—was stuck with the charge of a family tie to Hugo Stinnes; and "Eddy" Waetjen was simply regarded as a "patriot" who had helped support Hitler's expansionist goals in the early years of the Nazi regime. The most negative assessments were about the "so-called vice-consul" Gisevius, who was charged with "ruthlessness" in his choice of methods and according to an anonymous opposition figure from July 20 had not actively cooperated with this putsch.[95] Some of these assessments testified to the ignorance of their authors, and some were blatant fabrications,[96] but all in all, these prejudices were enough to make the American chargé-d'affaires in Bern, Leland Harrison, warn against granting liberties to the participants in the July 20 plot. "They might be inclined," he argued, to exploit these liberties for nationalist goals incompatible with the goals of the United States.[97]

Immediately after the end of the war Dulles made it his job to look up the last participants in the July 20 plot along with their family members. He found approximately 120 survivors of the Beck-Goerderer group, including many widows. Dulles saw it as his job to provide financial support, wherever possible, to the anti-Hitler conspirators and—as he explained in a 1947 letter to Bishop Bell—to work on making their sacrifice understood.[98] Thus it happened that Allen Dulles let Freya von Moltke, the young widow of Helmuth James Count von Moltke, fly to the American zone on November 19, 1945 together with her children. In addition, men like Joseph Wirth and Wilhelm Hoegner, who had loyally advised the OSS during the war, profited from Dulles's engagement. For example, Hoegner, in "view [of] services rendered" for the OSS, received a monthly stipend from the intelligence service for as long as his "son remains Suisse."[99]

It would be hard to determine what impact Allen Dulles had as a result of his engagement on behalf of moderate and conservative circles. It is clear that he failed to lift his chief informants—Gisevius, Waetjen, Kolbe etc.—into political positions. On the other hand, the overwhelming majority of the Germans he recommended did have successful careers in postwar Germany. Many of them were, in any event, predestined to assume public office or occupy some important position in German cultural life. Owing to the OSS's recommendation, their names came into the spotlight early, where they attracted the attention of the military government.[100]

IN THE SUMMER of 1944, a few days after the Faust Plan to infiltrate SI agents into the Reich had been approved, the procurement division of the OSS developed a program for the period of occupation immediately following the collapse of the Reich. At the heart of the so-called "Twilight" project was the effort to identify "pockets of Nazi resistance" and obtain information about the "underground" of fanatical Hitler supporters. A year later, in the early summer of 1945, the picture had changed fundamentally. There could be no longer any talk of a Götterdämmerung. The Alpine stronghold had turned out to be a chimera, and the "gods" were trying to leave for a more profane realm, attempting to flee the country, if they were not already awaiting a judicial ruling from the Allies. The main work of the OSS Secret Intelligence Branch now consisted of describing overall political developments and rustling up documents for the war crimes trials in Nuremberg.

In a situation like this, there was a gradual change in the ideological omens under which American intelligence was to be operating inside Germany. In June 1945 Frank Wisner foresaw an abundance of favorable opportunities if one were to use the War Crimes Organization of the OSS "as a cover" for moving into non-American zones.[101] At the same time, he got in touch with the "Organization Gehlen," that branch of counterintelligence that had been in charge of espionage in eastern Europe and the Soviet Union. Under the impact of the changing political constellations, the American secret intelligence service and the remnants of Hitler's counterintelligence began a closer collaboration.[102] The name "Operation Twilight" acquired an additional meaning. From now on, the hunt for Nazis was no longer always what it pretended to be. The United States saw itself confronting a new enemy.

Allen Dulles's attempts to deploy the "crown jewels" as guarantors of a liberal postwar order in Germany were by no means crowned with success. Admittedly, his activities rang in an era (after 1946) in which the successors of the OSS—the SSU and CIA—would no longer shy away from continuing their operations behind the scenes in eastern Europe.

VIII

The Dream of the Miracle War,
the Legacy of the OSS

THE END OF THE OSS AND THE ORIGINS OF THE MYTH

Despite Donovan's best efforts to keep it in place, the OSS was dissolved in September 1945. Neither in the government nor in Congress was there an influential group pushing to maintain the OSS in peacetime. What remained of the OSS was the Strategic Services Unit (SSU), a rump organization managed by John Magruder as a division of the War Department, along with a division in the State Department made up of former R&A staff.

The liquidation of the OSS was no isolated action, but was connected instead to the downsizing of the U.S. war apparatus and yet another "return to "normalcy." To be sure, there was no other government office that had protested so vehemently against its dissolution as had Donovan's secret intelligence service. The fight over the survival of the OSS was conducted using methods both public and covert, and it occasionally created the impression of a veritable bazaar of trickery and intrigue. Since 1943 the OSS Director had been forging plans for a centralized postwar intelligence service, and toward the end of the war some of his staff did not shy away from using subversive techniques that had been tested and proven in the shadow war against Hitler's Germany.[1] Thus, for example, late in the summer of 1945 Allen Dulles launched a series of articles in the *Saturday Evening Post* about the top-secret "Operation Sunrise" that were meant to bring home to a broad reading public how successful and dedicated the OSS had been. In this way Dulles was apparently parrying a counterblow against the anti-OSS press campaign of February 1945 in which, after Donovan revealed his plans for a postwar secret intelligence service, such newspapers as the *Chicago Tribune* and the *Washington Times-Herald* had denounced the project as a Gestapo-like super espionage system.[2]

Also among the critics of the OSS was John Franklin Carter, who toward the end of 1944 had already warned Roosevelt about a British infiltration of Donovan's organization and who, just a few months later, was telling Truman about Communist infiltration. In order to bring about the liquidation of the OSS and promote himself—as head of a small, informal central information office he envisioned—Carter was willing to use any means necessary. Although the bombastic journalist was gradually losing his influence after Roosevelt's death, he still succeeded in branding a number of people in the OSS staff and U.S. administration as persona non grata.[3]

Harry Truman would certainly have pushed for the liquidation of the OSS even without Carter's intervention. While Roosevelt was sympathetic to pursuing the idea of a major central secret intelligence service, Truman was opposed. When he put his signature on the order authorizing the liquidation of the OSS, the President remarked to Budget Director Harold Smith that he had envisioned a completely different kind of secret intelligence service.[4]

A few days later, an anonymous "obituary" arrived at the White House. On the OSS letterhead there was an illustration of a gravestone bearing a Latin inscription and gushing tears. The memorandum announced the early death of "Donovan's child" named "O.S.S." and speculated about the child's resurrection. It expressed the mood, widespread among the OSS staff, of discontent at the dissolution of the institution.

By the end of 1945, former members of the OSS turned their attention toward preserving the memory of Donovan's secret intelligence service. They founded an active Veterans of Strategic Services organization (VSS), which was supported by well-to-do members, organized trips all over the world, and arranged for meetings with members of resistance movements in western and southern Europe and the Far East.[6] After the war a Donovan Medal was awarded every other year to persons whose activities personified the spirit, tradition, and characteristics that distinguished General Donovan. The awardees included Allen Dulles, General Eisenhower, Earl Mountbatten of Burma, Margaret Thatcher, and the astronauts of Apollo 11.[7] It was not the R&A researchers, but rather the spies and saboteurs of the SI and SO whose courage and frontier mentality—which quickly became legendary—was to shape the postwar image of the OSS.[8]

By the start of 1946, Donovan had already been in touch with the major Hollywood film studios, which he urged to produce movies about the activities of the OSS's shadow warriors. To this end he guaranteed producers three weeks' access to a selection of secret OSS documents. The very same year three movies were produced that were to make a lasting impression on the image that two generations of Americans would form of the OSS.[9] Twentieth Century-Fox produced 13 *Rue Madeleine*, a movie that unmasked the activities of a Nazi double agent.[10] Warner Brothers produced the film *Cloak and Dagger* with a courageous and romantic Gary Cooper in the role of an OSS agent whose mission in Switzerland and Italy prevents the Germans from developing the atom bomb;[11] and Paramount produced the box office hit *O.S.S.*, which told the story of four agents (two of whom were killed) outfitted with OSS radio transmitters in France.[12] In the opening segment of the movie, Donovan characterized the story as a fictional tribute to the brave and inventive men and women of the OSS. *The New York Times* praised it as an outstanding spy story that had the factual believability of a documentary film, and Paramount took in $2.8 million at the U.S. box offices during its first year .[13]

In order to guarantee that the Americans would receive the most plausible and realistic picture of OSS operations, Donovan had arranged for a committee of specialists to advise the movie studios, and in the case of 13 *Rue Madeleine* he strictly forbade any explicit mention of the OSS: The screenplay had been complete for quite some time when the letters "O.S.S." were exchanged for "O-77"[14] because the operation portrayed did not seem authentic enough to the advisory committee. Donovan was convinced that Hollywood owed it to the nearly 25,000 members of the OSS and five times as many relatives and friends to have the activities of OSS agents appear in the right light.[15] In short, he did everything he could to present the most glorious possible picture of OSS professionalism and of its agents' genius and bravery.

OUTLINE OF THE SHADOW WAR: A SUMMARY

The first central secret intelligence service in the history of the U.S. was borne of a conviction that Hitler had been engaged in propaganda, espionage, and sabotage before 1939 and that subversion of future military enemies via "fifth columns" was what had prepared and rendered possible the Germans' phenomenal military triumphs. The concept of the COI was based on the wishful notion that a new kind of secret intelligence service, even beyond the traditional deployment of weapons and troops, could bring about a fundamental weakening of the enemy. Donovan dreamed about provoking an early collapse of the German Reich by identifying the adversary's psychic, moral, and economic weak points and activating resistance groups. To this end he recruited not only researchers from the country's best universities; he also took advantage of the enormous émigré potential of the U.S. by establishing the Foreign Nationalities Branch to get information about political activities abroad—an intelligence function whose renewal would be strongly endorsed by George Kennan after the war.[16]

Donovan's leadership of the secret intelligence service was not beholden to any rigid concept. Instead, he relied on the imagination and inventiveness of his division chiefs, to whom he guaranteed considerable leeway in a largely nonhierarchical government organization. His initial openness to the peace feelers of a man like Federico Stallforth, who in 1941 was supposedly trying to conclude peace with the U.S. on behalf of the German military opposition, was just as symptomatic of the intelligence director's fascination with unconventional projects as was the naive attempt at the beginning of 1941 to bribe the German emissary Hans Thomsen into issuing a public anti-Hitler declaration.

In spite of the shock of Pearl Harbor, concentrating on the chief enemy, Hitler, remained an immutable priority for American intelligence. Donovan, who had been courted by the British in 1940 and initiated by them into the handicraft of spying, could imagine no catastrophe worse than Great Britain's collapse. From the outset he did everything he could to concentrate military and intelligence resources on the Atlantic. To this end he was even ready to lose battles in the Pacific. A consequence of this fundamental decision was that the OSS collected a great deal of information on the German Reich and its allies and sent thousands of agents, analysts, and saboteurs to Europe between 1942 and 1945, while the Far Eastern theater of war was neglected and its ideological implications and underground wars as in China barely understood.[17]

The most serious turning point in the history of America's secret intelligence service took place in June 1941, when the COI split into the OWI and the OSS. As a result of the fundamental conflict between the FIS staffers around Robert Sherwood, who were inspired by the ideals of the New Deal and viewed "propaganda" as an instrument of democratic education, and William Donovan, who insisted that the secret intelligence service had to resort to the subversive weapons arsenal of psychological warfare, the OSS inherited the "dark" functions of its predecessor organization.

Donovan had not seen any problem in organizing subversion and open propaganda under one roof, but Sherwood and his people criticized the "un-American," immoral undertone of the dirty rumor campaigns and sabotage operations that were an inalienable component of the shadow war against Hitler to Donovan.

The COI and OSS had an image of the Reich's political and military strength that was quite different from that of the State Department and military intelligence services. Early in 1942 R&A researchers had uncovered the central weaknesses of the military supply apparatus on the Eastern Front. Nevertheless—in spite of the failure of the Barbarossa campaign and despite America's entry into the war—the researchers were not carried away by the kind of optimistic mood that prevailed in other government offices. The intelligence data with which R&A was operating frequently proved to be inadequate after 1942. That the OSS researchers nonetheless arrived at realistic assessments in their large-scale studies was due to the complex and methodical approach of the R&A, which did not always yield concrete results but did at least prevent hasty conclusions and, as in the case of the Economic Objectives Unit, led in practice to a successful general theory of strategic bombing.

The historians in the OSS, whose analyses were ideologically influenced by Franz Neumann's *Behemoth*, developed a sensitivity to the historical uniqueness and terroristic-repressive character of the Nazi regime. This helped make it possible for the OSS to reach appropriate assessments about the stability of the German home front and—in contrast to Adolf Berle in the State Department and the British secret service staffs—to avoid speculating about an imminent German collapse in either 1942 or 1943. How little the President showed an interest in the strategic analyses of the OSS was demonstrated at the Casablanca conference early in 1943, when the British and Americans settled on a military approach to Europe without consulting Donovan. Roosevelt's most important advisers were George Marshall and Henry Morgenthau. In contrast to these people, Donovan, whose memoranda showed fewer and fewer signs of Presidential attention as the war went on, shared only peripherally in the political-military discourse at the highest level. That Roosevelt, for example, was able to meet regularly with John Franklin Carter, his private spy administratively supported by the OSS, and that the President recruited Ernst "Putzi" Hanfstaengl as the interpreter of Hitler's mental world, although he showed only limited interest in SIGINT and the strategic analyses of the OSS demonstrates that Roosevelt did not fully understand and value the intelligence data he was getting from Donovan's agency.

No event did more to bring to light the sharp ideological tensions within the OSS than the founding of the National Committee for a Free Germany (Nationalkomitee Freies Deutschland, or NKFD) in Moscow in July 1943. While the liberal R&A analysts saw in the NKFD an effective force that could help topple the Nazi regime and tended to downplay any danger of a Bolshevik revolution, the conservative circles around James Grafton Rogers, Hugh Wilson, and John Wiley, who were able to prevail inside the OSS, were already anticipating the rise of a Communist, pro-Moscow government in postwar Germany. The fact that the intelligence service "parties" fought among themselves, and that each one was backed by a different faction from the community of German political émigrés, made things turn out in such a way that the OSS, as the only government office in the summer of 1943 advocating a German government-in-exile, failed to achieve this goal. The founding of the NKFD and the conviction, slowly crystallizing in the OSS at around the same time, that Hitler was going to lose the war, prompted the head of the OSS Planning Group, James Grafton Rogers, to criticize the American government's attitude of laissez faire, to push for anticipating what would happen after military victory, and finally to advocate (by cautiously distancing the OSS from Moscow and showing a willingness to rescind the demand for unconditional surrender) charting a new political course.

While Rogers resigned from his prominent OSS position when he recognized that the President was not prepared to make political concessions, a man like Allen Dulles, who took over the OSS outpost in Bern at the end of 1942, was able to undermine Roosevelt's demand for unconditional surrender in more subtle ways. Thus, the contacts he maintained to the resistance group around Beck and Goerdeler did not just serve intelligence purposes; they simultaneously served the aim of cautiously encouraging the anti-Hitler resistance, eliminating Hitler, and bringing about a substitute government. The information that the Bern head of the OSS cabled across the Atlantic in the course of the war surpassed everything that arrived in Washington from other OSS outposts. In Hans Bernd Gisevius and Eduard Waetjen, Dulles had two German informants working in counterintelligence, and in Fritz Kolbe (alias George Wood) he even had a direct link to the German Foreign Office. Contrary to all the legends, however, Kolbe's reports had hardly any major influence on the evaluations made by the OSS and on the organization's politics. When it was recognized how valuable the material presented by Wood really was, a good portion of its significance had already been lost. It was also a legend that Allen Dulles' telegrams about the production and technology of the V-rockets were solely responsible for the bombing of Peenemünde, for apparently the British had, for the most part, reached their decision to bomb Usedom quite independently of the material coming out of the Bern OSS.

Infiltrating agents into Germany was carried out by OSS headquarters in London without backing from the British . Not only did the British regard sending agents into the Reich as costly and risky; in addition, they believed that Ultra gave them a sufficiently effective and more convenient way to procure military intelligence. In the end, the infiltration of agents into the Reich was primarily indebted to the advance work done by the labor branch of the OSS, whose staff had contact addresses, cover stories, and a general concept for the top-secret "penetration of Germany," the so-called Faust Plan. Paul Hagen (alias Karl Frank), the Austrian who was controversial both among political émigrés and inside the OSS, had already called for establishing a Labor Division in 1942, and shortly thereafter the labor lawyer Arthur Goldberg put Hagen's ideas, which envisioned using the international trade union movement as an instrument, into practice. Although the agents infiltrated into Germany did not procure any relevant information, and although their mission to incite revolts was highly illusory and unrealistic, a mythical postwar history prevailed that celebrated the triumph of the Faust Plan along with the survival of most of the OSS agents. The attempt to get the OSS to cooperate with CALPO Communists and foreign workers intended for sabotage operations in the Reich backfired completely.

For the Morale Operations Branch of the OSS, success depended upon the use of every possible method in a subversive media war. By way of rumor campaigns, forged documents, radio, newspaper, and leaflet campaigns, the MO Branch's actions aimed at confusion and at stimulating an anti-Nazi resistance, an approach that demonstrated some success when one of the things inspiring the Bavarian Freedom Action to move was a series of subversive OSS radio broadcasts. With the recruitment of German prisoners of war as MO or "Sauerkraut agents" the OSS engaged in a violation of the Geneva Convention that was tacitly approved by Allied Headquarters and established the deniability policy that would become a trademark of the postwar CIA. Finally, the MO Branch made a genuinely American contribution with its secret radio operation "Musac" that systematically exploited a vacuum in Germany's entertainment culture and—in close cooperation with representatives of the U.S. advertising and entertainment industry—sought to undermine the morale of the Wehrmacht. After the war the importance of American entertainment as "Uncle Sam's No. 1 ambassador of goodwill."[18] would increase, and in the Cold War against the Soviet Union, entertainment made in America—jazz, rock, and pop music—even became ideological weapons.

THE LEGACY OF THE OSS

In more ways than one, the outcome of developments from the Second World War and of the politically charged arena in which the OSS arose was a metamorphosis of secret intelligence in the United States. In a country that had been largely critical of the culture of spying before World War II, the fear of Hitler and the shock of Pearl Harbor had made possible the establishment of a central intelligence service that used unheard-of methods and questioned time-honored intellectual paradigms. Thus, close cooperation with the British led to experimentation with forms and techniques of black propaganda that had been viewed as entirely un-American before the war. Donovan's philosophical premise that American democracy could only defend itself against totalitarian enemies by using its adversary's weapons was accepted and became part of the legacy for the CIA that was founded in 1947.

After 1945, what had seemed completely incompatible with the America of the 1930s—that a spy could also be a "gentleman" and that democracy could be defended with unorthodox methods—became an accepted axiom among a broad American public concerned about its country's political future and military preparedness. Furthermore, the originally quite European notion that power was knowledge and that science had an inherent force to it (Francis Bacon's *ipsa scientia potestas*) gained a foothold in America. The belief in the totality of information was reflected in the hundreds of thousands of reports, notes, interviews, maps, and periodicals that helped the OSS capture comprehensive, global knowledge about the enemy. Although the R&A researchers that had administered the OSS's store of knowledge subsequently left Donovan's agency and went on to work for the State Department or at universities, the CIA recruited only a few of them; therefore the main legacy of the interdisciplinary culture that had characterized the R&A researchers in the OSS was something it bequeathed to American universities.

How large the information deficit of the OSS could be in certain areas, in spite of the flood of incoming messages and the high analytic quality of the R&A division's reports, became apparent after the war with regard to the National Socialists' policy of annihilation, which got hardly any attention in Donovan's secret intelligence service. The reason for this puzzling shortcoming had to do with the fact that the OSS did not have the Ultra machine at its disposal and was therefore completely cut off from the most important source of information about the "mopping-up operations" of the SS. Indeed, the British Foreign Office and the State Department knew far more about the Holocaust than did the OSS.[19]

When Allied confidence about their ability to beat Hitler led to criticism of Roosevelt's harsh political line vis-à-vis Germany (during the "turning point of 1943"), it became apparent that influential circles in the OSS were now at work developing political goals and visions—extending well beyond mere military victory—that they were trying to implement using secret intelligence tools. It was a novelty in American history for someone like Allen Dulles to be using intelligence channels as a way of promoting the political candidates he favored for a stable and pro-Western postwar Germany. By the end of the 1940s, using covert methods in an attempt to influence the political landscape became almost conventional. In 1949 the CIA successfully supported Christian Democratic forces in Italy, it exercised influence on political relations in eastern Europe with operations like Radio Free Europe and Radio Liberty, and in 1953 Iran's Mohammed Mossadegh was overthrown with the aim of securing Western economic interests and containing Soviet influence, to name just a few examples. Indeed, the circles that shaped the physiognomy of the CIA were the very ones who had developed a soft spot for covert operations during the war. These were primarily Allen Dulles and William Casey. Thus, a paradoxical development took place. Although the deployment of secret intelligence agents in Nazi Germany and the black propaganda operations of the OSS were largely implemented in a way that tended to be dilettantish and experimental, they established a tradition of subversive warfare that became more and more widespread during the Cold War and that kept devouring more funds. Because the CIA had been organized along the lines of a wartime secret intelligence service, two functions usually kept strictly separate from each other in other secret intelligence services—intelligence-gathering, on the one hand, and covert operations, on the other—continued to be linked under one roof.

The significance of individual OSS projects was minor and—with the exception of the legendary "Operation Sunrise," which led to the surrender of German troops in northern Italy six days before the end of the war—had hardly any impact on the outcome of the Second World War. The sum total of all the single operations did amount to something weightier. If Donovan's secret intelligence service had not existed, the end of the war would have been drawn out for at least several weeks. Where America's assessment of the military situation was concerned, for example, it was not unimportant that Donovan's intelligence service was permanently warning against betting on a premature collapse of the Nazi regime, or that OSS analysts pinpointed weak points in the Third Reich's economy and infrastructure that led to their bombardment, or that the intelligence service's subversive radio broadcasts and infiltration of agents into Germany influenced the morale of the Wehrmacht and the civilian population. All this triggered uncertainty on the part of German counterintelligence and the Reich Security Service (Reichssicherheitsdienst) and led to a situation where many German forces that might otherwise have been deployed militarily got tied down.

Finally, it was one of the ironies of the OSS's history that all the exaggerations and misestimates of German strength should have ended up exerting greater influence on the institutional development of American secret intelligence than the many realistic and differentiated assessments made about the strength of the Third Reich's military, economy, and morale. The fear of a German "fifth column," an anxiety which (though it can only be viewed as neurotic) played a central role in establishing the secret intelligence service in 1941, did as much to consolidate the OSS as did the mistaken expectation about a German Alpine stronghold in 1944/45. In both cases Donovan knew that exaggerating the potential of the Germans would help legitimate the survival and growth of his secret intelligence service. The operations of the OSS in the Second World War, therefore, can only be comprehended against the background of a dual set of goals. On the one hand, the COI and OSS aimed at shortening the war by way of shadow operations; on the other hand, they definitely wanted to save the institutions of secret intelligence for service beyond war's end. Frequently, it is only possible to understand OSS intelligence diagnoses, assessments, and recommendations in light of the second goal.

With the dissolution of the OSS, Donovan's dream of a miracle war—in which he hoped to replace one part of the conventional army with a phalanx of spies, saboteurs, and propagandists—was far from being dreamed to its ultimate conclusion.

NOTES

INTRODUCTION

1. Charles Kebbe to Kay Halle, August 28, 1945 and September 14, 1945; Herbert S. Little to Broadcasting Section, Department of Interior, September 10, 1945, Recorded Presentation of MO, n.d. [September 1945], Folder 41, Box 76, Entry 99, Record Group (RG) 226, National Archives, College Park, Maryland (NA).

2. Jürgen Heideking, *Geschichte der USA* (Tübingen/Basel, 1996), p. 339.

3. The Spanish quote about the last word of kings comes from the first act of Calderón's play "In life everything is the truth and everything is a lie" (Pedro Calderón de la Barca, *En la vida todo es verdad y todo mentira*, ed. by Don Williams Cruickshank, London 1971). Richelieu had the motto engraved, in grammatically incorrect Latin (*ultimo ratio regum*), on Ludwig XIV's iron canons; the Prussians continued this tradition and adopted the watchword *ultima ratio regis* as their own.

4. In American English the term is used as a synonym for "secret war." See, for example, its usage by Leslie B. Rout, Jr. and John F. Bratzel, *The Shadow War: German Espionage and United States Counterespionage in Latin America during World War II* (Frederick, MD, 1986); Bradley F. Smith, *The Shadow Warriors: OSS and the Origins of the CIA* (New York, 1983). Robert M. Gates, *From the Shadows: The Ultimate Insider's Story of Five Presidents and How They Won the Cold War* (New York, 1996).

5. On Donovan see Corey Ford, *Donovan of OSS* (Boston, 1970); Richard Dunlop, *Donovan: America's Master Spy* (Chicago, 1982); Anthony Cave Brown, *The Last Hero: Wild Bill Donovan* (New York, 1982); Thomas Troy, *Donovan and the CIA* (Washington, D.C., 1980).

6. Donovan told the FBI that "the President knew he [Donovan] did not want this position [COI] because he would prefer to handle troops and that, when he accepted the post, it was upon the President's promise that Donovan could later handle troops if he would set up the coordinating agency." Edward A. Tamm [to J. Edgar Hoover], Memorandum for the Director, June 27, 1941, 94-4-4672–5X, Donovan File, Federal Bureau of Investigation (FBI) Archives, Washington, D.C.

7. Speech to the Erie County, NY, American Legion, November 11, 1939, cited by the *New York Times* (*NYT*) November 12, 1939.

8. This is especially true for the millions of individual dispatches making up the cable traffic. By contrast, there are excellent resources for tracking down the R&A Records, for the Foreign Nationalities branch, and (since 1998) even for OSS Headquarters Records.

9. B. F. Smith, "The OSS and Record Group 226: Some Perspectives and Prospects," in George C. Chalou, ed., *The Secrets War: The Office of Strategic Services in World War II* (Washington, D.C., 1992), p. 360. For more on the OSS records, see Richard Breitman, "Research in OSS Records. One Historian's Concerns," in ibid., pp. 103–108; Lawrence H. McDonald, "The OSS and its Records," in ibid., pp. 78–102; McDonald, "The Office of Strategic Services. America's First National Intelligence Agency," in *Prologue* 23 (1991), pp. 7–24.

10. Information from the archivist in charge of OSS documents at the National Archives, Dr. Lawrence McDonald, from the previous chief historian of the CIA, Prof. Dr. J. Kenneth McDonald, from Dr. Kay Oliver, and from the former Deputy Chief Historian of the State Department, Dr. Neal H. Petersen.

11. Within the framework of the OSS Oral History Project at Georgetown University (abbreviated subsequently as *OSSOHP*), a number of OSS experts conducted interviews between 1996 and 1998 with selected veterans of the American secret intelligence service. In addition to the author, the interviewing team consisted of Siegfried Beer (Graz), Betty A. Dessants (Florida State), Barry Katz (Stanford), Petra Marquardt-Bigman (German Historical Institute), Tim Naftali (Yale), and Maochun Yu (U.S. Naval Academy). The transcripts of the interviews were transferred to the National Archives in 2002.

12. Reliable accounts, such as Richard Harris Smith's history of the OSS or the memoirs of Elizabeth MacDonald were exceptions to the rule. See R. Harris Smith, *OSS: The Secret History of America's First Central Intelligence Agency* (New York, 1972); Elizabeth MacDonald, *Undercover Girl* (New York, 1947). By contrast, see Corey Ford and Alastair MacBain, *Cloak & Dagger: The Secret Story of OSS* (New York, 1945); Louis Huot, *Guns for Tito* (New York, 1945); Stewart Alsop and Thomas Braden, *Sub Rosa: The OSS and American Espionage* (New York, 1946); Nicol Smith and Clark Blake, *Into Siam: Underground Kingdom* (New York, 1945); Harvig Andersen, *The Dark City: A True Account of Adventures of a Secret Agent in Berlin* (New York, 1954); Donald C. Downes, *The Scarlet Thread: Adventure in Wartime Espionage* (New York, 1953); Roger Hall, *You're Stepping on My Cloak & Dagger* (New York, 1957); Robert Alcorn, *No Bugles for Spies: Tales of the OSS* (New York, 1962); idem., *No Banners, No Bands: More Tales of the OSS* (New York, 1965). See, in addition, the overview by the Veterans of Strategic Services: "Ex-OSS Persons about the OSS" (n. d., R. H. Smith Papers, Box 2, Hoover Institution, Stanford, CA).

13. The crass high point of this trend was reached in publications such as Benjamin Colby's, *'Twas a Famous Victory: Deception and Propaganda in the War with Germany* (New Rochelle, 1974). Allen Dulles's *The Craft of Intelligence* (New York, 1963) may be seen as less extreme, though still symptomatic.

14. Kermit Roosevelt, ed., *War Report of the OSS*. 2 vols. (New York, 1976), cited later here as WROSSKR, as well as Anthony Cave Brown, ed., *The Secret War Report of the OSS* (New York, 1976), cited later as WROSSACB.

15. See, for example, Gerhard Weinberg, *A World at Arms: A Global History of World War II* (Cambridge, UK 1994); Peter Hoffmann, *The History of the German Resistance 1933–1945* (Cambridge, MA, 1979); Klemens von Klemperer, *German Resistance against Hitler: The Search for Allies Abroad, 1938–1945* (Oxford, 1992); Klaus-Dietmar Henke, *Die amerikanische Besetzung Deutschlands* (Munich, 1995). Bradley F. Smith's monograph *Shadow Warriors* (1983), which offered an overview of the activities in Donovan's secret intelligence service without going into details about individual operations, marked a high point of this phase. His study was, at the same time, the last publication (using what was a manageable set of documents at the time) to provide an overall portrayal of the OSS. Smith's work, which came out in 1983, was based on OSS documents declassified in 1976 and transferred to the State Department by staff members from the R&A research division of the OSS. He was not able to look at the much more comprehensive "operational records" of the OSS, which the CIA began to release in 1980.

16. Among the areas of investigation researchers looking at the OSS tended to favor were the activities of individual protagonists, OSS departments, and agent teams. In addition, there were specialized or country studies that, as a rule, concentrated on the activities of individual OSS departments. The most important works in these fields have been done by Siegfried Beer, Fabrizio Calvi, Max Corvo, Betty A. Dessants, Arthur L. Funk, Peter Grose, Jürgen Heideking, Barry Katz, Clayton Laurie, Petra Marquardt-Bigman, Elizabeth MacIntosh, Timothy Naftali, Joseph Persico, Neal H. Petersen, Oliver Rathkolb, Gerald Schwab, Alfons Söllner, and Maochun Yu. They are listed in the bibliography.

17. The main publications to be mentioned are those by Barry Katz, Petra Marquardt-Bigman, and Alfons Söllner.

18. Neal H. Petersen, ed., *From Hitler's Doorstep: The Wartime Intelligence Reports of Allen Dulles 1942–1945* (University Park, PA, 1996), abbreviated later as *Dulles-WIR*. In addition, Jürgen Heideking and this author have edited several documents and sources, including Jürgen Heideking and Christof Mauch, eds., *USA und deutscher Widerstand: Analysen und Operationen des amerikanischen Geheimdienstes OSS*, (Tübingen/Basel, 1993), abbreviated later as *UUDW*; idem., *American Intelligence and the German Resistance to Hitler* (Boulder, CO, 1996), abbreviated later as *AmIntel*.

19. The only exception here is the OSS division for counterespionage, treated competently in the works of Timothy Naftali, since this department was dedicated to defending against enemy movements, not to attacking them—devoted, that is, not to the shadow war against Hitler, but to the war against Hitler's shadow war. See, especially, T. Naftali, "X-2 and the Apprenticeship of American Counterespionage" (Ph.D., Harvard, 1993).

20. On this, see Heike Bungert, *Das Nationalkomitee und der Westen: Die Reaktion der Westalliierten auf das NKFD und die Freien Deutschen Bewegungen 1943–1948* (Stuttgart, 1997).

21. OSS undertakings already depicted extensively in scholarly research—such as the spectacular "Operation Sunrise"—are deliberately not considered. On this, see Bradley F. Smith and Elena Agarossi, *Operation Sunrise: The Secret Surrender* (New York, 1979).

22. Friedrich Nietzsche, *Unzeitgemäße Betrachtungen*, (Leipzig, 1930), p.101ff.

1. THE SETTING

1. S. Alsop and T. Braden, *Sub Rosa: The OSS and American Espionage*, p. 15; Allen W. Dulles, *The Secret Surrender* (New York, 1966), pp. 4 ff; Lyman B. Kirkpatrick, Jr., *The Real*

CIA (New York, 1968), pp. 14ff; Arthur B. Darling, *The Central Intelligence Agency: An Instrument of Government to 1950*, with Introductions by Bruce D. Berkowitz and Allan E. Goodman (University Park/London, 1990), Introduction to Chapter I.

2. "Intrepid" was the telegraphic signature of the British military secret service MI-6, run by Brigadier General Sir Stewart Menzies, which Stephenson had used before the entry into the war. The name "Intrepid" was known mostly because of William Stevenson's autobiography. William Stevenson, *A Man Called Intrepid: The Secret War* (New York, 1976). For a critical view of Stevenson, cf. Thomas F. Troy, *Wild Bill and Intrepid: Donovan, Stephenson, and the Origin of CIA* (New Haven, 1996), pp. 159–164. On MI-6 see Nigel West [pseud.], *MI6: British Secret Intelligence Service Operations, 1909–1945* (New York, 1983).

3. In 1970 a study by Thomas Troy began to circulate within the CIA, classified "secret." In 1984, for the first time, Troy presented some of his theses publicly. See "CIA's British Parentage—and the Significance Thereof," paper delivered at the tenth annual meeting of the SHAFR, GWU, 3 August 1984, typescript. For more on this, see Troy, *Wild Bill and Intrepid*; Timothy J. Naftali, "Intrepid's Last Deception: Documenting the Career of Sir William Stephenson," in *Intelligence and National Security* 8 (1993), pp. 72–92; in addition, see the letter ("personal and confidential") of BSC in New York to James R. Murphy at the OSS, April 26, 1944, Box 1, J. Russell Forgan Papers, Hoover Institution on War, Revolution and Peace (later referred to as Hoover Institution) Stanford, CA.

4. On the quote attributed to Stimson, see David Kahn, *The Codebreakers* (New York, 1967), p. 178 and, for a dissenting interpretation, Rhodri Jeffreys-Jones, *American Espionage: From Secret Service to CIA*, (New York 1977), p. 134f.

5. On Casey's testimony before the Senate investigating committee, see Joseph Persico, *Casey: From OSS to CIA* (New York 1990), p. 363; Interview J. Persico, W. Casey, August 27, 1976, Folder Casey, Box 1, Persico Papers, Hoover Institution, Stanford, CA; William Donovan's comprehensive notes on secret intelligence during the American Revolution may be found in the William J. Donovan Papers, Collection on Intelligence in the Revolutionary Period, Columbia University Library, New York, NY. Corey Ford, Donovan's biographer, also wrote the monograph *A Peculiar Service* (Boston, 1965); CIA Director William J. Casey was the author of a publication entitled *Where and How the War Was Fought: An Armchair Tour of the American Revolution* (New York, 1976). Allen Dulles dedicated one chapter of his book on the handicraft of secret intelligence to the "Evolution of American Intelligence"—see *Craft of Intelligence*, pp. 29–47. There is a research overview that originally circulated inside the CIA and written by Walter Pforzheimer: "Intelligence in the American Revolution: A Review Article," in: Hayden B. Peake and Samuel Halpern, *In the Name of Intelligence. Essays in Honor of Walter Pforzheimer* (Washington, D.C., 1996), pp. 57–66.

6. John Bakeless, *Turncoats, Traitors and Heroes*, (Philadelphia, 1959); [Central Intelligence Agency], *Intelligence in the War of Independence* (Washington, 1976); C. D. Ameringer, *U.S. Foreign Intelligence* (Lexington, MA, 1990), pp. 17–27.

7. Rhodri Jeffreys-Jones, *American Espionage*, p. 11. Cf. further H. M. Wriston, "Executive Agents in American Foreign Relations" (Ph.D. dissertation, Harvard University, 1922), pp. 326ff.

8. On espionage during the Civil War, cf. the classic study by Harnet T. Kane, *Spies for the Blue and Gray* (Garden City, NY, 1954), and on the Southern states, see John Bakeless, *Spies of the Confederacy* (Philadelphia, 1970); Curtis Caroll Davis and Edwin C. Fishel have made major contributions toward demythologizing a literature based largely on legends and anecdotes. See C.C. Davis, "Companions of Crisis: The Spy Memoir as a Social Document,"

in *Civil War History* 10 (1964), pp. 385–400; E. C. Fishel, "The Mythology of Civil War Intelligence," in *Civil War History* 10 (1964), pp. 344–367; idem., *The Secret War for the Union: The Untold Story of Military Intelligence in the Civil War* (Boston, 1996). On the origins of the ONI, see the standard work by Jeffrey M. Dorwart, *The Office of Naval Intelligence: The Birth of America's First Intelligence Agency, 1865–1918* (Annapolis, 1983); on the MID, see Bruce W. Bidwell, *History of the Military Intelligence Division, Department of the Army General Staff 1775–1941* (Frederick, MD, 1986).

9. Nathan Miller, *Spying for America: The Hidden History of U.S. Intelligence* (New York, 1989), pp. 155–175.

10. Cf. C. Andrew, *For the President's Eyes Only* (New York, 1995), pp. 28ff.

11. Herbert O. Yardley, *The American Black Chamber* ([Indianapolis, 1931]New York, 1981); on this see David Kahn, "The Annotated 'The American Black Chamber'," in Cipher A. Deavours et al., eds., *Cryptology: Yesterday, Today and Tomorrow* (Norwood, 1987); James Bamford, *The Puzzle Palace*, (Boston, 1982 — rev. Harmondsworth, 1983); a criticial look at the State Department's attempts at coordination is Troy, *Wild Bill and Intrepid*, pp. 205 ff.

12. Robert Dallek, *F. D. Roosevelt and American Foreign Policy, 1932–1943* (New York, 1979), p. 336; Nicholas John Cull, *Selling War: The British Propaganda Campaign Against American "Neutrality" in World War II* (New York/Oxford, 1995), p. 143; Allan M. Winkler, *The Politics of Propaganda: The Office of War Information 1942–1945* (New Haven/London, 1978), p. 20 ff.

13. "FDR, Designating a Coordinator of Information," July 11, 1941, reprinted as Appendix C in T. Troy, *Donovan and the CIA* (Frederick, MD, 1981), p. 423.

14. In the last year of the war, the OSS budget came to $57 million, compared to the $2.5 million that had been available to military intelligence in the last year of the First World War. See R. Jeffreys-Jones, *American Espionage*, p. 172; Harry H. Ransom, *The Intelligence Establishment* (Cambridge, MA, 1970), p. 70.

15. Anthony Cave Brown, editorial introduction to Chapter 2, "The Structure of the OSS," SWROSS, p. 62. A structural table is reprinted in WROSSKR, in Ameringer, *U.S. Foreign Intelligence* on pp. 160–161, and in UUDW on p. 266.

16. Thomas F. Troy, *Donovan and the CIA*; "The History of Planning for Psychological Warfare and Strategic Services," Folder 44, Box 76, Entry 99, RG 226. SWROSS, p 65ff; on the divisions listed in the diagram but did not exist in reality see interview C. Mauch/ D. McLaughlin, October 7, 1996, OSSOHP.

17. In addition to the special operations, espionage, and training departments — there was a fifth category, the service department. The divisions under the "Chief of Service" included areas like the budget, civilian personnel, office services, supplies, and procurement. See the diagram "OSS Organization 1944" printed in WROSSKR and reproduced in Ameringer *U.S. Foreign Intelligence*, Fig.14–1, p. 166).

18. SWROSS, pp. 66–70; a comprehensive, illustrated history of the CB may be found in Folder 21, Box 73A, Entry 99, RG 226, NA.

19. SWROSS, pp. 73–77; on Stanley Platt Lovell (1890–1976), who was awarded the Presidential Medal for Merit in 1948 for his services to the OSS, see G. J.A. O'Toole, *The Encyclopedia of American Intelligence and Espionage: From the Revolutionary War to the Present* (New York/Oxford, 1988), pp. 281–282, as well as the inside OSS biography, *Stanley Platt Lovell: Special Assistant to the Director*, OSS, Folder 147, Box 97, Entry 99, RG 226, NA. Lovell's OSS memoirs are interesting, but frequently unreliable: Stanley Lovell, *Of Spies and Stratagems*

(Englewood Cliffs, NJ, 1963). A large number of photos, drawings, and explanations about how the R&D inventions functioned may be found in the files of the PB Branch (Entry 85), e.g. OSS Weapons October 1943 (R&D No.79), Folder 190, Box 8, Entry 85, RG 226, NA.

20. SWROSS, p. 76; William B. Breuer, *The Secret War with Germany* (Novato, CA, 1988); on the drugs, see SWROSS, p. 77 as well as O'Toole, *Encyclopedia*, p. 346ff., pp. 454–456, and Lawrence Zelic Freedman, "Truth Drugs," in *Scientific American* 202 (1960), pp. 145–154.

21. Alfons Söllner, ed., *Zur Archäologie der Demokratie in Deutschland*, Vol. 1 (Frankfurt, 1986), p. 25. Another positive characterization was made by Ludwell L. Montague, a member of the US Joint Intelligence Staff (JIS), Memorandum for Record, Intelligence Service, 1940–1950, [Montague Memoirs], Folder 99, Box 12, Troy Papers, RG 263, NA. Negative assessments about R&A were generally made by veterans of the OSS-SO branches. Thus, for example, General Singlaub in Interview Christof Mauch/Maochun Yu, John K. Singlaub, October 31, 1996, OSSOHP.

22. Report by Col. Richard Park, March 12, 1945, Folder 20, Box 6, Troy Papers, RG 263, NA; Memo for Record, Clayton Bissell, Col. Park's comments on OSS, OSS (3–6-43), MID, 334, RG 165, NA.

23. Cf. SWROSS, p. 77ff.; on recruiting R&A staff, see Barry Katz, *Foreign Intelligence*, especially pp. 8–13; Petra Marquardt-Bigman, *Amerikanische Deutschlandanalysen*, p. 25ff..

24. Cf. O'Toole, *Encyclopedia*, p. 345ff. The CID catalogue cards and records may be found—with the exception of biographies—in the National Archives in College Park, MD. The CID catalogue cards, although not catalogued in the official search registrars, are generally accessible; the CID records are made up of Entries 16, 19 and 21 of Record Group 226. Documents labeled with 'L numbers' (Entry 19) were not allowed to leave the library; the 'XL records' (Entry 21) could be lent out to institutions outside the OSS; all the other documents (Entry 16) could be used inside the OSS only. An overview of the biographical CID collection may be found in the confidential R&A-Memorandum "Outline of Material in Biographical Records," 16 October 1944, Folder 1171, Box 82, Entry 146, RG 226, NA. On the individual CID functions, see William J. Donovan to Brigadier General W. B. Smith. "Sub: The Office of Strategic Services; its Functions, Conception, Organization and Operations," August 17, 1942, Box 49, Entry 110, RG 226, NA. On the general layout of the R&A Branch, cf. Petra Marquardt-Bigman, *Amerikanische Geheimdienstanalysen*, pp. 24–33; there is an "insider report" about what went on inside the R&A and its work in the CID Library by the historian Dr. Arnold H. Price, "OSS Remembered," Price Family Papers, Hoover Institution, Stanford, CA.

25. Cf. Franz Neumann, *Behemoth* (New York, 2nd ed. 1944), esp. p. 348; an introduction to Neumann's thought is provided by Alfons Söllner, *Neumann zur Einführung* (Hanover, 1982). The significance of Neumann's *Behemoth* for the Central Europe analyses of R&A was repeatedly stressed by R&A researchers. On the influence that Neumann's classic study had on R&A staff members Carl Schorske and John Herz, cf. the impressive documentation of interviews by Rainer Erd, ed., *Reform und Resignation: Gespräche über Franz L. Neumann* (Frankfurt, 1985), pp. 153–182, esp. p. 158 ff.; the most comprehensive, ideologically colored, yet superb argumentation about Neumann's time at R&A is by Regina Ursula Gramer, "The Socialist Revolutionary Dilemma in Emigration: Franz L. Neumann's Passage Toward and Through the Office of Strategic Services, " M. A. thesis (typescript), The University of Arizona 1989.

26. The Coordinator of Information [W. J. Donovan] to The President [F. D. Roosevelt], December 20, 1941, Frame 488, Roll 1, MF 1642, Entry 190, RG 226, NA.

27. "The FN Branch Gets Itself Established" (October 1941-January 1942, 1, FNB History, Folder 27a, Box 74, Entry 99, RG 226, NA; OSS History (First Draft), Chapter XXXVI. Foreign Nationalities, pp. 1–43, especially p. 1ff.; 6, Folder 29, Box 74, Entry 99, RG 226, NA.

28. William J. Donovan to Secretary of State, January 13, 1942, Frame 488, Roll 1, MF 1642, Entry 190, RG 226, NA. J. Edgar Hoover, Director FBI, to General Donovan, September 25, 1942; Elmer Davis, Director OWI, to General Donovan, July 29, 1942; David Karr, Ass. Chief FLD, OWI, to DeWitt C. Poole, November 25, 1942, cited in OSS History (First Draft), Ch. XXXVI.

29. After the war, Poole became President of the CIA-financed National Committee for a Free Europe, see O'Toole, *Encyclopedia*, p. 375 ff.; a short inside OSS biography (entitled "DeWitt Clinton Poole, Chief, FNB of OSS") may be found in Folder 147, Box 97, Entry 99, RG 226, NA. In Poole's papers there are several memoranda, but also speeches, that clarify the DeWitt C. Poole's political philosophy, especially DeWitt C. Poole to Colonel Edward G. Buxton, September 18, 1943, Folder 4, Box 1, Poole Papers, The State Historical Society of Wisconsin (SHSW), Madison, WI and De Witt C. Poole, "Militant, Multi-National Democracy," July 3 1942, Speech Folder, Box 7, SHSW, Madison, WI.

30. A superb overview on the organizations and activities of X-2 is provided by the memorandum prepared by James R. Murphy for General Donovan, "Sub: X-2 Achievements to November 1, 1944, November 1944," Folder 98, Box 12, Troy Papers, RG 263, NA.

31. English differentiates between the two functions and calls the passive function, mostly made up of procuring information, counterintelligence (CI), while the active spying function is called counterespionage (CE). In his introduction to secret intelligence, brought out under a pseudonym, James McCargar strictly separated the two functions, designating one as "security" and the other as "espionage." See Christopher Felix (pseud.), *A Short Course in the Secret War* (New York, 1988), p. 126ff.

32. Cf. SWOSS, 85–96; on the meaning of the word X-2, see O'Toole, *Encyclopedia*, p. 342.

33. Allen Dulles, *The Craft of Intelligence* (New York/Evanston/London, 1963); Ameringer, *U.S. Foreign Intelligence*, p. 1 ff. and p. 9 ff.; SWROSS, p. 78; O' Toole, *Encyclopedia*, p. 347.

34. SWROSS, p 79 ff.; Interview Christof Mauch/Robert Houlihan, September 16, 1996, Lexington, KY, OSSOHP.

35. An especially bad reputation in this respect was won by a team of German agents in Algiers whose lethargy was quickly transformed into all manner of excess. Memorandum German Operations, pp. 5–11, n. d., Folder 187a, Box 37, Entry 99, RG 226, NA.

36. "A" meant that the source was "absolutely reliable," "B" stood for "previously or probably reliable," "C" designated "questionable reliability," and "D" was an indicator for "unreliability." Analogously, "1" meant "completely reliable first-hand information," "2" designated that the information could not be confirmed on the other end, "3" stood for "probably true," "4" indicated the "improbability" of the information. Memorandum Grading of Reports, October 19, 1942, Folder 103, Box 7, Entry 147, RG 226, NA. in the "War Report" of the OSS (SWROSS, p. 80 ff.), it is incorrectly reported that the "grading system" was first introduced in 1943. In addition to using this general grading system, Allen Dulles in Bern introduced a number of other systems, such as one for mood of the Germans (Code 0), where 1 meant "excellent" and 8 "agitated"; for the "source" Dulles used the letters "U"

through "Z," and for "information" the letters "M" through "P. " Cf. the comprehensive cable OSS Bern to OSS Washington, January 11, 1943, Folder 1079, Box 171, Entry 146, RG 226, NA.

37. In November 1943 Shepardson transferred from the management of the London SI outpost to Washington and promulgated the new orders on January 4. See SWROSS, p. 81; on Shepardson's time as head of the SI in London (Shepardson arrived in England at the end of May 1942), see the Bruce Diary, OSS against the War, ed. by N. D. Lankford, p. 22 and passim. There is a brief biography of Shepardson in Folder 147, Box 97, Entry 99, RG 226, NA.

38. On the Labor Section, see Arthur J. Goldberg to General William J. Donovan, May 10, 1943, "Attachment: Memorandum The Labor Section of the Office of Strategic Services," Box 2, Persico Papers, Stanford, CA; "Ongoing Projects" [Labor Section], January 8, 1944, Folder 273, Box 67a, WJD Papers, USAMI, Carlisle Barracks, PA, parts of which are reprinted in AmIntel, Doc 33, pp. 183–191.

39. On the goals of the OELR, see the memorandum jointly submitted by Paul Kohn, Dyno Löwenstein, Eva Levinski Pfister, and Toni Sender, n. d. [with brief biographies of the authors]. The memorandum went by turns from Toni Sender to Allen Dulles (May 27, 1942) and from Allen Dulles to Hugh R. Wilson (June 3, 1942); Folder 832, Box 66, Entry 168, RG 226, NA, also Memorandum Project: Manuals on the Labor scene in each of the Axis-Dominated European Countries, December 3, 1942, Folder 838, Box 65, Entry 168, RG 226, NA; on the very first activities of the OELR, "Report on the first three months of our activities," August 15—November 15, 1942, Folder 842, Box 66, Entry 168, RG 226, NA.

40. General Order No.9, January 3, 1943, cited here according to "MO Branch History" (Draft), Folder 32, Entry 99, RG 226, NA; on the establishment of the MO Branch, see the memo "Establishment of Morale Operations Branch and History, January to May 1943," Folder 97, Box 12, Troy Papers, RG 263, NA; on the definition of "psychological warfare" as a task, see "Provisional Basic Field Manual Psychological Warfare (as defined by J.C.S. 155/7/D)," 12 June 1943, Dec. File 1942–45, CCS 385 (2–22–43), RG 218, NA. An overview of the organizations of the MO Branch is provided by Clayton Laurie, Propaganda Warriors (Laurence, KS, 1996), pp. 140 ff., esp. Fig.7.2., p. 141.

41. James G. Rogers, Wartime Washington: The Secret O.S.S. Journal of James Grafton Rogers, 1942–1943, ed. by Thomas Troy (Frederick, MD, 1987), p. 164; critical voices from inside the OSS are recorded in the "Report to Executive Committee on MO Organization, Personnel and Operations, August 20, 1943," Box 126, Entry 136, RG 226, NA.

42. Symptomatic is an incident from April 1944, when the OSS Director asked the President to transfer Colonel Bryan Houston from the Office of Price Administration to the MO department ; FDR, however, flatly refused. Memorandum William J. Donovan to Franklin D. Roosevelt, April 3, 1944; G.Edward Buxton to Grace Tully, 8 April 1944; FDR to Bill [Donovan], April 13, 1944; James F. Byrnes to William J. Donovan, April 3, 1944, FDR Papers OF 4485, FDRL Hyde Park, NY.

43. SWROSS, pp. 119–133; on the training in the Congressional Country Club, cf. Interview C. Mauch, J. K. Singlaub; C. Mauch/R. Houlihan, OSSOHP; on the Curriculum of the MO School, see the eleven chapter-long "Outline of Course," Folder 40, Box 76, Entry 99, RG 226, NA.

44. U.S. Office of Strategic Services, Psychological Assessment Staff: Assessment of Men (New York, 1948), p. 10.

45. A. Söllner, *Archäologie der Demokratie*, p. 25.

46. Knightley, Phillip, *The Second Oldest Profession: The Spy as Bureaucrat, Patriot, Fantasist and Whore* (London, 1986), p. 241.

47. Interview Barry Katz, Alex Inkeles, Stanford, CA, April 18, 1997, OSSOHP.

2. DONOVAN ON THE OFFENSIVE AND AMERICA'S PATH TO WAR

1. Churchill's speech is reprinted in *Into Battle: Speeches by Winston S. Churchill*, compiled by Randolph S. Churchill (London, 1947), pp. 215–223.

2. On Roosevelt's thoughts about recruiting Stimson and Knox, see Grace Tully, *F.D.R. My Boss*, with a Foreword by William O. Douglas (New York, 1949), p. 242; on Knox, see George Henry Lobdell, "A Biography of Frank Knox" (Ph.D. Diss., University of Illinois, 1954); on the relationship between Donovan and Roosevelt, cf. Elliott Roosevelt, ed., *F.D.R. His Personal Letters 1928–1945*, Vol. IV (New York, 1950), p. 975 ff.; on the trip to England, see Donovan's diary entries of August 5 and 12, "Diary of Henry L. MD" (LOC Washington, D.C.); Henry L. Stimson and McGeorge Bundy, *On Active Service in Peace and War* (New York, 1948); Edgar A. Mowrer, *Triumph and Turmoil* (New York, 1968), pp. 314–317; Ronald Tree, *When the Moon Was High: Memoirs of Peace and War 1897–1942* (London, 1975), p. 126 ff.; SWROSS, p. 42 ff. Pacifists in the Senate and those who had spoken out against a third term for Roosevelt stated that the appointment of Stimson and Knox would drive us into the war. Cf. Harold L. Ickes, *The Secret Diary of H.L.I. Vol. III. The Lowering Clouds 1939–1941* (New York, 1954), diary entry from June 23, p. 215.

3. Bradley F. Smith, *Shadow Warriors*, pp. 20 ff.; William L. Langer and S. Everett Gleason, *The Challenge to Isolation 1937–1940* (New York, 1952), passim, esp. pp. 474 ff.; Robert A. Divine, *The Reluctant Belligerent*, 2nd ed. (New York, 1979), p. 92. Knox endorsed William Donovan as an appropriate candidate for another cabinet post when President Roosevelt offered him the postion of Navy Secretary; see Ickes's diary entry from December 24, *The Secret Diary*, III, p. 93.

4. Valentine Williams, August 1, 1940, "The Fifth Column (Memorandum)," 1, Box 207, RG 165, NA; William J. Donovan/Edgar Mowrer, *Fifth Column Lessons for America* (Washington D.C., 1940), p. 5. On the larger context, see Francis MacDonnell, *Insidious foes: The Axis Fifth Column and the American home front* (New York, 1995); Louis De Jong, *The German Fifth Column in the Second World War* (Chicago, 1956), p. 15.

5. On this, see Mowrer's memoirs, Edgar Ansel Mowrer, *Triumph and Turmoil: A Personal History of Our Times*, (New York, 1968) and NYT, March 4, 1977.

6. A brief character sketch of Donovan may be found in the unpublished memoirs of James B. Donovan: "Byways of Law," II, 1–2, Papers of James B. Donovan, Box 37, Hoover Institution, Stanford, CA; Biographical Papers, Box 109, Papers of Edgar A. Mowrer, Library of Congress, Manuscript Division (= LOCMD).

7. Corey Ford, *Donovan of OSS*, p. 96 ff; Allen W. Dulles, "William J. Donovan and the National Security" ("Adaptation from an address delivered in tribute to the father of central intelligence"), 73, SII, Box 1. RG 263, NA.

8. Details of the trip to England may be found in William Stephenson, *A Man Called Intrepid* (New York 1976), pp. 113–118; also Richard Dunlop, *Donovan: America's Master Spy* (New York, 1982), p. 209; Bradley F. Smith, *Shadow Warriors*, pp. 33–37; David Stafford, "Britain Looks at Europe, 1940. Some Origins of the SOE," in *Canadian Journal of History* 10 (1975), pp. 231–248; Donovan/Mowrer, *Fifth Column Lessons*, p. 2. On Orwell Lawrence

C. Soley, *Radio Warfare: OSS and CIA Subversive Propaganda* (New York, 1989), p. 51 and Asa Briggs, *The War of Words* (London, 1970), p. 159.

9. Donovan/Mowrer, *Fifth Column Lessons*. The Donovan-Mowrer pamphlet is a rare book. There is one copy each in the LOC Pamphlet Collection and in Box 16, Allen Welsh Dulles Papers, Seeley J. Mudd Library, Princeton, NJ.

10. Cf. Donovan/Mowrer, *Fifth Column Lessons*, p. 5 ff; Valentine Williams, August 1, 1940, "The Fifth Column" (Memorandum), 1, Box 207, RG 165, NA.

11. Donovan/Mowrer, *Fifth Column Lessons*, pp. 3–8.

12. On July 12, Kennedy had cabled Hull that his colleague Klemmer was working on an investigation about the Fifth Column. The British Embassy, according to Kennedy, was in a better position to obtain information than a newspaper man like Mowrer. Kennedy to Hull, July 12, 1940, 740.0011 EW 1939/4571 2/3, RG 59, NA. On Kennedy, see David E. Koskoff, *Joseph P. Kennedy: A Life and Times* (Englewood Cliffs, NJ, 1974); Dunlop, *Donovan*, pp. 203–205.

13. Among others, "Friedrich Sieburg the author, Otto Abetz," and "'pro-French' consuls like Nolde" were characterized by Donovan as Hitler's "agents."; Donovan/Mowrer, *Fifth Column Lessons*, pp. 8–9.

14. Ibid., p. 9.

15. Cf. ibid., pp.10–11.

16. Ibid., pp. 11–12. After the war was over, the United States Political Adviser for Germany had a confidential report prepared looking into the real extent of Fifth Column activities on the basis of Reich Foreign Ministry files: "Report regarding German Penetration of the United States," December 31, 1946, 862.20211/11–1346 RG 59, NA.

17. Donovan/Mowrer, *Fifth Column Lessons*, pp. 14–16.

18. Edmond Taylor, *The Strategy of Terror* (Boston, 1940), pp. 1–2. Cf., in addition, idem., "Strategy of Terror," in *Reader's Digest* (1940), pp. 89–92. On Taylor's life, see his autobiography *Awakening from History* (Boston, 1969 [London, 1971]). In 1941 a pamphlet-like book by Taylor was published summoning Americans to smash the Nazis' Fifth Column. E.T., *Smash Hitler's International* (New York, 1941).

19. FDR's *Fireside Chats*, ed. by Russell D. Buhite and David W. Lewy (Norman/London, 1992), p.161; Donovan/Mowrer, *Fifth Column Lessons*, p. 16. When, in June 1942, the Nazis made an isolated attempt to infiltrate a group of German agents via U–boats into America from the coast of New York, the eight-member team was tried on the spot. On German espionage in the U.S., cf. David Kahn, *Hitler's Spies: German Military Intelligence in World War II* (New York, 1978) and Ladislas Farago, *German Espionage in the United States and Great Britain During World War II* (New York, 1971).

20. Charles Lindbergh, *NYT*, April 24, 1941; Reply to Charles Lindbergh, *NYT*, April 30, 1941.

21. William Donovan to Gen. Sherman Miles, August 29, 1940; Valentine Williams, August 1, 1940, "The Fifth Column" (Memorandum), 3, Box 207, RG 165, NA; Smith, *Shadow Warriors*, p. 37.

22. David Reynolds, "Lord Lothian and Anglo-American Relations, 1939–1940" (Transactions of the American Philosophical Society, 73, part 2, 1983), pp. 25–29; Philip Goodhart, *Fifty Ships that Saved the World: The Foundation of the Anglo-American Alliance* (Garden City, N.Y., 1965); J.R.M.Butler, *Lord Lothian (Philip Kerr) 1882–1940* (London, 1960), p. 297; Henry Stimson, diary entries from August 6. and 12, 1940, Vol. 31, Roll 6, Stimson Diary, LOC; for Henry Luce role in the "Destroyers for Bases" deal cf. Henry R. Luce, *A Political Portrait of the Man who Created the American Century* (New York, 1994), pp. 9ff.

23. It is also no coincidence that OSS Colonel David K. E. Bruce, a man of letters and head of London's OSS headquarters, was reading Taylor's *Strategy of Terror* immediately after the Office of Strategic Service was founded—between Agatha Christie's *ABC Murders*, Emile Zola's *Nana*, and Alexander Woolcott's *While Rome Burns*. Diary entry of August 13 and 14, 1942, Nelson Douglas Lankford, ed., *OSS against the Reich: The World War II Diaries of Colonel David K.E. Bruce* (Kent, OH/London, 1991), p. 26.

24. Taylor's recommendations may be found in Memorandum Proposed Functions of OSS Committee, July 27, 1942, Papers of William Donovan, Box 99b, Vol.1, Tab A, USAMI, Carlisle Baracks, Pa. One of the German émigrés, Berlin native Werner H. Guttmann, became the COI adviser on Fifth Column matters. In October 1940 Guttmann had written the controversial "The Fifth Column—How Does It Work?" On Guttmann, see the OSS correspondence from the early part of 1942 and a curriculum vitae in: Folder 634, Box 46, Entry 168, RG 226, NA.

25. Interview Siegfried Beer/Joseph Kaplan, November 1, 1996, Washington, D.C. SCDLL, OSSOHP, Georgetown University.

26. Interview C. Mauch, S. Beer/Charlotte Bowman, January 18, 1997, Lexington, Vermont, OSSOHP; on Schorske's isolationism, see B. Katz, *Foreign Intelligence*, p. 167; T. Troy, *Donovan and the CIA*, p. 73 ff.; Memorandum re: William J. Donovan, and the Office of the Coordinator of Information, January 5, 1942, 94-4-4672–10, Donovan File, FBI Archives, Washington, D.C.

27. B. Katz, Foreign Intelligence, 1–13; Robin Winks, *Cloak and Gown: Scholars in the Secret War* (New York, 1987), passim; P. Marquardt-Bigman, *Amerikanische Geheimdienstanalysen*, pp. 25–33; R. Harris Smith, *OSS*, pp.1–35; Interview C.M./Robert Houlihan, September 16, 1996, Lexington, KY, OSSOHP; on the recruiting practices within the COI and OSS, see John Waller, *The Unseen War in Europe: Espionage and Conspiracy in the Second World War* (New York, 1996), pp. 216–220; the personal files are located in the History Office of the CIA and can only be viewed within the framework of the Freedom of Information Act (FOIA). The Personal Files of those rejected by the COI and OSS—for example, the files of John Wayne, who was turned down because of his inconstant life style—are found in Entry 92, RG 226, NA.

28. Interview Tim Naftali/Eloise Page, March 31, 1997, Washington, D.C.; Interview C. Mauch, P. Marquardt-Bigman/Arthur Schlesinger, Jr., June 9, 1997, New York, NY, OSSOHP.

29. Interview Christof Mauch, Siegfried Beer/Frederick Burkhardt, January 18, 1997, Bennington, Vt.; Interview Siegfried Beer/August Heckscher, March 25, 1997, New York, NY; Interview Siegfried Beer, Christof Mauch/Abram Flues, November 6, 1996, Chevy Chase, MD; Interview Siegfried Beer/David Crockett, January 16, 1997, Massachusetts, OSSOHP.

30. Interview Siegfried Beer/August Heckscher, March 25, 1997, New York, NY; Interview Tim Naftali/Eloise Page, March 31, 1997, Washington, D.C.; Interview C. Mauch, S.Beer/Charlotte Bowman, Bennington, Vt, January 18, 1997, OSSOHP.

31. Interview Barry Katz/H. Stuart Hughes, May 10, 1997, La Jolla, CA, OSSOHP.

32. Interview Christof Mauch/Richard Helms, April 21, 1997, Washington, D.C., OSSOHP.

33. Interview Christof Mauch, P. Marquardt-Bigman/Arthur Schlesinger, Jr., June 9, 1997, New York, NY, OSSOHP.

34. "Summary of 1942 Budget Request. Coordinator of Information," Thomas Troy Collection, Washington, D.C., reprinted in Troy, *Donovan and the COI*, p. 112.

35. Inland II geh. 57, K 208806, Auswärtiges Amt, Politisches Archiv (AA/PA) Bonn; Confidential Report, Federico Stallforth; Re: Frederico [!] Stallforth, n.d. [October 1941]; John A. Kingsbury to Harry L. Hopkins, November 6, 1941, File Categories of Isolationists, Box 301, Hopkins Papers, FDRL, Hyde Park, NY.

36. Among Federico Stallforth's acquaintances, the Morgans, Rockefellers, and Mellons stood out, in addition to General Dawes, Colonel Lindbergh, John Hayes Hammond, Henry Wallace, and Cordell Hull. In Germany, Stallforth maintained contact to Höpker Aschoff, Geheimrat [Privy Councillor] Albert, Geheimrat Hewel, and Dr. Markau, the former President of the German Chamber of Commerce in London. Inland II geh. 57, K 208806 and K 208775, AA/PA Bonn; Klemens von Klemperer, *German Resistance against Hitler: The Search for Allies Abroad, 1938–1945* (Oxford, 1992), p. 256, fn. 97; Armin Mruck, *The F. D. Roosevelt Administration and the German Anti-Hitler Resistance*, Towsend State University Lectures (Baltimore, 1987), p. 34. A 1996 FOIA request by the author to the FBI about Federico Stallforth has not been answered yet.

37. Amazingly, Stallforth always found financial backers for his machinations, and he knew how to exploit their credulity. One of his obscure projects in the summer of 1940 was to convey a peace plan going back to Hermann Göring, although the plan—owing to its exaggerated demands—did not resonate well either in London or in Washington. W. D. Whitney to COI, October 1, 1941, Safe Germany, Box 4, PSF, FDRL, Hyde Park, NY and corresponding files in the State Department, 840.000/390 and 740.0011/6061, RG 59, NA.

38. Inland II geh. 57, K 208806, K 208775, 217290–217298, AA/PA Bonn, Mruck, *The F. D. Roosevelt Administration*, p. 34 ff. On Stallforth's contacts with von Hassell, see Gregor Schöllgen, *Ulrich von Hassell 1881–1944: Ein Konservativer in der Opposition* (Munich, 1990), pp.125–129. On the British reaction to the German peace proposals of July 1940, cf. Winston Churchill, *The Second World War: Their Finest Hour* (Boston, 1949), p. 259 ff.

39. While Stallforth had emphasized that he would be exerting political pressure on people like "Hull, Wallace, Butler, Knudsen, Aldrich, Rockefeller [and] Lamont," Dieckhoff set the record straight on this statement by explaining that it was "precisely these men" who were "known [to be] our biggest opponents [!]." Inland II geh. 57, K 208775, AA/PA Bonn.

40. Diary entry from May 5, 1941, Ulrich von Hassel, *Aufzeichnungen vom Andern Deutschland: Die Hassell-Tagebücher 1938–1944*. Expanded edition based on handwritten diary, edited by Freiherr Hiller von Gaertringen with the assistance of Klaus Peter Reiß (Berlin, 1988), pp. 249 and 272.

41. W. D. Whitney to COI, October 1, 1941, "Safe Germany," Box 4, PSF, FDRL, Hyde Park, NY; Hoffmann, *History of the German Resistance* (Cambridge, MA, 1979), pp. 212, 44 ff.

42. During the first months of the war, London was inundated by peace feelers, so that at the beginning of 1941 Churchill issued a directive of "absolute silence." FO to Halifax, May 19, 1941, FO 371/26520; Miller (British Embassy Washington) to Balfour (FO), 371/24384, PRO, Kew; cf. G. Schöllgen, Ulrich von Hassell, 245 ff.; on the policy of absolute silence, see FO 371/26542/C610/324/P. On the broader context, see Klaus-Jürgen Müller and David Dilks, eds., *Großbritannien und der deutsche Widerstand 1938–1944* (Paderborn, 1994).

43. On this, see too Mother Mary Alice Gallin, O.S.U., *Ethical and Religious Factors in the German Resistance to Hitler* (Washington, D.C., 1955), p. 123; Stallforth to Gallin, June 23, 1955, Mary Alice Gallin Papers, Washington, D.C.; on the Welles mission at the beginning of 1940, cf., in addition to Welles' memoirs (*Time for Decision*, New York, 1944) esp. Stanley E. Hilton, "The Welles-Mission to Europe. February–March 1940: Illusion or Real-

ism?" in *Journal of American History* 58 (1971/72), pp. 73 ff. and Ulrich Schlie, *Kein Friede mit Deutschland*, p. 82 ff., p. 385.

44. Shortly after his first talk with Donovan, Stallforth phoned von Hassell, informing him that the proposals had fallen on "very fertile ground in America." On the report of Stallforth's Berlin secretary, see the diary entry of von Hassell from October 4, 1941, *Aufzeichnungen vom Andern Deutschland*, p. 276, and NS 19/3897, BA Koblenz.

45. Stallforth's view was that the ships for the Allies were of greater value than the currency was to the Axis powers. Cf., on this point, the comprehensive correspondence in the Hopkins Papers, especially Charles Lemmenmeier to Stallforth, August 29, 1941 with appendices; Protokoll einer Unterredung zwischen Lemmenmeyer und Dr. Meyer im Auswärtigen Amt September 9, 1941; Stallforth to Donovan, October 17, 1941, October 18, 1941; Donovan to Harry Hopkins, October 28, 1941.

46. William J. Donovan, Memorandum to the President, October 13, 1941, File COI 1941, Box 141, PSF, FDRL, Hyde Park, NY; Confidential Report, Federico Stallforth, n. d. [October 1941], File Categories of Isolationists, Box 301, Hopkins Papers, FDRL, Hyde Park, NY.

47. The letters were read and evaluated by COI staffers in Bermuda. William J. Donovan to President Roosevelt, Report on Germany—Spring and Autumn—1941, File COI 1941, Box 141, PSF, FDRL. Marlis G. Steinert, *Hitlers Krieg und die Deutschen: Stimmung und Haltung der deutschen Bevölkerung im Zweiten Weltkrieg* (Düsseldorf/Vienna, 1970), p. 227 ff.

48. William J. Donovan, Memorandum to the President, October 13, 1941, File COI 1941, Box 141, PSF, FDRL, Hyde Park, NY.

49. William J. Donovan to Harry L. Hopkins, October 28, 1941; Harry L. Hopkins to William J. Donovan, November 2, 1941, Box 301, Hopkins Papers, FDRL, Hyde Park, NY.

50. John Kingsbury to Harry Hopkins, November 5, 1941; Harry Hopkins to William J. Donovan, November 7, 1941; Harry Hopkins to John Kingsbury, November 7, 1941; John Kingsbury to Harry Hopkins (copy to Donovan), November 6, 1941, Box 301, Hopkins Papers, FDRL, Hyde Park, NY.

51. Memorandum [of the Board of Analysts], J. B. Baxter [to W. J. Donovan], December 12, 1941, Folder 1565, Entry 146, Box 113, RG 226, NA; W. J. Donovan, Memorandum to the President, December 12, 1941, frames 621 to 630, MF 1642, Entry 190, RG 226.

52. War Diary [= WD] OSS, Berne. Organization, 1, Berne OSS, CIA Box 11, FOIA-CIA.

53. [Whitney F. Shepardson], Talk with James Grafton Rogers, May 9, 1959, Folder Shepardson, Whitney, Box 10, MS #536, James Grafton Rogers Collection, Colorado Historical Society, Denver.

54. As Grace Tully recollected, Colonel Donovan first arrived at the White House around midnight and only talked with FDR for a few minutes. (Grace Tully, *FDR: My Boss*, New York, 1949), p. 258; cf. "The President's Appointments. Sunday, December 7, 1941" in Elliott Roosevelt, ed., *F.D.R. His Personal Letters 1928–1945*. Foreword by Eleanor Roosevelt (New York, 1940), Vol. 2, p. 1252; Corey Ford, *Donovan of OSS*, p. 116 ff.; and Troy, *Donovan and the CIA*, p. 116.

55. Cf. Christopher Andrew, *For the President's Eyes Only*, pp. 75–122. A comparative overview of the secret intelligence services' situation in 1941 is attempted by the CIA study [William Henhoeffer] *The Intelligence War in 1941: A 50th Anniversary Perspective* [Washington, D.C.] Paper of the Office of Training and Education/Center for the Study of Intelligence, 1992).

56. Roberta Wohlstetter, *Pearl Harbor: Warning and Decision* (Stanford, CA, 1962), p. 387, by way of summary. The central arguments in the controversy between orthodox and revisionist Pearl Harbor historiography had already been summarized by Hans L. Trefousse at the beginning of the 1980s; see *Pearl Harbor: The Continuing Controversy* (Malabar, FL, 1982).

57. In two superb studies, David Kahn has described how the Japanese "Purple" cryptography system was broken and persuasively explained why American military and government officials did not foresee the attack on Pearl Harbor. David Kahn, "The Intelligence Failure at Pearl Harbor," in *Foreign Affairs* (1991/92), pp. 138–152; idem., "Pearl Harbor and the Inadequacy of Cryptanalysis," in *Cryptologia* 15 (1991), pp. 273–294. Cf. David Kahn, "Did FDR Invite the Pearl Harbor Attack?" in *The New York Review of Books* 29 (1982), pp. 26–30, where the author discusses the Gordon Prange's outstanding book as well as John Toland's monograph: Gordon W. Prange, *At Dawn We Slept: The Untold Story of Pearl Harbor* (New York, 1991); John Toland, *Infamy: Pearl Harbor and Its Aftermath* (New York, 1982).

58. In mid-1940 Lovell had attempted to mediate between Philipp Kerr (Lord Lothian) and Hans Thomsen. See Lothian's memoranda to the Foreign Office from July 19 and 24, 1940, FO 371/24408/C8015 and FO 371/24408/ C1542. It is also evident from the German records that Thomsen and the "friend of peace" Lovell were in close contact with each other. Thomsen to Auswärtiges Amt, January 7, 1941, Büro Staatssekretär, USA, PA/AA, Bonn.

59. Malcolm Lovell to Colonel William J. Donovan, November 13, 1941; William J. Donovan to President Roosevelt, November 13, 1941; Malcolm Lovell to Colonel William J. Donovan, December 13, 1941; William J. Donovan to President Roosevelt, December 13, 1941, Box 147, PSF, FDRL, Hyde Park, N.Y.; cf. William L. Langer, *Our Vichy Gamble* (New York, 1947), p. 206 and (though with inadequate documentation) Anthony Cave Brown, *The Last Hero: Wild Bill Donovan* (New York, 1984), pp. 187 ff; see also Herzstein, *Henry R. Luce*, 171–174.

60. Bureau Memo, 3/14/46 re: Malcolm Lovell 100–25944–47, in: Memorandum Mr. Ladd to Mr. Rosen, July 15, 1953. Subject: William Joseph Donovan. Special Inquiry, 77–58706–48, Donovan File, FBI Archive, Washington, D.C.

61. In contrast to the First World War, when the German ambassador, Count Johann Heinrich von Bernstorff, was confronted with a hostile American position, at the moment (according to Thomsen) a friendly relationship prevailed between the U..S. and Germany. Malcolm Lovell to Colonel William J. Donovan, December 13, 1941; William J. Donovan to President Roosevelt, December 13, 1941, Box 147, PSF, FDRL, Hyde Park, N.Y.; on Bernstorff's peacemaking efforts, see Reinhard R. Doerries, *Washington—Berlin* 1908/1917, p. 238 ff.

62. It would take more than a year before Thomsen would shed his "illusions" and start complaining (within confidential circles) about the Führer's "showy display of [irresponsible] invincibility." Ulrich von Hassell, Tagebucheintrag vom 6. Juni 1943, in: U.v.H., Aufzeichnungen, p. 350 f..

63. William J. Donovan to FDR, December 16, 1941, Box 163, PSF; W. J. Donovan to FDR, January 24, 1942, Box 141, PSF, FDRL, Hyde Park, NY; on this, see B. F. Smith, *Shadow Warriors*, p. 100 ff.

64. Memorandum J.B. Baxter [to W.J. Donovan], December 12, 1941, Folder 1565, Entry 146, Box 113, RG 226, NA. The memorandum was immediately forwarded to the President. W. J. Donovan, Memorandum to the President, December 12, 1941, frames 621 to 630, MF 1642, Entry 190, RG 226.

65. Ibid.

66. The Position of Russia, in: Memorandum J.B. Baxter [to W.J. Donovan], 4–5.

67. Knowing about "Torch" would presumably have made the prognosis turn out differently. "Africa," in ibid., 6, December 12, 1941, Folder 1565, Entry 146, Box 113, RG 226, NA; W. Langer, *Our Vichy Gamble*, p. 206.

68. Bruce C. Hopper to Colonel William J. Donovan, Possibility of Russia's Defection, December 10, 1941, Folder 1565, Box 113, Entry 146, RG 226, NA. On Bruce Hopper, see B. F. Smith, *Shadow Warriors*, pp.125, 393.

69. Draft Memorandum, Observations on a Possible German Peace Offensive, 1, December 11, 1941, Folder 1565, Box 113, Entry 146, RG 226, NA; italic emphasis underlined in original.

70. Observations on a Possible German Peace Offensive, 2, December 11, 1941, Folder 1565, Box 113, Entry 146, RG 226, NA.

71. *The Public Papers and Addresses of Franklin D. Roosevelt*, ed. by Samuel I. Rosenman, Vol. 10 (New York, 1969), pp. 522–531.

72. Memorandum J.B. Baxter [to W.J. Donovan], December 12, 1941, Folder 1565, Entry 146, Box 113, RG 226, NA.

73. Coordinator of Information, "The German Military and Economic Position. Summary and Conclusion, December 12, 1941" (COI Monograph No.3), Donovan to FDR, December 12, 1941, Box 4, PSF, FDRL, Hyde Park, NY.

74. An undated version of the study from the first days of December may be found in the files of the State Department as an appendix to the letter James P. Baxter, 3d to Henry Villard, December 18, 1941, 862.20/1305 1/2, RG 59, NA. The State Department frequently received the COI analyses with some delay. The report of December 12, 1941 first arrived on Christmas eve. See James P. Baxter to Henry Villard, December 23, 1941, 103.918/113 (Germany), both in RG 59, NA.

75. The German Military and Economic Position, December 12, 1941, 103.918/ 113 (Germany), RG 59, NA.

76. Ibid., 21.

77. One of the reasons was that there was only fragmentary information available in December 1941, and that the COI economists were well aware of how much their conclusions needed revising. The authors of the study pointed out that the Eastern European Section [of R&A] was then working on a "special report" that would be taking a closer look at German gains in the Russia campaign. The German Military and Economic Position. Summary and Conclusion, 4, Fn 1, December 12, 1941, 103.918/113 (Germany), RG 59, NA.

78. "Die Stärke der deutschen Luftwaffe am 5.7.1941, 3.1.1942 und 31.4.1943," in WWR XI (1961), pp. 641–644. In the course of the war, monthly aircraft production figures would quadruple compared to the date from June 1941. Cf. "The Blitzkrieg War Economy" (= Appendix VIII), in Barry A. Leach, *German Strategy against Russia 1939–1941* (Oxford, 1973), p. 275.

79. David Kahn, "The United States Views [of] Germany and Japan in 1941," in Ernest R. May, *Knowing One's Enemies: Intelligence Assessment Before the Two World Wars* (Princeton, NJ, 1984), pp. 476–501.

80. Heideking, *Geschichte der USA*, p. 324.

81. Kahn, *U.S. Views of Germany and America*, p. 493. Author's emphasis.

82. Kahn, ibid.; F. H. Hinsley et al., *British Intelligence in the Second World War* (Cambridge, 1979), vol. 1, pp. 228 ff., 308; on the Germans' ruses, see Orville H. Bullitt, ed., *For the President. Personal and Secret: Correspondence between Franklin D. Roosevelt and William C.*

Bullitt (Boston, 1972), p. 421. For the period until 1939, see Wesley Wark, *The Ultimate Enemy: British Intelligence and Nazi Germany, 1933–1939* (Ithaca/London, 1985).

83. Cf. Howard V. Young, Jr., "Racial Attitudes of United States Navy Officers as a Factor in American Unpreparedness for War with Japan." Paper delivered at the Fifth Naval History Symposium, U.S. Naval Academy, Annapolis, October 2, 1981.

84. On this point, the author concurs with the assessment of B. F. Smith (*Shadow Warriors*, pp. 98 ff.) Even the few OSS memoranda that investigate Japan and Germany comparatively try to be extremely objective. Cf., for example, Lt. Colonel Carl O. Hoffmann via Lt. Colonel Edward L. Bigelow to The Planning Group, September 6, 1944, Folder 9, Box 565, Entry 92, RG 226, NA.

85. Even MID had assumed an air force size, at 11,000 planes, that was much too high for July 1941. U.S. Government, 79th Cong., 1st session, Joint Committee on the Investigation of the Pearl Harbor Attack, Hearings, 39 parts, Washington, D.C. 1946, XIV, 1336, on this point, see Kahn, "U.S. Views of Germany," p. 492. Characteristically, the British documents that Donovan send to Roosevelt in 1941 made up nearly a fifth of all the COI memoranda that reached the White House from COI headquarters. Entry 190, RG 226, NA. If the Americans still had access to relatively reliable information from Berlin (courtesy of military attachés' reports) until the outbreak of the war, after 1940 they were largely dependent on speculation, which only began to assume more realistic dimensions as the war dragged on. Cf., for example, the superb report of November 1939, Military Operations—General. An Estimate of the General Situation as of November 27, 1939, 862.20 MID Reports, RG 59, NA; here, too, see Wilhelm Deist, "Die Deutsche Aufrüstung in amerikanischer Sicht. Berichte des US-Militärattachés in Berlin aus den Jahren 1933–1939," in *Rußland-Deutschland-Amerika: Festschrift für Fritz T. Epstein zum 80.Geburtstag*, ed. by Alexander Fischer et al. (Wiesbaden, 1978), pp. 279–295. An additional factor was Hitler's longstanding aim of misleading his enemies with production and armaments figures that were too high, and the fact that even Göring misinformed him. See Central Intelligence Agency, ORD, *Covert Rearmament in Germany, 1919–1939: Deception and Misperception*, n.p. (= Washington, D.C.) 1979.

86. Coordinator of Information, *The German Supply Problem on the Eastern Front* (June 22—December 6, 1942 [sic; actually 1941]), March 25, 1942 (Monograph No. 6a), 103.918/113 (Germany), RG 59, NA.

87. Arnold H. Price, "OSS Remembered." Typescript, Price Family Papers, Hoover Institution, Stanford, CA. (revised version in author's possession.)

88. COI, *The German Supply Problem*, p. 5.

89. Cf., on this point and what follows, "Supply Requirements of the German Army in the Russian Campaign (= Chapter II)," in COI, *The German Supply Problem*, pp. 61–147, and Appendix to Chapter III: "Factors Affecting Railroad Capacity," p. 164 ff.

90. COI, *The German Supply Problem*, p.12 ff. and pp. 16–18. A map prepared by the COI entitled "Railroads on the Eastern Front" is in the monograph after p. 16.

91. Cf. "The German Campaign in Russia" (= Chapter I), in: COI, *The German Supply Problem*, pp. 31–60.

92. "Summary," in COI, *The German Supply Problem*, p. 28 ff.

93. Cf. *Deutschland im Zweiten Weltkrieg*, Vol. 2, p. 325 ff.

94. Cf. the outstanding accounts by Martin van Creveld, *Supplying War. Logistics from Wallenstein to Patton* (Cambridge, 1977), ch. 5; Klaus A. F. Schüler, *Logistik im Rußland-feldzug: Die Rolle der Eisenbahn bei Planung, Vorbereitung und Durchführung des deutschen*

Angriffs auf die Sowjetunion bis zur Krise vor Moskau im Winter 1941/42 (Frankfurt, 1987).

95. Thus, for example, Halder's notes contain relatively reliable figures (cf. the diary entry of September 12, 1941) and indicate an interest in the relative distribution of forces within the German military (diary entry of August 3, 1942). Yet it is obvious that Halder was repeatedly blinded by territorial gains and viewed the German situation much too optimistically. Generaloberst (Colonel General) Halder, *Kriegstagebuch*, ed. by Hans-Adolf Jacobsen (Stuttgart, 1963), Eintrag vom 31. Juli 1942 (entry for July 31. 1942); data for the beginning of the operation may be found in "German Intelligence Estimates of Soviet Army Strength" (= Appendix IV), in Leach, *German Strategy*, p. 270.

96. COI, *The German Supply Situation*, p. 1; G. Weinberg, *A World at Arms*, p. 264; the three million figure does not include the Waffen-SS. See *Deutschland im Zweiten Weltkrieg*, Vol. 2, p. 327; on the role of allies in the Eastern campaign, also consult the study by Peter Gosztony, which (however) does not contain any figures about the strength of the foreign armies; Gosztony, *Hitlers Fremde Heere: Das Schicksal der nichtdeutschen Armeen im Ostfeldzug* (Düsseldorf, 1976), p. 103 ff. The COI was not entirely off the mark with its estimate of 200 organized divisions for June 1941. On the whole, the Germans had more than 152 1/2 German divisions, as well as 14 Romanian and 21 Finnish ones, at their disposal. See "Distribution of German Divisions, June 1941" (Appendix VI), in Leach, *German Strategy*, p. 272.

97. An outstanding, still unsurpassed overview of partisans' activities in individual regions of the Soviet Union—dealing with historical background, ideology, successes and failures—is provided by John A. Armstrong, ed., *Soviet Partisans in World War II* (Madison, WI, 1964). Alexander Dallin, *German Rule in Russia, 1941–1945: A Study in Occupation Policies* (London, 1957), pp. 74 ff., 517 ff. and passim.

98. George Blau assumes there was a total of 625,000 horses, Werner Haupt as many as 750,000. See George Blau, *The German Campaign in Russia—Planning and Operations, 1940–42* (Washington, D.C., 1955), p. 41; Werner Haupt, *Die Schlachten der Heeresgruppe Süd* (Darmstadt, 1985), p. 16. R. L. Di Nardo and Austin Bay, "Horse-Drawn Transport in the German Army," in *Journal of Contemporary History* 23 (1988), pp. 129–142.

99. [Germany in the Third Winter of the War], March 26, 1942, David Bruce, Special Assistant [to Donovan] to The Honorable G. Howland Shaw, Department of State, March 26, 1942, Confidential File, 103.918/113 (Germany), RG 59, NA. Internal evidence and the classification "Most Secret" point to the material's British provenance.

100. [Germany in the Third Winter of the War], March 26, 1942, 3, Confidential File, 103.918/113 (Germany), RG 59, NA.

101. Foreign Nationalities, p.1 ff. in [OSS History. First Draft], Folder 29, Box 74, Entry 99, NA; additional figures and lists are found in "Foreign Nationality Groups in the U.S.A. Handbook," June 1943, Box 4, Entry 100, RG 226, NA.

102. "The FN Branch Gets Itself Established" (October 1941–January 1942), Folder 27a, Box 74, Entry 99, RG 226, NA. On the FNB, see Siegfried Beer, ed., "Exil und Emigration als Information. Zur Tätigkeit der Foreign Nationalities Branch (FNB) innerhalb des amerikanischen Kriegsgemeindienstes COI bzw. OSS, 1941–1945," in *Dokumentationsarchiv des österreichischen Widerstands, Jahrbuch 1989* (Vienna, 1989), pp. 132–137; Lorraine M. Lees, "National Security and Ethnicity: Contrasting Views during World War II," in *Diplomatic History* 11 (1987), pp.113–128.

103. Coordinator of Information to Attorney General, September 26, 1941, Folder 27c, Box 74, Entry 99, RG 226, NA.

104. In Harold B. Hoskins the Department had an official who was supposed to keep the Department informed about the activities of these movements. In reality, Hoskins's office had the function of keeping the "free movements" off the State Department's throat. Department of State, Press Release No. 600, Policy Regarding "Free Movements in the United States" December 10, 1941, Folder 28, Box 74, Entry 99, RG 226, NA; The FN Branch Gets Itself Established (October 1941–January 1942), p. 2 ff., Folder 27a, Box 74, Entry 99, RG 226, NA; Thomas Troy, Donovan and the CIA, 109.

105. Charles P. Kindleberger, *The Life of an Economist: An Autobiography* (Oxford, 1991), p. 69.

106. Poole and Wiley had, among other things, shared experiences at the American Embassy in Berlin. From 1926 to 1930 DeWitt Poole had been Counselor and John Wiley First Secretary at the Embassy. See Biographical Abstract, John Cooper Wiley (1898–1967), John C. Wiley Papers, FDRL, Hyde Park, NY. Poole was a co-founder of the School of Public and International Affairs at Princeton University (1930–1939). Biographical Abstract, Dewitt Clinton Poole (1885–1952), Poole Papers, SHSW, Madison, WI.

107. In reality, it had chiefly been Donovan's idea to tap the émigré pool for intelligence purposes. For tactical reasons, however, the COI Director stressed to the President and the Bureau of the Budget that the establishment of the Foreign Nationalities Branch was happening at the express wish of the State Department; for in either case the idea was to create the impression that the activity of the FNB was both wanted and (thus far) not covered by any other agency. Coordinator of Information [Donovan] to President [Roosevelt], December 20, 1941, Entry 190, frame 488, Roll 1, MF 1642, RG 226, NA; concerning the date and wording of the designation, see "The FN Branch Gets Itself Established" (October 1941–January 1942), 10, Folder 27a, Box 74, Entry 99, RG 226, NA; COI White House Books: Index and Approvals, Donovan Papers, Carlisle Barracks, PA.

108. Memorandum of Conversation between D.C. Poole and A. A. Berle, March 19, 1942, D.C. Poole to Colonel Donovan, March 20, 1942, here cited according to FNB History, ch.2, p. 32, Folder 27a, Box 74, Entry 99, RG 226, NA.

109. On Wiley's replacement, see FNB History, ch.2, especially pp. 24–27, Folder 27a, Box 74, Entry 99, RG 226, NA.

110. Preliminary Report of Frank Bohn on German-American Population in the United States and Work of German-American Congress for Democracy, November 30, 1941, INT-13GE-11, Entry 100, RG 226, NA.

111. Ibid.

112. Frank Bohn, Report Number Two, Part II, n.d., [presumably appendix for Frank Bohn to David Bruce, October 21, 1941], INT-13GE-4, Entry 100, RG 226, NA. On the effectiveness of Allied propaganda in the First World War, see "Psychological Warfare in the Mediterranean Theater. Part VI, Introduction," Box 14, C.D. Jackson Papers, Eisenhower Library, Abilene, KS.

113. Cf., for example, August Heckscher to John C. Wiley, German Propaganda, March 2, 1942; John C. Wiley to James P. Warburg, March 6, 1942, INT-13GE-44, Entry 100, RG 226, NA.

114. On the FBI checks, cf., for example, John Herz, *Wie ein Weltbild entstand: Autobiographie* (Düsseldorf, 1984), p.136. On the attitude of the State Department, see Memorandum of Conversation, Activities of Tibor Eckhardt here—question of foreign language groups, February 10, 1942, Berle Diary, Box 213, Berle Papers, FDRL, Hyde Park, NY. Adolf

A. Berle, Jr., Memorandum to the Secretary of State, December 20, 1942, Box 58, Berle Papers, FDRL, Hyde Park, NY.

115. On Baxter, Interview C. Mauch, S.Beer/Charlotte Bowman, Bennington, VT, January 18, 1997, OSSOHP. (Baxter's successor William Langer had a more open attitude toward the émigré question); on Neumann: Philip Horton to Mr. [John] Wiley, Interoffice Memo, October 26, 1942, sub: Franz Neumann, INT-13GE-410, Entry 100, RG 226, NA. On Neumann's role in the OSS, cf. esp. Rainer Erd, ed., *Reform und Resignation: Gespräche über Franz L. Neumann*, pp. 151 ff.

116. Eden to Lord Halifax, October 30, 1942, FO 371/30929/C10442 (excerpts quoted in Kettenacker, *Krieg zur Friedenssicherung*, p. 304, fn. 225).

117. Wiley's assessment here rested on information from an unnamed Austrian citizen who explained that the émigrés were "95% intellectuals"—and mostly without backing from inside the population. John C. Wiley, Memorandum to Colonel Donovan, January 20, 1942, INT-13GE-107, Entry 100, RG 226, NA.

118. [Views of German exiles], 1, March 4, 1942, INT-13GE-47, Entry 100, RG 226, NA. Next to propaganda, research was the second area in which the émigrés were able to cooperate with the U.S. government without eliciting major mistrust. On the work of German émigrés as researchers in R&A, see A. Söllner, *Archäologie der Demokratie*, pp. 7–40; B. Katz, *Foreign Intelligence*, p. 29 ff., P. Marquardt-Bigman, *Amerikanische Deutschlandanalysen*, pp. 67–73.

119. A. Heckscher to Mr. John C. Wiley, March 4, 1942; Report on interview with Thormann concerning propaganda to Germany, INT-13GE-46, Entry 100, RG 226, NA. Thormann had organized the German Freedom Radio (Deutscher Freiheitssender) in Paris. On the interventionist Council for Democracy, which had been founded in 1940 by (among others) C.D. Jackson, Archibald MacLeish, and Carl J. Friedrich, see Sydney S. Weinberg, "Wartime Propaganda in a Democracy: America's Twentieth-Century Information Agencies" (Ph.D., Columbia University, 1969) and Mark L. Chadwin, *The Warhawks. American Interventionists Before Pearl Harbor* (New York, 1968).

120. [Interview with Thormann], March 1, 1942, INT-13GE-46, Entry 100, RG 226, NA. In addition to Thormann, Father Odo (Württemberg) also took offense at this dilettantish propaganda. One of the things he criticized was the "Jewish voice" of the FIS commentator. Although certainly no anti-Semite—Odo informed American intelligence and the State Department about the crimes of the SS in Poland—the émigré priest said: "in present day Germany, propaganda sent out by a Jewish voice was simply out of the question. Far better to get Germans, preferably those who had quite recently been in Germany, who could not only talk good German but who could talk in the mentality of the people involved." Memorandum of Conversation, March 17, 1942, Berle Diary, Berle Papers, Box 213, FDRL, Hyde Park, NY.

121. Robert L. Reynolds to John C. Wiley, sub: German Propaganda, March 2, 1942 Robert L. Reynolds to John C. Wiley, sub: German Propaganda, March 2, 1942; A. Heckscher to John C. Wiley, Subject: German Propaganda, March 2, 1942, INT-13GE-44, Entry 100, RG 226, NA. Warburg, in the meantime, emphasized that Roosevelt himself had recently expressed the wish to give the Germans hope for a tolerable future. James Warburg to Robert Sherwood, March 12, 1942, Folder 8b, Box 71, Entry 99, RG 226, NA. On Heckscher, also see Winks, *Cloak and Gown*, p. 219.

122. On Poole's call for a counterrevolution, see "Remarks before Governmental Research Association at Princeton," September 5, 1940, Folder 5, Box 7, Poole Papers; Biography

[Poole, Dewitt Clinton (1885–1952)], Box 1, Poole Papers, State Historical Society of Wisconsin, Madison, WI.

123. [Walter Dorn], The German Political Emigration, IV, December 3, 1943, R&A 1568, RG 59, NA, excerpts reprinted in Söllner, *Archäologie der Demokratie*, I, pp. 63–90; a paraphrase of the R&A report may be found in Petra Marquardt-Bigman, *Amerikanische Geheimdienstanalysen*, p.115 ff. Cf., in addition, Interoffice Memo, Richard Rohman to John C. Wiley, sub: Further Report on German Emigration in the United States, April 6, 1942; German Refugees in the USA. Remarks on the Memorandum of February 16, 1942, INT-13GE-105, Entry 100, RG 226, NA.

124. See Chapter 8, section entitled "Excursus"

125. Cf. Department of State, Memorandum for the President June 24, 1944, sub: Funds for John Franklin Carter, Box 100, PSF, FDRL, Hyde Park, NY; Henry Field, Memorandum on Office of Coordinator of Information (COI), later Office of Strategic Services, April 5, 1963; idem., Memorandum on Ernst Hanfstaengl, 5f, October 29, 1965, Box 44, Henry Field Papers, FDRL, Hyde Park, NY. Where the money involving Field was concerned, this was the Emergency Fund for President, Allotment to State Department, Office of Secretary, 19–110/200002 (01).002, Allocation No. 92 (ibid., 6, fn.); John Franklin Carter to President Truman, April 24, 1945, Intelligence Reports, Box 14, Rose Conway File, Papers of Harry S. Truman, Truman Library, Independence, Missouri. Basic information on the budget of the Carter organization may be found in Boxes 2–4, Harold D. Smith Papers, FDRL, Hyde Park.

126. Brief Summary of the Principal Operations of this Unit (February 1941-November 1945), 9, appendix to John Franklin Carter to President Harry S. Truman, November 6, 1945, Rose Conway File, Papers of Harry S. Truman, Truman Library, Independence, Missouri. Among other things, early in 1944 Carter sent an election observer to London, and one year later Henry Field went to Moscow as the member of an international group of scientists. Ibid., p. 5 ff.

127. Cf. Interview Charles T. Morrissey, John Franklin Carter, February 9, 1966, Washington, D.C. (= Interview Morrisey, Carter), John F. Kennedy Library Oral History Project, John F. Kennedy Library, Boston, MA; duplicate in OHP: J.F.Carter, FDRL, Hyde Park, N.Y. In 1931 Jay Franklin's book *What We Are About to Receive* was published.

128. Interview Morrisey, Carter, 4, JFKL, Boston, MA; [Memorandum] Dr. Ernst Franz Sedgwick HANFSTAENGL, n.d., Box 44, Henry Field Papers, FDRL, Hyde Park, NY.

129. Cf. Interview Morrisey, Carter, 4, ibid., pp. 4–6. As a result of an editorial faux pas, Carter, the founder of the left-leaning New National Party, was linked to National Socialists in the U.S. Documents about this may be found in the John Franklin Carter Papers, American Heritage Center, University of Wyoming, Laramie, Wyoming.

130. Cf. Interview Morrisey, Carter, 11, JFKL, Boston, MA; *Ernst Hanfstaengl, The Missing Years* (London: Eyre and Spottiswoode, 1957), especially pp. 292 ff.

131. Brief Summary of the Principal Operations of this Unit (February 1941-November 1945), 2–3, John Franklin Carter to President Harry S. Truman, November 6, 1945, Rose Conway File, Papers of Harry S. Truman, Truman Library, Independence, Missouri; Henry Field to William Donovan, October 11, 1941, Box 44, Henry Field Papers, FDRL; some of the Polish Intelligence Reports are located in Box 99, PSF, FDRL, Hyde Park, NY. On Henry Field, see Memorandum on Office of Coordinator of Information (COI), later Office of Strategic Services, April 5, 1963, Box 44, Henry Field Papers, FDRL, Hyde Park, NY.

132. R. J. Campbell, British Embassy Washington, D.C. to John Franklin Carter, June 23, 1942, Box 44, Henry Field Papers, FDRL, Hyde Park, NY; Memorandum by Edward A. Tamm

(FBI) to [J. Edgar Hoover], March 13, 1942, File Hanfstangl [sic], 100–76954-[], FBI Archives, Washington, D.C. Among the various Hitler biographies, John Toland's standard work offers the most solidly attested details about the Hitler-Hanfstaengl relationship. John Toland, *Adolf Hitler* (Garden City, NY, 1976), especially pp. 128 ff., 140 ff., 172 ff., 181 ff., 323 ff.

133. Cf. Ernst Hanfstaengl, *Zwischen Weißem und Braunem Haus: Memoiren eines politischen Außenseiters* (Munich, 1970), p. 279 ff.

134. Joachim C. Fest, *Hitler: Eine Biographie* (Berlin—Frankfurt, 1973), p. 201.

135. [Memorandum], Dr. Ernst Franz Sedgwick HANFSTAENGL, n. d., (appendix to R. J. Campbell, British Embassy Washington, D.C. to John Franklin Carter, June 23, 1942), Box 44 Henry Field Papers, FDRL, Hyde Park, NY; Memorandum for the Director, re: Ernst Franz Sedgwick Hanfstaengl, alias Putzi Hanfstaengl, November 30, 1943, File Hanfstangl, 100–76954–39, FBI Archives, Washington, D.C. In the first memorandum cited above, a number of documents are analyzed that confirm Hanfstaengl's Nazi sympathies for the years 1938 and 1939. In addition, evidence is cited placing responsibility for the failure to reconcile with Hitler on Hanfstaengl's exorbitant demands and the outbreak of the war. On his internment in Canada, see Hanfstaengl, *The Missing Years*, pp. 292 ff. On the circumstances of Hanfstaengl's escape, there are several reports in addition to his own account. Cf., on this point, the File Hanfstangl in the FBI archive, especially Memorandum Robert C. Hendon to Mr. Tolson, re: Dr. Ernst Franz Sedgewick (Putzi) Hanfstaengl. Internal Security—G, April 1, 1944, 100–76954–45, FBI Archives, Washington, D.C. and L. B. Nichols, Memorandum for Mr. Tolson, January 29, 1943, 100–76954–12, FBI Archives, Washington, D.C. After Hanfstaengl's emigration, Hitler attempted to cover up the genuine differences he had with Hanfstaengl by accusing him of intolerable stinginess and avarice. Henry Picker, *Hitlers Tischgespräche im Führerhauptquartier. Vollständig überarbeitete und erweiterte Neuausgabe mit bisher unbekannten Selbstzeugnissen Adolf Hitlers, Abbildungen, Augenzeugenberichten und Erläuterungen des Autors: Hitler, wie er wirklich war* (Stuttgart, 1976), p. 423 ff., 424 fn.

136. Interview Morrisey, Carter, 12, JFKL, Boston, MA. (E. Hanfstaengl, *Zwischen Weißem und Braunem Haus*, p. 280).

137. R. J. Campbell, British Embassy Washington, D.C. to John Franklin Carter, June 23, 1942, Box 44, Henry Field Papers, FDRL, Hyde Park, NY; a copy went to Sumner Welles, "because of his personal interest in the scheme." Hanfstaengl gave Carter his word of honor that he would follow all the rules imposed on him. [Word of Honor to John Franklin Carter], Ernst S. Hanfstaengl, July 1, 1942, Box 44, Henry Field Papers, FDRL, Hyde Park, NY.

138. D. M. Ladd, Memorandum for the Director, re: Putzi Hanfstangel [sic], July 2, 1942, 100–76954–12, FBI Archives. Interestingly, as early as March 1942 William Donovan had already expressed an interest in extraditing Putzi Hanfstaengl and had already approached the FBI. Memorandum by Edward A. Tamm (FBI) to [J. Edgar Hoover], March 13, 1942, File Hanfstangl, 100–76954-[], FBI-Archives; letter to Edgar Hoover, Cleveland, Tennessee, n.d., File Hanfstangl, 10076954–23, FBI Archives, Washington, D.C.

139. Henry Field, Memorandum on Ernst Hanfstaengl, 6, October 29, 1965, Box 44, Henry Field Papers, FDRL, Hyde Park, NY.

140. Ibid., p 7 ff. Bush Hill belonged to a cousin of Henry Field, who was happy to evacuate the house. Under the circumstances, it was altogether advantageous that the driveways were completely overgrown and not passable for automobiles. Cf, in addition, Hanfstaengl, *Zwischen Weißem und Braunem Haus*, p. 381. On the FCC and its cooperation with the OSS,

see "The Radio Divisions and How They Operated," Ch. XVIII in Deuel History of the OSS, Folder 14, Box 73, Entry 99, RG 226, NA.

141. Ibid., 9. Cf., further, Memorandum on Ernst Hanfstaengl, p. 4 ff., October 29, 1965, Box 44, Henry Field Papers, FDRL, Hyde Park, NY. Details about the guard personnel may be found in the letter from Edward A. Tamms to J. Edgar Hoover (cc Mr. Ladd), January 7, 1944, 100–76954–40, FBI Archives, Washington, D.C. On Field's activities, cf. (in addition to his own records), E. Hanfstaengl, *Zwischen Weißem und Braunem Haus*, p. 383.

142. Henry Field, Memorandum on Ernst Hanfstaengl, 11f, October 29, 1965, Box 44, Henry Field Papers, FDRL, Hyde Park, NY.

143. Cf. ibid., pp. 9–12. Regarding the books that Hanfstaengl requested, none of his wishes went unfulfilled; he had at his disposal a superb private library, which even included the 20-volume Brockhaus encyclopedia.

144. Interview Morrisey, Carter, 11f, JFKL, Boston, MA.

145. Report on Conversations, December 24, 1943; J.F.C., Report on Hanfstaengl, December 28, 1943, Box 99, PSF, FDRL, Hyde Park, NY.

146. Notes on the Present Crisis, 1, September 23, 1943, Box 99, PSF, FDRL, Hyde Park, NY. The report was sent to FDR the same day, J.F.C. to F.D.R., Hanfstaengl Report on Allied Policy towards Germany, September 23, 1943, Box 99, PSF, FDRL, Hyde Park, NY.

147. Ibid., 1–2. The theme of Bolshevism vs. Christianity (Niemöller vs. Stalin) crops up in numerous Hanfstaengl comments. Cf. Hitler's Roofless Fortress Europe and Party-Member Number Zero, November 25, 1943; J.F.C. to F.D.R., Report from Putzi Hanfstaengl on Religious Situation in Germany, November 26, 1943, Box 99, PSF, FDRL, Hyde Park, NY. For the criticism of the Casablanca formula, see Hanfstaengl, *Zwischen Weißem und Braunem Haus*, p. 382.

148. Among other things, Hanfstaengl suggested sending Lochner to Switzerland, since he could establish contacts with the General Staff and German industrialists, and since people like Schacht frequently went to spas in Switzerland. Report on Putzi Hanfstaengl's Suggestions for Swiss Contacts, October 29, 1943; J.F.C., Report on Interview with Putzi Hanfstaengl [Interviewer Arthur Uphma Pope], December 6, 1943; Memorandum on Ernst Jünger, December 6, 1943, Box 99, PSF, FDRL, Hyde Park, NY. Hanfstaengl's aversion to Goebbels, by the way, was mutual (as the Goebbels diaries demonstrate). Cf., above all, the entries for August 8, 15, and 16, 1936, 19, for February 13, March 20, and April 13, 1937, and January 31, 1941. Joseph Goebbels, *Tagebücher 1924–1945*, vol 3, ed. by Ralf Georg Reuth (Munich/Zürich, 1992).

149. J.F.C., Report on Hanfstaengl, December 28, 1943, Box 99, PSF, FDRL, Hyde Park, NY.

150. Interview Morrisey, Carter, 16f, JFKL, Boston, MA. ON August 11, 1943 John Franklin Carter sent a report to FDR, requisitioned by Henry Field via Polish secret intelligence channels, which confirmed the German version of the events. Report on Katyn, August 11, 1943, Box 99, PSF, FDRL, Hyde Park, NY.

151. [Ernst Hanfstaengl], Adolf Hitler, December 3, 1942 [68 pages], Box 45, John Toland Papers, FDRL. On the basis of OSS material and published documents, Henry A. Murray prepared a 53-page analysis of Hitler's personality that, according to Carter, amounted to an unexpected vindication of Hanfstaengl's study: Henry A. Murray, M.D., "Analysis of The Personality of Adolph [sic] Hitler. With Predictions of His Future Behavior and Suggestions for Dealing with Him Now and After Germany's Surrender" (copy 1 of 30), October 1943; J.F.C., "Report on Psychiatric Analysis of Adolf Hitler," October 28, 1943; Henry Field, Memoran-

dum on Hitler's Psychology, October 29, 1943, Box 99, PSF, FDRL; Interoffice Memo, Henry Field to Major John McDonough, Subject: Biographical Sketch of Hitler, December 3, 1943, Box 45, John Toland Papers, FDRL. The Hitler study went both to Harry Hopkins and FDR; the latter obviously was very interested in it and called it "Hitler's Bedtime Story." The study was the first in the "Know Your Enemy" series. On the origins of the Hitler biography, see Memorandum on Ernst Hanfstaengl, p. 5 ff., October 29, 1965, Box 44, Henry Field Papers, FDRL, Hyde Park, NY.

152. John Franklin Carter, Memorandum for Miss Tully, "Fake Hitler" Suggestion, June 7, 1944, Box 100, PSF, FDRL, Hyde Park, NY.

153. Report on Suggested Fake Speech by Hitler to Aid Invasion, n. d., Box 100, PSF, FDRL, Hyde Park, NY.

154. E. Hanfstaengl, *Zwischen Weißem und Braunem Haus*, p. 383. It was, incidentally, clear to Henry Field, who detested "Hitler's piano player," that he was going to play a negative role in Hanfstaengl's memoirs ("I expect to figure as an uncompromising jailer"), Memorandum on Ernst Hanfstaengl, October 29, 1965, Box 44, Henry Field Papers, FDRL, Hyde Park.

155. Roosevelt's request for opinions dates from June 3.

156. G. Edward Buxton to Miss Grace Tully; G. Edward Buxton, Memorandum for the President, 7 June, 1944; Box 100, PSF, FDRL, Hyde Park, NY.

157. Although the position papers from the OSS and State Department did not give the project much of a chance, John Franklin Carter suggested in a letter to Roosevelt's secretary Grace Tully that the memoranda of Buxton and Stettinius should be interpreted positively, and that the plan now only needed to be accepted by the President. J.F. Carter, Memorandum for Miss Tully: "Fake Hitler" Suggestion, June 7, 1944, Box 100, PSF, FDRL, Hyde Park, NY. Edward Stettinius, Memorandum for the President, Proposal for Fake Hitler Propaganda, June 7, 1944, Box 100, PSF, FDRL, Hyde Park, NY. On Edward R. Stettinius, Jr. and his role as Chef of State Intelligence, see Troy, *Donovan and the CIA*, especially p. 222 ff.

158. E. Hanfstaengl, *Zwischen Weißem und Braunem Haus*, p. 382; on Hanfstaengl's world view, Sedwick Report, Part XLV, January 27, 1944, in which Hanfstaengl tells why there will never be a separate Russo-German peace or political "final accord" between the two nations; in addition, J.F.C., Report on Nazi Psychology and the Seven Years War, January 19, 1944, where Hanfstaengl discusses the contemporary relevance of the "Frederician legend," both in Box 100, PSF, FDRL, Hyde Park, NY.

159. Edward A. Tamms to J. Edgar Hoover (cc Mr. Ladd), January 7, 1944, 100–76954–40, FBI Archives, Washington, D.C. The danger that the location of Hanfstaengl's residence might leak out was magnified by the fact that the journalists Drew Pearson and Joseph Alsop lived across the street, where the courier who commuted back and forth between Bush Hill and Georgetown (Henry Field's residence) parked his motorcycle early every morning. Field also was apparently followed several times on his way to Hanfstaengl. Henry Field, Memorandum on Ernst Hanfstaengl, October 29, 1965, 13, Box 44, Henry Field Papers, FDRL, Hyde Park, NY.

160. J.F.C. Report on Security Arrangements for Putzi Hanfstaengl, January 17, 1944; Attorney General Francis Biddle to President Roosevelt, January 17, 1944; F.D.R, Memorandum for John Franklin Carter, Box 99, PSF, FDRL, Hyde Park, NY.

161. On September 3 Carter proposed that Roosevelt ask the British to end Hanfstaengl's POW status. Churchill replied in the negative. J.F.C. to F.D.R., Report on Letters from Putzi

Hanfstaengl to You and Mr. Churchill, September 3, 1943; F.D.R., Memorandum for Jack (!) Carter, September 15, 1943, Box 99, PSF, FDRL, Hyde Park, NY.

162. Cf. Hanfstaengl, *The Missing Years*, p. 298 ff.; idem., *Zwischen Weißem und Braunem Haus*, p. 385. Stettinius's view may be found in the Memorandum for the President, June 22, 1944, Box 100, PSF, FDRL, Hyde Park, NY. After Carter found out about Hanfstaengl's impending deportation, he turned to Roosevelt with a letter pleading for special protection for Hanfstaengl against attacks by Nazi POWs and against punitive hostilities from official British circles. Roosevelt gave his O.K., Report on Turning Putzi Hanfstaengl over to the British, July 7, 1944 (with "J.F.C. OK FDR" on the document, July 14, 1944), Box 100, PSF, FDRL, Hyde Park, NY. Carter kept President Roosevelt up to date for months to come on Hanfstaengl and his (mostly financial) affairs. The corresponding letters may be found in Box 100, PSF, FDRL, Hyde Park, NY.

163. "My self-appointed mission had failed, had been a failure for many months." Hanfstaengl, *The Missing Years*, p. 298; idem., *Vom Weißen zum Braunen Haus*, p. 384. As early as 1943, Hanfstaengl had been insisting that he could not see any indications of internal weaknesses in Nazi Germany, and that the war therefore had to be ended militarily if the U.S. was not going to alter its propaganda line. Hanfstaengl stuck to this position until he was extradited to the British. Cf., for example, Report on Conversations, December 24, 1943, Box 99, PSF, FDRL, Hyde Park, NY; Brief Summary of the Principal Operations of this Unit (February 1941-November 1945), 2, appendix to John Franklin Carter to President Harry S. Truman, November 6, 1945, Rose Conway File, Papers of Harry S. Truman, Truman Library, Independence, Missouri.

164. After the deportation there was a lot of tugging back and forth between Hanfstaengl and Carter, since Hanfstaengl viewed the Steinway grand piano as his property and requested that the proceeds from the instrument be sent to him, though this was a violation of the Alien Property Act. Cable from Putzi Hanfstaengl, JFC to FDR, January 4, 1945, Box 100, PSF, FDRL, Hyde Park, NY. Cf. Hanfstaengl, *Vom Weißen zum Braunen Haus*, pp. 380–383.

165. Interview Morrisey, Carter, 23f, JFKL, Boston, MA.

166. The volume dedicated to FDR is in the Roosevelt Library in Hyde Park. Ernst Hanfstaengl, ed., *Hitler in der Karikatur der Welt. Tat gegen Tinte – Ein Bildsammelwerk* (Berlin, 1933).

167. Cf. C. Andrew, *For the President's Eyes Only*, pp. 107, 156.

168. L.L. Montague, The Origins of National Intelligence Estimating, 64, Folder 99, Box 12, T. Troy Papers, RG 263, NA.

169. A history of the Foreign Information Service comprising 100 pages and written by Wallace Deuel may be found in Box 72, Entry 99, RG 226, NA.

170. For the War Theatre Building (WTB), which was conceived as the American counterpart to Churchill's War Office Rooms, 3.8 million dollars—roughly one third of the entire COI budget—were originally allocated. Summary of 1942 Budget Request. Coordinator of Information (with FDR's "O.K.," November 7, 1941), reprinted T. Troy, *Donovan and the CIA*, p. 112. On how the WTB was designed to be equipped, see Interview C. Mauch/D. McLaughlin, Garret Park, MD, October 7, 1996, OSSOHP. In a conversation with the author, Charles Kindleberger summarized the then current prejudices about the concept of visually presenting war planning with the sardonic remark: "They [the visual presentation people in COI] believed that generals can't read for more than 20 minutes without having to go to the bathroom and scratch themselves and so on. So they decided

to make Disney cartoons." (Interview C. Mauch/C. P. Kindleberger, January 17, 1997, Lexington, MA, OSSOHP.

171. On recruiting practice in the COI, see Laurie, *Ideology and American Propaganda*, p. 191 ff.; also John Houseman, *Front and Center* (New York, 1979), p. 45 ff.

172. Charlotte Bowman emphasizes that James Baxter was the one who made it possible in the first place to recruit military people for the R&A: "I think one of the things that he [Baxter] arranged for us was to be able to have working for us people in the services. We had allotments of army enlisted men and officers, Navy officers, even a few Marines." Interview S. Beer, C. Mauch/C. Bowman, January 18, Bennington, Vermont, OSSOHP. Sherwood's intentions and basic ideas about recruiting FIS personnel are formulated in several memoranda addressed to Donovan in the summer of 1941: R. Sherwood to W.J. Donovan, June 16, 1941; July 25, 1941 Folder 8b, Box 71, Entry 99, RG 226, NA; Sherwood to Donovan, July 31, 1941; August 18, 1941, Box 99b, WJD Papers, USAMI, Carlisle Barracks, Pa.; on recruitment practices, cf., in addition, T. Troy, *Donovan and the CIA*, p.74 ff.

173. Donovan's headquarters was located, as of September 1941 on 25th and E Street in Washington. Interview C. Beer, C. Mauch/C.Bowman, January 18, Bennington, Vermont, OSSOHP. Sherwood's FIS was located on 270 Madison Avenue, New York City; see T. Troy, *Donovan and the CIA*, p. 87.

174. Michaela Hönicke, "Know Your Enemy: American Images of Germany in World War II," 10, SHAFR Meeting June 19, 1993; author's emphasis.

175. On Donovan's conception of psychological warfare, see WROSSACB, p. 47; on Sherwood, cf. A.M. Winkler, *The Politics of Propaganda* (New York, 1978), pp. 9, 18, 27 ff.

176. Taylor, *Awakening from History* , p. 244 ff. On Woburn Abbey, see Soley, *Radio Warfare (New York, 1979)*, p. 25. On British training of COI/OSS agents, also see Sefton Delmer, *Black Boomerang* (London, 1962), p. 214 ff.; MO WD, Vol. 6, Basic Documents, Box 4, Entry 91, RG 226, NA.

177. Taylor, *Awakening from History* pp. 309 ff. and Edmond L. Taylor, Proposed Functions of OSS Committee, July 27, 1942, Box 99b, WJD Papers, USAMI, Carlisle Barracks, Pa.

178. Taylor, *Awaking from History*, p. 244; L. Soley, *Radio Propaganda*, p. 65.

179. Walter Langer received his doctorate in 1935 from Harvard's department of clinical psychology and studied psychoanalysis from 1937 to 1939 in Vienna and London, where he had been analyzed by Anna Freud. The stations of Langer's career through 1945 are listed, among other places, in Dr. Walter C. Langer to John Toland, April 6, 1972, Box 52, John Toland Papers, FDRL, Hyde Park, NY.

180. Walter C. Langer to Colonel Donovan, December 10, 1941 and November 13, 1941, Folder 8a (1 of 2), Box 71, Entry 99, RG 226, NA; Walter C. Langer, Recommendations and suggestions on Shortwave broadcasts to Germany, file World Situation 1941–42, Box 5, Entry 6H, RG 208, NA.

181. The proponents of the PFU also included Wallace Deuel, who otherwise stood completely behind Sherwood and, whenever possible, praised his political idealism. Wallace R. Deuel to Col. Donovan, sub: Report by Dr. Walter C. Langer, November 10, 1941, Folder 8a (1 of 2), Box 71, Entry 99, RG 226, NA. Wallace Deuel to Robert W. Bliss, July 3, 1942, Box 1, Wallace Deuel Papers, LOC, Washington, D.C.

182. Sherwood Memorandum, [Comments on memoranda of Dr. Walter C. Langer of November 13, 1941], n.d., Folder 8a (1 of 2), Box 71, Entry 99, RG 226, NA. The wide array of obstacles Langer encountered during his brief tenure as head of the PFU is listed in Walter C.

Langer to Colonel Donovan, December 10, 1941, Folder 8a (1 of 2), Box 71, Entry 99, RG 226, NA; on the work of the PFU, see Walter C. Langer to John Toland, Box 52, John Toland Papers, FDRL, Hyde Park, NY. After Langer was fired, to be sure, Donovan made him his special assistant (Special Psychological Consultant to General Donovan and the Office of Strategic Services); Langer to Toland, April 6, 1972, Box 52, John Toland Papers, FDRL, Hyde Park, NY.

183. The Clandestine War in Europe (1942–1945). Remarks of William J. Casey on receipt of the William J. Donovan Award at Dinner of Veterans of O.S.S., December 5, 1974, Folder Casey, Box 1, Persico Papers, Hoover Institution, Stanford. The philosopher, and later President of the ACLS, Frederick Burkhardt, reported that—in the context of "Operation Bughouse," which seized post satchels full of German documents in Bucharest in August 1944—there was one man belonging to the R&A team whose specialty was breaking into German safes. Interview C. Mauch, C. Beer/F. Burkhardt, January 19, 1997, Bennington, Vermont, OSSOHP.

184. Sherwood Memorandum, [Comments on memoranda of Dr. Walter C. Langer of November 13, 1941], n.d., Folder 8a (1 of 2), Box 71, Entry 99, RG 226, NA.

185. Vgl. WROSSACB, p. 44 ff.

186. Memorandum, Sherwood to F. D. Roosevelt [n.d.], Box 72, Entry 99, RG 226, NA; Robert Sherwood to William J. Donovan, October 20, 1941, OF 4485, FDRL, Hyde Park, NY.

187. Memorandum to the President (Personal and Confidential), March 19, 1942, COI Files, Box 128, PSF, FDRL, Hyde Park, NY.

188. Ibid., also 194 White House Memorandum for the Secretary of War, March 21, 1942; War Department Memo, May 18, 1942, COI Files, Box 128, PSF, FDRL, Hyde Park, NY.

189. Ibid.

190. On criticism of the Budget Director, Memorandum for the President, February 19, 1942; Memorandum for the President: Reorganization of War Information Services, March 7, 1942, Box 17, Harold Smith Papers, FDRL, Hyde Park, NY; on the debate between the COI and State Department, cf. Why State Department should not handle U.S. Foreign Propaganda, Nelson P. Poynter to Col. William J. Donovan, January 28, 1942, Folder 8b, Box 71, Entry 99, RG 226, NA. Cpt. Francis C. Denebrink was seconded from the armed forces and submitted proposals to the JCS for military uses of the COI., JCS Minutes of Meeting, March 2, 1942, No.23; [Cpt. Denebrink], Memorandum for General Smith, June 10, 1942, No.255, MF Reel 1, Records of the JCS, I: 1942–1945, MF Publication, Frederick, MD, n. d. At the beginning of 1942 the press was taking a special look at the "publicity cost" of the COI and of other government offices; see, for example, NYT, February 17, 1942, 4.

191. Arthur M. Schlesinger Jr., *The Coming of the New Deal* (Boston, 1959), pp. 527 ff., 583 ff.; Richard E. Neustadt, *Presidential Power* (New York, 1964), p.154 ff.; Dallek, *Franklin D. Roosevelt and American Foreign Policy*, p. 29.

192. In making this assessment, the author is going against the current conventional wisdom among researchers, which is to portray Donovan and Sherwood as losers but overlook the fact that, in light of pressures both from the public and from inside the government, there was really no alternative to dissolving and restructuring the COI. Thomas Troy calls the creation of the OSS "unwelcome news for him [Donovan]." Clayton Laurie's evaluation: "In reality the settlement of July 1942 was not a true victory for either side." Troy, *Donovan and the CIA*, p. 152; Laurie, *Propaganda Warriors*, p. 11.

193. Executive Order 9182: Consolidating Certain War Information Functions into an Office of War Information, June 13, 1942, reprinted as Appendix D in: T. Troy, *Donovan and the*

CIA, pp. 424–426; Military Order of June 13, 1942: Office of Strategic Services, June 13, 1942, reprinted as Appendix E, ibid., p. 427.

194. Roosevelt himself had proposed Elmer Davis as OWI Director. On this point, cf. Allen Winkler, who also quotes the bon mot attributed to Roosevelt about the "funny radio commentator." Winkler, *The Politics of Propaganda*, p. 34. The press, on the whole, reacted quite positively to Roosevelt's decision. *Time* called Elmer Davis a "Man of Sense" (June 22, 1942, p. 21), and only *Newsweek* mocked both Davis and the new information office. (June 22, 1942, p. 30). On E. Davis, see Roger Burlingame, *Don't Let Them Scare You: The Life and Times of Elmer Davis* (Westport, CT, 1974). In addition, biographical information and correspondence may be found in the Davis Papers, MD LOC, Washington, D.C. Milton Eisenhower, Eisenhower's younger brother, became associate director of the OWI and Archibald MacLeish, the poet and Director of the Library of Congress, became assistant director for policy development.

195. JCS 155/4/D, December 23, 1942. Approved December 22, 1942: Directive Functions of the Office of Strategic Services, reprinted as Appendix H, in: Troy, *Donovan and the CIA*, pp. 431–343.

196. Troy, *Donovan and the CIA*, p.124.

197. A few staff members, including Wallace Deuel and Edmond Taylor, decided to remain loyal to Donovan and not to Sherwood; they transferred from the COI-FIS to the OSS. Staff statistics may be found in the COI Statistical Report for Year Ending 30 June 1942, Box 81, Entry 99, RG 226, NA.; Executive Order 9182, Appendix D in: Troy, *Donovan and the CIA*, p. 424.

3. 1943: THE TURNING POINT

1. Memorandum by Adolf A. Berle, Political Propaganda Campaign Directed Toward Germany, Folder 70, Box 9, Entry 106, RG 266, NA, excerpts reprinted in *AmIntel*, Doc. 2, 20–24; *UUDW*, Doc.1, 15–17; Political-Propaganda Campaign, April 23, 1942, Box 214, Berle Papers, FDRL, Hyde Park, NY.

2. On Berle, see *Navigating the Rapids 1918–1971: From the Papers of Adolf A. Berle*, edited by Beatrice Bishop Berle and Travis Beal Jacobs, Introduction by Max Ascoli (New York, 1973); Jordan A. Schwarz, *Liberal: Adolf A. Berle and the Vision of an American Era* (New York/London, Free Press 1987); Toole, *Encyclopedia*, p. 65 ff.; in addition, [Biographical Sketch] in A. A. Berle Papers, FDRL, Hyde Park, NY. In the State Department Berle was in charge of the Office of Controls as well as the Office of Transportation and Communications. The former included not just the passport and visa departments vital to intelligence activities, but also the Division of Foreign Activity Correlation and the Special War Problems Division. See Organization of the Department of State, Folder General Correspondence, Box 35, L. Harrison Papers, MDLOC, Washington, D.C.

3. Berle, "Political Propaganda Campaign," *AmIntel*, Doc. 2, p. 20.

4. Memorandum by Adolf Berle, [Intelligence on German situation], July 15, 1941, Box 213, Berle Papers, FDRL, Hyde Park, NY.

5. A document from the German General Staff, which Berle had received via MAGIC, and which had already predicted the Germans' Russia campaign as early as December 1940, made Berle feel certain that his sources could basically be trusted. That Berle read intercepted Japanese-German radio traffic emerges from an April 23 memorandum. Allen Dulles emphasizes that Berle "of course, has access to material not available to me." In a talk with

Berle on April 30, representatives of the COI asked him about the nature of his sources. Berle did not provide clear information; however he did explain that he was convinced of the materials' "authenticity." Berle, "Political Propaganda Campaign," *AmIntel*, Doc. 2, p. 21; Allen Dulles to William J. Donovan, Suggestions for Psychological Warfare, May 8, 1942, Folder 70, Box 9, Entry 106, RG 266, NA; *AmIntel*, Doc.3, p. 23; *UUDW*, Doc.2, p.17; Memorandum of Conversation, Thursday, April 30th [1942], at Department of State between Assistant Secretary of State Adolph Berle, Robert E. Sherwood, Wallace Deuel, Edmond Taylor and James P.Warburg, Folder 1521, Box 111, Entry 146, RG 226, NA.

6. Berle, "Political Propaganda Campaign," *AmIntel*, Doc. 2, p. 20 ff.

7. The letter shows all the signs of a profound divide between the COI director and the FIS boss. Robert E. Sherwood to Colonel William J. Donovan, May 6, 1942, Folder 1521, Box 111, Entry 146, RG 226, NA.

8. Memorandum of Conversation, Thursday, April 30th [1942], at Department of State, Folder 1521, Box 111, Entry 146, RG 226, NA.

9. The document cannot be found in the OSS files. Presumably it has to do with the German General Staff's plan from 1940, which announced the Russia campaign of the summer of 1941 and made generally gloomy predictions for 1942. That Berle was not prepared to show the document to his interlocutors was attributable to the fact that it had been intercepted via MAGIC.

10. Memorandum of Conversation, Thursday, April 30th [1942], at Department of State, Folder 1521, Box 111, Entry 146, RG 226, NA.

11. Stalin's order is reprinted in *Stalin spricht: Die Kriegsreden vom 3. Juli 1941 bis zum 9. Mai 1945* (Stockholm, 1945), pp. 39–46; cf. too Josef Stalin, *On the Great Patriotic War for the Soviet Union: Speeches, Orders of the Day, and Answers to Foreign Press Correspondents* (London, 1944), p. 27.

12. Cf. L. Kettenacker, *Krieg zur Friedenssicherung*, p.198.

13. Cited here according to Berle, Political Propaganda Campaign, April 23, 1942, Folder 1521, Box 111, Entry 146, RG 226, NA.

14. Ibid.

15. Allen Dulles to William J. Donovan, Suggestions for Psychological Warfare, May 8, 1942, Folder 70, Box 9, Entry 106, RG 226, NA, UUDW, Doc.2, 17–18.

16. Woodrow Wilson's Secretary of State Robert M. Lansing had married one of John W. Foster's daughters. Foster was Dulles's maternal grandfather and Secretary of State under Benjamin Harrison. On this, see Leonard Mosley, *Dulles: A Biography of Eleanor, Allen and John Foster Dulles and Their Family Network* (New York, 1978).

17. Dulles, Suggestions for Psychological Warfare, May 8, 1942, Folder 70, Box 9, Entry 106, RG 266, NA, UUDW, Doc.2, 17f.

18. An outstanding glimpse into Donovan's work method is provided by the interview with his secretary Eloise Page. T. Naftali / E. Page, March 31, 1997, OSSOHP.

19. Colonel Donovan to Dr. Baxter, May 9, 1942, Folder 1521, Box 111, Entry 146, RG 226, NA. Donovan, who had fought in the First World War with the 165th Infantry of the U.S. Army in France, recalled the "general strike" that broke out in January 1918. In his view, it was not the instances of insubordination encountered in mid-1918 within the German Navy and Army that had induced Germany's collapse, but rather the "virus of revolution" that the German troops had carried with them from the east.

20. In reality, the aircraft carrier battle in the Coral Sea ended in a draw. Furthermore, eight days after Timoschenko's offensive from the Donez bridgehead, the Germans had started a

counter-offensive in the direction of Charkov. A Commentary on Some Aspects of the German Domestic and Military Situation, May 29, 1942, Folder 1521, Box 111, Entry 146, RG 226, NA.

21. A COI study from late in 1941 had demonstrated that only 60 of 100 airplanes reached their target's territory, 12 found their actual target, and of these only four hit its target. Furthermore, the losses were too high to sustain the operations. A Commentary on Some Aspects of the German Domestic and Military Situation, May 29, 1942, Folder 1521, Box 111, Entry 146, RG 226, NA. In fact, the destruction perpetrated by the RAF between the autumn of 1940 and early 1942 was held in check. In this period, 120 residential buildings on average were destroyed each month, and 219 people killed. In the following year, this figure increased tenfold for residential buildings and threefold for human deaths. Cf. Erich Hampe, ed., *Der zivile Luftschutz im zweiten Weltkrieg: Dokumentation und Erfahrungsberichte über Aufbau und Einsatz* (Frankfurt, 1963), p.147.

22. On this, cf. the R&A study "German Oil Position," February 24, 1942, R&A 89; "Oil and Germany Strategy," March 5, 1942, R&A 225, MF 1221, RG 59, NA.

23. A Commentary on Some Aspects of the German Domestic and Military Situation, 3b, May 29, 1942, Folder 1521, Box 111, Entry 146, RG 226, NA.

24. Table "Personelle Verluste des Heeres an der deutsch-sowjetischen Front, Dezember 1941 bis April 1942," in *Deutschland im zweiten Weltkrieg*, Vol. 2, p. 274. Total losses were put at 1,167,836. Ibid., p. 274. As German total losses on the Eastern Front—as in Stalingrad—climbed dramatically, the British and their military intelligence service G-2 underestimated the extent of these losses on the Eastern Front, while R&A came up with incredibly exact figures. Franklin Ford, who had a glimpse into the working methods of the R&A division that dealt with population studies explained that G-2 "generally underestimated the German casualties on the eastern front. They couldn't believe that, for example, when Stalingrad was surrounded by the Russians, the Germans didn't have one more circle to come around that. . . . But the OSS population study came and did a remarkable job in this, partly by making use of non-secret information: a close study of local newspapers, which would go ahead and mention casualties, where the total for the region didn't suggest that they were anywhere near that high." Interview C. Mauch/F. Ford, Lexington, Mass., January 17, 1997, OSSOHP.

25. Concretely, this study indicated that average consumers, such as housewives and office clerks, had just 1,500–1,600 calories per day at the end of the First World War; in 1942, by contrast, they got 2,400 calories. Heavy laborers at the end of 1918 received just 2,300–2,500 calories, but in 1942 they were getting at least 4,000 calories. A Commentary on Some Aspects of the German Domestic and Military Situation, 21–22, May 29, 1942, Folder 1521, Box 111, Entry 146, RG 226, NA.

26. A Commentary on Some Aspects of the German Domestic and Military Situation, besonders 10–21, May 29, 1942, Folder 1521, Box 111, Entry 146, RG 226, NA.

27. Summary, in ibid.

28. The report was commissioned by the JPWCC. Measures in the Event of Russian Collapse in 1942, June 1, 1942, Roll 6, MF 1642, Entry 190, RG 226, NA. On the background to the estimation of the USSR by the OSS, see Betty Abrahamsen Dessants, "Ambivalent Allies: OSS' USSR Division, the State Department, and the Bureaucracy of Intelligence Analysis, 1941–1945," in *Intelligence and National Security* 11 (1996), pp. 722–753.

29. In addition to Churchill's memoirs (*Hinge of Fate*), the complete Churchill-Roosevelt correspondence edited by Kimball as well as the Churchill-Roosevelt correspondence edited by Loewenheim et. al., the FRUS volume *Conferences at Washington and Casablanca*, pp. 488–496, provides a glimpse into the discussions between Roosevelt and Churchill at the

end of 1942; further, Dallek, *Franklin D. Roosevelt and American Foreign Policy*, esp. p. 366 ff. That Churchill at the end of 1942 was hardly committed to a clear-cut line is indicated by a key document from December 1942, Chief of Staff Minutes, COS Meeting, December 16, 1942, CAB 79/58 (Chiefs of Staff Minutes), PRO, Kew. That Roosevelt's plans for 1943 were still largely tentative during the summer of 1942 emerges from a memorandum sent by FDR to General Marshall, Admiral King, and Hon. Harry L. Hopkins, July 15, 1942, Box 4, Safe File, PSF, FDRL, Hyde Park, NY.

30. Colonel Donovan to Dr. Langer, November 26, 1942, Folder 2050, Box 139, Entry 146, RG 226, NA.

31. Discussion of the Board of Analysts Request from Col. Donovan, n. d., Folder 2050, Box 139, Entry 146, NA, RG 226. In addition to Charles Remer, Emile Despres and Donald C. McKay were among those taking part in the discussion. On the Board of Analysts (BOA), see the description of its tasks from September 19, Box 1, Entry 58, RG 226, NA. The negative assessment is from B. Katz, *Foreign Intelligence*, p. 4; also providing a critical perspective on the BOA is B. F. Smith, *Shadow Warriors*, p. 76 ff.

32. On Wiley's activity in the FNB see Ch. II.

33. [Board of Analysts], The Strategic Problem for 1943, [December 5, 1942], 1943, Folder 2051, Box 139, Entry 146, RG 226, NA. In the documents there are both internal and external indications of Wiley's authorship. See, for example, Fellers to Wiley, sub: Notes on Strategic Problem for 1943, January 14, 1943, Folder 2050, Box 139, Entry 146, RG 226, NA. Cf, too, the revised version from mid-January [John C. Wiley et al.], The Strategic Problem for 1943, January 16, 1943, Folder 2051, Box 139, Entry 146, RG 226, NA.

34. In the Board of Analysts discussions, Remer had favored attacking Burma and setting up American air bases in southern China. Discussion of the Board of Analysts Request from Col. Donovan, n. d., Folder 2050, Box 139, Entry 146, NA, RG 226.

35. Wiley saw that there was a special technical problem for psychological warfare operations owing to the fact that there was hardly any radio equipment in the countries occupied by Japan. The Strategic Problem for 1943, January 16, 1943, 6, Folder 2051, Box 139, Entry 146, RG 226, NA. Bonner Fellers, incidentally, was even less convinced than the OSS that psychological warfare actions could be implemented in the Pacific. See Fellers's comments on Basic OSS Psychological Warfare Plan for the Pacific, Box 3, Bonner Fellers Papers, Hoover Institution, Cal; on this, B. F. Smith, *Shadow Warriors*, p. 65, fn.103.

36. The basis for this assessment was, among other things, a study by Wayne C. Grover and H. Stuart Hughes. Wayne C. Grover/Lt. H.S. Hughes to Donald C. McKay, Attrition in the Pacific, December 2, 1942, Folder 2050, Box 139, Entry 146, RG 226, NA.

37. Cited here according to the final version of the BOA memorandum, The Strategic Problem for 1943, January 16, 1943, 6, Folder 2051, Box 139, Entry 146, RG 226, NA.

38. Ibid., 3, 9–15.

39. William Donovan to William L. Langer, December 17, 1942, Folder 2050, Box 139, Entry 146, NA, RG 226.

40. Fellers was a member of the OSS Planning Group, whose members were delegated by the Secretary of State, Chief of Staff, U.S. Army, Commander-in-Chief, U.S. Fleet, Chief of Naval Operations, and Director of Strategic Services. Memorandum James Grafton Rogers to Henry Morgenthau, February 6, 1943, 606:178, Roll 178, Morgenthau Diary, FDRL, Hyde Park, NY; William L. Langer to Colonel William J. Donovan, December 5, 1942, Folder 2050, Box 139, Entry 146, RG 226, NA.

41. The same opinion can already be found in a series of memoranda from the summer of 1942, Bonner F. Fellers Papers, Hoover Institution, Stanford CA; for biographical information, see Biographical Notes, Bonner Frank Fellers (1896–1973), Register, ibid..

42. Conclusions, in: [B. Fellers], The Strategic Problem for 1943, n. d. [ca. January 10, 1943], Folder 2051, Box 139, Entry 146, RG 226, NA (On dating and authorship, William L. Langer und John C. Wiley; Folder 2050, Box 139, Entry 146, RG 226, NA..

43. The Strategic Problem for 1943, 1–3, Folder 2051, Box 139, Entry 146, RG 226, NA.

44. Ibid., p. 5 ff. Fellers pointed out that the island of Hokkaido was not sufficiently secured and offered an outstanding base from which to launch a blow against the Japanese main island. For this reason he believed that it would be easy to convince the Japanese, and therefore the Germans, about a major operation in the Far East.

45. The British, to be sure, discovered the intelligence leak, but the warning they cabled to Cairo arrived too late to prevent Rommel's victorious strike. John W. Gordon, *The Other Desert War: British Special Forces in North Africa, 1940–1943* (New York. 1987), pp. 100–103; Hans-Otto Behrendt, *Rommel's Intelligence in the Desert Campaign, 1941–1943* (London, 1985), Appendix II; Kahn, *Codebreakers*, p. 472 ff.; Hinsley, *British Intelligence*, Vol. 2, p. 356 ff.; Vol. 5, p. 65.

46. Bonner Fellers to John C. Wiley, Sub: Strategic Problem for 1943 [with reference to the raw draft of Wiley"s memorandum], January 11, 1943, Folder 2050, Box 139, Entry 146, RG 226, NA.

47. Emile Despres to Dr. William L. Langer, sub: Notes from General Fellers, January 15, 1943, Folder 2050, Box 139, Entry 146, RG 226, NA. Despres was the head of the Economic Group (later Economic Section) of R&A; before he was on the staff of the COI/OSS he had been working in the Division of Research and Statistics of the Federal Reserve Board. See Katz, *Foreign Intelligence*, p. 98 ff.

48. As far as the critical importance of Romanian oil was concerned, the OSS had information largely identical with that of British secret intelligence. See B. F. Fellers to James G. Rogers, Sub: German Oil Supply, January 25, 1943, Folder 2050, Box 139, Entry 146, RG 226, NA. From the perspective of the R&A, some of the factors militating against bombing the refineries were 1) that these were hard to destroy and 2) that the raw oil extracted could also be processed by half of the refineries in operation. (Despres to Langer, January 15, 1943, Folder 2050, Box 139, Entry 146, RG 226, NA). Furthermore, the view in R&A was that the production sites for synthetic oil were easier to destroy than the oil facilities in Romania. This fundamental consideration was reflected in several R&A studies on the "Location of new synthetic oil plants and new oil fields in Germany," R&A 1628, 1628.1 etc. MF 1221, RG 59, NA.

49. That the establishment of a second front in 1943 would have been doomed to fail was something that Churchill repeatedly emphasized. (*The Second World War*, Vol. 3, p. 659 ff.; Vol. 4, p. 659). The opposite view was taken by, e.g., W. S. Dunn and J. Grigg. W. S. Dunn, *Second Front Now: 1943* (University, Ala., 1980); J. Grigg, *1943: The Victory That Never Was* (New York, 1980).

50. Fellers to Rogers, January 25, 1943; Fellers to Langer, Janaury 26, 1943; Langer to Board of Analysts, January 29, 1943, Folder 2050, Box 139, Entry 146, RG 226, NA.

51. Cf. here Dallek, *Franklin D. Roosevelt and American Foreign Policy*, especially pp. 369–379.

52. Bodo Scheurig, ed., *Verrat hinter Stacheldraht? Das Nationalkomitee "Freies Deutschland" und der Bund deutscher Offiziere in der Sowjetunion 1943–1945* (Munich, 1965); Bodo

Scheurig, *Freies Deutschland: Das Nationalkomitee und der Bund Deutscher Offiziere in der Sowjetunion 1939–1945* (Munich, 1960); Wolfgang Leonhard, *Die Revolution entläßt ihre Kinder* (Berlin, 1966), p. 227 ff.; for the most recent discussion, also see Peter Steinbach, "NKFD und Widerstand," in *Exilforschung* 8 (1990), pp. 61–91 and Gerd R. Ueberschär, ed., *Das Nationalkomitee "Freies Deutschland" und der Bund Deutscher Offiziere* (Frankfurt, 1996).

53. *Daily Worker*, July 22, 1943; partially reprinted in *NYT*, July 22, 1943.

54. James Grafton Rogers to General Magruder, Russian Manifesto of German Peace Offer, cc: Col. Buxton, Mr. Shepardson, Mr. Wiley, Col. Onthank, July 21, 1943, 22 July, 1943, Folder 100, Box 15, Entry 144, RG 226, NA; OSS Washington to OSS Bern [et al.], July 24, 1943, Box 165, Entry 134, RG 226, NA. Within two weeks, reactions poured in from all of the OSS outposts. The most concrete information came from Allen Dulles in Bern, who telegraphed Washington (by way of the legation) biographical information about the individual members of the NKFD as well as background information about the events in Stalingrad and Moscow. See, for example, the telegram Harrison for Victor, July 29, 1943, 103.918/455, RG 59, NA, as well as OSS Bern to Secretary of State, September 27, Folder 1078, Box 171, Entry 134, RG 226, NA; Telegram [OSS] Bern to Secretary of State, September 24, 1943, 103.918/1684, RG 59, NA.

55. Poole's authorship emerges from the document's specific idioms. Cf., additionally, DeWitt C. Poole to Col. Edward G. Buxton (personal and confidential), September 18, 1943 with appendix Excerpt from a Memorandum to the Planning Group, July 29, 1943, Folder 4, Box 1, DeWitt Poole Papers, SHSW, Madison, WI.

56. FNB, Memorandum for the Planning Group, July 29, 1943, ref: Memorandum of Dr. James Grafton Rogers, July 26, 1943, referring to the National Committee of Freies Deutschland, Folder 100, Box 15, Entry 144, RG 226, NA. The OSS Planning Group adopted the FNB theories on the origins of the NKFD, see Manifest to German People by Moscow National Committee for Free Germany, August 8, 1943, F091. Germany, ABC DF 1942–1948, OPD, RG 165, NA. On the Western evaluation of the NKFD, see Heike Bungert, "Ein meisterhafter Schachzug. Das Nationalkomitee Freies Deutschland in der Beurteilung der Amerikaner, 1943–1945," in Heideking/Mauch, *Geheimdienstkrieg gegen Deutschland*, pp. 90–121.

57. Graf Coudenhove-Kalergi was the President of the Pan-European Union, Milan Hodza the former prime minister of Czechoslovakia, Raoul Aglion led the Fighting French Delegation in New York. Julius Deutsch was a spokesman for the Austrian labor movement., Henry Ehrmann was active in "Neu Beginnen" ("New Beginning") alongside Paul Hagen; Stoyan Gavrilovich ran the Yugoslavian Information Center in the USA, Gerhart Seger edited the *Neue Volkszeitung* in New York, Albert Grzesinki was Chairman of the Association of Free Germans, and Greta Beigel had previously been editor of the Social Democratic newspaper *Der Tag* and now worked at OWI; Hans Simons was a former Prussian Finance Minister. Among the exiles cited in Poole's report there were, furthermore, Stefan de Ropp from the Polish Information Center; Sava Kosanovich, former Yugoslavian minister of state, Charles Davila, former Romanian envoy in Washington; Reinhold Schairer; Mrs. A.M. Brady from the Catholic Center of Information Pro Deo; Constantin Fotich, the Yugoslavian envoy in Washington, as well as Jan Ciechanowski, the Polish ambassador in Washington. Also questioned were personalities, like the American financier Arthur J. Goldsmith, who cultivated close ties to émigré groups and were well-versed in questions of European politics. On Goldsmith, see Richard Rhoman to John C. Wiley, sub: Arthur Goldsmith Group, July 1, 1942, INT-13GE-185, Entry 100, RG 226, NA.

58. FNB, Memorandum for the Planning Group, July 29, 1943, p.16 ff., Folder 100, Box 15, Entry 144, RG 226, NA. Cf. also DeWitt C. Poole, Memorandum for the Director of Strategic Services, July 27, 1943, Folder 96, Box 13, Entry 106, RG 226, NA. In the same collection there are numerous FNB memoranda composed between July and September 1943 and biographical notes on NKFD members, especially by Emmy C. Rado and Bernard Yarrow, who are not cited and discussed individually here. Folder 96 through Folder 105, Box 13, Entry 106, RG 226, NA.

59. FNB, Memorandum for the PG, July 29, 1943, 16–22, all emphases by author.

60. Schairer was a British subject and maintained close ties to Goerdeler. On this, as well as on Schairer's contacts to U.S government offices, see A[rthur] P[rimrose] Young, *The X-Documents* (London, 1974). FNB, Memorandum for the PG, July 29, 1943, 21. Also relevant John P. O'Keefe to Mr. John Wiley, sub: Reinhold Schairer and Arthur Goldsmith, August 31, 1942, INT-13GE-347, Entry 100, RG 226.

61. As an indication for this, Schairer cited (among other things) the attempt of the Soviet news agency TASS to get in touch with Friedrich Wilhelm Förster: TASS "asked him for a message to the 'Free Germany' group in Moscow. Evidently this was aimed at building up the Committee's position from the American side." Ibid.

62. Ibid., 22. On July 16, five days after the NKFD manifesto appeared, Roosevelt and Churchill, appealing to the Italians, called for the Fascist regime to be toppled and for a capitulation. On this, see too the R&A memorandum, The Soviet Union and 'Free Germany,' 2, July 27, 1943, Folder 100, Box 15, Entry 144, RG 226, NA.

63. In a confidential memorandum, the State Department's Russia experts had explained that the formation of the NKFD needed to be seen in conjunction with the dissolution of the Comintern, the founding of the Union of Polish Patriots in Moscow, the revival of Pan–Slavism, and the Soviet attitude toward the Roosevelt-Churchill appeal to the Italian public. The word from British embassy circles was that the foundation of the NKFD was an extremely clever propaganda move that probably represented a "trial balloon." FNB, Memorandum for the PG, July 29, 1943, 10–15. For the State Department's interest in the NKFD, also see Bernard Yarrow to J. C. Hughes, August 13, 1943, Folder 96, Box 13, Entry 106, RG 226, NA. On the larger context of the American and British reaction to the NKFD, see Heike Bungert, *Das Nationalkomitee und der Westen*.

64. FNB, Memorandum for the PG, July 29, 1943, pp. 20 ff., 26.

65. Biography D.C. Poole, Register D.C. Poole Papers, SHSW, Madison, WI.

66. In Princeton in September 1940 (at the time, still under the impact of the 1939 Hitler-Stalin-Pact), Poole had publicly called for democratic initiatives against totalitarianism. De-Witt C. Poole, A Project for Helping Strengthen Democratic Government in the United States. Remarks before Governmental Research Association at Princeton, September 5, 1940, 1,3, Folder 5, Box 7, D.C. Poole Papers, SHSW, Madison, WI. And see above, Chap. II.

67. DeWitt Clinton Poole, Militant, Multi-National Democracy, July 3, 1942, 2, Folder 1, Box 7, D.C. Poole Papers, SHSW, Madison, WI.

68. FNB, Memorandum for the PG, July 29, 1943, 28.

69. R&A-Memorandum, The Soviet Union and "Free Germany," July 27, 1943, esp. 2, Folder 100, Box 15, Entry 144, RG 226, NA.

70. Ibid., 12–15.

71. The Free Germany Manifesto and the German People, August 6, 1943, R&A 1033, MF 1221, RG 59, NA; also mentioned in P. Marquardt-Bigman, *Amerikanische Deutschlandanalysen*, p. 92.

72. In detail, there was talk about "reactivating" Articles 109, 114 through 118, 135, 152, 153, 169, 161, 165, 167, and 169. The Free Germany Manifesto and the German People, 3, August 6, 1943, R&A 1033, RG 59, NA.

73. On the R&A practice of surveying POWs in Italy, see the interview with the former Acting Chief of the CED of R&A, and later ACLS President, Frederick Burkhardt, C. Mauch, S. Beer/F. Burkhardt, January 18, 1997, Bennington, VT, OSSOHP.

74. On Marcuses's intellectual development, see Barry Katz, *Herbert Marcuse and the Art of Liberation: An Intellectual Biography* (London, 1982), along with the relevant essays in H.M., *Schriften, Bd.3. Aufsätze aus der Zeitschrift für Sozialforschung, 1934–1941* (Frankfurt, 1979).

75. The Free Germany Manifesto and the German People, 1, 4 ff., August 6, 1943, R&A 1033, RG 59, NA.

76. Nr. 356/43 g-IV A ld. AA Inland II G 32; Letter from August 6 and 13, 1943, R 58/211, BA Koblenz, cited here according to Marlis G. Steinert, *Hitlers Krieg und die Deutschen: Stimmung und Haltung der deutschen Bevölkerung im Zweiten Weltkrieg* (Düsseldorf/Wien, 1970), p. 399 ff.

77. Minutes of 172nd Meeting [OSS-PG], held on Thursday, 5 August 1943 at 1000 and 1430. Taking part in the discussion were Dr. James G. Rogers as well as Generals J. P. Smith, B. F. Fellers, also Cpt. Ward Davis, Comdr. C. H. Coggins, J. V. A MacMurray, Hugh Wilson, Edmond L. Taylor, Col. A. H. Onthank, and John Wiley. Folder 38, Box 5, Entry 144, RG 226, NA.

78. Memorandum from James Grafton Rogers, August 6, 1943, UUDW Doc 68, 222f.

79. See *NYT*, July 24, 1943.

80. [John Wiley], The National Committee of Free Germany ("Freies Deutschland") And Manifesto to the German People, Appendix "B," esp. 6–9, Folder 100, Box 15, Entry 144, RG 226, NA. John Wiley's authorship emerges from OSS-PG, Minutes of 172nd Meeting. Held on Thursday, August 5, 1943, Folder 38, Box 5, Entry 144, RG 226, NA.

81. Memorandum from James Grafton Rogers (OSS Planning Group) to the JCS, Manifesto to the German People by the Moscow National Committee of Free Germany, August 6, 1943, Folder 100, Box 14, Entry 144, RG 226, NA.

82. James Grafton Rogers, Office of Strategic Services. Notes and Comments, July 1961, OSS, Box 8, MS#536, James Grafton Rogers Papers, Colorado Historical Society, Denver. On Marshall's problems with Donovan, see George C. Marshall, *Interviews and Reminiscences for Forrest C. Pogue* (Lexington, Va., 1991), p. 483 ff.

83. Just a few R&A reports about the NKFD found their way to the White House, while (as a rule) the memoranda of the Planning Group at least got to the JCS, the White House, and the State Department. (See OSS HQ-Records, Entry 190, MF 1642, NA.) The exceptions were a few later R&A reports, such as the study published as JIC WS No.108, "The Free Germany Committee," MR 234, FDRL, Hyde Park, NY—on its authorship by the R&A, see "The Present Status of the Free Germany Committee," R&A 2878-S, February 2, 1945, Folder 883, Box 424, Entry 190, RG 226, NA.

84. On Roosevelt's conversation with Rogers, see James Grafton Rogers, Office of Strategic Services. Notes and Comments, July 1961, esp. p. 8 ff., OSS, Box 8, MS#536, James Grafton Rogers Papers, Colorado Historical Society, Denver.

85. Hugh R. Wilson to J.G. Rogers, January 10, 1944, Folder Wilson, Hugh, Box 7, MS#536, as well as Talk with James Grafton Rogers, Century Club, May 9, 1959, Folder

Whitney Shepardson, Box 10, MS#536, James Grafton Rogers Papers, Colorado Historical Society, Denver.

86. Memorandum, Irving H. Sherman to Hugh R. Wilson, August 3, 1943 Folder 101 (PG # 41), Box 15, Entry 144, RG 226, NA, reprinted in *AmIntel*, pp. 49–51. On Sherman and Wilson see W. Laqueur/R. Breitman, *Breaking the Silence* (New York1986), p. 207; A. C. Brown, *The Last Hero*, pp. 404, 514; Hugh R. Wilson. Special Assistant to the SSO Intelligence, ETO, Folder 147, Box 97, Entry 99, RG 226, NA; OSS to OSS Bern, June 30, 1943, Folder 1820, Box340, Entry 134, RG 226, NA.

87. A.H. Onthank, OSS PG: Save Germany Group, PG 41, August 6, 1943, Folder 101, Box 15, Entry 144, RG 226, NA; Memorandum, Irving H. Sherman to Hugh R. Wilson, August 3, 1943, ibid., reprinted in *AmIntel*, pp. 49–51.

88. Memorandum, Irving H. Sherman to Hugh R. Wilson, August 3, 1943 Folder 101, Box 15, Entry 144, RG 226, NA.

89. GLD in the U.S.A. (signed S. Aufhäuser, M. Brauer, R. Katz) to A. A. Berle, Folder 18, Box 3, Entry 142, RG 226, NA. A copy of the letter also went to Irving Sherman, whom Max Brauer knew to be interested in the establishment of a German exile committee. Rudolf Katz to I. Sherman, September 16, 1943, ibid.

90. Cf. The German Political Emigration, December 3, 1943, R&A 1568, RG 59, NA, partially reprinted in A.Söllner, *Archäologie der Demokratie I*, pp. 63–90, 77 ff.

91. [Resolution] August 1, 1943, Appendix to Rado to Hughes, August 28, 1943, Folder 103, Box 13, Entry 106, RG 226, NA.

92. [Resolution] No.2, n. d., appendix to Rado to Hughes, August 28, 1943, ibid.

93. Erklärung [Resolution] No.3, n.d. [= Mitte August], ibid. Emmy Rado calls future GDR Professor Hermann Budzislawski Dorothy Thompson's "research man"; Radkau designates him as Thompson's "ghostwriter." Emmy C. Rado to John C. Hughes and I. Sherman, August 28, 1943, Folder 103, Box 13, Entry 106, RG 226, NA. J. Radkau, *Die deutsche Emigration in den USA*, p. 71. On Eisenhower's statement, see Stephen E. Ambrose, *The Supreme Commander: The War Years of General Dwight D. Eisenhower* (Garden City, NY, 1970), p. 253, as well as A. E. Campbell, "Franklin Roosevelt and Unconditional Surrender," in Richard Langhorne, ed., *Diplomacy and Intelligence during the Second World War: Essays in Honour of F. H. Hinsley* (Cambridge, 1985), pp. 227 ff.

94. The statements by Sender and Weichmann may be found in the OSS files (Folder 103, Box 13, Entry 106 and in Folder 18, Box 3, Entry 142, RG 226, NA), there is a paraphrase of the Grzesinski memorandum by Emmy Rado. Emmy C. Rado to John C. Hughes and I. Sherman, August 28, 1943, Folder 103, Box 13, Entry 106, RG 226, NA.

95. The significance of GLD during the early years could be seen, not least of all, from the way that it received considerable financial support from the JLC. Here are indications of this in SOPADE IV, Rudolf Katz Collection, Hoover Institution, Stanford, CA Cf., too, Jack Jacobs, *Ein Freund in Not: Das Jüdische Arbeiterkomitee in New York und die Flüchtlinge aus den deutschsprachigen Ländern, 1933–1945* (Bonn, 1993), p.5 ff.

96. Emmy C. Rado to DeWitt Poole, Malcolm Davis et al., September 24, 1943, Folder 96, Box 13, Entry 106, RG 226; Emmy C. Rado to DeWitt C. Poole, October 29, 1943, Folder 18, Box 3, Entry 142, RG 226, NA; German Anti-Nazis in the United States still seeking National Committee October 15, 1943, INT-13GE-26, Entry 100, RG 226, NA. On Julius Deutsch, see his memoirs, *Ein weiter Weg: Lebenserinnerungen* (Zürich/Vienna, 1960).

97. A. A. Berle to Siegfried Aufhäuser, October 2, 1943, Folder 18, Box 3, Entry 142, RG 226, NA. Department of State, Press Release No.600, Policy Regarding Free Movements in the United States' December 10, 1941, Folder 28, Box 74, Entry 99, RG 226, NA.

98. A. A. Berle to M. B. Schnapper (Executive Secretary, American Council on Public Affairs), NYT, August 30, 1943, excerpts cited in A. A. Berle to Siegfried Aufhäuser, October 2, 1943, Folder 18, Box 3, Entry 142, RG 226, NA.

99. Ref. to PG-Meeting 216/1, September 25, 1943, Folder 101, Box 15, Entry 144, RG 226, NA.

100. Emmy C. Rado to Dewitt C. Poole, October 29, 1943, Folder 18, Box 3, En-try 142, RG 226, NA; DeWitt C. Poole to A.A.Berle, October 14, 1943, ibid.; ref. to PG-Meeting 216/1, September 25, 1943, Folder 101, Box 15, Entry 144, RG 226, NA; Irving H. Sherman to James G. Rogers, October 9, 1943, Folder 18, Box 3, Entry 142, RG 226, NA.

101. DeWitt C. Poole to Irving Sherman, October 22, 1943, Folder 18, Box 3, En-try 142, RG 226, NA, author's emphasis.

102. Emmy C. Rado to DeWitt Poole, sub: Dr. Proewig, August 17, 1943, Folder 18, Box 3, Entry 142, RG 226.

103. [Walter Dorn], The German Political Emigration, December 3, 1943, R&A 1568, RG 59, NA, partially reprinted in A. Söllner, *Archäologie der Demokratie I*, pp. 63–90; on Rado's thoroughgoing prejudices against Dorn, see Emmy Rado to John C. Hughes, May 25, 1943, Folder 19, Box 3, Entry 142, RG 226, NA. On Emmy Rado, see Elizabeth MacDonald, *Undercover Girl* (New York, 1947), p. 248 ff. C. Mauch, *Subversion and Propaganda*, p. 76, p. 88 ff.; condolence letter, Allen Dulles to Dr. Sandor Rado, January 3 1961, Box 97, Dulles Papers, Seeley G. Mudd Manuscript Library, Princeton, NJ.

104. Emmy C. Rado to DeWitt Poole, October 29, 1943, Folder 18, Box 3, Entry 142, RG 226, NA, emphasis by author. As early as August 24, the OSS had reported that Paul Hagen and Dorothy Thompson were trying to recruit Thomas Mann as chair of a Free German Committee, Irving H. Sherman to Hugh R. Wilson, August 24, 1943, ebd.

105. Irving H. Sherman to Hugh R. Wilson, November 6, 1943, Folder 18, Box 3, Entry 142, RG 226.

106. "It is recommended," the head of the FNB wrote, "that you say simply that the question of a German National Committee is naturally an important one and ought to be carefully considered with an eye to both the American and German interest and with that in mind you would be glad at some future mutually convenient time to receive Mr. Mann in your office and have a talk with him." Confidential letter, DeWitt Poole to A. Berle, November 10, 1943, ibid.

107. Only Horst Baerensprung had been let in on the decision after a conversation with Erika Mann. Emmy C. Rado to DeWitt Poole, John Hughes and Irving Sherman, November 23, 1943, Folder 18, Box 3, Entry 142, RG 226. More recently on this, Heike Bungert, VZG, xxx.

108. Emmy C. Rado to DeWitt C. Poole, December 8, 1943, Folder 18, Box 3, Entry 142, RG 226. In the same context, the *Mirror* cited something Thomas Mann had written in 1915, in which German militarism was characterized as a manifestation of German morality. *DM*, November 29, 1943. Cf., further, Hans Bürgin/Hans Mayer, *Thomas Mann: Eine Chronik seines Lebens* (Frankfurt, 1965), p. 178; J. Radkau, *Die deutsche Emigration in den USA*, pp. 200 ff. On the "Vansittartists" Stout, Ludwig Foerster etc., who founded the "Society for the Prevention of World War III" in December 1943, see J. Radkau, *Die deutsche Emigration in*

den USA, pp. 208–210. On Ludwig, see esp. his Testimony before the Committee on Foreign Affairs, House of Representatives 78th Congress on The German People, Friday March 26, 1943, Box 10, Phileo Nash Papers, Truman Library, Independence, MO.

109. OSS to OSS Bern, May 18, 1944, Folder 1056, Box 165, Entry 134, NA; Memorandum German Committee, February 8, 1944, Folder 18, Box 3, Entry 142, RG 226, NA. On Dorothy Thompson, see Peter Kurth, *American Cassandra: The Life of Dorothy Thompson* (Boston, 1990), esp. p. 350 ff.; on Paul Tillich, see Wilhelm Pauck/Marion Pauck, *Paul Tillich: Sein Leben und Denken*, Vol. 1 (Stuttgart, 1978); Friedrich Baerwald, "Zur politischen Tätigkeit deutscher Emigranten im Council for a Democratic Germany," in *VZG* 28 (1980), pp. 372–383. [FNB short biography] Paul Johannes Oskar Tillich, September 30, 1943, INT-13GE-863, Entry 100, RG 226, NA; Interview DeWitt C. Poole mit Professor Paul Tillich, February 14, 1944, New York, INT-13 GE-994, Entry 100, RG 226, NA; on the public impact of the CDG, see The Council for a Democratic Germany, June 20, 1944, Folder 41, Box 15, Entry 120, RG 226, NA.

110. Hans Franck an Paul Tillich, April 17, 1944, cited here according to J. Radkau, *Die deutsche Emigration in den USA*, p. 201.

111. Memorandum to the Planning Group, July 29, 1943; D.C. Poole to E.Buxton, September 18, 1943, Folder 4, Box 1, DeWitt Poole Papers, SHSW, Madison, WI.

112. R&A-PD, Current German Attitudes and the German War Effort (Report No.21), March 19, 1942, Box 1189, Entry 77, MID. Regional File (RF), RG 165, WNRC, Suitland, MD, and R&A 609, MF 1221, RG 59, NA.

113. See, for example, OSS Interim Report on German Morale (period March 4 to April 28, 1942); Box 1189, Entry 77, MID. Regional File (RF), RG 165, WNRC, Suitland, MD; J. Edgar Hoover to A. A. Berle, [April/May 1942]; ibid.; J. E. Hoover to A. A. Berle, July 24, 1942, ibid.

114. Report on conditions in Wurttemberg [!]. November 12, 1942; OSS to MID, November 16, 1942, Box 1189, Entry 77, MID. Regional File (RF), RG 165, WNRC, Suitland, MD; on the critical attitude of the population in Württemberg, see too the early report by Samuel W. Honacker (American Consul General) to American Embassy Berlin and Department of State Washington, December 14, 1940, Box 1190, Entry 77, MID. Regional File (RF), RG 165, WNRC, Suitland, MD; cf. too OSS Bern to OSS Washington (via Secretary of State), June 30, 1943, Box 307, RG 226, NA.

115. Memorandum for the Chief, MIS, sub: foreign Morale Information—from SI Branch, OSS, October 10, 1942, Box 1189, Entry 77, MID. Regional File (RF), RG 165, WNRC, Suitland, MD.

116. Charles C. Blakeney, Chief, PWB, War Department, MIS, December 16, 1942; Report on Intercepts, August and September 1942, ebd.; ONI, Special Warfare Report No. 1, Morale in Germany, June-December 1942, Folder 63, Box 213, Entry 92, RG 226, NA; Economic (Intelligence) Warfare, Series No.764, Special Report, The Effect of total Mobilization on German Morale, Box 1190, Entry 77, MID, RG 165, WNRC, Suitland, MD.

117. OSS Planning Group 37th Meeting, February 27, 1943, Box 5 Entry 144 RG 226, NA.

118. German Morale after Tunisia, June 25, 1943, R&A 933, MF 1221, RG 59, NA; on Neumann's authorship, see Harold Deutsch to William Langer, May 14, 1943, Box 5, Entry 38, RG 226, NA, as well as Katz, *Foreign Intelligence*, p. 209, fn. 25.

119. Handwritten remark, German Morale After Tunisia, June 25, 1943, Box 1190, Entry 77, MID, RG 165, WNRC, Suitland, MD.

120. It is worth noting that the thinking of the OSS about the concept of "public opinion" had a lasting influence on the postwar discourse concerning the phenomenon of public opinion under totalitarian conditions. Alexander Inkeles, for instance, working in the CED-R&A, later became an internationally recognized authority in this field. See, for example, Alex Inkeles, *Public Opinion in Soviet Russia* (Cambridge, MA, 1958); Interview B.F. Katz, A. Inkeles, Stanford, CA, March 1997, OSSOHP.

121. [Franz Neumann], German Morale after Tunisia, June 25, 1943, R&A 933, MF 1221, RG 59, NA; [Herbert Marcuse], Morale in Germany, R&A 1214, September 16, 1943, MF 1221, RG 59, NA.

122. William J. Donovan, Memorandum for the President, April 17, 1942, sub: Italian Plan, Box 148, PSF, FDRL, Hyde Park; Comments by the Office of Strategic Services on "Joint American-British Plan of Psychological Warfare for Italy" (JCS 139), Roll 34, Entry 180, MF A 3304, RG 226, NA; Psychological Warfare in the Mediterranean Theater. Part VI: A Study of Enemy Reactions to Allied Propaganda, September 10, 1945, Box 14, C.D. Jackson Papers, Dwight D. Eisenhower Library, Abilene, KS.

123. The Effect of the Italian Surrender upon Germany, October 20, 1943, R&A 1283, Box 1190, Entry 77, MID, RG 165, WNRC, Suitland, MD.

124. Germany. Axis Morale. Bombing of Civilians, n. d. (date of info: second half of August and first half week of September), Box 1190, Entry 77, MID, RG 165, WNRC, Suitland, MD; numerous additional Dogwood reports may be found in Boxes 589 through 592, Entry 92, RG 226, NA; on cooperation between Dogwood and the OSS Istanbul, see Barry Rubin, *Istanbul Intrigues: Espionage, Sabotage, and Diplomatic Treachery in the Spy Capital of WWII* (New York, 1992), p.167 ff.

125. German Morale at the End of 1943, R&A 1658, Box 1190, Entry 77, MID, RG 165, WNRC, Suitland, MD; the report was a sequel to the memorandum written by Marcuse and his colleagues, Morale in Germany, R&A 1214, September 16, 1943, MF 1221, RG 59, NA. On the Moscow Conference, see FRUS 1943, I, p. 589 ff.; Dallek, *Franklin D. Roosevelt and American Foreign Policy*, pp. 419 ff.; Hans-Adolf Jacobsen/Arthur L. Smith, Jr., eds., *World War II. Policy and Strategy. Selected Documents with Commentary* (Santa Barbara, CA, 1979), p. 277 ff.; on the Teheran Conference, see FRUS, The Conferences at Cairo and Teheran 1943, Washington 1961; Vojtech Mastny, "Stalin and the Prospects of a Separate Peace in World War II," in *American Historical Review* 77 (1972), pp. 1365–1388.

126. Cf. John Toland, *Adolf Hitler* (New York, 1976), p. xv ff.

127. W. S. Churchill, *The Second World War I*, p. 23; *Times* (London), September 11, 1939; David Dilks, ed., *The Diaries of Sir Alexander Cadogan 1938–1945* (London, 1971), p. 217; on the background, see L. Kettenacker, "Die britische Haltung zum Widerstand während des Zweiten Weltkriegs," in L. K., *Das "Andere Deutschland" im Zweiten Weltkrieg: Emigration und Widerstand in Internationaler Perspektive* (Stuttgart, 1977), p. 50 ff.; "Preußen-Deutschland als britisches Feindbild im Zweiten Weltkrieg," in Bernd Jürgen Wendt, ed., *Das britische Deutschlandbild im Wandel des 19. und 20. Jahrhunderts* (Bochum, 1984), pp. 145–168; Adolf M. Birke, "Warum Deutschlands Demokratie versagte: Geschichtsanalyse im britischen Außenministerium 1943/45," in *Historisches Jahrbuch* 103 (1983), pp. 395–410.

128. In Ernest R. May, *"Lessons" of the Past. The Use and Misuse of History in American Foreign Policy* (New York, 1973), p. 7; FRUS, The Conferences at Washington and Casablanca, 1943, Washington 1968, 505ff; C. Mauch, *Großbritannien, die Vereinigten Staaten und der Widerstand*, pp. 106–108.

129. S[igrid] S[chultz], What I saw of the German Revolution of 1918 and what I believe it showed, January 20, 1943, Folder 52, Box 239, Entry 92, RG 226, NA; Fredric R. Dolbear to Arthur Goldberg, January 23, 1943, ibid.

130. German Situation in 1918 and 1943, August 13, 1943, R&A 1043, RG 59, MF 1221, NA.

131. OSS Memorandum, The German Parallel—1918 and 1943, JIC WS April 28, 1943, Map Room 226, FDRL, Hyde Park, NY.

132. German Situation in 1918 and 1943, August 13, 1943, R&A 1043, RG 59, MF 1221, NA.

133. Report by the British War Cabinet's Joint Intelligence Sub-Committee, Probabilities of a German Collapse, September 1943, Sec 1-a JIC (43) 367 Final, ABC 381 Germany (29 January 43), RG 165, NA, excerpts reprinted in *AmIntel*, pp. 83–86.

134. Ibid. Research analyst Dr. Arnold Price, who worked in the R&A research division and later in the State Department's secret intelligence division, emphasized (in conversation with the author) that it was an unwritten law to stress potentially negative effects more strongly than positive ones.

135. Felix Gilbert, cited by Katz, *Foreign Intelligence*, p. 69.

136. German Situation in 1918 and 1943, August 13, 1943, R&A 1043; Possible Patterns of German Collapse, September 21, 1943, R&A 1483; The Process of Collapse, December 4, 1943, R&A 1477, MF 1221, NA.

137. Possible Patterns of German Collapse, September 21, 1943, R&A 1483, MF 1221, NA, excerpts reprinted in UUDW, Doc 9, 29–35; *AmIntel*, Doc 19b, 87–94. On the American critique of the British assessment, see U.S. Joint Intelligence Committee to JCS, Probabilities of a German Collapse, October 21, 1943, Germany Sec 1-B JIC 112/2, ABC 381, RG 165, NA, excerpts reprinted in *AmIntel*, pp. 94–96. Even the OSS autumn directors for psychological warfare warned against expecting an imminent collapse, Special Military Plan for Psychological Warfare against Germany, September 21, 1943, Folder 105, Box 15, Entry 144, RG 226, NA.

138. *Dokumente zur Deutschlandpolitik. First Series.* Vol. 3 (= DzD I/3). *Documents on British Foreign Policy Toward Germany*, Rainer A. Blasius ed. (Frankfurt, 1989), p.1095; 371/22986/C19495, FO, Kew; L. Kettenacker, "Die britische Haltung zum Widerstand während des Zweiten Weltkriegs," p. 54 ff. An indication that there were also voices on the American side identifying Prussianism with Hitlerism is, for example, Vice President Henry A. Wallace's speech, "Christian Bases of Peace," March 8, 1943, 243.172.4 (73/United States of America), World Council of Churches (WCC), Archiv des ökumenischen Rates der Kirchen (AÖRK), Geneva.

139. On the zeppelin and air battles during the First World War, see Sir Charles Webster/Noble Frankland, *The Strategic Air Offensive Against Germany, Vol. 1: Preparation* (London, 1961), pp. 6 and 34–48.

140. Cf. Williamson Murray, "Reflections on the Combined Bomber Offensive," in *MGM* 51 (1992), 73–94, 74.

141. Cf. Sir Arthur Harris, *Bomber Offensive* (London, 1947); further, Charles Messenger, *"Bomber" Harris and the Strategic Bombing Offensive, 1939–1945* (London, 1984), as well as Dudley Saward, *"Bomber" Harris* (London, 1985).

142. On the British strategy's difficulties, see Sir Charles Webster/Noble Frankland, *The Strategic Air Offensive Against Germany, Vol. 1: Preparation* (London, 1961). On the "Baedeker attacks," cf. Charles Whiting, *The Three-Star Blitz: The Baedeker Raids and the Start of Total War 1942–1943* (London, 1987). Without the last-minute interference of the

Prime Minister (vis-à-vis Marshall), the Americans would presumably have hardly been able to implement their concept of "daylight bombing." Churchill, not without a show of pride, indicates this in his autobiography. W. S. Churchill, *The Second World War: The Hinge of Fate* (Boston, 1950), pp. 678–680. Charles Kindleberger stressed that there was a specially trained flying squadron that bombed the Eder dam; he expounded further: "This scientist had a bomb made, designed as a round bomb with dimples on the ends. It began spinning inside to jump the net. The dams were protected by nets. So that you couldn't send a torpedo bomb in there. A torpedo bomb would have been stopped. But a rolling sphere jumped the net, rested against the edge of the dam and then sank and exploded." Interview C. Mauch/C. Kindleberger, January 17, 1997, *OSSOHP.*

143. Enemy [in the OSS War Diary erroneously Economic] Objectives Unit (= EOU). Preliminary Explanation, in: War Diary R&A Branch, OSS London (= WD R&A London), 1, Vol. 5 Economic Outpost with Economic Warfare Division (= EO/EWD), Box 3, Kindleberger Papers, Harry S. Truman Library, Independence, MO. The critical passages from the EOU War Diary were written by Walt Rostow. An adapted account focusing on the most important points of the EOU doctrine may be found as an article in the now largely declassified CIA journal *Studies in Intelligence*: Walt W. Rostow, The Beginnings of Air Targeting, SII, Box 3, RG 263, NA; on the founding of the EOU, cf. further Walt W. Rostow, "The London Operation: Recollections of an Economist," in *The Secrets War. The Office of Strategic Services in World War II*, edited by George C. Chalou (Washington, D.C., 1992), pp. 48–60, esp. p 48 ff. A list of EOU staff is reprinted as Appendix B, ibid., p. 59.

144. For a biography of Richard D'Oyly Hughes, see Walt W. Rostow, "The London Operation," p. 48 ff. There Rostow characterizes Hughes as a "truly major figure in the Allied effort." Rostow even dedicated his account of the pre-invasion bomber strategy to the memory of Hughes. See W. W. Rostow, *Pre-Invasion Bombing Strategy. General Eisenhower's Decision of March 25, 1944* (Austin, TX, 1981), on Hughes, ibid., p.17, p. 141 ff.

145. Cf. EOU Preliminary Explanation, in WD R&A London, 2–4, Vol. 5, EO/EWD; Harry S. Truman Library, Kindleberger Papers, Independence, MO. The complicated history of how the EOU was founded will not be offered here; it has been documented in detail in EO/EWD, Founding of EOU. April-September 1942, WD R&A London, 11–19, Vol. 5, Harry S. Truman Library, Kindleberger Papers, Independence, MO. Cf. further Charles P. Kindleberger, *Life of an Economist* (Cambridge, MA/Oxford, 1991), pp. 67–89, esp. p. 69.

146. On Harris's critique of "panacea targets," cf. Charles Webster and Noble Frankland, *The Strategic Air Offensive Against Germany, Vol. 2: Endeavour* (London, 1961), esp. p. 65 ff.

147. EOU Preliminary Explanation, in WD R&A London, 5f, 9; EO/EWD, Founding of EOU, 15, WD R&A London, Vol. 5, Box 3, Kindleberger Papers, Harry S. Truman Library, Independence, MO. The major accounts of the strategic air war overlook the specific working method and methodical orientation of the EOU; instead, they stress the analogies between the OSS-EOU and MEW. Cf., for example, C.Webster and N. Frankland, *The Strategic Air Offensive*, Vol. 1, p. 471.

148. C. Kindleberger, *Life of an Economist*, pp. 77–80; Interview C. Mauch/C. Kindleberger, January 17, 1997, *OSSOHP.*

149. In contrast to the British Air Ministry, the OSS in London had no access to Ultra. Only later, when the EOU was closely cooperating with the British in the so-called "Operation Octopus," was Walt Rostow initiated into the ULTRA secret. See ibid., as well as Interview B. Katz/W. W. Rostow, Austin, TX, February 3, 1997, *OSSOHP.*

150. After the war, this idea was systematically worked in the concept of "input-output theory" that was coined by OSS staffer and later Harvard Professor Wassily Leontief, which would later bring Leontief a Nobel Prize. Cf. C. Kindleberger, *Life of an Economist*, p. 75.

151. EOU Preliminary Explanation, in WD R&A London, 6f, WD R&A London, Vol. 5, Harry S. Truman Library, Kindleberger Papers, Independence, MO; Kindleberger, *Life of an Economist*, p. 74 ff.

152. CCS Directive for the Bomber Offensive from the United Kingdom, January 21, 1943, reprinted as Appendix 8 (p. xxviii), in Webster/Frankland, *Strategic Air Offensive*, Vol. 4: Annexes and Appendices (London, 1961), p.153 ff.

153. CCS Directive, January 21, 1943, ibid., p.154; cf. further Maurice Matloff, *Strategic Planning for Coalition Warfare 1943–1944* (Washington, D.C., 1959), p. 29.

154. Cf. John Ehrman, *Grand Strategy, Vol. 5: August 1943-September 1944* (London, 1956), p. 5 ff. Regarding the attack on Schweinfurt, cf. esp. Friedhelm Golücke, *Schweinfurt und der strategische Luftkrieg 1943: Der Angriff der U.S. Air Force vom 14. Oktober 1943 gegen die Schweinfurter Kugellagerindustrie* (Paderborn, 1988), as well as Thomas M. Coffey, *Decision over Schweinfurt: The U.S. 8th Army Air Force Battle for Daylight Bombing* (New York, 1977) and Martin Middlebrook, *The Schweinfurt-Regensburg Mission* (New York, 1983). On the evaluation made by the OSS of the British attacks against the Ruhr region and Hamburg, cf. Memorandum The Effect of Aerial Bombardment of the Ruhr on Axis War Potential, July 29, 1943, R&A 1005, MF 1221, RG 59, NA; Memorandum German Losses in the Hamburg Raids: 24 July to August 1943, September 18, 1943, R&A 1273, September 18, 1943, MF 1221, RG 59, NA; Damage to Fighter-Aircraft Production, in: Bomb Damage Report, 12ff, R&A 1044.3, October 1943, Folder 2173, Box 146, Entry 146, RG 226, NA.

155. The Combined Bomber Offensive from the United Kingdom (Pointblank) as approved by the CCS, May 14, 1943, reprinted as Appendix 23 in Webster/Frankland, *Strategic Air Offensive*, Vol. 4, pp. 273–283, citation 275. On the background to the AAF policy discussion, cf. further Wesley Frank Craven and James Lea Cate, eds., *The Army Air Forces in World War II, Vol. 2: Europe – Torch to Pointblank. August 1942 to December 1943* (Chicago, 1949).

156. Cf. W. W. Rostow, *Pre-Invasion Bombing Strategy*, p. 24 ff.; "Policy Planning and the Target Analysis of Industries," in WD R&A London, Vol. 5, EO/EWD, esp. pp. 54 ff., Harry S. Truman Library, Kindleberger Papers, Independence, MO. In the Pointblank memorandum, the OSS analysts are mentioned in one allusion: "A thorough study of those elements of the German military, industrial and economic system, which appeared to be profitable as bombing objectives, was made by a group of Operations Analysts consisting of eminent United States experts." Cf. The Combined Bomber Offensive from the United Kingdom (Pointblank) as approved by the CCS, May 14, 1943, reprinted as Appendix 23 in Webster/Frankland, *Strategic Air Offensive*, Vol. 4, p. 273.

157. E.O.U. Target Potentiality Report, German Fighter Aircraft, 1, May 3, 1943, Box 2, Kindleberger Papers, Harry S. Truman Library, Independence, MO.

158. Ibid. 1–9.

159. On the role of Hughes, see Policy Planning, p.54 ff., in WD R&A London, Vol. 5, EO/EWD, Box 3, Kindleberger Papers. The "specific assignments" prescribed for the Eighth Air Force are reprinted in WD R&A London, Vol. 5, EO/EWD, 75, Box 3, Kindleberger Papers. A relevant analysis of the German airplane industry is available in Memorandum C. P. Kindleberger to Colonel R. D. Hughes, March 15, 1943, in WD R&A London, Vol. 5, EO/EWD, 59–63, Box 3, Kindleberger Papers. The monthly production figure for two-motor

airplanes could be pushed back from 225 to 50 by the end of February 1944; cf. Policy Planning, p. 75, in WD R&A London, Vol. 5, EO/EWD, Box 3, Kindleberger Papers, Harry S Truman Library, Independence, MO.

160. W. W. Rostow, "The London Operation," p. 51.

161. Solly Zuckerman, *From Apes to Warlord* (New York, 1978). Cf., in addition, the autobiography of Lord Tedder, *With Prejudice* (London, 1966). On Zuckerman's autobiography, cf. the comprehensive critique by J. R. Killian Jr., "From Apes to Warlords. The Autobiography of Solly Zuckerman," Box 2, Kindleberger Papers, Harry S Truman Library Independence, MO.

162. Delay and Disorganization of Enemy Movement by Rail, n. d. [= January 22, 1944], Folder Barnett, Box 1, Entry 77, RG 226, NA. On the Italian bombing attacks, cf. Professor Zuckerman's Report on Air Attacks on Road and Rail Communications in Sicily and Southern Italy, December 28, 1943, AIR 37/49, PRO, Kew.

163. Tactical Targets and 'Operation Octopus.' January-September 1944, pp. 85–87, in WD R&A London, Vol. 5, EO/EWD, Box 3, Kindleberger Papers, Harry S. Truman Library, Independence, MO.

164. The triggering incident was Charles Kindleberger's review of Zuckerman's autobiography in *Encounter* 51 (1978), pp. 39–42; this was followed by Zuckermann's reply and Kindleberger's counter-response in *Encounter* 52 (1979), pp. 86–89; in 1980, finally, there was a literary controversy on the same matter between Rostow and Zuckerman in *Encounter* 55 (1980), pp. 100–102. See, further, Interview C. Mauch/C. Kindleberger, January 17, 1997, *OSSOHP*.

165. C. Kindleberger, *Life of an Economist*, p. 87. On the larger context, cf. Wesley Frank Craven and James Lea Cate, eds., *The Army Air Forces in World War II, Vol. 3: Argument to VE-Day. January 1944-May 1945* (Chicago, 1951), p. 372 ff.

166. Cf. Policy Planning, p. 80 ff., in WD R&A London, Vol. 5, EO/EWD, Box 3, Kindleberger Papers, Harry S Truman Library, Independence, MO; Harris' citation, ibid., p. 81. On Spaatz's attitude, cf. Memorandum Coombs to Kindleberger, January 2, 1944, Folder MAAF, Box 2, Entry 77, RG 226, NA; there is a brief portrait of Spaatz by Alfred Goldberg, "General Carl A. Spaatz," in Field Marshal Sir Michael Carver, ed., *The War Lords* (London, 1976), pp. 568–581.

167. Cf. WD R&A London, 70–73, Vol. 5, EO/EWD, Box 3, Kindleberger Papers; Memorandum The Value of Marshalling Yards as Targets. Mediterranean Experience (Summary), February 22, 1944; Memorandum to Col. R.D.Hughes, ODI, Target HQ, USSAEF, Subject: Bombing of Italian Railroads, February 8, 1944, both reprinted in WD R&A London, 70–73, Vol. 5, EO/EWD, Box 3, Kindleberger Papers, Harry S. Truman Library, Independence, MO, cf. further W. W. Rostow, *Pre-Invasion Bombing Strategy*, pp. 39–41.

168. Memorandum The Use of Strategic Air Power after March 1, 1944, reprinted in WD R&A London, 73–80, Vol. 5, EO/EWD, Box 3, Kindleberger Papers, Harry S Truman Library, Independence, MO.

169. Ibid. 76. On the significance of the surrender at Pantelleria on June 11, 1943, which took place as the result of severe bombing from the sea and air, cf. Josef Schröder's reliable account, *Italiens Kriegsaustritt 1943* (Göttingen, 1969).

170. Cf. C. Kindleberger, *Life of an Economist*, p. 84 ff.; likewise J. R. Killian, Jr., [critique of Zuckerman, *From Apes to Warlord*], 6–7, Box 2, Kindleberger Papers, Harry S Truman Library, Independence, MO.

171. Memorandum The Use of Strategic Air Power after 1 March 1944, WD R&A London, 77, Vol. 5, EO/EWD, Box 3, Kindleberger Papers, Harry S Truman Library, Independence, MO, 77.

172. Ibid., 79–80.

173. Cf. C. Kindleberger, *Life of an Economist*, p. 87; Wesley F. Craven and James Lea Cate, eds., *The Army Air Forces in World War II, Vol. 3: Argument to VE-Day. January 1944-May 1945* (Chicago, 1951), p. 72 ff.; S. Zuckerman, *From Apes to Warlord*, pp. 243 ff., 257. On the discussion with Spaatz, see WD R&A London, 80–82, Vol. 5, EO/EWD, Box 3, Kindleberger Papers; W. W. Rostow, *Pre-Invasion Bombing Strategy*, p. 32. In retrospect, the EOU staff criticized the USSTAF and its planning for not having taken into consideration the EOU Memorandum Outline Plan for Air Support of Overlord from February 17, 1944, which had supplemented the strategic oil plan with a tactical bridge plan. Cf. Outline Plan for Air Support of Overlord, including Table I: Tactical Target Systems by Type. Table II: Tactical Targets by Types of Aircraft, February 17, 1944, Box 1, Kindleberger Papers, as well as WD R&A London, besonders 91f, Vol. 5, EO/EWD, Box 3, Kindleberger Papers, Truman Library, Independence, MO.

174. Eisenhower's decision does not have to be analyzed and presented in any greater detail here, since it has been treated in the Air Force histories and in Rostow, *Pre-Invasion Bombing Strategy*, esp. pp. 3–6; 44 ff.; 72 ff. Policy Planning, in WD R&A London, 82ff, Vol. 5, EO/EWD, Box 3, Kindleberger Papers, Harry S. Truman Library, Independence, MO. Tedder's evaluation of the oil plan may be found in his autobiography, *With Prejudice* (London, 1966), p. 516 ff. On the overall context, of the Allied air war against the Deutsche Reichsbahn (German railway), cf. the outstanding study by Alfred C. Mierzejewski, *The Collapse of the German War Economy, 1944–1945: Allied Air Power and the German National Railway* (Chapel Hill, NC, 1988).

175. Diary entry from March 26, 1944, cited by Rostow, *Pre-Invasion Bombing Strategy*, p. 52.

176. Cf. W. F. Craven and J. L. Cate, eds., *The Army Air Forces in World War II*, Vol. 3, pp. 157–162 (there, too, is the G-2 quote). Curiously, the first experimental nighttime attacks of the British against railroad stations in March 1944 were very precise; cf. ibid., p. 27 ff. Although the Germans were no longer constructing train stations and heavy installations, it only took a short time for the switching stations to resume their operations. Cf. the SHAEF WIS, March 26, 1944, as well as the AG Weekly 'Neptune' Review of April 2, 1944; on this, see Hinsley, *British Intelligence in the Second World War*, Vol. 3, pp. 108 ff.; cf. further the British analyses for the first half of 1944, Bombing Attacks on French Railways, January to August 1944, AIR 40/371, PRO, Kew; [EOU] Evaluation of Rail Centre Attacks, 20 May 1944, Box 2, Kindleberger Papers, Truman Library, Independence, MO. Additional EOU and French secret intelligence service analyses may be found in Folder Barnett/ Transportation, Box 1, Entry 77, RG 226, NA.

177. Symptomatic is an episode recounted by Kindleberger. According to him, in the beginning of 1945 both the British and the Americans had interviewed the captured boss of the German transportation system in the west, General Colonel Höffner, in order to find out if attacks on bridges or on train stations were more effective. Both parties received the answer each was looking for (in spite of presumably objective interview conditions). Cf. Kindleberger, *Life of an Economist*, p. 86.

178. Diary entry from July 20, 1944, Bruce Diary, OSS *against the Reich*, ed. by N. D. Lankford, p. 113. On the success of the oil operations, also see W. W. Rostow, The London Operation, Appendix A, p. 57 ff.; idem, *Pre-Invasion Bombing Strategy*, pp. 78–80; The German Oil Position (June 1st 1944), Box 2, Kindleberger Papers, Truman Library, Independence, MO.

179. Albrecht Speer, *Erinnerungen* (Berlin, 1969), p. 357 ff. Five highly confidential reports by Speer (from June 30, 1944, July 28, 1944, August 30, 1944, October 5, 1944, and January 19, 1945) have been reprinted in English as Appendix 32 (The Report by Speer to Hitler on the Effects of the Attacks on Oil) in Webster and Frankland, *Strategic Air Offensive*, Vol. 4, pp. 321–340.

180. Sir Arthur Harris, *Bomber Offensive* (London, 1947), p. 220. Emphasis by author.

181. Arthur Schlesinger, "The London Operation. Recollections of a Historian," in G. C. Chalou, *The Secrets War*, p. 62. On the methodology of the EOU, cf. Katz, *Foreign Intelligence*, pp. 112ff.

182. "Insofar as OSS had any input . . . I think that the strategic bombing surveys and studies show that the input on the whole was bad enough in some cases, the wasted efforts and so on, but I think that it [OSS] tried to get on to more efficient use of this. For example, the zeroing in on railroads, rather than attacking personnel." Interview C. Mauch/F. Ford, January 17, 1997, Lexington, MA, *OSSOHP*.

183. Romania alone produced 50% of Germany's raw oil needs, SHAEF Weekly Report September 2, 1944, Box 2, Entry 6, RG 226, NA; B. N. McPhearson, *Kings and Desperate Men*, p. 138.

184. According to information from Professor Gregory D. Foster of the National Defense University (NDU) in Washington, D.C. (March 1997) the theories developed by the EOU still had relevance for the training of officers in the U.S. Army.

4. BERN: THE BIG WINDOW ONTO THE FASCIST WORLD

1. The house at Dufourstraße 26, on the corner of Thunstraße, had been rented out by the Legation. As of October 1, 1943, the adjoining building was also used as an OSS office. The secondary literature—which maintains, citing the account by R. Harris Smith (OSS, p. 204), that everyone knew where Dulles was operating—overlooks the fact that most OSS activities ran by the buildings in the Dufourstraße in Bern's embassy district. "SI and CE Activity," in War Diary. OSS, Berne, CIA Box 11, Berne OSS, Srodes Papers, Washington, D.C. The Bern war diary was released in the context of a FOIA request; quite a number of agents' names and descriptions of operations, however, have been blackened out. On Dulles's arrival in Bern, also see Telegram A. W. Dulles to OSS Washington, November 10, 1942, Box 307, Entry 134, NA; Telegram A. W. Dulles to OSS Washington, November 12, 1942, Box 171, Entry 134, RG 226, NA.

2. AWD, Statement of the Background, Education and Business Experience of Allen Welsh Dulles, Box 19, AWD Papers; Brooks Peters, A[llen] W[welsh], D[ulles], n.d., Folder OSS, Box 19, Dulles Papers, Seeley G. Mudd Manuscript Library, Princeton University Archives, Princeton, NJ. For a biography of Dulles, see the accounts by Peter Grose and Leonard Mosley; on John Foster and Allen Dulles, also see Nancy Lisagor and Frank Lipsius, *A Law Unto Itself: The Untold Story of the Law Firm of Sullivan and Cromwell* (New York, 1988). On the Bern OSS outpost, see too A. W. Dulles, *The Secret Surrender* (New York, 1966), p. 12 ff.; Jürgen Heideking, "Die 'Schweizer Straßen' des europäischen Widerstandes,"

in Gerhard Schulz, ed., *Geheimdienste und Widerstandsbewegungen im Zweiten Weltkrieg* (Göttingen, 1982), 143–187; *WROSSACB*, pp. 318 ff.

3. As head of the division for Near Eastern Affairs in the State Department, Dulles had procured illegal weapons for the Emperor of Abyssinia, Haile Selassie. As a result, he became a specialist on weapons dealing and arms control for the U.S. government. Brooks Peters, AWD, J-5/J-6, Folder OSS, Box 19, Dulles Papers, Seeley G. Mudd Manuscript Library, Princeton University Archives, Princeton, NJ. On Dulles's ties to John C. Wiley in the State Department, see Correspondence Dulles-Wiley, Box 6, Wiley Papers, FDRI., Hyde Park, NY.

4. W. Somerset Maugham, *Ashendon, or the British Agent* (London, 1928), p. 19; On Maugham's role as a British MI-1c agent, see Christopher Andrew, *Her Majesty's Secret Service* (New York, 1987), p. 209 ff.

5. The Lucy Ring, which (according to some evidence) may have been infiltrated by the British, made up a segment of the Swiss section of the Red Chapel (Red Three). On this outfit, see Anthony Read and David Fisher, *Operation Lucy: Most Secret Spy Ring of the Second World War* (London, 1980); Drago Arsenijevic, *Genève appelle Moscou* (Paris, 1981). Cf., also, Alexander Foote, *Handbook for Spies* (London, 1976). Foote, Lucy's dispatcher, explained that he passed on Ultra material to the Soviets for the British via Lucy.

6. Pierre Braunschweig, *Geheimer Draht nach Berlin: Die Nachrichtenlinie Masson-Schellenberg und der schweizerische Nachrichtendienst im Zweiten Weltkrieg* (Zürich, 1989); H. R. Kurz, *Nachrichtenzentrum Schweiz: Die Rolle der Schweizer Armee in Zwei Weltkriegen* (Frauenfeld, 1974).

7. Anthony Read and David Fisher, *Colonel Z: The Life and Times of a Master of Spies* (London, 1984); John Ferris, "Indulged in all too little? Vansittart, Intelligence and Appeasement," in *Diplomacy and Statecraft* 6 (1995), pp. 122–175. An outstanding, rather critical evaluation of British secret intelligence in Switzerland is provided by Neville Wylie, "'Keeping the Swiss Sweet.' Intelligence as a Factor in British Policy towards Switzerland during the Second World War," in *Intelligence and National Security* 11 (1996), pp. 442–467.

8. Leland Harrison and his associate, legation councilor J. Klahr Huddle, were the only ones put in the know about the true nature of Dyar's mission. War Diary. OSS, Berne. Organization, CIA Box 11, Berne OSS, Srodes Papers, Washington, D.C.

9. SI and CE Activity, in: War Diary. OSS, Berne, CIA Box 11, Berne OSS, Srodes Papers, Washington, D.C. Stalder rented an apartment in Bern; Loofbourow had initially taken up quarters at Alpenstraße 26 in Bern, but as of January 1943 he became vice-consul in Zürich, and Max Shoop lived in the Hôtel de la Paix in Geneva as well as in an apartment house at 1, Quai Gustave Ador. On AZUSA, see esp. Folder 86, Box 7, Entry 90; Box 589, Entry 88; Folder 65ff, Box 9, Entry 108, RG 226, NA. Further, Thomas Powers, *Heisenberg's War: The Secret History of the German Bomb* (New York, 1993).

10. 1,500 Nazis were forced by Swiss authorities to leave the country, although National Socialists like former Minister Dr. Köcher and the "infamous Nazi gangster Major Pabst" remained in the country. "SI, SO and CE. Preliminary," in War Diary. OSS, Berne, CIA Box 11, Berne OSS, Srodes Papers, Washington, D.C.

11. On Dulles's nightly telephone calls, see Brooks Peters, AWD, J-8—J-18, Folder OSS, Box 19, Dulles Papers, Seeley G. Mudd Manuscript Library, Princeton University Archives, Princeton, NJ, as well as Mary Bancroft, "Jung and his Circle," in *Perspectives* 6 (1975), p. 122, copy in Folder Bancroft, Box 1, Persico Papers, Hoover Institution, Stanford, CA. A selection

of Dulles telegrams was edited by Neal H. Petersen. From Hitler's Doorstep. *The Wartime Intelligence Reports of Allen Dulles, 1942–1945* (University Park, PA, 1996).

12. Brooks Peters, AWD, J-12—J-13, Folder OSS, Box 19, Dulles Papers, Seeley G. Mudd Manuscript Library, Princeton University Archives, Princeton, NJ; A. Dulles, *Germany's Underground*, pp. 130 ff.; idem., *Craft of Intelligence*, pp. 203 ff.; W. Laqueur and R. Breitman, *Breaking the Silence*, p. 168, 290 fn.; K. v. Klemperer, *German Resistance against Hitler*, p. 399, fn. The telegram that the Germans decoded is reprinted in Petersen's collection of Wartime Intelligence Reports (abbreviated from here on in as WIR). Telegram Dulles (via Burns and Victor) to Donovan, February 1, 1943, WIR-Doc 1–17, p. 35 ff. On the security problems, also see Bern Confidential File 1942, 830.02, RG 84, NA. Insinuations and additional indications about the undermining of the Bern OSS outpost may be found in Hoyt S. Vandenberg's postwar memorandum, Penetration and Compromises of OSS in Europe, n. d., Box 56, H. S. Vandenberg Papers, MDLOC, Washington, D.C.

13. "Wayne's List," which was released as a result of a FOIA request by Neal H. Petersen, and which Allen Dulles originally sent to Washington on December 4, contains 12 contact names, although they have been blacked out. Petersen, *From Hitler's Doorstep*, p. 563. On Moffat, see Hugh R. Wilson to Leland Harrison, October 29, 1940, General Correspondence, Box 29, L. Harrison Papers, MDLOC, Washington, D.C.

14. On the link to Sam Woods and Erwin Respondek, see John V. H. Dippel, *Two Against Hitler: Stealing the Nazis' Best-Kept Secrets* (New York, 1992); further, Telegram A. Dulles to OSS Washington, December 7, 1943, Box 165, Entry 134, RG 226, NA; Telegram A. Dulles To OSS Washington, December 16, 1943, Box 274, Entry 134, RG 226, NA.

15. On Schacht, see L. Harrison to Sumner Welles, May 8, 1941, Box 29, General Correspondence, L. Harrison Papers, MDLOC, Washington, D.C.; on "G" (= Gafencu), see AWD to L. Harrison, January 8, 1943, Box 33, General Correspondence, Harrison Papers, MDLOC, Washington, D.C.; L. Harrison to Cordell Hull, February 12, 1943, 862.00/4361, RG 59, NA; on Harrison's contacts with Schulte, see Walter Laqueur and Richard Breitman, *Breaking the Silence* (New York, 1986), p. 262 ff. Harrison had been in touch with Prince Max von Hohenlohe-Langenburg since the autumn of 1939. L. Harrison to Mr. Joyce, August 8, 1945, Box 47, Memoranda 1942–1947, Harrison Papers, MDLOC, Washington, D.C.

16. See, for example, Neal H. Petersen, "From Hitler's Doorstep: Allen Dulles and the Penetration of Germany," in George C. Chalou, ed., *The Secrets War: The Office of Strategic Services in World War II* (Washington, D.C., 1992), p. 275.

17. Fabian von Schlabrendorff, *Begegnungen in fünf Jahrzehnten* (Tübingen, 1979), p. 321 ff; W. Laqueur and R. Breitman, *Breaking the Silence*, p. 61 ff. The primary sources from the papers of Schulze-Gaevernitz in the BA/MA Freiburg archives were analyzed by Jürgen Heideking: Jürgen Heideking, "Gero von Schulze-Gaevernitz," in Michael Bosch and Wolfgang Niess, eds., *Der Widerstand im deutschen Südwesten 1933–1945* (Stuttgart, 1984), pp. 281–290. The report about Gaevernitz's Russia trip, along with a small file of correspondence, may be found in the Hoover Institution, Box 1, Schulze-Gaevernitz-Papers, Stanford, CA.

18. Charles Kindleberger, who met Gaevernitz in Switzerland in 1941, told the author: "One of the things that amused me very much was that he [Gaevernitz] supported himself in Switzerland, he said, by sending $500 in a check to New York and asking for them to put that into five $100 bills, which he'd then sell in Switzerland for $650, taking $500 and sending it back." Interview C. Mauch, Charles Kindleberger, January 18, 1997, Lexington, Mass., OSSOHP.

19. Klemens von Klemperer, *German Resistance Against Hitler*, p. 318.

20. On Bancroft, see his *Autobiography of a Spy* (New York, 1983) as well as Walter Scott's "Personality Parade: Mary Bancroft" (1978), Folder Bancroft, Box 1, Persico Papers, Hoover Institution, Stanford, CA Peter Grose has portrayed the relationship between Allen Dulles and Mary Bancroft with narrative latitude in P. Grose, *Gentleman Spy*, pp. 162–167 ff.; cf, M. Bancroft, *Autobiography of a Spy*, pp. 142 ff.

21. Mary Bancroft, "Jung and his Circle," in *Perspectives* 6 (1975), pp. 114–127, Copy in Folder Bancroft, Box 1, Persico Papers, Hoover Institution, Stanford, CA On Jung's political ideas during the war, see C.G. Jung, "Demokratie als erzieherische Aufgabe," in *Der Ruf*, August 15, 1945, copy in Folder 3, Box 598, Entry 92, RG 226, NA.

22. On Gisevius, cf. his memoirs: Hans Bernd Gisevius, *Bis zum bitteren Ende*, 2 vol. (Zürich, 1946), idem, *Bis zum bitteren Ende. Vom Verfasser auf den neuesten Stand gebrachte Sonderausgabe* (Hamburg, n. d.). Although the OSS boss disapproved of the telepathic communication between Mary Bancroft and Hans Bernd Gisevius and characterized it as pure "nonsense"—by no means did he wish to go down in history as a "footnote to one of Jung's cases"—he was enthusiastic about the analyses of this prominent psychologist. M. Bancroft, "Jung and his Circle," p. 123.

23. Burns [Dulles] to Director OSS, February 3, 1943, Folder 1079, Box 171, Entry 146, RG 226, NA; Telegram Dulles to Bruce, Box 307, Entry 134, Box 307, NA, RG 226, excerpts reprinted in *Amintel*, Doc. 9, 40; UUDW, Doc.5, 22.; diary entry M. Bancroft, February 9, 1943, reprinted in idem, "Jung and his Circle," pp. 123–124. A deep-rooted psychological difference between the Germans the French, in Jung's view, was that the Germans wanted to be loved and do not understand why they are not loved. ibid., p. 124. Jung later told Elizabeth Wiskemann that the Germans as a nation are probably unconsciously attempting to destroy themselves and commit suicide through this war. [Elizabeth-Report] to OSS-Bern, July 14, 1944, Folder 72/II, Box 5, Entry 125, RG 226, NA.

24. After it started becoming increasingly dangerous for counterintelligence agent Hans Bernd Gisevius to get across the border, Eduard Waetjen, also a counterintelligence agent, became an important informer for Dulles. On Waetjen, see Klemperer, *German Resistance Against Hitler*, p. 75 fn., as well as Laqueur/Breitman, *Breaking the Silence*, pp. 212–214. Another person held in high esteem by Dulles was the journalist Elizabeth Wiskemann, whose reports were transmitted to Allen Dulles by way of 493 (= Fred Loofbourow) or 224 (= Russell D'Oench). They may be found in Folder 72, 72/II, 72/III, 72/IV, 72/V, Box 5, Entry 125, RG 226, NA. Cf., too, her autobiographical publication, E. Wiskemann, *The Europe I Saw* (London, 1968).

25. Special mention goes to Wilhelm Hoegner, Joseph Wirth, and Otto Braun. On Hoegner, see his autobiography, *Der schwierige Außenseiter: Erinnerungen eines Abgeordneten, Emigranten und Ministerpräsidenten* (Munich, 1959), especially pp. 165 ff., as well as Peter Kritzer, *Wilhelm Hoegner: Politische Biographie eines bayerischen Sozialdemokraten* (Munich, 1979), pp. 95–170; on Wirth and his ties to Schellenberg, see *The Rote Kapelle: The CIA's History of Soviet Intelligence and Espionage Networks in Western Europe, 1936–1945* (Washington, D.C., 1979), p. 207, and John Waller, *The Unseen War in Europe*, p. 362 ff.; on Braun, siehe Hagen Schulze, *Otto Braun oder Preußens demokratische Sendung: Eine Biographie* (Frankfurt, 1977), esp. p. 802, also idem., "Rückblick auf Weimar: Ein Briefwechsel zwischen Otto Braun und Joseph Wirth im Exil," in VZG 26 (1978), pp. 144–185. Cf., further, Werner Mittenzwei, *Exil in der Schweiz* (Frankfurt, 1979) as well as Karl Hans Bergmann, *Die Bewegung 'Freies Deutschland' in der Schweiz 1943–1945* (Munich, 1974).

26. Telegram Allen Dulles to COI [sic], for 109 and 105, n. d., Folder 1079, Box 171, Entry 146, RG 226, NA. emphasis by author.

27. On German counterintelligence, see Heinz Höhne, *Canaris: Patriot im Zwielicht* (Munich, 1976), David Kahn, *Hitler's Spies*, as well as Paul Leverkuehn, *Der geheime Nachrichtendienst der deutschen Wehrmacht im Kriege* (Frankfurt, 2nd ed, 1957). Basic information on Hans von Dohnanyi and Hans Oster in particular may be found in Eberhard Bethge, *Dietrich Bonhoeffer: Theologe – Christ – Zeitgenosse*, (Munich, 6th ed., 1986).

28. OSS Bern to OSS Washington, January 13, 1943, Box 307, Entry 134, RG 226, NA as well as American Legation Bern to Secretary of State, January 13, 1943, Folder 1079, Box 171, Entry 146, NA, reprinted in *UUDW*, Doc 3, p. 18 ff. For the following, cf. esp. Jürgen Heideking, "Die 'Breakers'-Akte: Das Office of Strategic Services und der 20. Juli 1944," in Heideking/Mauch, *Geheimdienstkrieg*, pp. 11–50.

29. Allen Dulles to Donovan, May 6, 1942, Folder 70, Box 9, Entry 106, Entry 106, RG 226, NA.

30. Conversation with von Trott, January 1943, reported to Allen Dulles, file 4, Box XII, WCC, AöRK Geneva; Telegram OSS Bern to OSS Washington, January 14, 1943, Box 307, Entry 134, RG 226, NA (emphasis by author). On the meetings between Dulles and Visser t'Hooft, see Armin Boyens, *Kirchenkampf und Ökumene, 1939–1945: Darstellung und Dokumentation*, Vol. 2 (Munich, 1973).

31. Cf. OSS Bern to OSS Washington (via State Department), March 12, 1943, Box 307, Entry 134, RG 226, NA.

32. On the background to the Quebec Conference, see FRUS, *The Conference of Quebec 1944* (Washington, D.C., 1972); Dallek, *FDR and American Foreign Policy*, pp. 408 ff.; OSS Bern to OSS Washington, August 19, 1943, Folder 1817, Box 339, Entry 134, RG 226, NA, reprinted in *UUDW*, p 23 ff.

33. The Free Reports of February 23, 24, 25, 1943, OSS Bern to Secretary of State and OSS Washington may be found in Folder 1079, Box 171, Entry 146, RG 226, NA. OSS Bern to Secretary of State, February 25, 1943, ibid.

34. OSS Official Dispatch, Bern, via radiophone, sub: Allied Propaganda to Germany, n. d., Sept.-Dec. File, Box 72, MR, FDRL, Hyde Park, NY.

35. See above, ch. 3.

36. OSS Bern to OSS Washington, November 8, 1943, Folder 1821, Box 341, RG 226, NA, partly reprinted in *UUDW*, p. 73 ff.

37. OSS Dulles to OSS Bern, January 27, 1944, Folder 1368, Box 228, Entry 134, RG 226, NA.

38. OSS Bern (via Legation) to Secretary of State, April 7, 1943, Folder 1079, Box 171, Entry 146, RG 226, NA.

39. Leland Harrison to Mr. Joyce, August 8, 1945, Box 47, Memoranda 1942–1947, Box 47, LOC-MD, Washington, D.C.; OSS Bern to OSS Washington, April 7, 1943, Folder 1079, Box 171, Entry 146, RG 226, NA. On Hohenlohe's biography, see Bernd Martin, *Friedensinitiativen und Machtpolitik im Zweiten Weltkrieg 1939–1942* (Düsseldorf, 1974), p. 85, as well as Klemens von Klemperer, *German Resistance against Hitler*, p. 92.

40. "Bulls" was the code name for Dulles, "Paul" stood for Hohenlohe. The minutes of the "Bulls-Paul" conversation have been passed down several times, Aufzeichnung über Aussprachen mit Mr. Bull und Mr. Roberts [Recording of Discussions with Mr. Bull and Mr. Roberts], Sonntag, d.21.März 1943 [Sunday, March 21, 1943]; Unterredung Pauls: Mr.Bull, Schweiz [Conversation of Paul: Mr. Bull, Switzerland], Mitte Februar 1943 [mid-February

1943], OSS Bern, Box 5 CIA Archives, Srodes Papers, as well as in Roll 458, MF Publication T175, NA. Additional records, including the Memorandum Secret Allied Talks with Germany, European Section USSR Home Service, February 18, 1948, may be found in Box 37, Dulles, Papers, Seeley G. Mudd Manuscript Library, Princeton, NJ, and in Folder M.E. Hohenlohe-Langenberg/3, May 20, 1943, 862.20200, RG 59, NA.

41. That the documents might really have been forged after the fact, as the CIA claimed, can practically be excluded, since similar-sounding transmissions have surfaced in different sites. Its truthfulness may be estimated on the low side, however, since the author, Reinhard Spitzy, may have forged the text with its addressees, Himmler und Hitler, in mind. On this point, see Reinhard Spitzy, *So haben wir das Reich verspielt: Bekenntnisse eines Illegalen* (Munich, 2nd ed., 1987), p. 446 ff., esp. p. 456; Klemens von Klemperer, *German Opposition against Hitler*, p. 401, fn. Additional accounts of the Hohenlohe-Dulles conversations may be found in L. Mosely, *Dulles*, p. 145 ff.; Bernd Martin, "Deutsche Oppositions- und Widerstandskreise und die Frage eines separaten Friedensschlusses im Zweiten Weltkrieg," in Klaus Jürgen Müller, ed., *Der deutsche Widerstand 1933–1945* (Paderborn, 1986), p. 88 ff.; Christopher Simpson, *The Splendid Blond Beast: Money, Law, and Genocide in the Twentieth Century* (New York, 1993), pp. 122–124.

42. Leland Harrison to Mr. Joyce, August 8, 1945, Box 47, Memoranda 1942–1947, Box 47, MDLOC, Washington, D.C.; OSS Bern to OSS Washington, April 7, 1943, Folder 1079, Box 171, Entry 146, RG 226, NA; Memorandum 110 to Argus, March 30, 1945, Box 31, Entry 190, RG 226, NA.

43. That the Gestapo was reporting on Dulles's activity is confirmed, among other things, by the copy of conversation minutes from Director Richard Großmann, who witnessed a talk between the former Chancellor Joseph Wirth, Baron Godin, and Allen Dulles in Lucerne in May 1943. Abschrift Protokoll [Copy Minutes] Dr. Wirth—Baron Godin—Mr. Dulles, 22. Mai 1943 [May 22, 1943]. This and similar documents were sent as information to Dulles after the war by Robert Kempner in the course of the Nuremberg trials. Enclosures for Robert M. W. Kempner to Allen Dulles, January 28, 1948, Box 37 Dulles Papers, Seeley G. Mudd Manuscript Library, Princeton, NJ.

44. The occasion was an adventurous plan into which not only Major Steltzer had been initiated, but also Himmler, who wanted to move against Russia together with the Western allies. The Background of the George Story [handwritten, signed by Ernesto Kocherthaler], Allen Welsh Dulles Papers, File 6–1092, Box 5, CIA Archives/FOIA. (The author thanks J. Srodes for kindly providing a copy of the Kocherthaler document); OSS Bern to OSS Washington, December 27, 1944, CIA/FOIA.

45. OSS Bern to OSS Washington, January 27, 1944, Folder 3296, Box 235, Entry 146, RG 226, NA, partly reprinted in *AmIntel*, Doc 34, p. 191.

46. Bern Legation, Memorandum for the files, August 20, 1942, Enclosure to despatch No.12825, October 25, 1945, from American Legation, Bern, 862.00/10–2545, RG 59, NA.

47. OSS Bern to OSS Washington, Box 2, Entry 138, RG 226, NA. In January 1944 Leuschner was being considered as Vice-Chancellor. See the lists for a shadow cabinet in Hoffmann, *History of the German Resistance*, p. 367.

48. OSS Bern to OSS Washington, August 22, 1943, Box 273, Entry 134, RG 226, NA.

49. OSS Bern to OSS Washington, November 20, 1942, Box 171, Entry 134, RG 226, NA. On May 11, 1942 the American Legation in Bern had reported that a German general had approached Braun, who asked him if he would endorse a semi-military government supported

by the people ("appuyé sur le peuple") following a possible coup. The general had told Braun that the intra-German military opposition wanted to protect the Reich against Bolshevism and knew and respected the conservative Social Democrat Braun as a close friend of Hindenburg. Bern Legation, Memorandum for the files, May 11, 1942; on this, see Enclosure to despatch No.12825, October 25, 1945, from American Legation, Bern, 862.00/10–2545, RG 59, NA.

50. Dulles and Shepardson were neighbors in New York, and Dulles had recruited Shepardson for the COI. Conversation with Whitney Shepardson's son John in December 1996, Washington, D.C. On Shepardson's attitutude toward James Count von Moltke's "Herman-Plan," see Memorandum Whitney Shepardson, OSS-PG to General Donovan, April 3, 1944, Roll 52, MF 1462, Entry 190, RG 226, NA, reprinted in Heideking/Mauch, "Das Herman-Dossier. Helmuth James Graf von Moltke, die deutsche Emigration in Istanbul und der amerikanische Geheimdienst Office of Strategic Services," in VZG 40 (1992), pp. 621–623; OSS Dulles to OSS Bern, January 27, 1944, Folder 1368, Box 228, Entry 134, RG 226, NA; OSS-SI Washington (Shepardson) to OSS Bern, February 2, 1944, Folder 3269, Box 235, Entry 146, RG 226, NA.

51. Memorandum OSS for Secretary of State Cordell Hull, May 16, 1944, Box 234, Entry 146, RG 226, NA. As legitimation, the precedent of the Soviet Union's exclusive negotiations with Finland was cited.

52. J. Heideking, "Die Breakers-Akte," in Heideking/Mauch, *Geheimdienstkrieg*, p. 26.

53. Cf. ibid., pp. 22–27; *AmIntel*, pp. 191–233.

54. One of the first informants in this affair was apparently Massimo Magistrati ("Dan"), the Italian emissary in Bern. OSS Bern to OSS Washington, April 22, 1943, Folder 1079, Box 171, Entry 146, RG 226; OSS Bern to OSS Washington, April 17, 1943; OSS Bern to OSS Washington, April 24, 1943; OSS Bern to OSS Washington, April 30, 1943, ibid.

55. OSS Washington to OSS Bern, April 10, 1944, Box 2, Entry 138, RG 226, NA.

56. OSS Bern to OSS Washington, April 6 and 7, 1944, Box 2, Entry 138, RG 226, NA.

57. Ibid.

58. Telegram OSS Bern to OSS Washington and London, June 12, 1944, Box 192, Entry 134, OSS Washington to OSS Bern, June 17, 1944, Box 165, Entry 134, RG 226, NA; OSS Bern to OSS Washington, February 15, 1944, Box 170, Entry 134, reprinted in Dulles-WIR, Doc. 3–13, 218. One example of Dulles's informal contact to the resistance is his tie to Fritz P. Molden, see Interview S. Beer/Fritz P. Molden, Washington, D.C., November 5, 1996, OSSOHP.

59. OSS Washington to OSS Bern, April 10, 1944, Box 2, Entry 138, RG 226, NA; see too OSS Washington to OSS Madrid, May 29, 1944, Box 235, Entry 146, RG 226, NA.

60. In the cable and postal traffic with the British, the Breakers were called the "Wotan Group," see Box 2, Entry 138, RG 226, NA; Declaration of the Wotan Group, Folder 1, Box 557, Entry 92, RG 226, NA; OSS Washington (Donovan) to OSS London (David Bruce), July 28, 1944, Folder 3296, Box 235, Entry 146, RG 226, NA.

61. Cf. the cable from July 12, 13, and 15, 1944, OSS Bern to OSS Washington, Folder 58a, Box 14, Entry 99, RG 226, NA; Doc 45–49, in *AmIntel*, pp. 224–231; OSS to State Department, JCS and FDR, July 18, 1944, L 39980, Entry 21, RG 226, reprinted in Hoffmann, *History of the German Resistance*, Doc. 4, p. 749; *AmIntel*, Doc 49, p. 23 ff.

62. JIC 82, July 22, 1944, Germany Sec 1-B, ABC 381, RG 165, NA.

63. Allen W. Dulles to William J. Donovan, via radiotelephone, July 20, 1944, Folder 1, Box 557, Entry 92, RG 226, NA, partially reprinted in *AmIntel*, Doc.50, pp. 233–235.

64. OSS Bern to General Thomas J. Betts, July 21, 1944, Folder 63, Box 4, Entry 134, RG 226, NA, *AmIntel*, Doc 51, p. 235 ff.; W. J. Donovan to FDR, July 22, Folder 58a, Box 14, Entry 99, RG 226, NA, *AmIntel*, Doc 53, pp. 243–249; see too *FRUS 1944*, I, pp. 510–513.

65. On this point, see the memorandum of July 22, 1944 sent to Warren (State Department), McGovern (JCS), General Marshall, General Magruder, and the Map Room of the House, which, as formulated late in the afternoon of July 22, no longer contained a list of measures. L 39971, Entry 21, RG 226, NA; cf. J. Heideking, "Breakers-Akte," p. 46 fn.

66. Interview C. Mauch/F. Ford, Lexington, MA, January 17, 1997, *OSSOHP*. Franklin Ford, "The Twentieth of July in the History of the German Resistance," in *AHR* 51 (1945/46), pp. 609–626.

67. Stockholm/Despatch 4040, Encl. 2, Position of German Communists in Questions of the Day (Meeting of August 1), August 3, 1944, CDF 103.918/9–1944, RG 59, NA.

68. Memorandum by Walter Langer, July 26, 1944, MF Roll 52, Entry 190, RG 226, NA, reprinted in *UUDW*, pp. 101–105.

69. "The Attempt on Hitler's Life and Its Consequences," July 27, 1944, R&A 2387, RG 59, NA, excerpts reprinted in *AmIntel* Doc 60, pp. 260–272. Officially, as Paul Zimmer explained in an interview with Barry Katz on June 17, 1985, Franz Neumann was the author of the R&A study. To be sure, the report betrays linguistic and ideological formulae that are obviously attributable to Marcuse. See B. Katz, "Foreign Intelligence," p. 210, fn.; on this point, see too J. Heideking, "Die Breakers-Akte," p. 30 ff.; P. Marquardt-Bigman, *Amerikanische Geheimdienstanalysen*, p. 109 ff.; C. Mauch, "Subversion und Propaganda," pp. 56–60.

70. OSS Bern to OSS Washington, July 21, 1944, Box 273, Entry 134, RG 226, NA; OSS Washington to FDR, July 22, 1944, Box 168, PSF, FDRL, Hyde Park.

71. Peter Hoffmann, "Colonel Claus von Stauffenberg in the German Resistance to Hitler: Between East and West," in *Historical Journal* 31 (1988), pp. 629–650.

72. Memorandum Charles S. Cheston to JCS, January 1945, Folder 58a, Box 14, Entry 99, RG 226, NA. As early as July 22, Leiber had reported that the German Anti-Hitler-generals were split into a pro-Western group and a pro-Russian group. "Report by Informed German Sources in Rome on the Situation in Germany," OWI-London, Intelligence Section, to Dr. Eugene N. Anderson, OSS Washington, July 24, 1944, 88111, Box 983, Entry 16, RG 226. NA; on Lieber, also see [H. Stuart Hughes], OSS Interview with Pater Leiber, August 18, 1944, Box 14, Entry 136, RG 226, NA, reprinted in *UUDW*, Doc. 44, pp. 123–125.

73. F.H. Hinsley, British Intelligence, III/1, p. 362 ff.; regarding the first indications about German rocket research passed on to the British, in some cases anonymously—via Oslo –see F. H. Hinsley, British Intelligence I, p. 508 ff; On the Oslo Report, see Reginald V. Jones, *The Wizard War: British Scientific Intelligence, 1939–1945* (New York, 1978), p. 67 ff., further, Arnold Kramish, *The Griffin* (Boston, 1986), p. 99 ff; on the initial information about Peenemünde, see too Jozef Garlinski, *Hitler's Last Weapons: The Underground War Against the V1 and V2* (London, 1978), p. 44 ff.

74. Telegram OSS Bern to OSS Washington, February 5, 1943, Box 171, Entry 134, RG 226, NA; OSS Bern to OSS Washington, February 27, 1943, Box 307, Entry 134, RG 226, NA.

75. On Theodor Buchhold, see Walter Dornberger, *V-2* (New York, 1954), p. 232.

76. Constance Babington Smith, *Evidence in Camera* (London, 1958), 200 ff.; R. V. Jones, *Wizard War*, pp. 339, 349 ff.; AIR 41/7, *Photographic Reconnaissance*, Vol. II, pp. 110, 127, cited in F. H. Hinsley, *British Intelligence*, III/1, pp. 363, 367.

77. Hugh T. Cunningham (Chief, Steering Division) to Dr. Lester C. Houck, Washington, October 16, 1946, Folder 579, Box 73, Entry 108B, RG 226, NA.

78. Garlinski estimates that the cost for a V-1 rocket was 125 English pounds, but 12,000 for a V-2. J. Garlinski, *Hitlers Last Weapons*, p. 70. The British, as Weinberg emphasizes, regarded the rocket construction as a bluff. Adding to their confusion was the simultaneous development of four different systems. G. Weinberg, *World at Arms* (Cambridge, 1993), p. 564; Jürgen Rohwer/Eberhard Jäckel, *Die Funkaufklärung und ihre Rolle im Zweiten Weltkrieg* (Stuttgart, 1979), p. 366.

79. R. V. Jones, Wizard War, p. 355 ff.

80. OSS Bern to OSS Washington, May 29, 1943, Box 307, Entry 134, RG 226, NA; Telegram OSS Bern to OSS Washington, June 24, 1943, Box 307, Entry 134, RG 226, NA. On December 16, 1943, as a follow-up to the report from "493" (Loofbourow) and "Flute" (Professor Paul Scherrer), Dulles cabled Washington that the V-weapon was designated by the name A-4 and would be driven by a liquid propellant. December 16, 1943, Folder 1821, Entry 134, RG 226, NA.

81. [Report from Switzerland, June 24, 1943], sub: Rocket Weapon, Box 3, Entry 107, RG 226, NA. On the accuracy of the V-1, which improved extremely between December 1943 and May 1944, see R. V. Jones, *Wizard War*, Fig. 22, p. 368, Fig. 27, p. 414.

82. On the diversionary maneuvers, see Gordon Welchman, *The Hut Six Story: Breaking the Enigma Codes* (New York, 1982), p. 420 ff.; on the planning, F. H. Hinsley, *British Intelligence* III/1, p. 381 ff.; on their effects, see R. V. Jones, *Wizard War* pp. 346–348. The victims included the head of the Luftwaffe General Staff, Hans Jeschonnek, who was driven to suicide by the attack on Peenemünde, as well as by differences of opinion with Göring. The OSS immediately speculated about the nature of Jeschonnek's death, see Telegram OSS Bern to OSS Washington, September 15, 1943, Folder 1819, Box 340, Entry 134, RG 226, NA.

83. On this, see the scanty references in J. Persico, *Piercing the Reich*, p. 56 ff.; W. Laqueur/R. Breitman, *Breaking the Silence*, p. 176; N. Petersen, *From Hitler's Doorstep*, p. 567 fn; B. F. Smith, *Shadow Warriors*, p. 223.

84. CAB 120/748, JIC 955/43 of July 1943, Hinsley, III/1, 379. The OSS really did occasionally overestimate the danger of a German deployment of gas weapons; see, for example, OSS Bern for Victor (American Legation Bern to Secretary of State), March 4, 1943, FW 103.918/1065F, RG 59, NA. As a rule, however, Donovan did not make the connection between gas weapons and the miracle weapon. On this point, see the summary R&A report, Secret Weapons, November 2, 1943, Enclosure to Francis P. Miller to Whitney Shepardson, November 22, 1943, Box 265, Entry 108, RG 226, NA.

85. F. H. Hinsley, *British Intelligence*, III/1, p. 378 ff.

86. OSS London to OSS Washington, February 17, 1944. Folder 1565, Box 274, Entry 134, RG 226, NA.

87. Stanley P. Lovell to Allen Dulles, July 27, 1962; Allen Dulles to Stanley P. Lovell, July 30, 1962, Box 19, Dulles Papers, Seeley G. Mudd Manuscript Library, Princeton, NJ. In his memoirs, he then downplayed his misestimation. Stanley P. Lovell, *Of Spies and Stratagems*, pp. 126–130.

88. A History of the Survey of Foreign Experts from its Inception in September 1942 to December 31, 1944, Eric W. Staight, Chief, Survey of Foreign Experts to Mr. Conyers Read, Director, OSS History Project, Folder 53, Box 77, Entry 99, RG 226, NA.

89. Eric Staight to Frederic R. Dolbeare, Folder 43, Box 3, Entry 107, RG 226, NA.

90. In one report from Istanbul in August, it said: "Assembly plants and other accessory manufacturers for radio rockets are located at Oswiecim." The Istanbul report received a grade of "C-o" and was, to be sure, first disseminated within the OSS on October 14, 1943. It went out to the sabotage division SO, among other departments. The camp was described as "the great concentration camp of 65.000 people. . . . The group includes 32,000 Jews from Poland, France, Belgium and Jugoslavia, and they are worked in groups of 100, each under a Kommandant. The camp is highly protected and fortified. . . . Many prisoners are political." Memorandum, sub: Radio Rocket Bomb, Box 3, En-try 107, RG 226, NA; on Auschwitz, also see Memorandum: Further Developments on Peenemünde Products, November 2, 1943, Frederic R. Dolbear to Eric W. Staight, November 2, 1943; Memorandum OSWIECIM, November 30, 1943, both ibid.

91. On Dora-Mittelbau, see W. Dornberger, *V-2*, p. 204 ff; R.V. Jones, *Wizard War*, p. 454; J. Garlinski, *Hitler's Last Weapon*, p. 104 ff., and esp. Manfred Bornemann, *Geheimprojekt Mittelbau* (Munich, 1971). OSS-London received lots of information from "reliable Dutchmen" and "reliable Belgians," see the material in Box 3, Entry 107, RG 226, NA.

92. OSS Bern to OSS Washington, September 9, 1943, Folder 1819, Box 340. Entry 134, RG 226, NA; see too Laqueur/Breitman, *Breaking the Silence*, p. 175. On September 15 Dulles reported that one of his sources had put the damage in Peenemünde at "eighty to ninety per cent." The underground electrical generator facility, however, remained undamaged. OSS Bern to OSS Washington, September 15, 1943, Box 273, Entry 134 as well as Box 340, Entry 134, RG 226, NA.

93. The name Johann is also decoded in the cables as Johan. The most important cables may be found scattered among hundreds of "folders" in Entry 134, RG 226, NA. Additional information about the V-weapons in Entry 108B as well as in Box 1 through 8, Entry 108; Box 6, Entry 26, Entry 190, RG 226, and Box 15, RG 84, NA.

94. OSS Bern to OSS Washington, September 15, 1943, Box 340, Entry 134, RG 226, NA; [Johann-Report], September 15, 1943, ibid.; Report from OSS London, Germany: Military/Technical, sub: V-3, Report Date 15, 1944, Box 264, Entry 108, RG 226, NA; R&A Report Secret Weapons, November 2, 1943, Enclosure to Francis P. Miller to Whitney Shepardson, November 22, 1943, Box 265, Entry 108, RG 226, NA. On the zeppelin and Rax factories, see too R. V. Jones, *Wizard War*, p. 454.

95. Not all of the technical specifications were correct. At 40 tons, Loofbourow put much too high an estimate on the weight and, at 800 km/h, too low an estimate on the weapon's speed; by contrast, the specifications about the range, ignition, and catapulting mechanism were accurate. OSS Bern to OSS Washington, December 9, 1943, Box 274, Entry 134, RG 226, NA, partially reprinted in Dulles-WIR, Doc.2–87, 175. On Loofbourow, see Powers, *Heisenberg's War*, p. 271 ff.

96. See the map in Hinsley, *British Intelligence*, III/1, between p. 402 and p. 403. Dulles was presumably the first one to report about the exact location of the rocket installations in the Pas de Calais. Harry S. Truman, July 18, 1946, Citation to Accompany the Award of the Medal for Merit to Allen W. Dulles, July 18, 1946, Dulles Papers, Seeley G. Mudd Manuscript Library, Princeton, NJ.

97. That the OSS in Bern also identified a number of launching ramps is proven by the cable traffic in Entry 134; see, for example, OSS Bern to OSS Washington, March 7, 1944, Box 307, Entry 134, RG 226, NA. On photographic intelligence and Ultra, see esp. F. H. Hinsley, *British Intelligence*, III/1, pp. 433–455.

98. Weinberg, *World at Arms*, p. 565.

99. German Morale. February and March 1944. Based on an Analysis of 1674 Letters written to German Prisoners of War in American Camps, July 15, 1944, Box 144, Entry 136, RG 226, NA. Rhoda Metraux, German Morale. December 1943 and January 1944. Based on an Analysis of 2045 Letters written to German Prisoners of War in American Camps, 7 June 1944, 25, fn., Box 144, Entry 136, RG 226, NA. The somewhat different morale of German prisoners of war in America has been investigated by M. I. Gurfein and Morris Janowitz, "Trends in Wehrmacht-Morale," in *Public Opinion Quarterly* 10 (1946) pp. 78–84.

100. M. Steinert, *Hitlers Krieg und die Deutschen*, p. 460 ff.

101. OSS Bern to OSS London, June 27, 1944, Box 26, Entry 139, RG 226, NA.

102. Thus far, it has not been possible to identify Agent 328. He was a Frenchman married to a German woman, and he had excellent contacts to trade unions. In one telegram, 328 is designated as René; conceivably, this was René Bertholet.

103. OSS Bern to OSS London, June 27, 1944, Box 26, Entry 139, RG 226, NA.

104. M. Steinert, *Hitlers Krieg und die Deutschen*, p. 512.

105. N. Petersen, *From Hitler's Doorstep*, Doc 4–86, p. 382.

106. At the beginning of July, for example, the informant had reported that Berlin did not have any information with which to assess the damage caused by V-1 rockets in southern England. OSS Bern to OSS Washington, July 6, 1944, CIA/FOIA, Srodes Papers.

107. W. S. Stephenson to W.J. Donovan, November 15, 1944, Box 1, J. Russell Forgan Papers, Hoover Institution, Stanford, CA. According to another assessment, Kolbe was characterized as the "prize intelligence source of the war." Memorandum of Information for the Joint U.S. Chiefs of Staff, sub: OSS Operations in Switzerland 1942–1945, Box 67A, William J. Donovan Papers, USAMI, Carlisle Barracks, Pa.

108. On this point, see the internal CIA publication by Anthony Quibble, "Alias George Wood," in *SII* 10 (1966), pp. 69–90, 69, Entry 193, RG 226, NA. Also important, though it needs to be read with caution and a critical eye, is the fictionalized report (based on interviews with Gerald Mayer and Fritz Kolbe) by Edward P. Morgan, "The Spy the Nazi's Missed," in *True Magazine*, July 1950, copy in Box 3, Persico Papers, Hoover Institution, Stanford, CA; thoroughly unreliable is the article by Emile C. Schurmacher, "Allen Dulles and the Spy House at 2430 E Street, N.W.," Folder Swiss Operations, Box 4, ibid.

109. Kocherthaler, a German born in Spain, had been flown into Switzerland after the Spanish Civil War. He was a friend of the Basle banker, who, in turn, kept closely in touch with Gerald Mayer. On Kocherthaler, see OSS Bern to OSS Washington, December 27, 1944, CIA/ FOIA.

110. Ernesto Kocherthaler, The Background of the George Story, Allen Welsh Dulles Papers (CIA), Box 5, file 6–1092, FOIA/CIA. By way of Sauerbruch, Kolbe had also gotten to know Alfred Graf von Waldersee, who belonged to the resistance.

111. In September 1945 Kolbe was asked by staff members at the Department of State about what had driven him to work for the Americans. His answer was: "What profit [has] a man if he conquers the whole world and loses his own soul." Interrogation of Fritz Kolbe, De-Witt C. Poole Mission, Sept.23–24, 1945, Department of State, MS, cited by Mary Alice Gallin, "Ethical and Religious Factors," p. 129.

112. Kocherthaler, The Background of the George Story, Allen Welsh Dulles Papers (CIA), Box 5, file 6–1092, FOIA/CIA; A. Quibble, "Alias George Wood," in: *SII* 10 (1966), pp. 70–72. The girlfriend in Berlin was Sauerbruch's secretary Maria Fritsch.

113. On August 25 Dulles checked whether the OWI telegram that Kolbe quoted from memory, and whose code had apparently been broken, really did exist. OSS Bern to OSS Washington and London, August 25, 1943, Box 273, Entry 134, RG 226, NA.

114. In Bern only Gerald Mayer and "493" knew about Fritz Kolbe (alias Georg Kaiser or Georg Merz). Even Dulles' close associate Gaevernitz never learned about Fritz Kolbe's mission during the war. OSS Washington to OSS Bern, November 24, 1944, Box 590, Entry 88, RG 226, NA; OSS Washington to OSS Bern, September 21, 1944, Box 590, Entry 88, RG 226, NA. OSS Bern to OSS London, August 21, 1943, Box 339, Entry 134, RG 226, NA; OSS Bern to OSS Washington, Folder 1021, Box 158, Entry 134, RG 226, NA.

115. OSS Bern to OSS London and OSS Washington, October 9, 1943, Box 273, RG 226, NA. Material on deciphering some of the key codes may be found in OSS Bern to OSS London and Washington, October 8, 1943, Box 274, RG 226, NA as well as OSS Bern to OSS Washington (#1455–1457), December 28, 1943, Box 298, Entry 134, RG 226, NA. The code system for the Kappa cable traffic was extremely complex. In order to mislead, apparently, letters from the Greek alphabet were covered with several different layers of coding. OSS Bern to OSS Washington (#1463–1465), December 28, 1943, Box 298, Entry 134, RG 226, NA. Different colors designated different countries (yellow, for example, stood for Turkey, blue for Sweden, red for France), code words with five letters (by contrast) designated institutions, persons, or places (e.g.. "Grand" stood for 'Foreign Office,' "Bramt" for Ribbentrop's office, or "Milit" for 'Ambassador von Papen').

116. A. Quibble, "Alias George Wood," p. 74; OSS Bern to OSS Washington, December 30, 1943; OSS Bern to OSS Washington, October 31, 1943.

117. OSS Bern to OSS Washington, January 1, 1944, CIA/FOIA.

118. At the end of 1942 [1932, inaccurately, in the original] there were 24 sabotage operations against trains, compared to 293 for the same time period in 1943; the murder rate, correspondingly, had increased from 15 to 195. OSS Bern to OSS Washington, January 8, 1944, CIA/FOIA; OSS Bern to OSS Washington, April 17, 1944, CIA/FOIA; OSS Bern to OSS Washington, January 4, 1944, CIA/FOIA.

119. OSS Bern to OSS Washington, Box 298, Entry 134, RG 226, NA. The "Confidential Reich Matter" ("Geheime Reichssache") from November 4 mentioned the SD-Agent Moystisch assigned to evaluate the material. See also M. L. Moyzisch, *Operation Cicero* (London, 1969). Cf., in addition, A. Quibble, "Alias George Wood," p. 77, as well as OSS Bern to OSS Washington, Box 298, Entry 134, RG 226, NA, OSS Bern to OSS Washington December 31, 1943, CIA/FOIA; OSS Bern to OSS Washington, undated (= February 21, 1944), CIA/FOIA.

120. See, too the memoirs of the British ambassador Hugh Montgomery Knatchbull-Hugessen, *Diplomat in Peace and War* (London, 1968).

121. A certain amount of delay, to be sure, was the result of the fact that the Kappa material first went to X-2 and only then was forwarded from there to "Broadway." OSS London to OSS Washington, January 6, 1944, CIA/FOIA.

122. When asked who Cicero might be, "Wood" answered that there was no way to find out who Cicero is. OSS Bern to OSS Washington, undated (= February 21, 1944), CIA/FOIA.

123. Nigel West, *MI-6. British Secret Intelligence Service Operations 1909–1945* (London, 1983), p. 200 ff.

124. Memorandum for the President, January 10, 1944, Roll 18, MF 1642, Entry 162, RG 226, NA. Owing to a lack of other sources, for McCormack's correspondence the author is relying on the CIA study "Alias George Wood," pp. 78, 81. According to that study, at the

end of January the "Boston Series" was no longer sent out to FDR, just to Berle. The OSS in London, too, enormously restricted dissemination of the Kappa material. Some dispatches went to Ambassador Winant, while the bombing damage reports that were not attributed to any source were forwarded to the usual channels. OSS London to OSS Washington, January 6, 1944, CIA/FOIA.

125. OSS Bern to OSS Washington, December 29, 1943, Box 298, Entry 134, RG 226, NA.

126. A. Quibble, "Alias George Wood," p. 81 ff; OSS Bern to OSS Washington, April 11, 1944, CIA/FOIA.

127. A comprehensive report about the distribution of the Kappa material may be found in "Rhythm" (Russell Forgan) to "110," February 10, 1945, Folder 120, Box 7, Entry 125, RG 226, NA.

128. Bern to Director OSS, Secretariat, Magruder, "105" (D. Bruce) and "Jackpot" (unidentified), April 12, 1943, Roll 18, MF 1642, Entry 162, RG 226, NA.

129. Dulles occasionally characterized the Allied front he anticipated for France—along with the Italian, Russian, and Balkan fronts—as a "fourth front."

130. OSS Bern to OSS Washington, April 17, 1944, CIA/FOIA.

131. OSS Bern to OSS Washington, May 15, 1944, CIA/FOIA.

132. A. Quibble, "Alias George Wood," p. 88 ff.; OSS Bern to OSS Washington, April 7 1945, Box 7, Entry 90, RG 226, NA; Dulles-WIR, Doc.5–88, 493.

133. Quibble raises the question as to why the reports were transmitted across X-2 channels. In reality, none of Quibble's notorious scapegoats—Bissell in G-2, Berle in the State Department, and McCormack from MIS—was responsible; rather, it was Dulles himself. A. Quibble, "Alias George Wood," p. 88. OSS London to OSS Washington, January 6, 1944, CIA/FOIA.

134. Interview C. Mauch/R. Helms, April 14, 1997, Washington, D.C. OSSOHP.

135. At the beginning of April, Kolbe arrived in Switerland with a five-day visa, and Dulles assigned him the job of obtaining messages about the Alpine redoubt. OSS Bern to OSS Washington, April 4, 1945, Folder 86, Box 7, Entry 90, RG 226, NA.

136. OSS Mission for Germany, to Inter-Division Coordinating Committee on German Government Personnel, Lt. Col. Howard P. Jones, Chairman, sub: German Government Personnel, August 6, 1945, XL 22686, Entry 19, RG 226, NA.

137. Apparently, first Kolbe and then later Köcher were arrested by the Swiss authorities. Kolbe, On behalf of Dulles, Kolbe had attempted to prevent Köcher from burning the Foreign Office documents located in Bern. Following his visit, Köcher was arrested by the Swiss, but in the end he was released from custody. Since the Swiss authorities had learned that Köcher was illegally helping Nazis to get across the German border and distributing gold coins hidden in the basement of the legation, the Swiss emissary was arrested and interned. The Swiss federal councillor Pilet-Golaz, who had originally spoken out strongly on Köcher's behalf, rescinded his words of support under pressure from the military police, and Köcher, who told the diplomats interned with him that Kolbe had betrayed him, committed suicide. Köcher's denunciation ultimately reflected back on Kolbe. Ernesto Kocherthaler, The Background of the George Story, Allen Welsh Dulles Papers, File 6–1092, Box 5, CIA Archives/FOIA. The possibility cannot be entirely excluded that the Swiss authorities learned about Köcher's machinations from Kolbe.

138. Apparently, "Wood" was working for the OSS when he had his accident, see "Black" to "110," August 8, 1945, Folder Berlin, Box 151, Entry 88, RG 226, NA. Between 1945 and 1948

"George" had received a total of $6199.25 as well as 20,000 Swiss francs. On October 12, 1948 he was issued a U.S. visa, with the CIA supporting the application. Richard Helms to Allen Dulles, February 19, 1948; April 21, 1945; October 11, 1948; October 12, 1948; Fred Stalder to Allen Dulles, May 11, 1948, Box 35, Dulles Papers, Seeley G. Mudd Manuscript Library, Princeton, NJ.

139. Remarks by Allen W. Dulles. Veterans of Strategic Services. Dinner—January 22, 1962 (talking points note), Box 22, Dulles Papers, Seeley G. Mudd Manuscript Library, Princeton, NJ.

140. OSS Bern to OSS Washington, January 3, 1944, Folder 1565, Box 274, Entry 134, RG 226, NA. Interview Christof Mauch/Erika Glaser Wallach, July 4, 1993, Warrenton, VA.

141. The spying activities of the Rhine skippers were probably denounced a number of times, since they were arrested "frequently" and "without apparent cause." OSS Bern to OSS Washington, October 21, 1943, Folder 1821, Box 341, Entry 134, RG 226, NA; OSS Bern to OSS Washington, October 21, 1943, Folder 1021, Box 158, Entry 134, RG 226, NA; OSS Bern to OSS Washington, June 23, 1943, Folder 1819, Box 339, Entry 134, RG 226, NA; OSS Bern to OSS Washington, December 1, 1943, Folder 1821, Box 340, Entry 134, RG 226, NA.

142. OSS Bern to OSS Washington, March 10, 1943, Box 171, Entry 134, RG 226, NA as well as Folder 1079, Box 171, Entry 146, RG 226, NA. The report was sent out via the State Department and at a time when Dulles knew that the Germans could crack the code. On April 1 there followed a report in which it said that the killing of Jews on the spot (as opposed to deportation to Poland) about which Dulles had reported in March had to be suspended owing to protests. OSS Bern to OSS Washington, April 1, 1943, Folder 1079, Box 171, Entry 146, RG 226, NA. On December 30, to mention yet another example, Kolbe reported that Obersturmbannführer Kappler had been instructed to dispatch 8000 Jews living in Rome to northern Italy for liquidation. OSS Bern to OSS Washington, December 30, 1943, Box 298, Entry 134, RG 226, NA.

143. W. Laqueur/R. Breitman, *Breaking the Silence*.

144. In October 1943, for example, Dulles received $3000 and was able to obtain 60 Swiss visas. OSS Bern to OSS Washington, October 30, 1943, Box 341, Entry 134, RG 226, NA; OSS Washington to OSS Bern, June 23, 1943, Folder 1820, Box 340, Entry 134, RG 226, NA.

145. Harry S. Truman, July 18, 1946, Citation to Accompany the Award of the Medal for Merit to Allen W. Dulles, July 18, 1946, Dulles Papers, Seeley G. Mudd Manuscript Library, Princeton, NJ.

146. Penetration and Compromises of OSS in Europe, n.d., Box 56, Hoyt S. Vandenberg Papers, MDLOC, Washington, D.C.

147. On this, see SWROSS, pp. 294 ff.

5. MEDIA WAR AND BLACK PROPAGANDA

1. This retrospective assessment derives from a secret document of the Morale Operations Branch History, which—in contrast to other departmental histories—is characterized by a high degree of institutional self-criticism. MO Branch History, Box 75, Entry 99, RG 226, NA. One of the people who rejected recruiting by the MO was Richard Helms. Interview C. Mauch/R. Helms, April 14, 1997, *OSSOHP*.

2. One Oechsner, see above, Ch. II.

3. JCS 155/7/D, Directive. Functions of the Office of Strategic Services, April 4, 1943, reprinted as Appendix J in: T. Troy, *Donovan and the CIA*, pp. 436–438.

4. In the MO Branch History, it said: "Elmer Davis was quoted as saying that OWI was not doing 'black,' might never do it, but would not relinquish the right to do it." MO Branch History, Box 75, Entry 99, RG 226, NA.

5. MO Branch History, Box 75, Entry 99, RG 226, NA. In the field, MO was subordinated to the Psychological Warfare Board, which (among other things) threw propaganda leaflets from the sky, broadcast "Voice of America" programs, and hung American posters in cities. On the organization of the PWB, see Schematic Organization of PWB, January 1943, Box 34, Entry 99, RG 226, NA; on the operations, see Laurie, *Propaganda Warriors*, pp. 154–158. On the operations in northern Africa, also see the Whitaker Report (filmed by the OSS), Guy V. Thayer, Jr. to Lt. Col. O.C. Doering, May 16, 1944, Box 28, Entry 90, RG 226, NA.

6. The best account of the OSS leaflet operations is the several hundred page long Psychological Warfare Report by Lt. Colonel Heber Blankenhorn, Combat Propaganda in Africa, Italy, United Kingdom and France, 1943–1944, Heber Blankenhorn Papers, Hoover Institution, Stanford, CA

7. On Langer ch. 4.

8. Operational Plans for Planting Rumors Concerning Hitler, February 1943; Origin of MO Campaign on Hitler; Memorandum for the Walter Langer File on Hitler, April 23, 1944, from Frederick Oechsner; Hitler To Speak Rumor; Example of an MO "Plan" Rumor "Where is Hitler," n. d.; Weekly MO Directive- June 20/44 (European), Folder 306 (3 of 3), Box 69, Entry 99, RG 226, NA. "Comebacks" to the "Where is Hitler"-Operation may be found in *NYT*, November 8, 11, 1944; ES, November 12, 1944, WP November 11, 1944; WP, November 6–7, 11, 13, 14, 19, 1944, PI, November 18, 1944. The authors of the comebacks included Drew Pearson and Louis P. Lochner. The final version of Langer's report is available in paperback: Walter C. Langer, *The Mind of Adolf Hitler: The Secret Wartime Report* (New York, 1972); see, in addition, MO Branch History, Box 75, Entry 99, RG 226, NA; Material for Leaflet Propaganda, n. d. [1943], Folder 2149, Box 160, Entry 139, RG 226.

9. Worksheets on Morale; The A B C's of Wartime Rumor, n. d. Folder 2147, Box 160, Entry 139, RG 226, NA. Additional basic texts circulating through the OSS came from Major Alex Trousdell, PWB, Cairo, Rumours as a Weapon of Attack on German Troops, July 12, 1944, Folder 780, Box 78, Entry 144, RG 226, NA.

10. MO Branch History, Box 75, Entry 99, RG 226, NA; PG Minutes of 410th Meeting. Held on Monday May 22, 1944; PG Minutes of 411th Meeting. Held on Tuesday May 23, 1944, Folder 42, Box 6, Entry 144, RG 226.

11. Hand-written commentary [author unidentifiable] on Lieut. Patrick Dolan to Dr. James Grafton Rogers, sub: German Subversive Leaflet, August 17, 1943, Folder 2396, Box 175, Entry 139, RG 226, NA.

12. Hand-written commentary [Dolan] to Mueller, Folder 2396, Box 175, Entry 139, RG 226, NA.

13. "Flugschrift, Nur für Erwachsene! Nur für Nationalsozialistische Männer und Frauen! Vertrauliche Information für Opfer von Luftangriffen, Berlin, den 15.September 1943"; Robert H. Knapp to Dr. James Grafton Rogers, August 16, 1943, sub: Accompanying Subversive Pamphlet Text; Lieut. Patrick Dolan to Dr. James Grafton Rogers, sub: German Subversive Leaflet, August 17, 1943; Leaflet (Instructions for Sexual Impotency), n. d., Folder 2396, Box 175, Entry 139, RG 226, NA.

14. Just months before, incidentally, the British had developed a similar project that spread via underground contacts within the Wehrmacht and instructed soldiers about the art of sim-

ulating diseases. E. Cushing to Carl Devoe, September 16, 1943, Folder 2396, Box 175, Entry 139, RG 226, NA.

15. Ibid.

16. MO Draft Branch History, 18f, Box 75, Entry 99, RG 226, NA. Relevant examples of MO Weekly Directives to OSS outposts in Europe may be found, above all, in Box 113, Entry 134, RG 226 and in Box 318, Entry 134, RG 226, NA. For the feedback on some of the rumors, see HT, September 20, 1944, copy in Folder 2150, Box 161, Entry 139, RG 226, NA.

17. MO Draft Branch History, 23–27, Box 75, Entry 99, RG 226, NA.

18. Memorandum by the OSS Morale Operations Branch in London. Suggestions for a German Underground Plan, August 31, 1943, Folder 2316, Box 175, Entry 139, RG 226, NA, partly reprinted in *AmIntel*, Doc.17, 60–69; C. Mauch, "OSS Subversive Warfare and the German Resistance to Hitler," paper presented at the SMH Annual Conference, Arlington, VA. April 1996. According to an anonymous MO veteran, Dr. Hamilton was in charge of "assessment training" in the OSS.

19. On the NKFD and the reactions of the OSS, see above, Ch. III.; see also suggestions for a German Underground Plan, August 31, 1942, Folder 2316, Box 175, Entry 139, RG 226, NA. H[eber] B[lankenhorn], Memorandum for Colonel Solbert, sub: Propaganda by Army Leaflets, June 26, 1942, Folder 2072, Box 155, Entry 139, RG 226, NA.

20. Die MO Branch's naïve ideas were attributable, not least of all, to the fact that in the late summer of 1943 there was hardly any notion of what social realities and conditions were like in National Socialist Germany. Early in September 1943 Rae Smith admitted quite bluntly in a telegram to Patrick Dolan: "With regard to the German underground, we have practically no information and nothing has been done about it," OSS London to OSS Washington, September 6, 1943, Folder 852, Entry 134, RG 226, NA. On discussions about the MO plan within the OSS Planning Group, see esp. Minutes of 207th Meeting, September 15, 1943, and Minutes of 209th Meeting, September 17, 1943, Folder 38, Box 5, Entry 144, RG 226, NA.

21. The discussions about the Hamilton plan by the MO are located in Box 175, Entry 139, RG 226, NA.

22. An outstanding description of the projects planned by the OSS and of the evaluation of political and psychological factors in the Reich may be found in OSS-PG 45/1, Special Military Plan for Psychological Warfare Against Germany, September 27, 1943, Folder 105, Box 15, Entry 144, RG 226, NA.

23. Radiotelephone Allen W. Dulles (OSS Bern) to William J. Donovan, 20 July 1944, NA, RG 226, Entry 92, Box 557, Folder 1; see, too, Heideking/ Mauch, *American Intelligence*, pp. 233 ff.

24. Memorandum William J. Donovan to President Roosevelt, July 24, 1944, NA RG 226, Entry 99, Box 14, Folder 58a. On this point and what follows, also see Mauch, "Dream of a Miracle War," p. 138 ff.

25. Memorandum K[enneth] D. Mann to William J. Donovan, Brief of Sauerkraut Missions I-II-III-MO-Rome, December 19, 1944 (Washington History Office Operations Files, Series 23), NA, RG 226, Entry 99, Box 88, Folder 5. Interview with Barbara Podoski, October 29, 1993, Washington, D.C.

26. Interview C. Mauch, C. Beer / F. Burkhardt, January 18, 1997, Bennington, VT, OS-SOHP; The Story of the Sauerkrauts, MO-MEDTO, 2677th HQ-Detachment OSS (Prov.), May 1945, 3, Box 102 A, Donovan Papers, USAMI, Carlisle Barracks, Pa.

27. Interview C. Mauch / B. Podorski, September 11, 1996, Washington, D.C., OSSOHP; on Eddie Lindner, a Viennese-born journalist, see Interview S. Beer/E. Lindner, 1997, Westport, Conn., *OSSOHP.*

28. Biographical Sketches in: The Story of the Sauerkrauts, MO-MEDTO, 2677th HQ-Detachment OSS (Prov.), May 1945, 27–34, Box 102 A, Donovan Papers, USAMI, Carlisle Barracks, Pa.; Memo on Averso operation on [!] July 1944, Barbara Lauwers Papers, Washington, D.C.; Authors' interview with Barbara Podorski (Lauwers), October 29, 1993, Washington, D.C.

29. Haseneier's charcoal sketches of Operation Sauerkraut are located in Box 14, Entry 99, RG 226, NA; see, in addition, Sourkraut [sic!] Operation #3—MO of OSS, Box 20, Entry 90, RG 226, NA. Interestingly, the cartoonist Saul Steinberg was an MO agent with the rank of lieutenant belonging to the OSS unit in charge of "Operation Sauerkraut."

30. Details about the course of individual Sauerkraut missions may be found in an article by Clayton D. Laurie, "The 'Sauerkrauts.' German Prisoners of War as OSS Agents, 1944–1945," in *Prologue* 26 (1994), pp. 49–59.

31. MO Branch History, Box 75, Entry 99, RG 226, NA. From the comprehensive chapter on "Prisoners of War" in the War Diary (Office of the Director, October, November, December 1944, Folder 148, Box 211, Entry RG 226, NA), it emerges, of course, that the MO agents hardly brought any military intelligence back with them at the end of 1944. On the importance of the interviews with POWs in the estimation of the OSS, see Memorandum for the JCS, Sub: Interrogation of Prisoners of War, August 19, 1944, Entry 162, roll 18, MF 1642, RG 226, NA. "Comebacks" on "Sauerkraut" Operations from March 1945 may be found in MO/MEDTO Field Report—April 1945, Excerpt in Box 69, Entry 99, RG 226, NA.

32. Chief MO [Kenneth Mann] to Director OSS [William Donovan], Brief of Sauerkraut Missions I-II-III-MO-Rome, December 1944, Folder 5, Box 88, Entry 99, RG 226, NA; Lt. Jack Daniels to 2677 Reg. OSS (Prov), September 17, Sub: Report on Initial Observed Results of Effect of Propaganda Disseminated in Operation Sauerkraut II, Box 51, Entry 154, RG 226, NA; Brief of Sauerkraut Missions. Final Conclusions, December 19, 1944, Box 88, En-try 99, RG 226, NA; Edward F. [Lindner], Final Report Sauerkraut 3, October 8, 1944, Box 41, Entry 154, RG 226, NA; Final Conclusion [on Sauerkraut], Folder 306, Box 69, Entry 99, RG 226, NA.

33. "We told them what had happened in Wolfschanze and that they would actually help save lives if they would bring the news to the front line soldier, because the front line soldier doesn't know that back in Germany there is turmoil, that the war is over."

34. Report by J. R. Pershall, September 22, 1944, Box 16, Entry 110, RG 226, NA.

35. Chief MO [Kenneth Mann] to Director OSS [William Donovan], Brief of Sauerkraut Missions I-II-III-MO-Rome, December 1944, Folder 5, Box 88, Entry 99, RG 226, NA; Edward F. Zinder, [Lindner], Final Report Sauerkraut 3, October 8, 1944, Box 41, Entry 154, RG 226, NA; Edward F. Zinder [= Lindner] Final report "Sauerkraut" operation Team "Marie" only, October 5, 1944; Intelligence report, "Sauerkraut 3 ops," team Marie, October 5, 1944, Folder 2173, Box 162, Entry 139, RG 226; Interview S. Beer/ E. Lindner, 1997, Westport, Conn., OSSOHP. Interview C. Mauch, C. Beer/ F. Burkhardt, January 18, 1997, Bennington, VT, OSSOHP.

36. U.S. War Department, Rules of Land Warfare, Par. 36, 82, 104; Art. 9 and 31 of the Geneva Convention (1929) and Annex to the Hague Convention (1907), Art. 23. On the position of the JCS rejecting this view at the end of 1943, see OPD 383.6 (30 Nov 43), Memo-

randum for the Secretariat, Joint Chiefs of Staff, December 8, 1943, CCS 385 (11–28–43), Dec File 1942–1945, RG 218, NA; MO in the War Against Germany, n. d. [Project] To be prepared for the President, JCS, Chief-PWD, and others, Folder 132, Box 95A (126), Entry 99, RG 226, NA; Ch. "Prisoners of War," War Diary, Office of the Director, October, November, December 1944, Folder 148, Box 211, Entry RG 226, NA. In an interview with the author, Barbara Lauwers emphasized: "I earned a degree in Law and had one semester at the Ecole de Droit in Paris and there I studied History of treaties and the Geneva Convention so I was aware of the fact that what OSS was doing was not altogether kosher," September 11, 1996, Washington, D.C., OSSOHP. On how the SI and William Casey used prisoners of war, also see J. Persico, *Casey: From the OSS to the CIA* (New York, 1990), p. 72 ff.

37. In an encounter with Willi Haseneier, she reminded him: "I also remember sitting in the jeep next to the driver and waiting for some of you to emerge from a Roman dwelling after an afternoon of faun with call girls. It was my chore to pay for your well deserved pleasures after a successful mission across the lines. But I was wondering how this expenditure will be explained to the US taxpayer by the disbursing OSS officer. Ja das waren Zeiten. [Yes, those were the days.]" Interview C. Mauch / B. Podorski, September 11, 1996, Washington, D.C., OSSOHP.

38. Cf. "Prisoners of War," War Diary, Office of the Director, 80; ibid., 27, October, November, December 1944, Folder 148, Box 211, Entry RG 226, NA.

39. The OSS Directorate had originally envisioned deploying the German agents for postwar work in reeducation. "Prisoners of War," War Diary, Office of the Director, p. 50 ff., October, November, December 1944, Folder 148, Box 211, Entry RG 226, NA. Eddie Lindner, Suggested Recompense for POW Agents of Sauerkraut Operations, November 26, 1945; Eddie Lindner, Sauerkraut Agents, November 30, 1945, Box 123, Entry 136, RG 226, NA. Eddie Lindner had disseminated reports that some of the agents, among them Hans Tappert and Willi Haseneier, were refusing to return to the POW camp. Instead, they raided a gambling casino in Rome, which earned them a prison stay in postwar Italy. Interview, S. Beer / E. Lindner, May 1, 1997, OSSOHP.

40. Heber Blankenhorn, Adventures in Propaganda. Letters from an Intelligence Officer in France, Boston 1919; idem., "The War of Morale: How America 'Shelled' the German Lines with Paper," in *Harper's*, September 1919, pp. 510–524; idem., "The Battle of Radio Armaments," in *Harper's*, December 1931, pp. 83–91.

41. On Blankenhorn's activities during the Second World War, see his comprehensive report Combat Propaganda in Africa, Italy, United Kingdom and France 1943–1944, Psychological Warfare Report by Lt. Colonel Heber Blankenhorn, Hoover Institution, Stanford, CA

42. The relevant document here is German Military Morale in the Light of Prisoner of War Interrogations, April 26, 1944, R&A 2020.1, Folder 1491, Box 107, Entry 139, RG 226, NA, further: Monthly Review of Economic and Morale Factors Bearing on German Unconditional Surrender, December 24, 1943 to April 26, 1944, R&A 2215.1–5, RG 59, NA.

43. The documents from early 1944 about Blankenhorn's project were already missing during the war, so that the account here is based on reports and correspondence from the beginning of 1945. W. B. Kantack, Capt., A. C., Reports Officer, re: Soldiers Committees: History of MO Project (Black), 1944–1945, Report by Lt. Col. H. Blankenhorn, January 1945, Box 601, Entry 92, RG 226, NA; on the background, see [Heber Blankenhorn], Propaganda in 1917–1918, Folder 2290, Box 173, Entry 139, RG 226, NA as well as [Heber Blankenhorn], Situation, War Department, 1942, Folder 2290, Box 173, Entry 139, RG 226, NA.

44. Soldiers Committees: History of MO Project (Black), 1944–45, 2f, Report by Lt. Col. H. Blankenhorn, January 1945, Box 601, Entry 92, RG 226, NA.

45. Ibid., 2 as well as Secretariat OSS to Acting Director, sub: History of MO Plan for the Establishment of Soldiers Committees in the Wehrmacht, February 2, 1945, Box 601, Entry 92, RG 226, NA.

46. Authorization and Approvals in: Soldiers Committees, 14–18, Report by Lt. Col. H. Blankenhorn, January 1945, Box 601, Entry 92, RG 226, NA; Edward L. Bigelow, Deputy Director-SSO to William J. Donovan, February 21, 1945; David Williamson, Chief Eu.& Med. Section-MO to Lt. Col. Roller, January 18, 1945, Box 601, Entry 92, RG 226, NA.

47. Secretariat to Acting Director, sub: History of MO Plan for the Establishment of Soldiers Committees in the Wehrmacht, February 1945, Box 601, Entry 92, RG 226, NA.

48. Most of the issues of the original OKW reports may be found in the Captured Documents Section of SHAEF. Of what were originally 12 MO documents, the only ones located among the OSS files are the "Sondernummer der Mitteilungen für das Offizierskorps. Chefsache, Juli 1944," Box 601, Entry 92, RG 226, NA; Adventures of the Leaflet, "Directives to the Officer Corps," in *Soldiers Committees*, pp. 19–22, Report by Lt. Col. H. Blankenhorn, January 1945, ibid.

49. "Sondernummer der Mitteilungen für das Offizierskorps. Chefsache, Juli 1944," Box 601, Entry 92, RG 226, NA. Ludendorff and Hindenburg were often cited as model generals, because they had recognized just in time that the "completely meaningless war" had to be "ended." "Your Cease-Fire" Folder 2302, Box 174, Entry 139, RG 226, NA.

50. Adventures of the Leaflet, "Directives to the Officer Corps," in *Soldiers Committees*, p. 21 ff., Report by Lt. Col. H. Blankenhorn, January 1945, Box 601, Entry 92, RG 226, NA.

51. David Williamson to Lt. Col. John S. Roller, January 18, 1945; David Williamson to Lt. Col. John S. Roller, January 24, 1945; Edward Bigelow to William Donovan, February 21, 1945; Colonel Lowman to Mr. Bigelow, February 23, 1945, Box 601, Entry 92, RG 226, NA.

52. Example of MO Newspaper 'Das Neue Deutschland' (DND), Box 68, Entry 99, RG 226, NA; additional material and "feedback" on DND may be found in Box 16, 75, 86–89, RG 226, NA as well as in Box 31, Entry 154, RG 226, NA. On this, and on the following, see C. Mauch, "Subversion und Propaganda," pp. 62–65 as well as idem., "Dream of a Miracle War," pp. 138–140; C. Laurie, *Propaganda Warriors*, p. 199 ff.

53. Letter from Eddie Lindner to the author, November 5, 1993.

54. See, for example, Telegram OSS-MO Washington to OSS Bern, June 28, 1944, Box 14, Entry 134, RG 226, NA: "Please be on the alert for a publication called 'Neues Deutschland,' which will claim to be the mouthpiece of an underground liberal party in the Reich. . . . Make foreign and allied correspondents (OWI included) think that it is genuine."

55. The New Plan, n. d. [August 1944], Folder 306, Box 69, Entry 99, RG 226, NA.

56. Aufruf zum 'Volkssturm' gegen die Partei, DND im Oktober des sechsten Kriegsjahrs ["Call for a 'People's Attack' against the Party, DND in October of the sixth year of the war"], n. d. Folder 214, Box 102, Entry 190, RG 226, NA.

57. Neues Leben blüht aus den Ruinen / Neues Leben wird wieder ersteh'n! / Dem Neuen Deutschland alle wir jetzt dienen; / das Dritte Reich, das muss dann untergeh'n! / Klein Klassenkampf! / Kein Rassenhass! / Kein Führer, kein Monarch! // Dem Neuen Deutschland als Freie Menschen dienen; / Das Neue Deutschland wird für ewig steh'n!; Marching Tune of the Movement 'Das Neue Deutschland,' n.d. Folder 1594, Box 115, RG 226, NA. A facsimile of the DND hymn is reprinted in *UUDW*, p. 258.

58. Of subversive propaganda was produced under the management of Colonel John T. Whitacker and introduced into OSS and Army circles. A copy of the film is located among the OSS holdings. From POW interviews in Italy it emerges that there had been warnings about Allied material from the air. This made the newspapers smuggled in by the Sauerkraut agents, by contrast, all the more effective, since their Allied origin was not suspected. Chief MO [Kenneth Mann] to Director OSS [William Donovan], Brief of Sauerkraut Missions I-II-III-MO-Rome, December 1944, Folder 5, Box 88, Entry 99, RG 226, NA; Edward F. Zinder, [Lindner], Final Report Sauerkraut 3, October 8, 1944, Box 41, Entry 154, RG 226, NA.

59. MO Newspaper 'Das Neue Deutschland;' "Comebacks" on Das Neue Deutschland, MO/MEDTO Field Report, 15–30 April 1945, both in Box 69, Entry 99, RG 226, NA.

60. MO Interrogations of German PWs, May and June 1945, July 7, 1945, Folder 306, Box 69, Entry 99, RG 226, NA.

61. Operation Annie, April 6, 1945, Folder 65b, Box 15A, Entry 99, RG 226, NA. In the same set of holdings one also finds the "Annie Scripts" and reactions of the German public to 'Radio 1212' ("First Reactions to Annie"); NYTM February 17, 1946; Howard Becker, "Nature and Consequences of Black Propaganda," in *ASR* 14 (1949), p. 231 as well as in Daugherty/Janowitz, *Psychological Warfare Casebook*, p. 677; Soley, *Radio Warfare*, 138–145.

62. A comprehensive treatment on this point in L. Soley, *Radio Warfare*, p. 45 ff.; "U.S. Takes Over Short Waves to Win Air Propaganda War," in *Newsweek*, October 9, 1942, p. 31; W. J. Donovan to FDR, sub: Memorandum of Establishment of Service of Strategic Information, June 10, 1942, Box 141, FDRL, Hyde Park, NY.

63. On the larger context, see MacGregor Knox, *Mussolini Unleashed 1939–1941: Politics and Strategy in Fascist Italy's Last War* (Cambridge, 1982), esp. pp. 129–135.

64. In reality, the radio transmitter usually broadcast on irregular frequencies, while the attempts to transmit on Radio Rome's wavelength could be successfully upset by the Italians. Wallace Carroll, *Persuade or Perish* (Boston, 1948), p. 30; Soley, *Radio Warfare*, p. 104 ff.; "Underground at Globe: A grim Anti-Nazi-Film," in *New York World-Telegram*, June 23, 1941, p. 8; *NYT*, June 23, 1941, p. 13; MO Draft Branch History, Box 75, Entry 99, RG 226, NA; An Example of Black (Italian) 'Italo Balbo,' Folder 306, Box 69, Entry 99, RG 226, NA; F. Oechsner to William Donovan, August 24, 1943, Folder 158, Box 32, Entry 99, RG 226, NA; "Comeback" from Black Radio Italo Balbo, September 8, 1943, Box 16, Entry 99, RG 226, NA as well as Folder 306 (3 of 3), Box 69, Entry 99, RG 226, NA.

65. General Beck Speaks Again, October 31, 1944; Folder 1539, Box 115, Entry 139, RG 226; Beck I (Final), ibid.; "Var det general Beck?, Was ist general Beck?," pp. 1, 18 in *Aftonbladet*, November 1, 1944; MO Draft Branch History, Box 75, Entry 99, RG 226, NA; Summary of MO Operations, April 23, 1945, April 23, 1945, Box 123, Entry 136, RG 226, NA; Operation Joker, Box 6, Entry 91, RG 226, NA; L. Soley, *Radio Warfare*, p. 136 ff., C. Mauch, "Subversion und Propaganda," p. 65 ff.; C. Laurie, *Propaganda Warriors*, p. 205. Beck's address may be found in Audiovisual Records, RG 226.01, NA and it partially reprinted in *UUDW*, Doc.74b, pp. 243–249.

66. Eisenhower to War Department, January 5, 1945, Proposal SCAF 166, Europe Sec 1-B, ABC 384, RG 165, NA; Memorandum by the Representatives of the British Chiefs of Staff. Plan "Matchbox," CCS 771, January 18, 1945, ibid.; partially reprinted in *UUDW*, Doc 77a and b, pp. 254–257.

67. On Operation Musac, see Lothar Metzl, Report on Musac Operation, n.d. [= April/May 1945]. After the operation was concluded, one copy was sent to Donovan, another to the MO

Reports Office. Col. Mann to David Williamson, 7 May 1945, NA RG 226, Entry 139, Box 172, Folder 2280; on the "Soldatensender" ("Soldiers Station") and Aspidistra, cf. Secret War Report, p. 531; Use of Aspidistra to Break Down German Resistance, January 19, 1945, JCS 1218/1, Records of the Joint Chiefs of Staff (= JCS Records) MF, Part I: 1942–1945, Roll 11, 469ff; Aspidistra History, PRO, FO 898/43; [Memo on] Aspidistra, January 30, 1942, PRO, FO 898/349; The Psychological Warfare Division Supreme Headquarters Allied Expeditionary Force, An Account of its Operation in the Western European Campaign 1944–1945, Bad Homburg 1945, 55. On the Milton Bryant complex, cf. Soley, *Radio Warfare*, p. 25.

68. On the "Soldatensender" ("Soldiers Station"), cf. the not always reliable memoirs of the British secret intelligence staffer and journalist Delmers, from whom the idea for the station derived: Sefton Delmer, *Black Boomerang* (London, 1962;) on the popularity of the Soldiers Station, see the memorandum from SHAEF, PWD, Listening to Allied Radio Broadcasts by German Civilians Under the Nazis, June 5, 1945, Papers of Daniel Lerner, Box 87, Hoover Institution: "Nature and Consequences of Black Propaganda," in A *Psychological Warfare Casebook*, p. 677.

69. Lothar Metzl, Report on Musac Operation, n. d. [April/May 1945], Folder 2279, Box 172, Entry 139, RG 226, Entry 139, RG 226, NA.

70. Smith's telegrams #35014 and #35994 are, to be sure, not among the files, but there is a summary in Edward Cushing to Samuel Scrivener, April 11, 1944, Folder 1, Box 487, Entry 92, RG 226, NA. It was not known in the OSS that Friedrich Hollaender (mistakenly called Hollander in the files) had, in fact, begun his career as the in-house composer for revues in the Berlin cabaret "Schall und Rauch"—and that he had also been active as a writer of lyrics.

71. Cf. Edward Cushing to Samuel Scrivener, April 11, 1944, Folder 1, Box 487, Entry 92, RG 226, NA; on Weston Howland, who also worked for the FNB and VPB of the OSS, see The FN Branch Gets Itself Established (October 1941-January 1942, 18f, FNB History, Folder 27a, Box 74, Entry 99, RG 226, NA, as well as the first draft of the unpublished OSS History, Chapter XXXVI. Foreign Nationalities, 42, Folder 29, Box 74, Entry 99, RG 226, NA, and also O'Toole, *Encyclopedia*, p. 235; Michael Burke, *Outrageous Good Fortune: A Memoir* (New York, 1982); James K. Lyon, ed., *Brecht in den USA* (Frankfurt, 1994); Patty Lee Parmalee, *Brecht's America* (Columbus, Ohio, 1981); United States Congress Committee on Un-American Activities. Hearings Regarding the Communist Infiltration of the Motion Picture Industry. Devoted to the Hearings of October 20, 21, 22,23, 24, 27, 28, 29 and 30, 1947, Washington, D.C. 1947; Bertolt Brecht, *Briefe*, 2 volumes, ed . by Günter Glaeser (Frankfurt, 1981); Sander Gilman, "Bertolt Brecht and the FBI," in *The Nation*, November 30, 1974, pp. 560–562; Sander Gilman, "'Man schenkt mir große Aufmerksamkeit.' Notes to the FBI File on Bertolt Brecht," in *German Life and Letters* XXIX, April 1976, pp. 322–329.

72. E. R. Richer to Samuel Scrivener, May 17, 1944, Facsimile in: Lyon, ed., *Brecht in den USA*, p. 139.

73. Samuel Scrivener, Jr. to Lt. Col. Kenneth D. Mann, April 15, 1944, Folder 1, Box 487, Entry 92, RG 226, NA.

74. Dr. Wolfgang Jeske, Frankfurt a. M. to author, April 4, 1995.

75. Graham Aldis to Lt. Col. K.D. Mann (through David Williamson), May 10, 1944, Folder 1, Box 487, Entry 92, RG 226, NA. The last-mentioned candidate was Stefan Samek, who in the end was hired (after all) as a (second) writer for the OSS operation. The other candidates remained anonymous in Aldis's memorandum.

76. Biographical information on Metzl may be found in Heinz Greul, *Bretter, die die Zeit bedeuten* (Munich, 1971); Klaus Budzinski, *Die Muse mit der scharfen Zunge: Vom Cabaret zum Kabarett* (Munich, 1962); Rudolf Weys, *Carabet and Kabarett in Wien* (Vienna Munich, 1970). A brief overview is provided by the lexicon entry in the *Biographisches Handbuch der deutschsprachigen Emigration nach 1933*, vol. 1 (Munich, 1980). The entry "worked for U.S. govt." refers to a successful career in the Central Intelligence Agency, which Metzl joined in 1947 as a Research Analyst. He died in Washington, D.C. on September 6, 1989 as the result of a heart attack. I owe this information to his daughter Paula Ackerman (message from December 5, 1995).

77. Edward Cushing had already requisitioned him on February 18, 1944. Edward Cushing to Samuel Scrivener, April 11, 1944, NA, Folder 1, Box 487, Entry 92, RG 226, NA.

78. From a report about Musac it emerges that Metzl could compose up to eight texts a week. David Williamson to Major George C. Dibert, November 3, 1944, NA, RG 226, Entry 92, Box 487, Folder 1. On Musac's budget, see Memorandum, Soldatensender Entertainment Project, Executive Officer, MO Branch [David H. Winton] to Charles A. Bane, July 6, 1944, NA, RG 226, Entry 169, Box 12, Folder 108. Summary reports about "Musac" are located, among other places, in the files of the OSS History Office, Memorandum on Musac Project, NA, RG 226, Entry 99, Box 16, Folder 67; Pancake-Musak Project, RG 226, Entry 99, Box 69, Folder 306. A handwritten report about Musac is part of the MO Draft History, NA, RG 226, Entry 99, Box 75, Folder 32, pp. 94–98.

79. The Board of Review to The Chief, MO Branch, Evaluation of Current Projects, March 29, 1945, NA, RG 226, Entry 139, Box 172, Folder 2280; David Williamson to Col. Mann, Musac Project [Final Report by Lothar Metzl], May 7, 1945 (ibid.). On this and what follows, cf. Soley, *Radio Warfare*, pp. 124–127. Soley's account is primarily based on after-the-fact reports of the OSS History Office and reveals a number of mistakes. It did not occur to him that a real person by the name of Lothar Metzl was concealed behind "Metzyl."

80. In the run-up to the broadcast, there was a discussion about the dangers for the Soldiers Station that might occur as a result of the Musac cover being blown. David H. Winton to Major Alcorn, 24 May 1944, NA, RG 226, Entry 169, Box 12, Folder 108.

81. Thus, for example, only $500 per week were available for the permanent orchestra. See David H. Winton to Charles A. Bane, 6 July 1944, NA, RG 226, Entry 169, Box 12, Folder 108.

82. A series of tape recordings are located in the holdings of the National Archives; see, for example, NA, Audiotapes 226.03; 226.07; in addition, there are records in the private possession of Ms. Paula Ackerman, Washington, D.C.

83. On the individual artists, cf. Musac Project, Final Report, 7 May 1945, NA, RG 226, Entry 139, Box 172, Folder 2280 as well as Interoffice Memo, Edward Cushing to Mrs. R.K. Hirsch, November 28, 1944, NA, RG 226, Entry 92, Box 487, Folder 2. Six years after the war, Marlene Dietrich requested that the OSS musical recordings of 1943 be released for commercial production. In a letter to General Donovan she wrote: "I hold the original cuttings and signed a letter at the time that I would not use them commercially. I would be grateful if you would help me to get a release so that the Columbia Corporation where I am recording now can bring them out." Donovan granted Dietrich's request. Marlene Dietrich to General Donovan, July 24, 1951, Betty McIntosh Papers, Leesburg, Va.

84. Musac Project, Final Report, May 7, 1945, NA, RG 226, Entry 139, Box 172, Folder 2280; on the reaction to Metzl's texts, MO London to [Col. K.D.] Mann, July 7, 1944, NA, RG 226, Entry 134, Box 330, Folder 1793.

85. MO London to [Col. K.D.] Mann, June 15, 1944, NA, RG 226, Entry 134, Box 330, Folder 1793.

86. Musac Project, Final Report, May 7, 1945, NA, RG 226, Entry 139, Box 172, Folder 2280.

87. Ferne in der alten Zeit/ Traeumten wir von Seligkeit:/ Unsere Zukunft war so hell,/ Und doch, wie schnell / War alles aus. / Dunkel wird noch manches Jahr sein . . . Dunkel ist die Nacht / Wie das Leben. / Wir schweben in die Nacht / Hingegeben / An Tanzmusik und Rhythmus / Der Gegenwart / Doch fern im Regen harrt / Der Tod; Musac Project, n. d., NA, RG 226, Entry 139, Box 172, Folder 2279.

88. Wenn auf Reisen man geht / Und kein Woertchen versteht / Von der heimischen Sprache des Landes, / Kommt man immer sich vor / Wie der Ochs vor dem Tor, / Denn man sagt was und keiner verstand es. / Im Hotel der Portier, / Auf der Wiese der Stier, / Ja die biegen sich alle vor Lachen. / Doch der Mann von Kultur, / Der studiert immer nur, / Und er konzentriert sich auf Sprachen: // O der Gau- / O der Gau- / Der Gauleiter lernt ploetzlich spanisch. / Denn der Gau- / Denn der Gau- / Der Gauleiter ist ja ganz panisch. / Und die Gau- / Leiter Frau / Die packt voller Eifer die Koffer, / Denn die ganze Menage, / Die ganze Baggage, / Verflüchtigt sich nach Madrid. / Ole! // Ja der Gau- / Ja der Gau- / Der Gauleiter lernt auch japanisch. / Denn der Gau- / Leiter Schlau / Verlaesst sich nicht ganz auf sein spanisch. / Auch die Gau- / Leiter Frau / Hat schon einen flotten Kimono, / Und passiert was dem Franco, / Sind sie nicht va banquo, / Und ziehen nach Tokio. / Banzai!; Ferdinand The Bull. Singer: Sig Arno, Series 1-Record 19d, NA, RG 226, Entry 139, Box 172, Folder 2279. The folder contains the Musac Recordings of Series 1, i.e., texts with an openly propagandistic character.

89. Ustravic London to Col. Mann, July 1, 1944; July 6, 1944; July 24, 1944, NA, RG 226, Entry 134, Folder 1793. On Musac's budget, see Evaluation of Current Projects, NA, RG 226, Entry 139, Box 172, Folder 2280 as well as Memorandum Musac Project, Col. K. D. Mann to The Board of Review, November 24, 1944, NA, RG 226, Entry 92, Box 487, Folder 1.

90. Lt. Commander Reichner to Mr. [David] Williamson, October 4, 1944, cited in Lothar Metzl to Edward Cushing, October 17, 1944, NA RG 226, Entry 92, Box 487, Folder 2.

91. Lothar Metzl to Edward Cushing, October 17, 1944, NA, RG 226, Entry 92, Box 487, Folder 2; Edward Cushing to Samuel Scrivner, Jr. [for transmission to Ira Ashley], January 6, 1945, NA, RG 226, Entry 92, Box 487, Folder 1.

92. *The New Yorker*, October 7, 1944, cited in Edward Cushing to David Williamson, November 28, 1944, NA, RG 226, Entry 92, Box 487, Folder 1.

93. Interoffice Memo Musac Project, Edward Cushing to David Williamson (Questionnaire as an appendix to this memo), November 28, 1944, NA, RG 226, Entry 92, Box 487, Folder 1; Memo MUSAC, Samuel Scrivener to Edward Cushing, November 30, 1944, ebd.

94. Evaluation of Current Projects, Col. K.D. Mann to The Board of Review, March 29, 1945, NA, RG 226, Entry 139, Box 172, Folder 2280.

95. [Gesprochen] Na hoer doch auf . . . Nicht doch! . . . / Was faellt dir ein? // Verschone mich mit deiner Verfuehrungskunst. / Du hast keine Aussicht auf meine Gunst. / Benimm dich doch wie ein Gentleman, sonst sind wir quitt! / Bei mir beisst man auf Granit. // Ich bin wie der Westwall / und ich falle auf keinen Fall. / Ich bin wie der Westwall, / ja, ich bin's ueberall. / Ich sag dir nur eines: / Haende weg von meinem Knie. / Ich bin wie der Westwall— / bei mir stehts du immer machtlos nur vis-à-vis. // Und wenn wir mal zusammen ins Kino gehn, / will ich mir in Ruhe den Film ansehn. / Drum kaufe keine Logensitze fuer uns zwei, / denn ich bin ja nicht dabei. // Ich bin etc. // Und wenn das Militär auch Soldaten braucht—

/ mein Enthusiasmus ist ausgeraucht. / Drum gib es auf, denn ich halte die Balanz. / Winde mir den Jungfernkrantz. // [Gesprochen] Was faellt dir ein . . . // Ich bin etc. // [Gesprochen] Wie oft muss ich dir denn noch sagen, // Ich bin wie der Westwall?; "Ich bin wie der Westwall" ["I am like the Westwall"], Record Number 12, Musac Lyrics, NA, RG 226, Entry 139, Box 172, Folder 2286.

96. Viele junge Poeten / und alte Propheten, / die prophezein: / bald wird alles zu Ende sein / zwischen Oder und Rhein. / Aber Seher und Dichter, / sie sehen schon Lichter / im Morgenschein, / denn sie schaun in die Zukunft hincin, / und sie sehn, o wie schoen! / dort ein besseres Deutschland erstehn. / Ja im Vierten Reich, / zieht der Friede ins Haus, / und der Fuehrer zieht aus. / Ja im Vierten Reich / wird kein Himmler zum Himmel mehr schrein. / Statt Kanonen gibts Butter. / Dann wird jede Mutter / so gluecklich sein, / den im schoenen, im / Vierten Reich / sperrt man Deutschlands Verfuehrer dann ein. / Und die Arbeiterklasse / marschiert auf der Strasse / am ersten Mai, / und sie singen: Wir sind wieder frei / von der Bluttyrannei. / Jeder Pastor und Priester / auf neue geniesst er / der Freiheit Schein, / und er spendet das Brot und den Wein / ohne dass ihm der Hass / folget bis in die Kirche hinein. / Ja, im Vierten Reich / zieht der Herrgott ins Haus / under der Goering zieht aus, / denn das Vierte Reich / wird das Land der Gerechtigkeit sein. / Wenn die Nazis verkrachen / wird Deutschland erwachen / und auferstehn, / denn im schoenen, im Vierten Reich / wird kein Goebbels mehr luegen, / kein Funk mehr betruegen, / kein Hitler mehr bruellen, / kein Himmler mehr killen, / kein Schirach befehlen, / kein Ribbentrop stehlen, / kein Rosenberg schnaufen, / und kein Ley sich besaufen—/ im Vierten Reich / werden all zum Teufel sie gehn!; Im Vierten Reich ["In the Fourth Reich"], Record Number 30, NA, RG 226, Entry 139, Box 172, Folder 2286. Another version of the text, with some handwritten changes, is located in Folder 2, Box 487, Entry 92, RG 226, NA. The title song was sung by John Hendrik.

97. Interoffice Memo, Musac Project, Edward Cushing to Mrs. R. K. Hirsch, November 28, 1944; Musac Project, Folder 2, Box 487, Entry 92, RG 226, NA. Musac Project, Final Report, May 7, 1945, Folder 2280, Box 172, Entry 139, RG 226, NA.

98. Evaluation of Current Projects, Col. K.D. Mann to The Board of Review, March 29, 1945; Final Report, Musac Project, David Williamson to Col. Mann, May 7, 1945, Folder 2280, Box 172, Entry 139, RG 226, NA. Scripts of the Musac productions as well as an English-language outline are located in Folder 2, Box 487, Entry 92, RG 226, NA.

99. Cited in Final Report, Musac Project, David Williamson to Col. Mann, May 7, 1945, Folder 2280, Box 172, Entry 139, RG 226, NA.

100. Ustravic, London to OSS [Washington], May 20, 1944, Folder 1793, Entry 134, RG 226, NA.

6. PENETRATION OF GERMANY

1. Especially Joseph Persico, *Piercing the Reich* (New York, 1979).

2. David Stafford, *Britain and European Resistance, 1940–1945: A survey of the Special Operations Executive, with Documents* (Toronto/Buffalo, 1980), p. 187; cf. B. Sweet-Escott, *Baker Street Irregular* (London, 1965), p. 116 ff.; on the Venlo incident, cf. the account of British Secret Service officer Captain Sigismund Payne Best (who took part in the incident), *The Venlo Incident* (London, 1950); also M.R.D. Foot, "Britische Geheimdienste und deutscher Widerstand," in Müller/Dilks, eds., *Großbritannien*, p. 162 ff.; Klemens von Klemperer, *German Resistance against Hitler*, pp. 160–162, 201. On the position of the Foreign Office vis-à-vis the resistance, cf. the tendentious but important studies by Richard Lamb, *The Ghosts of Peace*

1935–1945 (Wilton, 1987) as well as idem., "Das Foreign Office und der deutsche Wider-stand," in Müller/Dilks, eds., *Großbritannien*, pp. 53–82; further, Mauch, *Großbritannien, die Vereinigten Staaten und der Widerstand gegen den Nationalsozialismus*, pp. 102–108.

3. Since the British documents about the London negotiations are not available, the ac-count is mainly based on the reports of OSS Major Aubrey H. Harwood. OSS Activities, July 1944, Folder 117, Box 93, Entry 99, RG 226, NA; Report by Major Aubrey H. Harwood on OSS SI Activities, November 4, 1944, Folder 64a, Box 11, Entry 99, RG 226, NA; B. N. McPherson, "Kings and Desperate Men," p. 156 ff.; on Brook, his educational background, and his role in France, cf. the peripheral mentions in M. R. D. Foot, *SOE in France*, especially pp. 49, 222n, 241, 337, 386n, as well as Robin Brook, "The London Operation: The British View," in G. Chalou, ed., *The Secrets War* (Washington, D.C., 1992), p. 69 ff., 369 ff.

4. Brook, "The London Operation," p. 73. Conversation Sir Robin Brook with author, July 12, 1992 in Washington, D.C.

5. McPherson, "Kings and Desperate Men: The United States Office of Strategic Services in London and the Anglo-American Relationship, 1941–1946" (PhD. diss. University of Toron-to, 1995), p. 158. On the discussion about the recruitment of POWs, cf. the monthly sum-maries—cited in brief excerpts by McPherson (ibid.)—in the War Diary of the department of British Military Intelligence responsible for POWs, department 19 (a): MI 19(a) War Diary, WO 165/41, PRO London.

6. On the problems of forged papers, see McPherson, "Kings and Desperate Men," p. 91.

7. The biggest discrepancy of opinion between the Secret Intelligence Branch of the OSS and the British existed in the autumn of 1943, when the British Chiefs of Staff (BCS) pre-sented a memorandum that demanded approval f all SI operations by British military au-thorities. [Commentaries on] Paper of the British Chiefs of Staff, October 8 1943, Box 264, Entry 108, RG 226, NA.

8. Robin Brook, "The London Operation," p. 72 ff., confirms that the main effort of the English pertained to Operation Overlord.

9. Memorandum Future Office of Strategic Services Operations in Central Europe, Sep-tember 2, 1944, Folder 61, Box 220. Entry 92, RG 226, NA. The memorandum to the Presi-dent is not in the Roosevelt Library. There is a reference to this in Memorandum Donovan to Roosevelt, December 1, 1944, Box 155, PSF, FDRL Hyde Park, NY.

10. European Theater Office Report, September 12, 1944, Folder 36, Box 8, Entry 99, RG 226, NA; Stewart W. Herman to Col. Haskell, September 13, 1944, Folder 5, Box 2, Entry 99, RG 226, NA; B. N. McPherson, "Kings and Desperate Men," p. 159. On Stewart W. Herman, see Gerhard Besier, ed., "Ökumenische Mission in Nachkriegsdeutschland: Die Berichte von Stewart W. Herman über die Verhältnisse in der evangelischen Kirche 1945–1946," in *Kirchliche Zeitgeschichte* 1 (1988), pp. 151–187; J. Heideking, "USA und deutsche Kirchen: Beobachtung, Planungen und Besatzungspolitik," in Anselm Doering-Manteuffel/Joachim Mehlhausen, eds., *Christliches Ethos und der Widerstand gegen den Nationalsozialismus in Europa* (Stuttgart/Berlin/Cologne, 1995), pp. 119–138, esp. pp. 122 and 132–134. The book he started writing in Bad Nauheim—Herman was interned there from the end of 1941 to the be-ginning of 1942—about the situation of the churches in National Socialist Germany was pub-lished in 1942 by Harper & Brothers: *It's Your Souls We Want* (New York, 1942). In German: *Eure Seelen wollen wir: Kirche im Untergrund* (Munich/Berlin, 1951).

11. R. Harris Smith, OSS, p. 224; on the advance in the West, see G. Weinberg, *A World at Arms*, pp. 750 ff., 761ff.; on the future of the OSS, see B. F. Smith, *Shadow Warriors*, p. 270;

Memoranda 13 February 1945, March 5, File 6–17–42, CCS 111, RG 218, NA; Future Office of Strategic Services Operations in Central Europe, September 2, 1944, Folder 61, Box 220. Entry 92, RG 226, NA; on the financial situation, job assignments, and problems in the different OSS divisions, see Memorandum Secretariat to Director, August 21, 1944, Folder 96, Box 86, Entry 99, RG 226, NA as well as Monthly Progress Reports, Box 86, Entry 99, R 226, NA; on the Jedburgh teams that were shipped into Asia, see Interview C. Mauch, M. Yu/Gen. John K. Singlaub, November 1996, *OSSOHP*; Interview M. Yu/Col. Frank Mills, November 1996, *OSSOHP*; on the US home front, see esp. John M. Blum, *V Was for Victory: Politics and American Culture during World War II* (New York, 1976) as well as Richard Polenberg, *War and Society: The United States 1941–1945* (Philadelphia, 1972).

12. The problems that arose from Eisenhower's expectation of winning the war in France are described by Casey, Penetration, p. 3 ff., Folder Casey, Box 1, Persico Papers, Hoover Institution, Stanford, CA.; on Donovan's and David Bruce's assessment of the invasion, see the diary entry of David Bruce, June 4, 1944, Lankford, ed., *OSS against the Reich*, p. 53 ff; on the contribution of the R&A, see B. D. Rifkind, *OSS and Franco-American Relations*, p. 275 as well as William R. Corson, *The Armies of Ignorance: The Rise of the American Intelligence Empire* (New York, 1977), p. 201.

13. Interview J. Persico, W. Casey, August 27, 1976, 9–10, Folder Casey, Box 1, Persico Papers, Hoover Institution, Stanford, CA., pp. 9–10.

14. On this point, cf. the information provided by Casey in Interview J. Persico, W. Casey, August 27, 1976, 10, Folder Casey, Box 1, Persico Papers, Hoover Institution, Stanford, CA. On Goldberg, see "Art. Goldberg, Arthur Joseph (August 8, 1908-): attorney, diplomat, secretary of labor, U.S. Supreme Court justice, intelligence officer," in O'Toole, *Encyclopedia*, p. 207; R. Harris Smith, *OSS*, pp. 12, 12d as well as J. Persico, *Piercing the Reich*, p. 20 ff. Further, Memorandum re: Arthur J. Goldberg, May 6, 1942, 100–7764–5, Arthur Goldberg File, FBI, Washington, D.C. (released as a result of a FOIA inquiry by the author with the FBI).

15. Robert M. Gates, *From the Shadows: The Ultimate Insider's Story of Five Presidents and How They Won the Cold War* (London: Simon and Schuster, 1996), p. 198.

16. Memorandum Observations in MEDTO, Lieutenant W. J. Casey to Colonel David Bruce and Colonel J. R. Forgan, August 21, 1944, Folder 163a, Box 33, Entry 99, RG 226, NA.

17. Interview J. Persico, W. Casey, August 27, 1976, 9–10, Folder Casey, Box 1, Persico Papers, Hoover Institution, Stanford, CA., pp. 9–10; Goldberg's worries with regard to mistrust of the OSS Labor Division were briefly noted by Bruce, diary entry from July 13, 1944, N. D. Lankford, ed., *OSS against the Reich*, p. 108.

18. Mosley, *Dulles*, p. 114; a plethora of memoranda about the German emigrés and their contracts to the COI/OSS may be found in Boxes 10 through 12 as well as 37, Entry 106, RG 226, NA.

19. Among the countless emigré reports or COI/OSS memoranda that assessed Hagen's role, only a few of the relevant ones are mentioned here: [Albert C. Grzesinski on Hagen], Emmy Rado to Colonel Buxton, March 20, 1942, Box 12, Entry 106, RG 226, NA; Memorandum on Neu Beginnen Group, Emmy C. Rado to Mr. Lithgow Osborne, Mr. DeWitt C. Poole, Mr. George Pratt, October 16, 1942, FNB-Int-13-GE-369, Entry 100, RG 226, NA; Office Memorandum, Subject: Paul Hagen, Arthur J. Goldberg to Allen W. Dulles, July 11, 1942, Box 12, Entry 106, RG 226, NA; Memorandum by Willy Brandt, Oppositional Movements in Germany, September 25, 1943, FNB-INT-13 GE-928, Entry 100, RG 226, NA (Am-Intel Doc 21); Labor Groups in Exile May 24, 1944, CID#72928, Entry 16, RG 226, NA.

20. Cf., by contrast, Memorandum German Emigration in the USA, May 1, 1942. The unidentified author, presumably Wenzel Jaksch, stated that Hagen belonged to the Communist party until 1932, Box 12, Entry 106, RG 226, NA; Hagen's statement may be found in A Conversation with Paul Hagen [furnished by a friend of DeWitt C. Poole], Box 12, Entry 106, RG 226, NA.

21. When Hagen wanted to leave the USA for Canada, he was denied approval for reentry. A friend of the extremely conservative DeWitt C. Poole who interviewed him for the COI under the pretext of discussing his book with him observed that Hagen presumably recognized the real reason for the conversation and had been warned by Wallace Deuel. Office Memorandum Arthur J. Goldberg to Allen W. Dulles, July 11, 1942 with confidential FNB enclosure, A Conversation with Paul Hagen, Box 12, Entry 106, RG 226, NA. The author's 1993 FOIA inquiry about Karl Frank (Paul Hagen) has, to date, not been processed by the FBI.

22. Paul Hagen, *Will Germany Crack?* (New York, 1942); "Best Book on Germany, Present and Future. Detached and Factual, Despite an Underground Past, Paul Hagen Assays Trends in Nazidom," *NYHT* June 14, 1942; "What of Hitler's Home Front? Mr. Hagen Studies the Destructive Forces Within Germany Itself," *NYT* June 14, 1942.

23. A.W. D. [= Dulles] to Mr. Goldberg, n. d.; A.J.G. [= Goldberg] to Dulles, May 12, 1942; [Paul Hagen] Memorandum How to Prepare Collaboration with the Anti-Nazi Underground Movement, April 10, 1942, Box 12, Entry 106, RG 226, NA. The latter is reprinted in *AmIntel*, Doc 1. Cf., further, Arthur J. Goldberg to Allen W. Dulles, May 23, 1942 and Memorandum [Paul Hagen], Cooperation with the German Labor Movement, folder 89, Box 12, Entry 106, RG 226, NA.

24. Hagen admitted in a conversation with an OSS agent that he had deliberately exaggerated the oppositional role of the rural population. A Conversation with Paul Hagen, 1, Box 12, Entry 106, RG 226, NA.

25. If—through passive resistance and work slowdowns—business production were only reduced by 10 percent, this reduction (according to Hagen's estimate) would be higher than the total sum of the lease and loan payments made by the USA to its European allies.

26. See also *UUDW*, Doc. 52, pp. 155–158.

27. Especially with regard to the second point, incidentally, Hagen was thinking (not least of all) about himself when he suggested his own name—along with that of Paul Hertz and Jakob Walcher—for a German COI Labor committee.

28. The memorandum is undated, but it obviously comes from May 1942. On May 23 it was forwarded to Allen Dulles by Arthur Goldberg, with a request for discussion, and it shows up in the records of several OSS departments. Arthur J. Goldberg to Allen W. Dulles, Sub: German Labor Contacts, Folder 89, Box 12, Entry 106, RG 226, NA.

29. Formally, the memorandum cited was a commentary on a "Neu Beginnen" fundamental document about the "coming war": Memorandum Accompanying Comment to "The Coming World War," containing: I. The Aims of the Revolutionary Socialists; II. Greater Germany, III. Soviet Germany as the Dominant Power in Europe. Rado regarded the memorandum as something written by an exiled Czech. Emmy C. Rado to Mr. Lithgow Osborne, Mr. DeWitt C. Poole, Mr. George Pratt, October 16, 1942, FNB-Int-13-GE-369, Entry 100, RG 226, NA. On the NB publication "Der kommende Weltkrieg" (Der kommende Weltkrieg. Aufgaben und Ziele des deutschen Sozialismus. Eine Diskussionsgrundlage, Paris n. d. [= 1939]); also see Memorandum Germany. Labor Groups in Exile, 13–14, Folder 337, Box 38, Entry 106, RG 226, NA.

30. Memorandum Emmy C. Rado to Colonel Buxton, March 20, 1942, Box 12, Entry 106, RG 226, NA. The largest part of Grzesinski's literary estate is located at the IISG, Amsterdam; a number of exile manifestos, however, are also in Entry 106 of the OSS files, RG 226, NA.

31. Hugh R. Wilson to Mr. Allen W. Dulles, May 28, 1942, Box 12, Entry 106, RG 226, NA; on Wilson, also see A. C. Brown, *The Last Hero*, p. 514; B. F. Smith, *Shadow Warriors*, pp. 376, 390 ff.; Interview J. Persico, G. v. Arkel, Tapes 59–61 (Gerhard van Arkel), Persico Papers, Hoover Institution, Stanford, CA; David Williamson is cited in Hugh R. Wilson to Allen Dulles, June 9, 1942, June 9, 1942, Folder 70, Box 9, Entry 106, RG 226, NA.

32. See Paul Hagen (American Friends of German Freedom) to Arthur Goldberg, June 10, 1942 as well as Arthur J. Goldberg to Allen W. Dulles, June 11, 1942, Folder 88, Box 12, Entry 106, RG 226, NA. Hagen named Werner Wille, Georg and Vera Eliasberg, Fritz Schmidt, Charles Yost, Esther Brunauer, Friedrich Adler, Emil Kirschmann, Eva Jeremias, Dr. Paul Hertz, Lene Boegler, and Maurice Goldbloom as witnesses to his travels.

33. The Purpose of the Labor Section, in George O. Pratt to David K. E. Bruce, Sub: Plans for Proposed Operations on the Continent—Labor Desk, March 23, 1944, Folder 493, Box 48, Entry 110, RG 226, NA.

34. The liaison in the SIS was Alfred R. Rickmann. On the SIS, see Phillip Knightley, *The Second Oldest Profession*, pp. 117–118; F. H. Hinsley et al. *British Intelligence*, Vol. 1, 1979, p. 278; Kim Philby, *My Silent War* (London, 1968), p. 4. On Rickmann, see Craig Graham McKay, *From Information to Intrigue: Studies in Secret Service Based on the Swedish Experience, 1939–1945* (London, 1993). Dieter Nelles, "'Landesverrat' als Widerstand! Die Zusammenarbeit der Internationalen Transportarbeiterföderation (ITF) mit dem englischen Geheimdienst 1939–1945," p. 4 ff. and idem., "Ungleiche Partner: Die Zusammenarbeit der Internationalen Transportarbeiterföderation (ITF) mit den westalliierten Nachrichtendiensten 1938–1945," typescript n. d.., p. 17 ff. Nelles bases his argument on the correspondence of Edo Fimmens, especially the letter Brief Karl to Fimmen, May 31, 1939; Fimmen to Brandt and Enderle, June 29, 1939 159/3/C/a/92, and 78, MRC Warwick as well as Brandt to Fimmen, July 9, 1939 and Fimmen to Enderle, July 6, 1939, folder 21, records of ITF, ASD.

35. Hugh Dalton had advocated bringing Hans Vogel, Erich Ollenhauer, as well as Curt Geyer and Fritz Heine, to London. Anthony Glees, *Exile Politics during the Second World War: The German Social Democrats in Britain* (Oxford, 1982), esp. p. 118.

36. Conrad Pütter, "Deutsche Emigranten und britische Propaganda: Zur Tätigkeit deutscher Emigranten bei britischen Geheimsendern," in G. Hirschfeld, ed., *Exil in Großbritannien*, p. 106 ff.; Francis L. Carsten assumes that about 450 German emigrants were active in the IC. F. L. Carsten, "Deutsche Emigranten in Großbritannien 1933–1945," in ibid., p. 152. For the larger context, see Lothar Kettenacker, "Der Einfluß der deutschen Emigranten auf die britische Kriegszielpolitik," in ibid., pp. 80–105; Werner Röder, "Deutschlandpläne der sozialdemokratischen Emigration in Großbritannien 1942–1945," in VZG 17 (1969), pp. 72–86; Werner Link, ed., *Mit dem Gesicht nach Deutschland. Eine Dokumentation über die sozialdemokratische Emigration*, edited by Erich Matthias (Düsseldorf, 1968); Johannes Klotz, *Das "kommende" Deutschland: Vorstellungen und Konzeptionen des sozialdemokratischen Parteivorstandes im Exil 1933–1945 zu Staat und Wirtschaft* (Cologne, 1983); Jan Foitzik, "Revolution und Demokratie: Zu den Sofort- und Übergangsplanungen des sozialdemokratischen Exils für Deutschland 1943–1945," in IWK 3 (1988), pp. 308–341; [OSS Labor Division], The German Political Emigration in Great Britain, August 1943, George O. Pratt to Mr. Whitney H. Shepardson, August 25, 1943, Box 205, Entry 108, RG 226, NA.

37. W. Röder, *Die deutschen sozialistischen Exilgruppen*, p. 188; A. Glees, *Exile Politics*, p. 115.

38. A. C. Brown, ed., *The Secret War Report*, p. 82.

39. Memorandum Labor Division of OSS, Arthur J. Goldberg to Colonel William J. Donovan, February 23, 1943, Box 2, Persico Papers, Hoover Institution, Stanford, CA.

40. Jan Foitzik, "Revolution und Demokratie," p. 322. On the OSS Labor Division's assessment of the ISK, see Memorandum The German Political Emigration in Great Britain, August 1943, George O. Pratt to Mr. Whitney H. Shepardson, August 25, 1943, Box 205, Entry 108, RG 226, NA; on the significance of the ITF in Goldberg's calculation, see Memorandum The Labor Section of the Office of Strategic Services, Arthur J. Goldberg to General William J. Donovan, May 10, 1943, Box 2, Persico Papers, Hoover Institution, Stanford, CA.

41. Memorandum Labor Division of OSS, Arthur J. Goldberg to Colonel William J. Donovan, February 23, 1943, Box 2, Persico Papers, Hoover Institution, Stanford, CA. On Goldberg's and Pratt's professional background, see Persico, *Piercing the Reich*, p. 19.

42. To General William J. Donovan, May 10, 1943, Attachment: Memorandum The Labor Section of the Office of Strategic Services, Box 2, Persico Papers, Stanford, CA.

43. R&A Preliminary Report on the Comite "Allemagne Libre" Pour L' Ouest (CALPO), n. d. [December 1944], folder 882, Box 424, Entry 190, RG 226, NA. After the war Goldberg stated that he kept his distance from the Communists. Interview Burton Hersh with Arthur Goldberg, November 24, 1986, cited here by Burton Hersh, *The Old Boys, The American Elite and the Origins of the CIA* (New York/Toronto, 1992), p. 138.

44. Arthur J. Goldberg to Colonel E. F. Connely, via Lt. Floyd M. Muller, sub: Recruitment for Faust Project, November 1943; Plan for Penetration of Germany for Intelligence Purposes, August 15, 1944; George O. Pratt to Whitney H. Shepardson (attn. Major Arthur J. Goldberg), August 22, 1944, Box 553, Entry 92, RG 226, NA; Memorandum by the Planning & Operations Board, ETO, September 26, 1944, folder 153, Box 212, Entry 190, RG 226, NA; Memorandum The Purpose of the Labor Section, Plans for Proposed Operations on the Continent—Labor Desk, George O. Prattt to David K. E. Bruce, Colonel, AUS, via William Maddox, Major, AUS, March 23, 1944, Folder 493, Box 48, Entry 110, RG 226, NA.

45. SHAEF/17240/25/Ops (C), GCT/370–15(Ops (C), Sub: Subversive and Coup de Main activities of SOE and OSS in Germany, October 5, 1944 (released as the result of a FOIA request by the author), FOIA-CIA; Clandestine supply to Foreign Workers, November 22, 1945, folder 1252, Box 284, Entry 190, RG 226, NA. J. Heideking, "Amerikanische Geheimdienste und Widerstandsbewegungen im Zweiten Weltkrieg," in Gerhard Schulz (ed.) *Partisanen und Volkskrieg: Zur Revolutionierung des Krieges im 20. Jahrhundert* (Göttingen, 1985), pp. 147–177.

46. Mauch, "Subversion und Propaganda," p. 67 ff.; Memorandum by OSS Adviser Kurt Bloch. The Opposition Potential of the Foreign Workers in Germany, INT 13-GE-599, Entry 100, RG 226, NA, partially reprinted in *AmIntel*, Doc 6, 32–34, UUDW, Doc 61, 187–189.

47. The Foreign Laborer in Germany as an MO Target, September 30, 1943 R&A 1243, RG 59, NA, partially reprinted in UUDW, Doc 62, 189–192.

48. John Steinbeck, *The Moon is Down* (New York, 1942).

49. Operation Braddock II, November 16, 1944, folder 1271, Box 286, Entry 190, RG 226, NA; Reactions of Appeal to Foreign Workers, ibid.; Enemy Sabotage in the Reich Involving the Cooperation of Foreign Workers and Supply of Sabotage Material by Enemy Aircraft, in: Special Supplement to the German Criminal Policy Gazette, November 3, 1944; OSS Pro-

gram against Germany [October 24, 1944], folder 101, Box 167, Entry 190, RG 226, NA; Memorandum, Resistance Activities in Berlin, December 3, 1944, OSS-Report on Bomb Damage. Sabotage. Foreign Workers, December 3, 1944, Entry 108, RG 226, NA; Daniel Lerner, "raddock II" in William E. Daugherty/ Morris Janowitz, *A Psychological Warfare Casebook*, p. 416; idem., *Sykewar: Psychological Warfare against Germany D-Day to VE-Day* (New York, 1949), p. 259 ff.; for a critical look at the effect of Braddock II, see Howard Becker, "Nature and Consequences of Black Propaganda," in *A Psychological Warfare Casebook*, p. 677.

50. SHAEF, Minutes of Meeting on Special activities in Germany, January 10, 1945, folder 1266, Box 286, Entry 190, RG 226, NA; Clandestine supply to Foreign Workers, November 22, 1945, folder 1252, Box 284, Entry 190, RG 226, NA; SHAEF/17240/13/Ops (C), CCT 322–2/Ops (C), sub: OSS (SO) an SOE activities in Germany, January 29, 1945, (released as a result of a FOIA request by the author.), FOIA-CIA.

51. Memorandum by M. Quinn Shaughnessey, Secretary, Plans & Operations Staff, sub: CALPO, January 15, 1945; CALPO—Minutes of inter-branch meeting held in Director's Office, January 10, 1945, folder 2296, Box 174, Entry 139, RG 226, NA; Relations with CApo, October 1944-January 1945, n. d. folder 149, Box 212, Entry 190, RG 226, NA; C. Mauch, "Dream of a Miracle War," p. 140 ff.; on the perception of CALPO by the Western allies, see H. Bungert, *Das Nationalkomitee*, p. 128 ff.

52. "Activity and Role of the Comite 'Allemagne Libre' Pour L' Ouest" [= Statement issued by CALPO October 7, 1944]; R&A Preliminary Report on the Comité "Allemagne Libre" Pour L' Ouest (CALPO), n. d. [December 1944], Box 424, Entry 190, RG 226, NA. Lt. Williams to Lt. Martin, sub: Brief of Information in CALPO File, February 14, 1945, ibid.

53. Agenda for Meeting of The Plans and Operations Staff, January 15, 1945, folder 52, Box 5, Entry 169, RG 226, NA; Relations with CApo, October 1944-January 1945, n. d. folder 149, Box 212, Entry 190, RG 226, NA. In an interview with the author, Arthur Schlesinger, Jr. emphasized that he was suspicious from the outset about Noel Field, the Quaker Communist whom Schlesinger officially received in 1944 as a delegate from CALPO. To be sure, he (Schlesinger) then had the reputation—by his own account—of being thoroughly anti-Communist compared to his colleagues in R&A. Interview C. Mauch/A. Schlesinger, June 9, 1997, New York, NY, OSSOHP; R. Harris Smith, OSS, 228.

54. CALPO—Minutes of inter-branch meeting held in Director's Office, January 10, 1945, folder 2296, Box 174, Entry 139, RG 226, NA as well as folder 21, Box 2, Entry 115, RG 226, NA; Agenda for Meeting of The Plans and Operations Staff, January 15, 1945, folder 52, Box 5, Entry 169, RG 226, NA; A. E. Jolis, Labor Division, SI to Thomas G. Cassady, Chief SI, Paris, Major E. F. Black, Director's Office, Major S. F. Runkle, X-2, J. R. Murphy, X-2, February 2, 1945, Box 424, Entry 190, RG 226, NA.

55. Budget for Agents Recruited through CALPO for SO Branch Controlled Operations into Germany, to: Chief, Special Funds Branch, OSS, ETO, February 22, 1945, folder 52, Box 5, Entry 169, RG 226, NA.

56. R&A France: Political. Report on CALPO Meeting, folder 883, Box 424, Entry 190, RG 226, NA; Gerald E. Miller, Chief SO Branch to Chief, Plans and Operations Staff, SO Branch Use of German Nationals, Recruited through CALPO for "Coup de Main" Special Operations, February 5, 1945, folder 21, Box 2, Entry 115, RGG 226, NA; Only for a brief time in November 1944, and on a purely unofficial basis, had SHAEF permitted cooperation between OSS/SOE and CALPO. Memorandum Major Black to Mr [Stewart] Herman, November 24, 1944, November 24, 1944, and, on the "'Hands off' policy," OSS Washington to

OSS Bern, December 3, 1944, in: Relations with CApo, October 1944—January 1945, n. d. folder 149, Box 212, Entry 190, RG 226, NA.

57. Edwin A. Willard, the Commanding Officer of OSS-ETO, approved the projects for coup de main activities and sabotage operations, as did William C. Jackson, the head of the Plans & Operations Division. E. A. Willard, sub: Approval of SO Branch CALPO Projects, March 21, 1945; W. C. Jackson to Chief, SO Branch, March 3, 1945, Box 2, Entry 115, RG 226, NA; Report to C.O. SCI- France, sub: Organizations Operating in Riviera District, January 9, 1945, Box 424, Entry 190, RG 226, NA; SAINT, Paris to Commanding Officer, 6th and 12th Army Group SCI Det., Box 424, Entry 190, RG 226, NA; Special Sabotage Operations Against Nazi and Gestapo Personnel, March 31, 1945, folder 2113, Box 122, Entry 148, RG 226, NA; Covering Report For OSS/ETO, 1–15 April, 1945, April 18, 1945, folder 153, Box 212, Entry 190, RG 226, NA; on the planned deployments of CALPO agents in Austria, see H. Bungert, *Nationalkomitee*, p. 204 ff.

58. R. E. S. Thompson to George O. Pratt, Final Operations Report, May 28, 1945: "At the outset of German operations a loss of 50% had been anticipated," Box 49, Entry 110, RG 226, NA.

59. "The Bach Section," in London War Diary, Vol.6, pp. 137–162, Roll 4, MF 1623, RG 226, NA; Operations Report, DIP, SI, OSS, ETO, May 28, 1945, Appendix H, Box 49, Entry 110, RG 226, NA; Appendix H. Operations Report, DIP, SI, ETO [on Bach Section], May 28, 1945, 1945, Box 49, Entry 110, RG 226, NA.

60. On Kappius, see Helga Grebing, ed., *Lehrstücke in Solidarität: Briefe und Biographien deutscher Sozialisten 1945–1949* (Stuttgart, 1983), p. 343 ff.; J. Foitzik, "Revolution und Demokratie," p 331 ff.

61. A "safe address" was defined by the Labor Division as an address with a telephone or other contact options where the agent could stay for longer than one night—as a rule, with ISK, SPD, or "Neu Beginnen" members. Carl A. Auerbach to George O. Pratt, Chief, Labor Div., SI, sub: Addresses inside Germany, October 9, 1944, folder 147, Box 32, Entry 190, RG 226, NA.

62. Hartmut Pietsch, "Die Entwicklung des politischen Systems in den Städten des Ruhrgebietes 1945–1948," phil. Diss., Bochum, 1977, p. 274 ff. Pietsch did not know that Kappius had been infiltrated by the OSS; K.-D. Henke, *Die amerikanische Besatzung*, p. 645 ff.; Werner Link, *Die Geschichte des Internationalen Jugend-Bundes (IJB) und des Internationalen Sozialistischen Kampfbundes (ISK): Ein Beitrag zur Geschichte der Arbeiterbewegung in der Weimarer Republik und im Dritten Reich* (Meisenheim am Glan, 1964), pp. 313–315, 321; J. Persico, *Piercing the Reich*, pp. 76–88; SWROSS, p. 545–546 ff.; Memorandum Colonel Lada Mocarski to General Donovan, Intelligence Penetration of Germany, February 6, 1945, Box 14, Entry 99, RG 226, NA; London War Diary, Vol.6, 380–394, Roll 4, MF 1623, RG 226, NA.

63. William Casey, Penetration of Germany, 8–10, Box 1, Persico Papers, Hoover Institution, Stanford, CA; J. Persico, *Piercing the Reich*, pp. 163–165; comprehensively on this point: London War Diary, Vol.6, p. 335 ff., Roll 4, MF 1623, RG 226, NA.

64. Agent Teams Successfully Dispatched to Germany, May 15, 1945, folder 59, Box 14, Entry 99, RG 226, NA.

65. R. E. S. Thompson to George O. Pratt, Report and Analysis of SI Operations in Germany, May 26, 1945, Box 49, Entry 110, RG 226, NA.

66. Ibid. as well as London War Diary, Vol.6, Roll 4, MF 1623, RG 226, NA; J. Persico, *Piercing the Reich*, pp. 171ff, 211–215, 320–322. While the OSS War Report emphasized that

the team only made contact once with London, (*SWROSS*, pp. 550 ff.), a report from May 15 maintained that there was a total of four radio contacts. Agent Teams Successfully Dispatched to Germany, May 15, 1945, folder 59, Box 14, Entry 99, RG 226, NA.

67. Agent Teams Successfully Dispatched to Germany, May 15, 1945; SI Operations Germany, April 7, 1945, folder 59, Box 14, Entry 99, RG 226, NA.

68. Van Arkel had taken over the Bern Labor Section in September 1944; prior to that, he was active as an agent in Algiers. The only staff associate available to work with van Arkel was the socialist-oriented stepdaughter of Noel Field, Erika Glaser (later Wallach). Interview Christof Mauch/Erika Wallach, Warrenton, Va., July 4, 1993. G. P. Van Arkel to George O.Pratt, sub: Diverse, n. d. [November 20, 1944, Pratt], folder 147 Box 32, Entry 190, RG 226, NA.

69. G. P. van Arkel to George O. Pratt, December 11, [1944], folder 147 Box 32, Entry 190, RG 226, NA.

70. Berthold Viertel, who lived in Hollywood, let himself be interviewed several times by the Foreign Nationalities Branch of the OSS. The corresponding documents may be found in Entry 100, RG 226, NA; J. Persico, *Piercing the Reich*, p. 114 ff.

71. One of the "tourists" was shot in Mannheim. OSS agent George Howe immortalized him in his bestseller *Call it Treason* (1949), which was turned into a film by Anatole Litvak. After the war, at the instigation of two OSS veterans, the murdered agent's brother, Immo Stabreit, later Germany's ambassador to Washington, received a scholarship to attend Harvard University. Interview Christof Mauch/Peter Sichel, New York, NY, July 13, 1993.

72. Casey, William J., *The Secret War Against Hitler* (Washington, DC 1988), p. 216.

73. The undated manuscripts for Donovan's Labor Day Speech are located in Box 67a, William J. Donovan Papers, USAMI, Carlisle Barracks, Pa.

74. Agent Teams Successfully Dispatched to Germany, May 15, 1945, folder 59, Box 14, Entry 99, RG 226, NA.

75. I owe this information to Nicholas Scheetz. The document, from which there is no permission to quote, is in the Anthony Cave Brown Papers, Georgetown University, Washington, D.C.

76. "399" (Arkel) to Devoe, February 16, 1945, folder 148, Box 32, Entry 190, RG 226, NA.

77. Railroad Strike, "399" to "304" (G.O.Pratt), February 23, 1945, folder 148, Box 32, Entry 190, RG 226, NA; also see [van Arkel], Program for Work with German Railroad Workers, December 2, 1944, folder 147, Box 32, Entry 190, RG 226, NA.

78. Gerald Schwab, *OSS Agents in Hitler's Heartland*, p. 147 ff.

79. If the Nazis had succeeded in defending the Alps, the "30 intelligence operatives" who were holding up in the region of the redoubt on May 1, 1945 would have played a major role. Edward G. Buxton, Memorandum of Information for the Joint U.S. Chiefs of Staff, sub: OSS Penetration of Germany, June 1945, folder 59, Box 14, Entry 99, RG 226, NA.

7. GÖTTERDÄMMERUNG: BETWEEN WAR AND PEACE

1. Rodney G. Minott, *The Fortress That Never Was: The Myth of Hitler's Bavarian Stronghold* (New York/Chicago/San Francisco, 1964). Cf., in addition, Chester Wilmot, *The Struggle for Europe* (New York, 1952), pp. 690–698; John Ehrman, *Grand Strategy* (London, 1956), pp. 131–163; Milton Shulman, *Defeat in the West* (London, 1947), pp. 315–323; Gerhard Weinberg, *World at Arms* Cambridge, 1994), p. 817; Arthur Brysant, *Triumph in the West* (London, 1959), pp. 425–482; W. Churchill, *The Second World War: Triumph and Tragedy* (New York, 1962), VI, pp. 391–400.

2. Eisenhower to CCS, SCAF 279, April 14, 1945, folder German armistice, RG 84, NA; B. F. Smith, Secret Surrender, 24.

3. For the OSS—in addition to his correspondence with Allen Dulles—Minott was only able to fall back on an R&A report about southern Germany, which is located in the Hoover Library: South Germany. An Analysis of the Political and Social Organization, the Communications, Economic Controls, Agriculture and Food Supply, Mineral Resources, Manufacturing and Transportation Facilities of South Germany, Washington 1944 (= R&A 232) This report rests exclusively on generally available information. After the completion of the Habilitationsschrift on which this book is based, an excellent article by Timothy Naftali appeared which confirms some of the findings of this chaper, see: Naftali, "Creating the Myth of the Alpenfestung: Allied Intelligence and the Collapse of the Nazi Police State," in Günter Bischof and Anton Pelinka, eds., Austrian Historical Memory and National Identity (New Brunswick/ London 1997, 203–246).

4. Jon Kimche, Spying for Peace: General Guisan and Swiss Neutrality (London, 1962), pp. 27–57, especially p. 52 ff.; Trial of the Major War Criminals before the International Military Tribunal, Nuremberg, November 14, 1945 to October 1, 1946, XXI, Nuremberg 1948, 9; Minott, Fortress, p. 10 ff.

5. After the German defeat in Italy, Field Marshall Rommel talked to Gauleiter Hofer for the first time about the question of a southern defense line in the Alps. Cf. Georg Ritter von Hengl, General der Gebirgstruppen, The Alpine Redoubt, MS # B-461, World War II German Military Studies (= WWIIGMS), ed. by Donald S. Detwiler (New York/London, 1979), Vol. 23. The studies prepared in the context of the Foreign Military Studies Program are cited here in the selected edition that Detweiler edited in English, since this version is generally accessible.

6. Details may be found in Gauleiter Franz Hofer's report, National Redoubt, 5–12, WWIIGMS, Vol. 23, MS # B-458.. Cf., in addition, Hengl, MS # B-461, The Alpine Redoubt (General), 1, ibid. as well as Minott, Fortress, p. 12 ff.; Wilhelm Hoettl, Hitler's Paper Weapon (London, 1945), p. 148.

7. The report transmitted by Dulles on September 1 (radiotelephone # 205) was forwarded three days later to the Joint Chiefs of Staff. Memorandum Charles S. Cheston to Joint U.S. Chiefs of Staff, 4 September 1944, 975, Roll 18, MF 1642, Entry 162, RG 226, NA; A. Dulles, The Secret Surrender, p. 29.

8. South Germany. An Analysis. R&A 232, RG 59, NA.

9. Telegram OSS London to OSS (SI) Washington, September 21, 1944, folder 813, Box 165, Entry 134, RG 226, NA. An OSS report categorized as "relatively reliable" had taken note of the training for special guerrilla war units on October 16. In the same month construction of SS munitions depots in Bad Tölz and of camps for mountain troups in the Garmisch-Mittenwald region was reported. Synopsis in The Alpine Redoubt.

10. Nazi Plans for Underground Resistance, November 16, 1944, JIC WS 97, 20–25, MR 234, FDRL, Hyde Park, NY; J. Persico, Piercing the Reich, p. 10.

11. JICWS 97, 20.

12. Ibid. The text Dulles cabled to Washington went immediately to President Roosevelt. Telegram OSS Bern to Director OSS, February 13, 1945 and February 14, 1945; Memorandum Donovan to Roosevelt, 14 February 14 and 15, 1945, Box 155, PSF, FDRL, Hyde Park, NY.

13. JICWS 97, 25.

14. Even the Daily Worker (DW) in New York reported about the redoubt and the "werewolves" in National Socialist Germany. Its correspondents, to be sure, assumed that the Nazi

underground would fall apart. The first DW articles appeared on Christmas Eve of 1944; Minott, *Fortress*, p. 28 ff.

15. The memorandum to the President is not in the Roosevelt Library; A reference may be found, however, in Memorandum Donovan to Roosevelt, December 1, 1944, Box 155, PSF, FDRL, Hyde Park, NY; Memorandum Charles S. Cheston to Joint U.S. Chiefs of Staff, September 4, 1944, 975, Roll 18, Entry 162, MF 1642, RG 226, NA; Memorandum Future OSS Operations in Central Europe, September 2, 1944, folder 61, Box 220. Entry 92, RG 226, NA. In contrast to subsequent assertions, even William Casey regarded the redoubt as a realistic danger. Casey to Donovan December 12, 1944, Box 17, Entry 1, RG 226, NA.

16. Memorandum W.J. Donovan to F. D. Roosevelt, December 1, 1944, folder OSS, Box 155, PSF, FDRL, Hyde Park, NY.

17. Telegram OSS Bern to Director OSS, February 13, 1945, Box 155, PSF, FDRL, Hyde Park, NY.

18. This was true, in the first place, for the *Nationalzeitung*, which to all appearances was fed by German agents. Newspaper reports from the *Nationalzeitung* frequently went to the President; see, e.g., Memorandum Donovan to Roosevelt February 14 and 15, 1945, Box 155, PSF, FDRL, Hyde Park, NY.

19. Telegram OSS Bern to OSS Washington, March 3, 1945, W. J. Donovan to F. D. Roosevelt, March 6, 1945, Box 155, PSF, FDRL, Hyde Park, NY.

20. Telegram OSS Bern to OSS Washington, March 27, 1945; W. J. Donovan to F. D. Roosevelt, March 28, 1945, Box 152, FDRL, Hyde Park, NY.

21. OSS Bern [Dulles] to OSS Washington Director [Donovan], April 6, 1945, folder 86, Box 7, Entry 90, RG 226, NA.

22. See the methodological discussion about 'Criteria Employed in the Test' and 'Sources Used," in R&A No.3005, 5–9, ibid.

23. Report No. B-2176, Bern to Paris/Caserta/Washington, March 29, 1945, folder 45, Box 6, Entry 108, RG 226, NA. A 51-page Survey of Reported Activities is available as the appendix to The Alpine Reduit. Second Survey of Available Intelligence Summer 1944 to End of March 1945, OSS Detachment (Main) APO 413 U.S. Army RAL 148.3, April 24, 1945, X 1695, WWII Collection, Marshall Library, Lexington, VA.

24. The Alpine Redoubt. An Interim Survey of Available Intelligence (Summer 1944 to Mid-February 1945), OSS Detachment (Main) APO 413 U.S. Army, February 22, 1945, RAL 148, X 1695; The Alpine Redoubt. An Interim Survey of Available Intelligence (Summer 1944 to Mid-February 1945), March 20, 1945, R&A No.3005, X 1704, WWII Collection Marshall Library, Lexington, VA.

25. See Conclusions, in: R&A No.3005, 26–36 as well as in RAL 148, 23–29, ibid.

26. RAL 148.1, The Alpine Reduit. Economic Capabilities, April 10, 1945, X 1697, WWII Collection, Marshall Library, Lexington, VA. On the German side, the situation was evaluated even more negatively. Von Hengl assumed that supplies and materials at the end of April only sufficed for a few weeks. See Georg Ritter von Hengl, The Alpine Redoubt, 10, WWI-IGMS, Vol. 23, MS # B-461.

27. RAL 148.3 The Alpine Reduit. Second Survey of Available Intelligence Summer 1944 to End of March 1945, April 24, 1945, X1695, WWII Collection, Marshall Library, WWII Collection, Lexington, VA.

28. G. J. A. O'Toole, *Encyclopedia*, p. 422 ff.; F. H. Hinsley, *British Intelligence*, III/2, (London, 1970/1990), pp. 712 ff.

29. MI 14 Appreciation of January 4, 1945 as well as Notes on Germany's Last Stand, February 4, 1945, WO 208/4314. The POW interviews may be found in a report from March 18, 1945, WO 208/4319, MI 14/10/12/45, see Hinsley, British Intelligence, III/2, p. 712 ff. The OSS was fundamentally skeptical about the value of POW interviews. These opinions, meanwhile, seemed to point in the direction of there being no alpine fortress ("that no such thing was possible"). The Alpine Redoubt, 9, March 30, 1945, R&A No.3005, X 1704, WWII Collection, Marshall Library, Lexington, VA.

30. Hinsley, British Intelligence, III/2, p. 717. The kernel of truth about taking hostages was that the Nazis had transformed the Itterschloß (Itter palace) in Brixlegg into a fortress for more than 50 prominent prisoners, including Edouard Daladier, Maurice Gamelin, and Paul Reynaud. J. Persico, Piercing the Reich, p. 205.

31. Hinsley, British Intelligence, p. 717 ff.; J. Ehrmann, Grand Strategy, 6, 1956, 132–34; MID Memorandum, Expected Developments of April 1945 in the German Reich, 2 April 2, 1945, sec. 12, 014.Germany (7–10–42), CAD, RG 165, NA.

32. Gauleiter Franz Hofer, The Alpine Fortification & Defense Line. A Report on German and U.S. Views of the Alpine Redoubt, in 1944 Annex #1: Alpen-Reduit, USA-Diplomatic Representation in Switzerland, Father of Germany's Alpine-Fortification, the "Festung Alpen," 1–2, WWIIGMS, Vol. 23, MS # B-457.

33. Gauleiter Hofer, National Redoubt, 5–11, WWIIGMS, Vol. 23, MS # 458. Accordingly, the Hofer memorandum of November 6, 1944 was first forwarded by Martin Bormann to Hitler in March 1945. Cf., also, Gauleiter Franz Hofer, The Alpine Fortification & Defense Line, Annex # 3: The Alpine-Fortification ("Fuehrer-Vorlage") (Proposal Submitted to Hitler for Decision): The Forwarding of the USA "Alpen-Reduit" Report to the "Fuehrer-Hauptquartier" and My Own Opinions and Deductions, WWIIGMS, Vol. 23, MS # B-457.

34. Von Hengl had drawn attention to how the Austrian population had already become war-weary by the end of April. Georg Ritter von Hengl, Report on the Alpine Fortress, 25 April 1946, pp. 8 ff., WWIIGMS, Vol. 23, MS # B-459.

35. JIC SHAEF (45) 3 (Final), Ability of the German Army in the West to Continue the War, March 10, 1945, X 1701, WWII Collection, Marshall Library, Lexington, VA; AGTS 14–3, RG 260, NA.

36. JIC SHAEF (45) 3 (Final), 2, Marshall Library, X 1701, WWII Collection, Marshall Library, Lexington, VA.

37. Eisenhower to General Marshall, March 31, 1945, X 1698, WWII Collection, Marshall Library, Lexington, VA.

38. Memorandum G.C. Marshall to President Roosevelt, Probable Developments in the German Reich, [April 2 1945], Marshall Library, WWII Collection, X 1699.

39. See Chapter 4.

40. The recommendation to publish came from George Marshall: Memorandum G. C. Marshall to Roosevelt, April 2 1945; Note "Immediate Release," April 5 1945; Eisenhower to Roosevelt, March 31, 1945; Col. F. McCarthy to Gen. Hull, March 29, 1945, X 1698, WWII Collection, Marshall Library, Lexington, VA.

41. It is clear that the American press in March and April was anything but reserved or measured in its reporting on the subject of the Alpine fortification. In any event, numerous myths and deceptive pictures about the Nazis' final struggle were already circulating; NYT April 8, 1945; Life Magazine, April 9, 1945, p. 38 ff.; Minott, Fortress, p. 87 ff.

42. Cf. Hinsley, *British Intelligence*, III/2, p. 714. Symptomatic of the overheated dispatches was a report from February 20, 1945, which was sent—via OSS channels—to Paris, London, Caserta, and Washington, and which stated emphatically that the Nazis were undoubtedly preparing a last bitter struggle. Report No. B-1715, Germany, the Maquis Problem, folder 33, Box 4, Entry 108, RG 226, NA.

43. Cf., for example, "Reich Army Rebels: Uprisings Led by Revolt in the Cradle of Nazism Sweep South Germany," *NYT* April 29, 1945, pp. 1, 19.

44. Franz Obermaier/Josef Mauerer, *Aus Trümmern wächst das neue Leben. Bilder aus der bayerischen Nachkriegszeit – Eine Chronik für Stadt und Land*, (Munich, n.d.), pp. 5–17; Kurt Preis, *München unterm Hakenkreuz, 1933–1945*, (Munich, 1989), pp. 204–212. A critical perspective, by contrast, in Joachim Brückner, *Kriegsende in Bayern 1945: Der Wehrkreis VII und die Kämpfe zwischen Donau und Alpen* (Freiburg, 1987), p. 187 ff.; Klaus-Dietmar Henke, *Die amerikanische Besetzung Deutschlands* (Munich, 1995), pp. 854–861. Cf., further, Heike Bretschneider, *Der Widerstand gegen den Nationalsozialismus in München 1933–1945* (Munich, 1968); Hildebrand Troll, "Aktionen zur Kriegsbeendigung im Frühjahr 1945," in Martin Broszat, Elke Fröhlich, Anton Großmann, eds., *Bayern in der NS-Zeit*, IV, p. 660 ff.

45. B.F. Smith/Aga Rossi, *Operation Sunrise* (New York, 1979), p. 62; Soley, *Radio Warfare*, 147–148; Mauch, "Subversive Kriegführung," p. 66.

46. OSS Bern to OSS Washington, March 23, 1945, NA, RG 226, Entry 90, Box 7, Folder 86. Dulles did not meet with Heintze personally; instead, he received the information via an agent, Prince Alois von Auersperg (OSS-Code 502), a counterintelligence agent working for the German Consulate in Bern. On this, see Telegram OSS Bern to OSS Washington, November 10, 1944, Box 277, Entry 134, RG 226, Dulles-WIR, Doc 4–101, 396f; Petersen, ed. *From Hitler's Doorstep*, p. 396.

47. Faulhaber's good reputation had become solidified over the years, so that different OSS informants such as Willy Brandt, Father Georg Leiber, and Hans Schönfeld commended the Munich cardinal's qualities as an opposition figure. [Brandt], Opposition Movements in Germany, September 25, 1943, reprinted in *AmIntel*, Doc 21, p. 104; Interview with Father Leiber, August 18, 1944, ibid., Doc. 65, p. 281; Memorandum by Hans Schönfeld, [September 1944], ibid., Doc 70c, p. 304. Heideking/Mauch, *American Intelligence*, pp. 104, 281, 304.

48. OSS Bern to OSS Washington, March 23, 1945, NA, RG 226, Entry 90, Box 7, Folder 86.

49. A. Dulles, *The Secret Surrender* (London, 1967); A. Dulles/Gero von Schulze-Gaevernitz, *Unternehmen "Sunrise" – Die geheime Geschichte des Kriegsendes in Italien* (Düsseldorf, 1967); Catherine Schiemann, "Der Geheimdienst beendet den Krieg. "Operation Sunrise" und die deutsche Kapitulation in Italien," in Heideking/Mauch, *Geheimdienstkrieg*, pp. 142–165; Peter R. Black, *Ernst Kaltenbrunner, Ideological Soldier of the Third Reich* (Princeton, NJ, 1984).

50. OSS Bern to OSS Washington, March 24, 1945, Box 7, Entry 90, RG 226, NA, RG 226.

51. Cf., e.g., William J. Donovan, Memorandum for the President, March 27, 1945; [William J. Donovan], Memorandum for Information to the Secretary of State, March 27, 1945, 153ff, Roll 21, MF 1641, RG 190, NA; G. Edward Buxton, Memorandum for the Secretary of State, April 9, 1945; G. Edward Buxton, Memorandum for Information for the Joint Chiefs of Staff, Roll 68, Entry 180 (Donovan MF), RG 226, NA; G. Edward Buxton to the President, April 9, 1945, Box 153, PSF, FDRL, Hyde Park, NY.

52. It was noted, moreover, that Captain Wenig was a member of the group; it was not known, however, if he would show up in Bavaria on time. OSS Bern to OSS Washington, March 26, 1945, folder 86, Box 7, Entry 90, RG 226, NA. On the role played by Schulze-Gaevernitz and on his biographical background, see Jürgen Heideking, "Gero von Schulze-Gaevernitz," in Michael Bosch/Wolfgang Niess, eds., *Der Widerstand im deutschen Südwesten 1933–1945* (Stuttgart, 1984), pp. 281–290.

53. Ibid.

54. OSS Bern to OSS Paris (Dulles and Schulze-Gaevernitz to Forgan and Gamble), April 7, 1945, folder 86, Box 7, Entry 90, RG 226, NA. Copies of the cable also went out to the OSS in London, Caserta, and Washington.

55. OSS Bern to OSS Paris, April 7, 1945, NA, RG 226, Entry 90, Box 7, Folder 86. On the move of government offices to southern Germany, see Hinsley, *British Intelligence*, III/2, p. 713 ff.

56. G. Edward Buxton, Memorandum for Information for the Joint Chiefs of Staff, NA, RG 226, Entry 180 (Donovan MF), Roll 68; G. Edward Buxton to the President, April 9, 1945, Box 153, PSF, FDRL, Hyde Park, NY.

57. Cf. Preis, *München unter Hakenkreuz*, pp. 205 ff.

58. The text of the proclamation is reprinted in Obermaier, *Aus Trümmern wächst das neue Leben*, pp. 9–10. On criticism of the proclamation, see Lutz Niethammer, *Die Mitläuferfabrik: Entnazifizierung am Beispiel Bayerns* (Berlin, 1982), p. 182 ff.

59. Whether von Epp was forced in front of the microphone with a revolver to his head, as OSS staffer Howard Becker maintained, cannot be determined. Howard Becker, "The Nature and Consequences of Black Propaganda," in *American Sociological Review* 14 (1949), p. 232.

60. Freedom Action Bavaria, May 26, 1945, in Freedom Action Bavaria (Freiheitsaktion Bayern, FAB), Office of Strategic Services Mission for Germany European Theater of Operations APO 655 U.S. Army Field Intelligence Study 1, June 27, 1945, folder 36, Box 7, Entry 124, RG 226, NA.

61. Preis, *München unterm Hakenkreuz*, p. 208.

62. Cf. ibid., p. 209.

63. OSS Field Report Freedom Action Bavaria, May 26, 1945, NA, RG 226, Entry 124, Box 7, folder 36.

64. Preis, *München*, p. 211; on 'Werwolf' cf. Perry Biddiscombe, *Werewolf!: The History of the National Socialist Guerrilla Movement 1944–1946* (Toronto: Toronto University Press 1988).

65. While Popitz, Hassell, and Schacht were in touch with each other, there are no indications that von Epp was in touch with this group. In Hassell's diary entries Ritter von Epp is not mentioned even once. Ulrich von Hassell, *Aufzeichnungen vom Andern Deutschland.*

66. No record of any conversation between Kesselring and von Epp has come down in any of Kesselring's volumes of memoirs. Albert Kesselring, "Soldat bis zum letzten Tag," 1953; "Gedanken zum Zweiten Weltkrieg," 1955.

67. OSS Field Report Freedom Action Bavaria, May 26, 1945, NA, RG 226, Entry 124, Box 7, folder 36.

68. Cf. Howard Becker, "Nature and Consequences of Black Propaganda," p. 230; Peter R. Black, *Ernst Kaltenbrunner: Ideological Soldier of the Third Reich* (Princeton, NJ, 1990).

69. This characterization of Howard Becker comes from Sefton Delmer, an Englishman who grew up in Germany and who produced subversive radio broadcasts for the British. Delmer's autobiographically tinged study of the British radio war contains numerous telling

characterizations; in detail, however, Delmer's report is frequently faulty. Sefton Delmer, *Black Boomerang* (New York, 1962), p. 253. and Howard Becker, *German Youth: Bond or Free* (New York, 1947). cf. further, Soley, *Radio Warfare*, pp. 146, 154f.

70. In the brief summary of the operation published in 1949, Howard Becker was not able to mention the names "Capricorn" and "Hagedorn," since the OSS documents had not yet been released. Instead of Hagedorn, Becker used the code name "Holly," and "Capricorn" was called "Operation Frolic." Howard Becker, "The Nature and Consequences of Black Propaganda," pp. 230–31, citation 231.

71. MO Branch Progress Report, April 30, 1945, folder 1168, Box 81, Entry 148, RG 226, NA. on Stephan Schnabel, whose name also appears in OSS documents as Stephen or Stefan, see C. Laurie, *Propaganda Warriors*, p. 83; Morale Operations Branch, Progress Report, March 15, 1945, Box 81, Entry 148, RG 226, NA; Black Radio "Capricorn"; Memo Capricorn, folder 67, Box 16, Entry 99, NA; MO Branch, Progress Report, Feb. 16–23, 1945, February 28, 1945; Chief MO Branch OSS, John S. Roller to Brig. General Robert A. McClure, sub: MO "Black" Radio Program "Capricorn," February 16, 1945, Box 113, Entry 139, RG 226, NA.

72. Cited here according to Radio "Hagedorn" in MO History, Vol. III, Box 113, Entry 139, RG 226, NA.

73. This is especially interesting against the background of how German newspapers and radio stations were continuously warning about "pseudo-German radios" toward the end of the war. The individual warnings were summarized in FCC reports, see for example FCC (European Section. German Reich Affairs), Nazis Warned on Pseudo-German Radios, March 29, 1945, folder 2034, Box 150, Entry 139, RG 226, NA.

74. The FAB under Occupation, in Freedom Action Bavaria (Freiheitsaktion Bayern, FAB), OSS Mission for Germany-ETO, FISt 1, June 27, 1945, folder 36, Box 7, Entry 124, RG 226, NA.

75. OSS Washington to OSS Bern, July 26, 1943, folder 1820, Box 340,Entry 134, RG 226, NA.

76. OSS Bern to OSS Washington, February 15, 1944 (Tel. 2068–73), folder 1077, Box 170, RG 226, NA.

77. OSS Bern to OSS Washington, February 15, 1944 (Tel. 2054–56), Dulles-WIR, Doc. 3–13, 218, February 15, 1944, Box 170, Entry 134, RG 226, NA; OSS Bern to OSS Washington, February 15, 1944 (Tel. 2057–61), February 15, 1944, folder 565, Box 274, Entry 134, RG 226, NA, partially reprinted in Dulles-WIR, Doc. 3–14, 218f. On February 21. February OSS central headquarters in Washington requested, for the first time, information about persons for the postwar occupation. OSS Washington to OSS Bern, Box 275, Entry 134, RG 226, NA. On "Ted" or "643" [Schulte], also see Telegram OSS Bern to OSS Washington, August 16, 1944, folder 1390, Box 231, Entry 134, RG 226 as well as OSS Bern to OSS Washington, March 25, 1943, Box 165, Entry 165, RG 226, NA; OSS Bern to OSS Washington, August 20, 1944, Box 193, En-try 134, RG 226, NA.

78. OSS Bern to OSS Washington, June 12, 1944, Box 192, Entry 134, RG 226, NA, Dulles-WIR, Doc 3–149, p. 307 ff.

79. OSS Washington to OSS Bern, 109 to 110, June 17, 1944, folder 1056, Box 165, Entry 134, RG 226, NA.

80. The Attempt on Hitler's Life and Its Consequences, July 27, 1944, R&A 2387, RG 59, NA.

81. German Government Personnel, Allen W. Dulles to Inter-Division Coordinating Committee on German Government Personnel, Lt. Col. Howard P. Jones, Chairman, August 6, 1945, XL 22686, Box 314, Entry 19, RG 226, NA.

82. As early as January 15, 1944, Dulles had cabled Washington that "Leo" or "817" [Hoegner], who lived at Westbühlerstraße 30, had been of great help and indeed a key informant. Telegram OSS Bern to OSS Washington, folder 1021, Box 158, Entry 134, RG 226, NA; March 16, 1943, Box 165, Entry 134, RG 226, NA. Dulles telegraphed some biographical data about Hoegner to Washington on August 2, 1944, Box 231, Entry 134, RG 226, NA.

83. On the Gisevius-Sauerbruch connection, see the reports by "Elizabeth" from the end of 1944 and start of 1945, Box 5, Entry 125, RG 226, NA.

84. Telegram 110, Berlin to Lee and Hughes, Amzon, Box 151, Entry 88, RG 226, NA. On Müller, see his memoirs, *Bis zur letzten Konsequenz: Ein Leben für Frieden und Freiheit* (Munich, 1975).

85. Short biographical remarks about Wilhelm Hoffmann may be found in the introduction to a festschrift for Peter Hoffmann: Francis R. Nicosia/Lawrence D. Stokes, eds., *Germans Against Nazism: Nonconformity, Opposition and Resistance in the Third Reich: Essays in Honour of Peter Hoffmann* (New York, 1990).

86. [General List] and Supplementary List (Possible Candidates who are under further investigation), XL 22686, Box 314, Entry 19, RG 226, NA.

87. Telegram 110 Amzon to Black USCON, Box 151, Entry 88, RG 226, NA. On the "White List," see Henric L. Wuermeling, *Die Weiße Liste: Umbruch der politischen Kultur in Deutschland 1945* (Frankfurt, 1981).

88. Some of the "crown jewels" were deployed as American agents. Gordon M. Stewart, to Whitney H. Shepardson, B. L. Penrose, Jr., Hans Tofte, January 26, 1946 and January 31, 1946, sub: SI Germany, folder 559, Box 70, Entry 108B, RG 226; R. Harris Smith, OSS, 236f; Interview C. Mauch/F. Ford, OSSOHP; Interview C. Mauch/R. Helms, OSSOHP.

89. Telegram 110, Berlin to Lee and Hughes, Amzon, Box 151, Entry 88, RG 226, NA. Hans Peter Schwarz, *Adenauer: Der Aufstieg. 1876–1952* (Stuttgart, 1986), p. 658 ff. and Henning Köhler, *Adenauer: Eine politische Biographie* (Berlin/Frankfurt, 1994), pp. 724–737.

90. "I'm not at all convinced that if there had been some, in retrospect, unbelievable change in the course of the war, that he [Gisevius] wouldn't have been able to make a case for himself." Interview C.Mauch/Franklin Ford, Lexington, MA, January 17, 1997, *OSSOHP.*

91. Ibid.

92. E. K. M. to Huddle, June 26, 1945, Activities of Remnants of Subversive Movement, Bern Confidential File 1945, RG 84, NA; Memorandum from 6435 [unidentified], sub: Nazi Underground Activities, n.d., ibid. ; Dr. Schönfeld and the International Church Group at Geneva, Enclosure to despatch No. 12825, October 25, 1945, from American Legation, Bern, Switzerland, ibid.

93. On Kolbe, see chapter 4.

94. Comprehensive on this subject: Laqueur/Breitman, *The Man Who Broke the Silence*, pp. 232–236.

95. Gero von Schulze-Gaevernitz to Allen Dulles, October 22, 1945, N 524/6 BA-MA Freiburg, on this, see Laqueur/Breitman, *The Man Who Broke the Silence*, p. 237 as well as J. Heideking, "Gero von Schulze-Gaevernitz," pp. 281–290; Telegram Bastedo to 110 (Dulles), October 19, 1945, Box 152, Entry 88, RG 226, NA; "Eddy" Waetjen, Enclosure to despatch No. 12825, October 25, 1945, from American legation, Bern, Switzerland, Activities of Remnants of Subversive Movement, Bern Confidential File 1945, RG 84, NA. German Legation and Consulates' Turnover, from #2217 [unidentified], May 8, 1945; Report Dr. Gisevius (Continued), May 12, 1945; Confidential Report: More About Dr. Gisevius, May 23, 1945, Activities

of Remnants of Subversive Movement, Bern Confidential File 1945, RG 84, NA. On Gisevius, also see Klaus Urner, *Der Schweizer Hitler-Attentäter* (Frauenfeld, 1980), p. 20 ff.

96. Memorandum from 6435 [unidentified], sub: Nazi Underground Activities, n.d., Activities of Remnants of Subversive Movement, Bern Confidential File 1945, RG 84, NA.

97. Leland Harrison to Secretary of State (Copy to USPOLAD), sub: The July 20, 1944, attempt to effect a coup d'état in Germany and its present-day political significance as seen from Switzerland, Activities of Remnants of Subversive Movement, Bern Confidential File 1945, RG 84, NA.

98. Conversation with Allen Dulles, Office Memorandum October 25, 1945, Activities of Remnants of Subversive Movement, Bern Confidential File 1945, RG 84, NA; Allen Dulles to Bishop Bell, July 5, 1947, Bell Papers MS 47, especially 47.183, Lambeth Palace Library, London. After the war, Bishop Bell founded an assistance program for the surviving relatives of the victims from the German resistance. Money was collected to support families, and young Germans, including Marion Countess Dönhoff, were invited to Great Britain. Dulles hoped, in 1947, to establish an American sister organization. The July 20th Memorial Fund General Information, Bell Papers, 47.259–260; 47.304. Lambeth Palace Library, London. See, in addition, Christiane Toyka-Seid, "Gralshüter: Notgemeinschaft oder gesellschaftliche 'Pressure Group'?. Die Stiftung 'Hilfswerk 20.Juli 1944' im ersten Nachkriegsjahrzehnt," in *Der 20.Juli 1944. Bewertung und Rezeption des deutschen Widerstands gegen das NS-Regime* (Cologne, 1994), pp. 157–169.

99. Telegram [Richard] Helms to Suhling, AMZON, November 19, 1945, Box 152, Entry 88, RG 226, NA; Telegram 110 [Allen Dulles], Berlin to [John A.] Bross, London, September 26, 1945, Box 151, Entry 88, RG 226, NA; 110 [Allen Dulles] and 257 [Robert P. Joyce], Bern to [Lt. Philip] Bastedo, Berlin, October 21, 1945, Box 152, Entry 88, RG 226; Telegram 110 and 476 to 257 and 1049, September 19, 1945, Box 151, Entry 88, RG 226, NA.

100. In this context, the role of Emmy C. Rado, who since 1943 (initially in New York, later in London, Bern, and Berlin) was compiling black and white lists of German Nazis and anti-Nazis, can hardly be overestimated. Rado devoted special attention to church circles in Germany. Mortimer Kollender to Arthur J. Goldberg, June 8, 1943, folder 841, Box 66, Entry 168, RG 226, NA; William Langer to John C. Hughes, August 21, 1943, folder 4, Box 1, Entry 159, RG 226, NA; Field Unit, NYC of Biographical Records, folder 5, Box 1, Entry 159, RG 226, NA; John C. Hughes to David C. Shaw, The Confessional Church in Germany, March 3, 1945, folder 6, ibid.; Emmy C. Rado to General William J. Donovan, September 19, 1944, Entry 180, Roll 125, MF A 3304, RG 226, NA. See, further, the lists by SHAEF-PWD, Subject: PWD "White List" of Persons in Germany Believed to be Anti-Nazi or Non-Nazi, December 5, 1944, XL 20085, Box 242 as well as XL 20312, Box 294, Entry 19, RG 226, NA; the only—admittedly highly deficient—publication is by Edward L. Field, *"Retreat to Victory": A Previously Untold O.S.S. Operation* (Surfside Beach, SC, 1991).

101. Twilight Program, August 8, 1944, folder 5, Box 553, Entry 92, RG 226, NA; OSS Detachment ETOUSA to Supreme Commander, SHAEF, February 17, 1945, folder 493/II, Box 48, Entry 110, RG 226, NA; Philip Bastedo, Plans and Operations Staff to Colonel J. R. Forgan, OSS Activities upon Collapse or Surrender of Germany, February 20, 1945, folder 1251, Box 284, Entry 190, RG 226; SI Plans and Material on Hand for Twilight I and II, S.A. Callisen to Lt. N.P. Bastedo, March 7, 1945, ibid.; William J. Casey to James R. Forgan, sub: SI Post Collapse Plans, February 26, 1945, folder 281, Box 222, Entry 190, RG 226, NA; Lt. R.M. Helms to Deputy Chief, SI/ETO, March 8, 1945, sub: Staff Personnel for Germany in Twilight II, folder 276, Box

222, Entry 190, RG 226, NA; Memorandum by Frank Wisner, June 14, 1945, FOIA-CIA; Interview C. Mauch/R. Helms, April 21, 1997, *OSSOHP*.

102. On Gehlen, see his memoirs, *Der Dienst: Erinnerungen 1942–1971* (Mainz, 1971) as well as E. H. Cookridge, *Gehlen: Spy of the Century* (London, 1971) and Mary Allen Reese, *General Reinhard Gehlen: The CIA Connection* (Fairfax, VA., 1990).

8. THE DREAM OF THE MIRACLE WAR AND THE LEGACY OF THE OSS

1. The earliest elaborated sketch for a postwar intelligence service is dated September 1943, William J. Donovan, The need in the United States on a permanent basis as an integral part of our military establishment of a long-range strategic intelligence organization, with attendant "subversion" and "deception of the enemy" functions, September 17, 1943, Box 264, Entry 108, RG 226, NA. See, further, Memorandum for the President by William J. Donovan, November 18, 1944; Substantive Authority Necessary in Establishment of Central Intelligence Service, reprinted as Document 1, in: William M. Leary, ed., The Central Intelligence Agency. History and Documents, n. p. [Mobile, Alabama] 1984, pp. 123–125.

2. T. Troy, *Donovan and the CIA*, pp. 287–304; B. F. Smith, *Shadow Warriors*, pp. 309–419; Allen Dulles to John Foster Dulles, August 20, 1945, John Foster Dulles Papers, Box 26, Seeley G. Mudd Library, Princeton, NJ;Brooks Peters article on AWD, n. d., Box 19, Allen Dulles Papers, Seeley G. Mudd Library, Princeton, NJ; Fabian von Schlabrendorff, "Our Two Tries to Kill Hitler"; Allen Dulles, "One of the Boldest and Bravest of the Anti-Nazis," Folder 12, Box 8, Francis Pickens Miller Collection, Marshall Library, Lexington, VA; CDT, February 9, 1945; WTH, February 9, 1945, February 11, 1945; NYT, February 10, 1945, February 13, 1945; WP, February 16, 1945; William J. Donovan, Memorandum for the President, February 23, 1945; William J. Donovan, Memorandum for the Joint Chiefs of Staff, February 15, 1945, Box 155, PSF, FDRL, Hyde Park, NY.

3. On September 25, 1945 Carter sent Truman a September 21 report that, among other things, denounced the staff of the Visual Presentations Branch as socialists and Communists. One of the staff, Carl Marzani, who was a member of the Communist party, was imprisoned for several years. The others stopped receiving commissions from the U.S. government. Report on Various Rumors Concerning the Office of Strategic Services, John Franklin Carter to President Truman, September 25, 1945, Rose Conway File, Papers of Harry S Truman, Truman Library, Independence, Missouri. A memorandum dealing with Carter's accusations, based on all the OSS veterans mentioned by Carter and still living, is in the possession of the author. Donal McLaughlin to C.M., Ref: Response to Jay Franklin Carter's declassified report of 9/25/45, "Report on Various Rumors Concerning the Office of Strategic Services," May 29, 1997; Interview C. Mauch/Donal McLaughlin, October 7, 1996, *OSSOHP*.

4. Harold Smith, Conference with President Truman September 13, 1945; Harold Smith, Conference with Harry Truman, September 20, 1945, Box 3, Harold Smith Papers, FDRL, Hyde Park, NY.

5. The inscription reads: "Hic iacet inconsecrata in terra infans illicitus Gulielmi Donovan intempeste abortus, parum quidem tarde occisusquem homines O.S.S. nuncupare solebant. Resurgam? Natus est MCMXL,Obiit MCMXLC. Siste viator pro infelicem lacrimam relinquite." Memorandum OSS (pictor ignotus, scriptor ignotus) to Harry S. Truman, sub: Tempora mutantur, October 12, 1945; attachments: Harry S Truman to General Donovan, n. d. [October 1945], Harry S Truman to Secretary of State, n. d. [October 1945]; Box 4, Safe File, PSF, FDRL, Hyde Park, NY.

6. The documents of the Veterans of Strategic Services (VSS) are located in Donovan's law offices in Rockefeller Plaza, New York, NY and are administered by VSS President Geoffrey M. T. Jones. Additional smaller collections are scattered among the Allen Dulles Papers, Seeley G. Mudd, Library, Princeton, NJ as well as in Box 4, Shepardson Papers, FDRL, Hyde Park, NY.

7. The Donovan Medal, in: William J. Casey, The Clandestine war in Europe (1942–1945). Remarks of William J. Casey on receipt of the William J. Donovan Award at Dinner of Veterans of O.S.S., December 5, 1974, Folder Casey, Box 1, Persico Papers, Hoover Institution, Stanford, CA

8. Only a tiny percentage of VSS members belonged to the R&A Branch. Most were recruited from the ranks of SI, SO, X-2, and MO.

9. James Robert Parish/Michael R. Pitts, *The Great Spy Pictures* (Metuchen, NJ, 1974), p. 358; Jay Robert Nash/Stanley Ralph Ross, *The Motion Picture Guide* (Chicago, 1986), VI, p. 2214; James I. Deutsch, "I Was a Hollywood Agent." The Office of Strategic Services in the Movies of 1946, April 21, 1997, SMH Conference, Arlington, Va. Since the OSS files were already under lock and key in 1946, the documents in question were ones that the Hollywood directors were unable to inspect; presumably they were portions of the microfilms illegally produced by Donovan, Entry 180, MF A 3304, RG 226, NA.

10. *13 Rue Madeleine*. Released by Twentieth Century-Fox Film Corp., December 1946. Produced by Louis De Rochemont. Directed by Henry Hathaway. Screenplay by John Monks Jr. and Sy Bartlett. 16mm print, FCA 3540–3542, LOC, Washington, D.C.

11. *Cloak and Dagger*. Released by Warner Bros. Pictures, September 1946. Produced by Milton Sperling. Directed by Fritz Lang. Screenplay by Albert Maltz and Ring Lardner Jr., based on an original story by Boris Ingster and John Larkin. VBE 7077–7078, LOC, Washington, D.C. The title of the film was taken from the book by Corey Ford and Alastair MacBains that came out in 1945, *Cloak and Dagger: The Secret Story of OSS* (New York, 1945). The film script was written by former OSS-SO agent Michael Burke. On Burke, see R. Harris Smith, *OSS*, p. 189; E. Hymoff, *OSS in World War II*, pp. 167, 250; O'Toole, *Encyclopedia*, pp. 84 ff.; *NYT* February 7, 1987 as well as the memoirs of Michael Burke, *Outrageous Good Fortune: A Memoir* (Boston, 1984); Larry Langman/David Ebner, *Encyclopedia of American Spy Films* (New York, 1990), p. 71; Lotte H. Eisner, *Fritz Lang* (New York, 1977), p. 267. On Lang, also see Paul M. Jensen, *The Cinema of Fritz Lang* (New York, 1969).

12. *O.S.S.* Released by Paramount Pictures, May 1946. Produced by Richard Maibaum. Directed by Irving Pichel. Screenplay by Richard Maibaum. 16mm print FCA 3160–3163, LOC, Washington, D.C. After "O.S.S." Maibaum wrote the first four screenplays for the first four James Bond movies.

13. Deutsch, "I Was a Hollywood Agent," pp. 6 ff.; *NYT*, May 27, 1946; In box office terms, *O.S.S.* ranked above a classic like *My Darling Clementine*, which also appeared in 1946, "60 Top Grossers of 1946," in *Variety*, January 8, 1947, p. 8.

14. The final script dated May 13, 1946 is still called "Donovan and OSS." Information from James Deutsch, February 1997.

15. [Col. Forgan] to General William J. Donovan, March 1, 1946; Twentieth Century Film Corporation to William Casey, March 19, 1946; William J. Donovan to Mr. Louis de Rochemnt, July 3, 1946; Memorandum of Comments of Messr. Forgan and Doering Regarding Script "13 Rue Madeleine," dated May 13, 1946; *NYT* August 25, 1946, Box 1, Russell Forgan Papers, Stanford, CA

16. In Kennan's view, the lack of information about the foreign nationals prevented the Americanization, i.e. the integration of these groups into American life. William E. Griffith to Mr. DeWitt C. Poole (strictly private), sub: Mr. Kennan's Interest in the Foreign Nationality Field, January 4, 1951, Folder 7, Box 1, Poole Papers, State Historical Society of Wisconsin, Madison, WI.

17. Among other things, this was related to the fact that McArthur maintained his own secret intelligence service. In October 1944 there were only 106 OSS agents in China. The secret intelligence service did not become active in the Far East until 1945. Maochun Yu, *OSS in China: Prelude to War* (New Haven/London, 1997), p. 226.

18. Cedric Larson, "Music—a Medium for Psychological Warfare," in W. Daugherty/M. Janowitz, eds., *Psychological Warfare Casebook* (Baltimore, 1958), p. 580.

19. Richard Breitman, *Official Secrets: What the Nazis Planned, what the British and Americans knew* (New York, 1998).

BIBLIOGRAPHY

From among the wealth of published sources and literature used in this book, the only titles listed below will be those closely connected with the theme of this study. Each one of the titles not listed is cited in full the first time it is mentioned in the footnotes.

UNPUBLISHED SOURCES

The overwhelming majority of archival research for this account was carried out prior to 1995 in the National Archives of the United States. At that time, OSS records were in what is today "Archives I" in Washington, D.C. as well as in Suitland, MD. At the end of 1995 the OSS records were transferred to College Park, MD.

1. Items in the National Archives, Washington, D.C./ College Park, Maryland

MODERN MILITARY BRANCH

RG 165 Records of the War Department General and Special Staffs
ABC Files
RG 218 Records of the Joint Chiefs of Staff (JCS)
JCS Historical Office
Edward P. Lilly Papers on Psychological Warfare
RG 226 Records of the Office of Strategic Services
Entry 1 General Correspondence, 1942–1946
Entry 16 R&A Intelligence Reports (Regular Series), 1941–1945
Entry, 19 Intelligence Reports (XL Series), 1941–1945

Entry 21 Intelligence Reports (L Series), 1941–1945
Entry 58 Minutes of Meetings
Entry 77 Enemy Objectives Unit of the Economic Warfare Division, 1943–1945
Entry 85 Visual Presentation Branch Files, 1942–1945
Entry 88 Overseas Cable File
Entry 90 Records of the Washington Radio & Cable and Field Photo Branch
Entry 91 History of OSS
Entry 92 COI/OSS Central Files
Entry 97 Algiers File
Entry 99 OSS History Office Collection
Entry 100: Records of the Foreign Nationalities Branch (C 0002)
Entry 106 Records of the New York Secret Intelligence Branch
Entry 107 Records Relating to a Survey of Foreign Experts
Entry 108 Washington Registry SI Field Files
Entry 108b Washington Registry SI Field Files
Entry 110 Field Intelligence Reports, Theater Officer Correspondence,

Draft Histories

Entry 120: Washington CI Files
Entry 125 Field Station Files, Bern, Stockholm, Caserta
Entry 134 Washington Registry Radio & Cable Files
Entry 136 Washington and Field Station Files: Algiers, Austria, Bari, Caserta, Denmark. London, Paris, New York
Entry 138 Washington X-2 Branch Record.
Entry 139 Washington and Field Station Files: Cairo, Caserta, New York, Paris, Stockholm
Entry 142 New York SI Branch Records
Entry 144 Field Station Files, Algiers, Austria, Bari, Belgium, Cairo
Entry 146 Miscellaneous Washington Files. Budget & Finance, CD, General Counsel, History Project, Intelligence Service, R&A, R&D, Secretariat, Security, SI, SO
Entry 147 New York and London Files
Entry 148 Field Station Files: Holland, Istanbul. London, New York, Paris, Stockholm
Entry 154 Field Station Files: Bari, Bukarest, Caserta, Cairo
Entry 159 New York SI Records
Entry 162 Records of the Director's Office, Minutes and Correspondence with the Navy, State and War Departments and with FDR (MF 1642)
Entry 168 Field Station Files: London, Madrid, New York, Paris, Stockholm
Entry 169 Records of Washington/London Special Funds Branch
Entry 171 Washington X-2 Personalitites Files
Entry 180 Director OSS Official Files (A 3304)
Entry, 190 Field Station Files: Athens, Bari, Bern, Cairo, Casablanca, Caserta, Lisbon. London, Madrid, Paris and Rome
Entry, 193 Boston Series (MF 1740)
RG 243 Records of the U.S. Strategic Bombing Survey
RG 260 Records of U.S. Occupation Headquarters, World War II
RG 263 Central Intelligence Agency
Office of Strategic Services (OSS) Oral History Project Transcripts

Studies in Intelligence
Thomas Troy Papers
RG 331 Allied Op and Occ. H.Qs, Headquarters 6th Army
RG 457 Records of the National Security Agency (SRH-006)

MODERN DIPLOMATIC BRANCH

RG 51 Records of the Office of Management and Budget [BOB]
RG 59 Records of the Department of State
General Diplomatic Files
Final Reports of the Research and Analysis Branch (M 1221)

MOTION PICTURE AND SOUND RECORDINGS BRANCH

RG 64 Conference Proceedings "The Secrets War. The Office of Strategic Services in World
     War II"
RG 226 OSS Motion Pictures and Sound Recordings

NATIONAL RECORD CENTER, SUITLAND, MARYLAND

RG 84 Records of the Foreign Service Posts of the Department of State
RG 153 Records of the Office of the Judge Advocate General (Army)
RG 332 ETOUSA
General Records, European Theater of Operations (ETO)
ETO, Historical Records
RG 331 Allied Operational and Occupation Headquarters, WWII
Intelligence Division
Military Intelligence Division
Intelligence Section
RG 319 Records of the Army Staff
Military Intelligence G-2
"ID"-Files
Army Intelligence Decimal Files
RG 165 Records of the War Department.
General and Special Staffs Military Intelligence Division

LIBRARY OF CONGRESS, WASHINGTON, D.C

Pamphlet Collection
Manuscript Division
Elmer Davis Papers
Wallace Deuel Papers
Edgar Ansel Mowrer Papers
John Toland Papers
Henry Stimson Papers
Hoyt S. Vandenberg Papers
Film Collection
Cloak and Dagger. Released by Warner Bros. Pictures, September, 1946, VBE 7077–7078
O.S.S. Released by Paramount Pictures, May, 1946, FCA 3160–3163

13 Rue Madeleine. Released by Twentieth Century-Fox Corp., December, 1946, FCA 3540–3542

FEDERAL BUREAU OF INVESTIGATION, WASHINGTON, D.C.

William J. Donovan Files
Arthur Goldberg File
Putzi Hanfstaengl File

FRANKLIN D. ROOSEVELT LIBRARY, HYDE PARK, NEW YORK

Adolf A. Berle Papers
John Franklin Carter (Oral History Transcript)
Oscar S. Cox Papers
Henry Field Papers
Stanley High Papers
Papers of Harry L. Hopkins
Joint Intelligence Committee Weekly Summaries (Map Room Files)
Henry M. Morgenthau, Jr. Papers
Henry M. Morgenthau, Jr. Diary
Oral History Transcripts
Franklin D. Roosevelt Papers, President's Secretary's File
Franklin D. Roosevelt Papers, Official File
Franklin D. Roosevelt Papers, Map Room Files
Whitney Hart Shepardson Papers
Sherwood Collection (Hopkins Papers)
Harold D. Smith Papers
John Toland Papers
John Wiley Papers
John Winant Papers

HARRY S TRUMAN LIBRARY, INDEPENDENCE, MISSOURI

Papers of Eben A. Ayers
Papers of Charles Kindleberger
Papers of Philleo Nash
Naval Aide Files
Papers of Harry S Truman: President's Secretary's Files
Rose Conway File

EISENHOWER LIBRARY, ABILENE, KANSAS

Papers of Dwight D. Eisenhower
Papers of C.D. Jackson
John F. Kennedy Library, Waltham, Massachussetts
Oral History Project: John Franklin Carter
James P. Warburg Papers

U.S. MILITARY HISTORY INSTITUTE, CARLISLE BARRACKS, PENNSYLVANIA

Papers of William J. Donovan

Interview Collection of Forrest C. Pogue (for The Supreme Command, 1946–1952)
Seeley G. Mudd Library, Princeton, New Jersey
Allen Welsh Dulles Papers
John Foster Dulles Oral History Project
George Kennan Papers

GEORGE C. MARSHALL RESEARCH LIBRARY, LEXINGTON, VIRGINIA
George C. Marshall Papers
Francis P. Miller Papers
Special Collection of World War II Documents

JOSEPH MARK LAUINGER LIBRARY, GEORGETOWN UNIVERSITY, WASHINGTON, D.C.
Anthony Cave Brown Papers
Russell J. Bowen Collection (Intelligence Literature)

HARVARD UNIVERSITY LIBRARY, CAMBRIDGE, MASSACHUSSETTS
Heinrich Brüning Papers
William Langer Papers

COLUMBIA UNIVERSITY LIBRARY, NEW YORK, NEW YORK
Oral History Projects: DeWitt C. Poole
William J. Donovan Papers: Collection on Intelligence in the Revolutionary Period

AMERICAN HERITAGE CENTER, UNIVERSITY OF WYOMING, LARAMIE, WYOMING
John Franklin Carter Collection

STATE HISTORICAL SOCIETY OF WISCONSIN, MADISON
DeWitt Clinton Poole Papers

STATE HISTORICAL SOCIETY OF COLORADO, DENVER
James Grafton Rogers Collection

HOOVER INSTITUTION ARCHIVES, STANFORD, CALIFORNIA
James B. Donovan Papers
Bonner F. Fellers Papers
J. Russell Forgan Papers
Gero von Schulze-Gaevernitz Papers
Richard Harris Smith Papers
M. Preston Goodfellow Papers
Rudolf Katz Collection
Daniel Lerner Papers
Price Family Papers
Leland Round Papers
Combat Propaganda in Africa, Italy, United Kingdom and France, 1943–1944, Psychological
    Warfare Report by Lt. Colonel Heber Blankenhorn

2. Archives in Great Britain, the Federal Republic of Germany, and Switzerland

PUBLIC RECORD OFFICE. LONDON (KEW)

AIR 37 Records of the Air Ministry, RAF (AEAF)
AIR 40 Records of the Air Ministry (Directorate of Intelligence)
CAB 79 Minutes of the Chiefs of Staff
FO 371 Records of the Foreign Office (Political Files)
FO 898 Political Warfare Executive
WO 165, Records of the War Office, War Diaries, WOD, 1942–1945
WO 204 Records of the Allied Force [Mediterranean] Headquarters

LAMBETH PALACE LIBRARY. LONDON

Papers of Bishop Bells Papers MS 47
Modern Records Centre, Warwick University, Warwick
Papers of the International Transport Workers Federation

BUNDESARCHIV KOBLENZ

NS, 19: Persönlicher Stab Reichsführer SS
Auswärtiges Amt, Politisches Archiv, Bonn
Büro Staatssekretär, USA
Abteilung Inland II geh.

ARCHIV DES ÖKUMENISCHEN RATES DER KIRCHEN, GENF

Papers of the World Council of Churches

3. Privately Owned Literary Estates and Documents

Mother Mary Alice Gallin Papers, Washington, D.C.
Barbara Podorski-Lauwers Papers, Washington, D.C.
Eddie Lindner Papers, Westport, CT
James Srodes Papers, Washington, D.C.

4. Interviews and Conversations with Contemporaries

The place name after the name refers to the site of the interview; the asterix designates an interview by telephone.

Paula Ackermann, Washington, D.C.*; Robert Alder, Bern, Schweiz; Charlotte
Bowman, Bennington, VT; Sir Robin Brook, Washington, D.C.; John T. Brown, George-
town, D.C.; Frederick Burkhardt, Bennington, VT; Wolf Eckardt*; A. Gil Flues, Chevy
Chase, MD; Franklin Ford, Lexington, Mass.; Gregory D. Foster, Washington, D.C.*;
Robert Houlihan, Lexington, KY; Geoffrey M.T. Jones, New York, N.Y.; Charles
Kindleberger, Lexington, Mass.; Edward Linder, Westport, CT*; Elizabeth McIntosh,
Washington, D.C.; Leesburg, Va.; Bar-bara Lauwers Podoski, Washington, D.C.; Arnold
H. Price, Washington, D.C.; Sterling, Va.; Harry L. Rositzke, Warrenton, VA; Arthur
Schlesinger, jr., New York, NY; John W. Shepardson, Denver, CO*; Washington, D.C.;
Peter Sichel, New York, N.Y.; John K. Singlaub, Arlington, VA; Erika (Glaser) Wallach,

Warrenton, Va.; John Waller, Arlington, VA*; Washington, D.C.; Eleanor Weis (Grecay), Long Island, NY; John Weitz, New York, N.Y.

PUBLISHED SOURCES

(Includes memoirs, correspondence, and contemporary writings)

Alsop, Stewart/Thomas Braden. *Sub Rosa. The OSS and American Espionage*. New York, 1946.

Baker, Richard Brown. *The Year of the Buzz Bomb. A Journal of London, 1944*. New York, 1952.

Beer, Siegfried, ed. Exil und Emigration als Information. Zur Tätigkeit der Foreign Nationalities Branch (FNB) innerhalb des amerikanischen Kriegsgemeindienstes COI bzw. OSS, 1941–1945. In: *Dokumentationsarchiv des österreichischen Widerstands, Jahrbuch, 1989*. Vienna, 1989, pp. 132–144.

Berle, Beatrice Bishop/Travis Beal Jacobs, eds. *Navigating the Rapids, 1918–1971. From the Papers of Adolf A Berle*. Introduction by Max Ascoli. New York, 1973.

Blumenson, Martin, ed. *The Patton Papers, Vol. 2, 1940–1945*. Boston, 1974.

Borsdorf, Ulrich/Lutz. Niethammer, Eds., *Zwischen Befreiung und Besatzung. Analysen des US-Geheimdienstes über Positionen und Strukturen deutscher Politik, 1945*, Wuppertal, 1976.

Breuer, William B. *The Secret War with Germany*. Novato, CA., 1988.

Brown, Anthony Cave, ed. *The Secret War Report of the OSS*. Edited with an introduction by A.C.B. New York, 1976.

Buhite, Russell D./David W. Lewy, eds. *FDR's Fireside Chats*. Norman, OK/London, 1992.

Bullitt, Orville H., ed. *For the President. Personal and Secret. Correspondence Between Franklin D. Roosevelt and William C. Bullitt*. Boston, 1972.

Carroll, Wallace. *Persuade or Perish*. Boston, 1948.

Chandler, Alfred D., Jr., et al., eds. *The Papers of Dwight David Eisenhower, Vol. III. The War Years*. Baltimore, 1970.

Churchill, Winston. *Memoirs*. Boston, 1948.

Churchill, Winston. The Second World War, Vol 2. *Their Finest Hour*. Boston, 1949.

Churchill, Winston. The Second World War, Vol 4. *The Hinge of Fate*. Boston, 1950.

Churchill, Winston. *Into Battle: Speeches by Winston S. Churchill*. Compiled by Randolph S. Churchill. London, 1947.

Corvo, Max. *The O.S.S. in Italy, 1942–1945: A Personal Memoir*. New York, 1990.

Dear, Ian. *Sabotage and Subversion: The SOE nd OSS at War*. London, 1999.

De Jong, Louis. *The German Fifth Column in the Second World War*. Chicago, 1956.

Delmer, Sefton. *Black Boomerang*. London, 1962.

Doerries, Reinhard R., ed. *Die Geschichte von Nachrichtendiensten in den deutsch-amerikanischen Beziehungen in Frieden und Krieg—Intentionen und Wirklichkeiten*. Heidelberg, 2001, 161–188.

Dokumente zur Deutschlandpolitik. First Series, Vol. 3.: Documents on British Foreign Policy Toward Germany, Rainer A. Blasius, ed., Frankfurt, 1989.

Donovan, Robert J. *Conflict and Crisis: The Presidency of Harry S. Truman. 1945–1948*. Columbia, MO, 1996.

Donovan, William J./Edgar Mowrer. *Fifth Column Lessons for America*. Washington D.C., 1940.

Eisenhower, Dwight D. *Crusade in Europe*. New York, 1948.

Foreign Relations of the United States, 1933–1945. Washington, D.C., 1959–1969.

Foreign Relations of the United States, 1943/I (General). Washington, D.C., 1963.

Foreign Relations of the United States, 1944/I (General). Washington, D.C., 1966.

Foreign Relations of the United States, The Conferences at Washington and Quebec (1943). Washington, 1961.

Foreign Relations of the United States. The Conferences at Cairo and Tehran (1943). Washington, D.C., 1955.

Foreign Relations of the United States. The Conferences at Washington (1942) and Casablanca (1943), Washington, 1968.

Foreign Relations of the United States. The Conference of Quebec, 1944. Washington, D.C., 1972.

Franklin, Jay (= John Franklin Carter). *The Catoctin Conversation*. New York, 1947.

Gisevius, Hans Bernd. *Bis zum bitteren Ende*. 2 vols. Zurich, 1946.

Goebbels, Joseph. *Tagebücher, 1924–1945*. Georg Reuth von Ralf, ed. 5 vols, Munich/Zurich, 1992.

Hagen, Paul. *Will Germany Crack?* New York, 1942.

Halder, Franz. *Generaloberst Halder. Kriegstagebuch*. Hans-Adolf von Jacobsen, ed. 3 vols, Stuttgart, 1963.

Hanfstaengl, Ernst. *Zwischen Weißem und Braunem Haus. Memoiren eines politischen Außenseiters* Munich: R.Piper, 1970.

Hanfstaengl, Ernst. *Unheard Witness*. Philadelphia/New York, 1957.

Harris, Sir Arthur. *Bomber Offensive*. London, 1947.

Hassell, Ulrich von. *Aufzeichnungen vom Andern Deutschland. Die Hassell-Tagebücher. 1938–1944*. Berlin, 1988.

Heideking, Jürgen/Christof Mauch, Eds., "Das Herman-Dossier. Helmuth James Graf von Moltke, die deutsche Emigration in Istanbul und de amerikanische Geheimdienst Office of Strategic Services." in: VZG 40 (1992), 567–623.

Heideking, Jürgen/Christof Mauch, Eds., *USA und deutscher Widerstand. Analysen und Operationen des amerikanischen Geheimdienstes im Zweiten Weltkrieg*. Tübingen/Basel, 1993.

Heideking, Jürgen/Christof Mauch, eds. *American Intelligence and the German Resistance to Hitler*. Boulder, CO, 1996..

Hoegner, Wilhelm. *Der schwierige Außenseiter. Erinnerungen eines Abgeordneten, Emigranten und Ministerpräsidenten*. Munich, 1959.

Ickes, Harold L. *The Secret Diary of H.L. Ickes*. 2 vols. New York, 1954.

Kimball, Warren F. ed., *Churchill & Roosevelt: The Complete Correspondence*. Princeton, NJ: Princton University Press, 1984.

Lankford, Nelson Douglas, ed. *OSS Against the Reich. The World War II Diaries of Colonel David K.E. Bruce*. Kent, Ohio, 1991.

Leary, William M., ed. *The Central Intelligence Agency. History and Documents*, n.p. [Mobile, Alabama], 1984.

Leverkuehn, Paul, *Der geheime Nachrichtendienst der deutschen Wehrmacht im Kriege*. Frankfurt, 1957 (English German Military Intelligence. London, 1954).

Link, Werner, ed. *Mit dem Gesicht nach Deutschland. Eine Dokumentation über die sozialdemokratische Emigration, bearbeitete von Erich Matthias*. Düsseldorf, 1968.

Loewenheim, Francis L., et al., eds. *Roosevelt and Churchill:Their Secret Wartime Correspondence*. New York: Da Capo Press, 1990 (originally published 1975).

Lovell, Stanley, Of Spies and Strategems, Englewood Cliffs, NJ, 1963.

Mendelsohn, John, ed. *Covert Warfare. Intelligence, Counterintelligence and Military Deception During the World War II Era.* 18 Vols. New York/London, 1989.

Mowrer, Edgar, A. *Triumph and Turmoil: A Personal History of Our Times.* New York, 1968.

Nelles, Dieter/Hermann Knüfken. "Über den Widerstand der Internationalen Transportarbeiter Föderation gegen den Nationalsozialismus und Vorschläge zum Wiederaufbau der Gewerkschaften in Deutschand—zwei Dokumente, 1944/45, eingeleitet von D.N." in:, 1999. *Zeitschrift für Sozialgeschichte des 20. und 21. Jahrhunderts,* 7 (1993), 64–87.

Nicholas, H.G., ed. *Washington Despatches, 1941–1945. Weekly Political Reports from the British Embassy.* London, 1981.

Oechsner, Frederick et al. *This Is the Enemy.* Boston, 1942.

OSS London Special Operations Branch and Secret Intelligence Branch War Diaries. 13 Vols. [Washington, D.C.], 1945; 8 MF reels, Frederick, MD, 1985 (University Publications of America. Microfilms).

Petersen, Neal H., ed. *From Hitler's Doorstep. The Wartime Intelligence Reports of Allen Dulles, 1942–1945.* University Park, 1996.

Picker, Henry, *Hitlers Tischgespräche im Führerhauptquartier. Vollständig überarbeitete und erweiterte Neuausgabe mit bisher unbekannten Selbstzeugnissen Adolf Hitlers, Abbildungen, Augenzeugenberichten und Erläuterungen des Autors: Hitler, wie er wirklich war.* Stuttgart, 1976.

Rathkolb, Oliver, ed. *Gesellschaft und Politik am Beginn der Zweiten Republik. Vertrauliche Berichte der US-Militäradministration aus Österreich, 1945, in englischer Originalfassung.* Vienna, 1985.

Roosevelt, Elliott, ed. *F.D.R.: His Personal Letters, 1928–1945.* New York, 1950.

Schlabrendorff, Fabian von. *Begegnungen in fünf Jahrzehnten.* Tübingen, 1979.

Sender, Toni. *Autobiographie einer deutschen Rebellin.* Frankfurt, 1981.

Sherwood, Robert. "The Power of Truth: Radio a Vital Factor in War." In: *Vital Speeches* 9 (1942), 61–62.

Singlaub, John K., with Malcolm McConnell. *Hazardous Duty. An American Soldier in the Twentieth Century.* New York, 1991.

Smith, Bradley F. OSS Jedburgh Teams I. New York, 1989.

Smith, Bradley F. OSS Jedburgh Teams II. New York, 1989.

Speer, Albrecht. *Erinnerungen.* Berlin, 1969.

Stalin spricht. Die Kriegsreden vom 3. Juli, 1941 bis zum 9. Mai, 1945, Stockholm, 1945.

Stalin, Josef. *On the Great Patriotic War for the Soviet Union. Speeches, Orders of the Day, and Answers to Foreign Press Correspondents.* London, 1944.

Stimson, Henry L./McGeorge Bundy. *On Active Service in Peace and War.* New York, 1948.

Taylor, Edmond. *Awakening from History.* Boston, 1969 (London, 1971).

Taylor, Edmond L. *Smash Hitler's International.* New York, 1941.

Taylor, Edmond L. *The Strategy of Terror.* Boston, 1940.

Tedder, Arthur William. *With Prejudice.* London, 1966.

Tully, Grace. *F.D.R. My Boss.* New York, 1949.

U.S. Office of Strategic Services. *Psychological Assessment Staff. Assessment of Men.* New York, 1948.

Welles, Sumner. *Time for Decision.* New York, 1944.

Wiskemann, Elizabeth. *The Europe I Saw.* London, 1968.

World War II German Military Studies. A collection of 213 special reports on the Second World War prepared by former Officers of the Wehrmacht for the United States Army, edited by Donald S. Detwiler, et al. New York, 1979.

Zuckerman, Solly. *From Apes to Warlords: The Autobiography (1904–1946) of Solly Zuckerman.* . New York, 1978.

NEWSPAPERS AND PERIODICALS

Chicago Daily News; Chicago Daily Tribune; The Daily Mirror; The Daily. Worker; The Evening Star; Deutscher Staatsanzeiger; Encounter; Nationalzeitung (Basel); *Newsweek; New York Herald-Tribune; New York Times; Philadelphia. Inquirer; Time Magazine; Veterans of OSS Newsletter* (New York); *Washington Post; Washington Times Herald.*

LITERATURE

Ameringer, Charles D. *U.S. Foreign Intelligence. The Secret Side of American History.* Lexington, MA/Toronto, 1990.

Andrew, Christopher. *For the President's Eyes Only. Secret Intelligence and the American Presidency from Washington to Bush.* New York, 1995.

Andrew, Christopher. *Her Majesty's Secret Service.* New York, 1987.

Baerwald, Friedrich. "Zur politischen Tätigkeit deutscher Emigranten im Council for a Democratic Germany." In: VZG 28 (1980), 372–383.

Bank, Aaron. *From OSS to Green Berets. The Birth of Special Forces.* Novato, 1986.

Becker, Howard. "The Nature and Consequences of Black Propaganda." In: *American Sociological Review* 14 (1949), 221–235.

Beer, Siegfried, et al. "Die Widerstandsgruppe Maier-Messner und der amerikanische Kriegsgeheimdienst OSS in Bern, Istanbul und Algier, 1943/44." In: "Dokumentationsarchiv des österreichischen Widerstandes" (1993), 75–100.

Beer, Siegfried. Von Alfred Redl zum "Dritten Mann." "Österreich und Österreicher Innen im internationalen Geheimdienstgeschehen, 1918–1947." In: *Geschichte und Gegenwart* 16 (1997), 3–25.

Bennett, Ralph. *Ultra and Mediterranean Strategy.* New York, 1989.

Besier, Gerhard, ed. "Ökumenische Mission in Nachkriegsdeutschland. Die Berichte von Stewart W. Herman über die Verhältnisse in der evangelischen Kirche, 1945/46." In: *Kirchliche Zeitgeschichte* 1 (1988), 151–187.

Biddiscombe, Perry. *Werewolf!: The History of the National Socialist Guerrilla Movement, 1944–1946.* Toronto, 1988.

Bidwell, Bruce W. *History of the Military Intelligence Division, Department of the Army General Staff 1775–1941.* Frederick, MD, 1986.

Biographisches Handbuch der deutschsprachigen Emigration nach, 1933, hrsg. vom Institut für Zeitgeschichte München und von der Research Foundation for Jewish Immigration, Munich, 1980, 1983.

Black, Peter R. *Ernst Kaltenbrunner. Ideological Soldier of the Third Reich.* Princeton, NJ, 1984.

Blum, John M. *V Was for Victory: Politics and American Culture During World War II.* New York, 1976.

Boyens, Armin. *Kirchenkampf und Ökumene, 1939–1945. Darstellung und Dokumentation* vol. 2, Munich, 1973.

Braunschweig, Pierre. *Geheimer Draht nach Berlin. Die Nachrichtenlinie Masson-Schellenberg und der schweizerische Nachrichtendienst im Zweiten Weltkrieg.* Zürich, 1989.

Breitman, Richard. *Research in OSS Records. One Historian's Concerns.* In: G. Chalou, ed., *Secrets War* [q.v.], 103–108.

Breitman, Richard. *Official Secrets. What the Nazis Planned, What the British and Americans Knew.* New York, 1998.

Bretschneider, Heike. *Der Widerstand gegen den Nationalsozialismus in München, 1933–1945.* Munich: 1968.

Briegel, Manfred/Wolfgang Frühwald, eds. *Die Erfahrung der Fremde. Kolloquium des Schwerpunktprogramms 'Exilforschung' der DFG.* Weinheim, 1988.

Briggs, Asa. *The War of Words.* London, 1970.

Broszat, Martin et al., eds. *Bayern in der NS-Zeit.* Munich, 1977.

Brown, Anthony Cave. *"C": The Secret Life of Sir Stewart Menzies. Spymaster to Winton Churchill.* New York, 1987.

Brown, Anthony Cave. *The Last Hero: Wild Bill Donovan.* New York, 1984.

Brückner, Joachim. *Kriegsende in Bayern, 1945. Der Wehrkreis VII und die Kämpfe zwischen Donau und Alpen.* Freiburg, 1987.

Brysant, Arthur. *Triumph in the West, 1943–46. Based on the Diaries and Autobiographical Notes of Field Marshal The Viscount Alanbrook, K.G., O.M.* London, 1959.

Bungert, Heike. " 'Den deutschen Widerstandswillen brechen.' Anglo-amerikanische Pläne zur Gründung eines deutschen Komitees als Antwort auf das NKFD." In: *Überschär, Das Nationalkomitee "Freies Deutschland" und der Bund Deutscher Offiziere,* pp 52–63.

Bungert, Heike. *Das Nationalkomitee und der Westen. Die Reaktion der West alliierten auf das NKFD und die Freien Deutschen Bewegungen, 1943–1948.* Stuttgart, 1997.

Campbell, A. E. "Franklin Roosevelt and Unconditional Surrender." In: Richard Langhorne, ed., *Diplomacy and Intelligence During the Second World War: Essays in Honour of F. H. Hinsley.* Cambridge, 1985, 219–241.

Carroll, Wallace. *Persuade or Perish.* Boston, 1948.

Casey, William J. *The Secret War Against Hitler.* Washington, D.C., 1988.

Chalou, George, ed. *The Secrets War. The Office of Stratetic Services in World War II.* Washington, D.C., 1992.

Cline, Marjorie W., et al., eds. *Scholar's Guide to Intelligence in Literature.* Bibliography of the Russell J. Bowen Collection in the Joseph Mark Lauinger Memorial Library, Georgetown University, Frederick, MD, 1983.

Constantinides, George C. *Intelligence and Espionage. An Analytical Bibliography.* Boulder, CO, 1983.

Corson, William R. *The Armies of Ignorance: The Rise of the American Intelligence Empire.* New York, 1977.

Craven, Wesley Frank/James Lea Cate, eds. *The Army Air Forces in World War II, Vol.2: Europe — Torch to Pointblank. August, 1942 to December, 1943.* Chicago, 1949.

Craven, Wesley Frank/James Lea Cate, eds. *The Army Air Forces in World War II, Vol.3: Argument to VE-Day. January, 1944–May, 1945.* Chicago, 1951.

Cull, Nicholas John. *Selling War: The British Propaganda Campaign Against American "Neutrality" in World War II.* New York, 1995.

Dallek, Robert. *Franklin D. Roosevelt and American Foreign Policy, 1932–1945*. New York, 1979.

Daugherty, William E. with Morris Janowitz, eds. *A Psychological Warfare Casebook* Baltimore, MD, 1958.

Deavours, Cipher A. et al., eds. *Cryptology Yesterday, Today and Tomorrow*. Norwood, 1987.

Deist, Wilhelm. "Die Deutsche Aufrüstung in amerikanischer Sicht. Berichte des US-Militärattachés in Berlin aus den Jahren, 1933–1939." In: Alexander von Fischer, et al., eds. *Rußland-Deutschland-Amerika. Festschrift für Fritz T.Epstein zum 80.Geburtstag*. Wiesbaden, 1978, 279–295.

Delmer, Sefton. *Black Boomerang*. London, 1962.

Dessants, Betty Abrahamsen. "Ambivalent Allies. OSS' USSR Division, the State Department, and the Bureaucracy of Intelligence Analysis, 1941–1945." In: *Intelligence and National Security* 11 (1996), 722–753.

Dippel, John V.H. *Two Against Hitler. Stealing the Nazis' Best-Kept Secrets*. New York, 1992.

Doering-Manteuffel, Anselm/Joachim Mehlhausen, eds. *Christliches Ethos und der Widerstand gegen den Nationalsozialismus in Europa*. Stuttgart/Berlin/Köln, 1995.

Doerries, Reinhard R. *Washington-Berlin, 1908/1917*. Düsseldorf, 1975 (English-language version: *Imperial Challenge*. Chapel Hill, 1989).

Donovan, William J. "Secret Movements, Espionage and Treachery." In: Thorsten V. Kalijarvi et al., eds., *Modern World Politics*, 3rd edition. New York, 1953, 308–312.

Dornberger, Walter. *V-2*. New York, 1954.

Dulles, Allen W. *The Secret Surrender*. New York, 1966.

Dulles, Allen/Gero von Schulze-Gaevernitz. *Unternehmen "Sunrise". Die geheime Geschichte des Kriegsendes in Italien*. Düsseldorf, 1967.

Dunlop, Richard. *Donovan. America's Master Spy*. New York, 1982.

Ehrman, John. *Grand Strategy*. London, 1956.

Erd, Rainer, ed. *Reform und Resignation. Gespräche über Franz L. Neumann*. Frankfurt, 1985.

Fichter, Michael. *Besatzungsmacht und Gewerkschaften. Zur Entwicklung und Anwendung der US-Gewerkschaftspolitik in Deutschland, 1944–1958*. Opladen, 1982.

Fischer, Alexander. *Sowjetische Deutschlandpolitik im Zweiten Weltkrieg, 1941–1945*. Stuttgart, 1975.

Foitzik, Jan. "Revolution und Demokratie. zu den Sofort- und Übergangsplanungen des sozialdemokratischen Exils für Deutschland, 1943–1945." In: IWK 3 (1988), 308–341.

Förster, Jürgen. *Stalingrad. Risse im Bündnis, 1942/43*. Freiburg, 1975.

Foot, M. R. D. *Resistance. An Analysis of European Resistance to Nazism, 1940–1945*. New York, 1977.

Foot, M. R. D. *SOE in France*. London, 1966; Frederick, MD, 1984.

Ford, Corey. *Donovan of OSS*. Boston, 1970.

Ford, Franklin L. "The Twentieth, of July in the History of the German Resistance." In: AHR 51 (1945/46), 609–626.

Fussell, Paul. *Wartime: Understanding and Behavior in the Second World War*. New York/Oxford, 1989.

Gallin, Mother Mary Alice. *Ethical and Religious Factors in the German Resistance to Hitler*. Washington, D.C., 1955.

Garlinski, Jozef. *Hitler's Last Weapons. The Underground War Against the V1 and V2*. London, 1978.

Golücke, Friedrich. *Schweinfurt und der strategische Luftkrieg, 1943. Der Angriff der U.S. Air Force vom 14. Oktober, 1943 gegen die Schweinfurter Kugellagerindustrie.* Paderborn, 1988.

Grose, Peter. *Gentleman Spy. The Life of Allen Dulles.* Boston/New York, 1994.

Gurfein, M.I./Morris Janowitz. "Trends in Wehrmacht-Morale." In: *Public Opinion Quarterly* 10 (1946) 78–84.

Hass, Gerhard. *Von München bis Pearl Harbor. Zur Geschichte der deutsch-amerikanischen Beziehungen, 1938–1941.* East Berlin, 1965, 223–229.

Heideking, Jürgen. *Geschichte der USA.* Tübingen/Basel, 1996.

Heideking, Jürgen. "Amerikanische Geheimdienste und Widerstandsbewegungen im Zweiten Weltkrieg." In: Gerhard Schulz, Partisanen und Volkskrieg (qv.), 147–177.

Heideking, Jürgen. "Gero von Schulze-Gaevernitz." In: Michael Bosch/Wolfgang Niess, eds., *Der Widerstand im deutschen Südwesten, 1933–1945.* Stuttgart, 1984, 281–290.

Heideking, Jürgen. "Die 'Schweizer Straßen' des europäischen Widerstandes." In: Gerhard Schulz, ed. *Geheimdienste und Widerstandsbewegungen im Zweiten Weltkrieg.* Göttingen, 1982, 143–187.

Heideking, Jürgen/Christof Mauch, eds. *Geheimdienstkrieg gegen Deutschland. Subversion, Propaganda und Nachkriegsplanungen des Office of Strategic Services im Zweiten Weltkrieg.* Göttingen, 1993.

Henke, Klaus-Dietmar. *Die amerikanische Besetzung Deutschlands.* Munich, 1995.

Herzstein, Robert Edwin. *Henry R. Luce: A Political Portrait of the Man Who Created the American Century.* New York, 1994.

Hindley, Meredith. "The Strategy of Rescue and Relief. The Use of OSS Intelligence by the War Refugee Board in Sweden, 1944–1945." In *Intelligence an National Security* 12 (1967), 145–165.

Hinsley, Francis Harry, et al. *British Intelligence in the Second World War.* 5 vols. New York/London, 1979–1990.

Hirschfeld, Gerhard, ed. *Exil in Großbritannien. Zur Emigration aus dem. nationalsozialistischen Deutschland.* Stuttgart, 1983.

Höhne, Heinz. *Canaris: Patriot im Zwielicht.* Munich, 1976.

Hoffmann, Peter/Claus Schenk. *Graf von Stauffenberg und seine Brüder.* 2nd ed. Stuttgart, 1992.

Hoffmann, Peter. *The History of the German Resistance, 1933–1945.* Cambridge, MA, 1979.

Howard, Michael. *Strategic Deception* (British Intelligence in the Second World War, Vol. 5). New York, 1990.

Hymoff, Edward. *The OSS in World War II,* revised and updated edition. New York, 1986.

Jeffreys-Jones, Rhodri. *American Espionage. From Secret Service to CIA.* New York, 1977.

Jeffreys-Jones, Rhodri. *The CIA and American Democracy,* New Haven/London, 1988.

Kahn, David. *The Codebreakers.* New York, 1967.

Kahn, David. *Hitler's Spies. German Military Intelligence in World War II.* New York, 1978.

Katz, Barry M. *Foreign Intelligence: Research and Analysis in the Office of Strategic Services, 1942–1945.* Cambridge MA/London, 1989.

Kettenacker, Lothar, ed. *Das 'Andere Deutschland' im Zweiten Weltkrieg. Emigration und Widerstand in internatioaler Perspektive.* Stuttgart, 1997.

Kettenacker, Lothar. *Krieg als Friedenssicherung: Die Deutschlandplanung der britischen Regierung während des Zweiten Weltkrieges.* Göttingen/Zürich, 1989.

Kimche, Jon. *Spying for Peace. General Guisan and Swiss Neutrality.* London, 1962.

Klemperer, Klemens von. *German Resistance against Hitler. The Search for Allies Abroad, 1938–1945*. Oxford, 1992.

Klotz, Johannes. *Das "kommende" Deutschland. Vorstellungen und Konzeptionen des sozialdemokratischen Parteivorstandes im Exil, 1933–1945 zu Staat und Wirtschaft*. Köln, 1983.

Knightley, Phillip. *The Second Oldest Profession. The Spy as Bureaucrat, Patriot, Fantasist and Whore*. London, 1986. (German: *Die Geschichte der Spionage. im 20. Jahrhundert. Aufbau und Organisation, Erfolge und Niederlagen der großen Geheimdienste*. Berlin, 1990).

Krammer, Arnold. *Deutsche Kriegsgefangene in Amerika, 1942–1946*. Tübingen, 1995.

Krammer, Arnold. "Deutsche Zivilinternierte in den USA, 1941–1945." In: VZG 44 (1996), 581–603.

Krammer, Arnold. *Deutsche Zivilinternierte in den USA, 1941–1945*. Tübingen, 1998.

Kurz, H.R. *Nachrichtenzentrum Schweiz. Die Rolle der Schweizer Armee in Zwei Weltkriegen*. Frauenfeld, 1974.

Langer, Walter C. *The Mind of Adolf Hitler. The Secret Wartime Report*. New York, 1972.

Langhorne, Richard, ed. *Diplomacy and Intelligence During the Second World War. Essays in Honour of F.H. Hinsley*. Cambridge, 1985.

Laqueur, Walter/Richard Breitman. *Breaking the Silence*. New York, 1986.

Laurie, Clayton D. "Black Games, Subversion, and Dirty Tricks. The OSS Morale Operations Branch in Europe, 1943–1945." In: Prologe 25 (1993), 259–271.

Laurie, Clayton. *The Propaganda Warriors. America's Crusade Against Nazi Germany*. Lawrence, KS, 1996.

Lees, Lorraine M. National Security and Ethnicity. Contrasting Views During World War II." In: Diplomatic History 11 (1987), 113–128.

Link, Werner. *Die Geschichte des Internationalen Jugendbundes (IJB) und des Internationalen Sozialistischen Kampfbundes (ISK). Ein Beitrag zur Geschichte der Arbeiterbewegung in der Weimarer Republik und im Dritten Reich*. Meisenheim, 1964.

Lovell, Stanley P. *Of Spies and Strategems*. Englewood Cliffs, NJ, 1963.

Löwenthal, Richard. "Konflikte, Bündnisse und Resultate der deutschen politischen Emigration." In: VZG 39 (1991), 626–636.

MacPherson, Brian Nelson. "Kings and Desperate Men. The United States Office of Strategic Services in London and the Anglo-American Relationship, 1941–1946." Ph. D. University of Toronto, 1995.

Marquardt-Bigman, Petra. *Amerikanische Geheimdienstanalysen über Deutschland, 1942–1949*. Munich, 1995.

Masterman, J.C. *The Ultra Secret*. London, 1974.

Mauch, Christof. "Central Intelligence Agency." In: Rüdiger B. Wersich, ed., *USA-Lexikon* Berlin, 1996, 147–149.

Mauch, Christof. "Dream of a Miracle War. The OSS and Germany, 1942–1945." In: *Prologue* 27 (1995), 134–143.

Mauch, Christof. "Großbritannien, die Vereinigten Staaten und der Widerstand. gegen den Nationalsozialismus. Perzeptionen und politische Dilemmata." In: Anselm Doering-Manteuffel/Joachim Mehlhausen, eds, *Christliches Ethos und der Widerstand gegen den Nationalsozialismus in Europa*. Stuttgart/Berlin/ Köln, 1995, 102–118.

Mauch, Christof. "Intelligence." In: Rüdiger B. Wersich, ed., *USA-Lexikon*. Berlin, 1996, 394–396.

Mauch, Christof. "Subversion und Propaganda. Der Widerstand gegen den Nationalsozialismus im Kalkül des amerikanischen Geheimdienstes OSS." In: *Heideking/Mauch, Geheimdienstkrieg gegen Deutschland*, 51–89.

Mauch, Christof. "Das Dritte Reich im Visier der amerikanischen Geheimdienste. Projekte, Operationen, Politik," Reinhard R. Doerries, ed. *Die Geschichte von Nachrichtendiensten in den deutsch-amerikanischen Beziehungen in Frieden und Krieg—Intentionen und Wirklichkeiten.* Heidelberg, 2001, 161–188.

May, Ernest R., ed. *Knowing One's Enemies. Inteligence Assessment before the Two World Wars.* Princeton, NJ, 1984.

May, Ernest R. *"Lessons" of the Past. The Use and Misuse of History in American Foreign Policy.* New York, 1973.

McDonald, Lawrence. "The Office of Strategic Services. America's First National Intelligence Agency." In: *Prologue* 23 (1991), 7–24.

Messenger, Charles. *"Bomber" Harris and the Strategic Bombing Offensive, 1939–1945.* London, 1984.

Minott, Rodney G., *The Fortress that never was. The Myth of Hitler's Bavarian Stronghold.* New York,/Chicago/San Francisco, 1964.

Moltmann, Günter. *Amerikas Deutschlandpolitik im Zweiten Weltkrieg.* Heidelberg, 1958.

Moon, Tom. *This Grim and Savage Game: OSS and the Beginning of U.S. Covert Operations in World War II.* New York, 2000.

Mosley, Leonard, Dulles. *A Biography of Eleanor, Allen and John Foster Dulles and Their Family Network.* New York, 1978.

Mruck, Armin. *The F. D. Roosevelt Administration and the German Anti-Hitler Resistance.* Baltimore, 1987 (= Towsend State University Lectures).

Müller, Klaus-Jürgen/David Dilks, eds. *Großbritannien und der deutsche Widerstand, 1933–1944.* Paderborn, 1994.

Naftali, Timothy J. "Creating the Myth of the Alpenfestung: Allied Intelligence and the Collapse of the Nazi Police State." In: Günter Bischof and Anton Pelinka, eds., *Austrian Historical Memory and National Identity.* New Brunswick, NJ/ London, 1997, 203–246.

Naftali, Timothy. "Intrepid's Last Deception. Documenting the Career of Sir William Stephenson." In: *Intelligence and National Security* 8, 1993, 72–92.

Naftali, Timothy. "X-2 and the Apprenticeship of American Counterespionage, 1942–1944." Ph.D. Harvard, 1993.

Niethammer, Lutz. *Die Mitläuferfabrik. Entnazifizierung am Beispiel Bayerns* Berlin, 1982.

O'Toole, G. J. A. *The Encyclopedia of American Intelligence and Espionage. From the Revolutionary War to the Present.* New York/Oxford, 1988.

O'Toole, G. J. A. *Honorable Treachery.* New York, 1991.

Parrish, Thomas. *The Ultra Americans. The U.S. Role in Breaking the Nazi Codes.* New York, 1986.

Pauck, Wilhelm/Marion Pauck. *Paul Tillich. Sein Leben und Denken,* vol. 1. Stuttgart, 1978.

Pavlovic, Vojislav. *The Presumed Indifference: The OSS in Yugoslavia 1943–1944.* Belgrade, 1997.

Peake, Hayden B./Samuel Halpern, eds. *In the Name of Intelligence. Essays in Honor of Walter Pforzheimer.* Washington, D.C., 1994.

Persico, Joseph. *Casey: From the OSS to the CIA.* New York, 1990.

Persico, Joseph. *Piercing the Reich. The Penetration of Nazi Germany by Secret Agents During World War II.* New York, 1979.

Persico, Joseph. *Roosevelt's Sececret War: FDR and World War II Espionage.* New York, 2001.

Petersen, Neal H. *American Intelligence, 1775–1990. A Bibliographical Guide.* Claremont, California, 1992.

Pietsch, Hartmut. "Die Entwicklung des politischen Systems in den Städten des Ruhrgebietes, 1945–1948." Phil. Diss. Bochum, 1977.

Pinck, Dan C., Geoffrey M. T. Jones, and Charles T. Pinck. *Stalking the History of the Office of Strategic Services: An OSS Bibliography.* Boston, 2000.

Polenberg, Richard. *War and Society. The United States, 1941–1945.* Philadelphia, 1972.

Pogue, Forrest C., George C. Marshall. *Organizer of Victory.* New York, 1973.

Powers, Thomas. *Heisenberg's War. The Secret History of the German Bomb.* New York, 1993.

Radkau, Joachim. *Die deutsche Emigration in den USA. Ihr Einfluß auf die amerikanische Europapolitik, 1933–1945.* Düsseldorf, 1971.

Ranelagh, John. *CIA: A History.* London, 1992.

Röder, Werner. "Deutschlandpläne der sozialdemokratischen Emigration in Großbritannien, 1942–1945." In: VZG 17 (1969), 72–86.

Rostow, Walt Whitman. *Pre-Invasion Bombing Strategy. General Eisenhower's Decision of March 25, 1944.* Austin, Texas, 1981.

The Rote Kapelle. *The CIA's History of Soviet Intelligence and Espionage Networks in Western Europe, 1936–1945.* Washington, D.C., 1979.

Salter, Michael, ed. "60 Years OSS: New Research on the Office of Strategic Services. *The Journal of Intelligence History* 2 (2002).

Salter, Michael. "The Prosecution of Nazi War Criminals and the OSS: The Need for a New Research Agenda. *The Journal of Intelligence History* 2 (2002), 77–119.

Scheurig, Bodo. *Freies Deutschland. Das Nationalkomitee und der Bund Deutscher Offiziere in der Sowjetunion, 1939–1945.* Munich, 1960.

Scheurig, Bodo, ed. *Verrat hinter Stacheldraht? Das Nationalkomitee "Freies Deutschland" und der Bund deutscher Offiziere in der Sowjetunion, 1943–1945.* Munich, 1965.

Schlie, Ulrich. *Kein Friede mit Deutschland. Die geheimen Gespärche im Zweiten Weltkrieg, 1939–1941.* Munich/Berlin, 1994.

Schöllgen, Gregor. *Ulrich von Hassell 1881–1944. Ein Konservativer in der Opposition.* Munich, 1990.

Schüler, Klaus A. F. *Logistik im Rußlandfeldzug. Die Rolle der Eisenbahn bei Planung, Vorbereitung und Durchführung des deutschen Angriffs auf die Sowjetunion bis zur Krise vor Moskau im Winter, 1941/42.*, Frankfurt, 1987.

Schulz, Gerhard. Englische Geheimdienste und europäische Widerstandsbewegungen. In: Schulz, *Partisanen und Volkskrieg* (qv), 19–78.

Schulz, Gerhard, ed. *Partisanen und Volkskrieg. Zur Revolutionierung des Krieges im 20. Jahrhundert.* Göttingen, 1985.

Schulz, Gerhard. "Zur englischen Planung des Partisanenkriegs am Vorabend des Zweiten Weltkriegs." In: VfZ 30 (1982), 322–358.

Schulze, Hagen. "Rückblick auf Weimar. Ein Briefwechsel zwischen Otto Braun und Joseph Wirth im Exil." In: VZG 26 (1978), 144–185.

Schwab, Gerald. *OSS Agents in Hitler's Heartland.* Westport, CT/London, 1996.

Schwarz, Jordan A. *Liberal: Adolf A. Berle and the Vision of an American Era.* New York,/London, 1987.

Sherwood, Robert. *Roosevelt and Hopkins.* New York, 1948.

Smith, Bradley F. *Shadow Warriors. OSS and the Origins of the CIA.* New York, 1983.

Smith, Bradley F. *Sharing Secrets with Stalin. How the Allies Traded Intelligence, 1941–1945.* Lawrence, KS, 1996.

Smith, Bradley F. *The Ultra-Magic Deals And the Most Secret Special Relationship, 1940–1946.* Novato, CA, 1993.

Smith, Bradley F./Elena Agarossi. *Operation Sunrise. The Secret Surrender.* New York, 1979.

Smith, Richard Harris. *OSS: The Secret History of America's First Central Intelligence Agency.* London, 1972 (Los Angeles/London, 1981).

Soley, Lawrence C. *Radio Warfare. OSS and CIA Subversive Propaganda.* New York, 1989.

Söllner, Alfons, ed. *Zur Archäologie der Demokratie in Deutschland.* Vol. 1: *Analysen von politischen Emigranten im amerikanischen Geheimdienst, 1943–1945.* Bd. 2: *Analysen von politischen Emigranten im amerikanischen Außenministerium, 1946–1949.* Frankfurt, 1986.

Söllner, Alfons. "Wissenschaftliche Kompetenz und politische Ohnmacht. Deutsche Emigranten im amerikanischen Staatsdienst, 1942–1949." In: Thomas Koebner et al., eds. *Deutschland nach Hitler. Zukunftspläne im Exil und aus der Besatzungszeit, 1939–1949.* Opladen, 1987, 136–150.

Söllner, Alfons. "Office of Strategic Services and State Department." In: Rainer Erd, ed., *Reform und Resignation*(qv), 151–182.

Stafford, David. *Britain and European Resistance, 1940–1945. A Survey of the Special Operations Executive, with Documents.* Toronto/Buffalo, 1980.,

Steinert, Marlis G. *Hitlers Krieg und die Deutschen. Stimmung und Haltung der deutschen Bevölkerung im Zweiten Weltkrieg* Düsseldorf/Vienna, 1970.

Taylor, Edmond L. *Awakening from History.* London, 1971.

Toland, John. *Adolf Hitler.* New York, 1976.

Troy, Thomas F. *Donovan and the CIA. A History of the Establishment of the Central Intelligence Agency.* Frederick, MD, 1981.

Troy, Thomas F. *Wild Bill and Intrepid. Donovan, Stephenson, and the Origin of CIA.* New Haven/London, 1996.

Ueberschär, Gerd R., ed. *Das Nationalkomitee "Freies Deutschland" und der Bund Deutscher Offiziere.* Frankfurt, 1996.

Waller, John H. *The Unseen War in Europe. Espionage and Conspiracy in the Second World War.* New York, 1996.

Wark, Wesley. *The Ultimate Enemy. British Intelligence and Nazi Germany., 1933–1939.* London, 1985.

Warner, Michael. "Prolonged Suspense: The Fortier Board and the Transformation of the Office of Strategic Services." *The Journal of Intelligence History* 2 (2002), 65ff.

Weinberg, Sydney S. "Wartime Propaganda in a Democracy. America's Twentieth-Century Information Agencies." Ph.D. Dissertation, Columbia University, 1969.

Weinberg, Gerhard. *A World at Arms. A Global History of World War II.* Cambridge, 1994.

Wendt, Bernd Jürgen, ed. *Das britische Deutschlandbild im Wandel des, 19. und 20. Jahrhunderts.* Bochum, 1984.

Winkler, Allan M. *The Politics of Propaganda. The Office of War Information, 1942–1945.* New Haven/London, 1978.

Winks, Robin. *Cloak and Gown. Scholars in the Secret War, 1939–1961.* New York, 1987.

Winterbotham, F. W. *The Ultra Secret.* New York, 1974.

Wylie, Neville. " 'Keeping the Swiss Sweet': Intelligence as a Factor in British Policy Towards Switzerland during the Second World War." In: *Intelligence and National Security* 11 (1996), 442–467.

Yu, Maochun. *OSS and China: Prelude to Cold War.* New Haven/London, 1997.

INDEX